Mauritius and African Human Rights Law

Roopanand Mahadew

Mauritius and African Human Rights Law

A Critical Assessment of Challenges and Prospects

Springer

Roopanand Mahadew
Department of Law
University of Mauritius
Reduit, Mauritius

ISBN 978-3-032-08831-4 ISBN 978-3-032-08832-1 (eBook)
https://doi.org/10.1007/978-3-032-08832-1

This Springer imprint is published by the registered company Springer Nature Switzerland AG
The registered company address is: Gewerbestrasse 11, 6330 Cham, Switzerland

Foreword

It is a great honour for me to provide the preface to this book. This book could not have come at better time than now. After over three decades of the adoption of the Universal Declaration of Human Rights and gains made so far during this time, the world is at a critical juncture, where respect for human rights is under great threats. We are witnessing the activities of anti-rights and measures adopted by states that are capable of undermining human rights and reversing the gains made so far. Some countries are adopting laws that make it difficult for civil society groups and human rights defenders to operate within their jurisdictions. More importantly, some countries have continued to adopt draconian laws that criminalise consensual sexual activities between two adults. These developments are of great concerns to us and remind us of the need for us to remain vigilante and remain resolute in our efforts at ensuring the promotion and protection of human rights of everyone without distinction. This aligns well with one of the main goals of the Sustainable Development Goals—not to leave anyone behind. If no one must be left behind, states and other stakeholders must recommit to ensuring the promotion and protection of human rights worldwide. This book serves as an important contribution to the debate about ensuring that the hard-fought victory exemplified by the various international and regional human rights instruments adopted does not become illusory.

The book discusses the human rights situation in Mauritius and Africa as a whole. It traces the historical development of Mauritius and its demography before tracing the evolution of human rights discourse in the country. The author reminds us that civil and political rights as well as socio-economic rights are not only interrelated and indivisible but are also equally important. In line with the UDHR, the book highlights the need for states, including Mauritius to adopt measures and policies towards the realisation of all human rights. More importantly, the book discusses the need for states to pay special attention to vulnerable and marginalised groups who are often on the receiving sides of human rights violations. In this regard, attention is given to the human rights changes by women, children, persons with disabilities, sexual minorities and older persons. Due to deteriorating economic situations in the world fuelled by the financial crisis and pandemic such as

COVID-19, the inequality between the haves and the have nots has deepened over the years. This has raised some human rights concern, which this book has discussed.

It is also interesting that this book examines the role of the regional human rights bodies, such as the African Commission on Human and Peoples' Rights, the African Committee of Experts of the Rights on the Welfare of the Child and the African Court on Human and Peoples' Rights in ensuring the realisation of human rights in Africa. The book points out some of the important progress and achievements in promoting and protecting human rights by these bodies but at the same highlighting the challenges and missed opportunities over the years. It identifies institutional challenges and poor implementation of the decisions of these bodies as major areas of concerns. Also, the need for the African Union to provide financial support for these institutions was raised by the author.

Overall, this book has made a significant contribution to knowledge on human rights in Mauritius and Africa as a whole. It is one of the first books to discuss in detail the human rights norms and standards in Mauritius and the influence of the African Human Rights system on Mauritius. The book will be useful for students, academics, researchers, policy makers, civil society organisations, and international institutions and bodies.

Centre for Human Rights
University of Pretoria,
Pretoria, South Africa

Ebenezer Durojaye

Acknowledgements

I read somewhere that writing a book is harder than one thinks and more rewarding that one can ever imagine. I have now experienced this feeling. None of this would have been possible without some people who deserve a word of mention and gratitude. I am eternally grateful to my wife Bhavna who has been extremely supportive and my harshest critic throughout this journey. The warmth of my children Mayra and Krishiv has been so comforting during the hard phases of this endeavour. My parents and Sapna, my sister, deserve a special mention for having always believed in me. A very special thanks to Mansha Mohee, a brilliant scholar, who has been instrumental in the conceptualisation of this book as well as the main brain behind the third chapter of his book. She should have formally been part of this book but some sweet circumstances did not allow. I genuinely look forward to work with you Mansha. I finally dedicate this book to Professor Frans Viljoen and Professor Ebenezer Durojaye who have been my mentors and inspirational figures in my humble journey as an academic and researcher.

Contents

Chapter 1
Introduction

Abstract This chapter offers the context and establishes a setting for the discussion of this book. Notably, the author felt compelled to write a thorough analysis of the African human rights framework and Mauritius' involvement with it. This is driven by the lack of research and literature on the topic, which hampers scholars, researchers, lawyers, legislators, judges, and anyone who aspires to work with this human rights framework. The necessity of this study is justified by the fact that the African human rights system is extremely important and relevant to Mauritius. This chapter provides for a historical, political, and socio-economic background of Mauritius before embarking on establishing the connection between Mauritius and the Organisation of African Unity as well as its successor, the African Union. It then paints a picture of the salient features of the African human rights architecture as a background against which the subsequent chapters would be developed.

1.1 Historical, Political, and Socio-Economic Background of Mauritius

Mauritius is an African island state of an area of 2040 square kilometres located 500 miles off the east coast of Madagascar. With Port Louis as its capital city, the Republic of Mauritius consists of the Island of Mauritius (hereafter referred to as Mauritius) and other dependencies such as Rodrigues Island, Agalega Island, Cargados Carajos Shoals (also known as St. Brandon), and the Chagos Archipelago.[1] It should be underlined that together with Chagos Archipelago, Tromelin Island is the subject of sovereignty claims between Mauritius and its former coloniser.[2] The terrain of Mauritius is of volcanic nature, and it is surrounded by coral reefs with a central plateau rimmed by mountains. It has a tropical climate with cyclonic seasons

[1] See Britannica 'Mauritius' (17 February 2023) available at https://www.britannica.com/place/Mauritius (accessed 22 February 2025).

[2] Khalid (2013), p. 128.

R. Mahadew, *Mauritius and African Human Rights Law*,
https://doi.org/10.1007/978-3-032-08832-1_1

from December to April. As of July 2022, the population of the Republic of Mauritius, including the Island of Mauritius, the Island of Rodrigues and Agalega, and St. Brandon, stood at 1,262,523.[3] In terms of ethnic groups, 68% of Mauritians are Indo-Mauritians, 27% are Creoles, 3% are Sino-Mauritians, while 2% are Franco-Mauritians, and in terms of religions, 48% are Hindus, 23.6% are Roman Catholic, 16.6% are Muslim, 8.6% are other Christian, and 2.5% follow other religions.[4]

The island of Mauritius was known to Arab and Malay seafarers since the tenth century AD, and Portuguese sailors made the first voyage there in the sixteenth century, but it was unoccupied until the Dutch colonisation in 1638.[5] The following several centuries saw merchants, artisans, planters, and their slaves as well as traders settling in Mauritius. The Dutch, who left the colony in 1710, gave the island its name in honour of Prince Maurice of Nassau.[6] In 1715, the French occupied Mauritius and changed its name to Ile de France. Under the French East India Company, it developed into a thriving colony.[7] The island was used as a naval and merchant ship station during the Napoleonic wars when the French government acquired it in 1767. The British conquered Mauritius in 1810, and the Treaty of Paris, signed 4 years later, officially recognised their possession of the island. The Napoleonic code of law and other French institutions were upheld. Even today, more people speak French than English.

The slaveholders and slaves who were brought in to work the sugar fields are where the Mauritius Creoles get their origin.[8] With the abolition of slavery in 1835, immigrants from the Indian subcontinent arrived in Mauritius in the nineteenth century to serve as indentured labourers. Indo-Mauritians (mainly Hindus, though also Muslims and Christians) are descended from these immigrants.[9] Most of the great sugar plantations are still in the ownership of Franco-Mauritians, who are also involved in trade and banking.[10] Political power transitioned from the

---

[3] Statistics Mauritius 'Population' available at https://statsmauritius.govmu.org/Pages/Statistics/ESI/Population/Pop_Vital_Jan-Jun22.aspx (accessed 20 February 2025)—Island of Mauritius (1,217,588), Island of Rodrigues (44,661) and Agalega and St Brandon (274).

[4] It should be noted that the last census that was conducted on the lines of ethnicity and religion dates back to 1972. In addition, section 3 of the First Schedule to the Constitution of Mauritius provides that *the population of Mauritius shall be regarded as including a Hindu community, a Muslim community, and a Sino-Mauritian community, and every person who does not appear, from his way of life, to belong to one or other of those three communities shall be regarded as belonging to the general population, which shall itself be regarded as a fourth community.*

[5] Cheke (2001), p. 347.

[6] Turner (2014), p. 847.

[7] Johnson (2006)

[8] Miles (1999), p. 211.

[9] Claveyrolas (2017), pp. 174–189.

[10] Salverda (2008), p. 93.

Franco-Mauritians supported by the Creoles to the Indo-Mauritian Hindus as the Indo-Mauritian community grew in size and the voting age was raised.[11]

The first steps towards Mauritius' independence were the 1947 elections for the newly established Legislative Assembly. After 1961, when the British agreed to allow for more self-government and eventual independence, an independence push gathered traction.[12] In the face of opposition from Franco-Mauritian and Creole supporters of Gaetan Duval's Parti Mauricien Social Democrate (PMSD), a coalition comprising of the Mauritian Labour Party (Ptr), the Comité D'Action Musulman (CAM), and the Independent Forward Bloc (IFB), a traditionalist Hindu political party, won a majority in the Legislative Assembly Election of 1967.[13] Locals viewed the election as an independence referendum. After a period of communal unrest that was subdued with the help of British troops, Sir Seewoosagur Ramgoolam, the leader of the Mauritian Labour Party and the colonial government's chief minister, was appointed the country's first Prime Minister on 12 March 1968.[14]

The politics of Mauritius are dynamic and marked by alliance and coalition building. With the majority of political parties being centrist, the national consensus favours democratic politics and a reasonably open economy with a robust private sector.[15] On 12 March 1992, Mauritius acceded to the status of a Republic. The most notable consequence was that Queen Elizabeth II was replaced as head of state by a Mauritian President. According to the 1992 revised Constitution, Parliament continued to hold the reins of political power, and the President's role was essentially ceremonial. The President is chosen by the National Assembly upon recommendation of the Prime Minister.[16] The prime minister, who serves as head of government and is also the leader of the ruling party in the legislature, is joined by around 24 other ministers in the Council of Ministers (cabinet), which is in charge of directing and overseeing the administration.[17] Up to 70 representatives can serve in the unicameral National Assembly. Sixty-two are chosen by universal suffrage, and the Electoral Supervisory Commission may select up to eight 'best losers' from the runners-up using a method intended to provide minority ethnic communities with at least some representation.[18]

With a per capita income of $9106.2 as of 2021 and a 2021 GDP at market prices estimated at $11.53 billion, Mauritius is among the most prosperous and dynamic economies in Africa.[19] Sugar, textiles, tourism, and financial services form the foun-

---

[11] Mehta (1995), p. 4.

[12] See Houbert (1981), pp. 75–105.

[13] See Kadima and Kasenally (2005), pp. 133–164.

[14] Hookoomsing (2003), pp. 25–44.

[15] Carroll and Carroll (1999), p. 181.

[16] Mathur (1997), p. 184.

[17] Darga and Joomun (2005), pp. 95–110

[18] Mahadew (2015), p. 135.

[19] The World Bank 'GDP per capita - Mauritius' available at https://data.worldbank.org/indicator/NY.GDP.PCAP.CD?locations=MU (accessed 20 February 2025).

dation of the economy. Information and communications technology, hospitality, seafood, real estate development, renewable energy, healthcare, and training and education have recently emerged as significant industries, drawing significant investment from both domestic and foreign companies.[20] As Mauritius entered the new millennium in 2000, its economy suffered from the phase out of long-standing trade privileges and preferences in sugar and textiles, the cornerstones of its growth strategy.[21] In order to open up the economy, to further facilitate trade, to enhance the investment climate, and to attract foreign direct investment, the government launched an economic reform program in 2005.[22] These changes boosted the growth rate by lowering unemployment, creating new economic sectors, and diversifying the economy. This helped in cushioning the impact of the Eurozone crisis and the global economic slump, paving the way for Mauritius to restore rapid growth in 2010.[23]

The success of the Mauritian economy is credited to its free market and its long tradition of private entrepreneurship, resulting in a dynamic and strong private sector. With cutting-edge telecommunications equipment, such as international leased lines and high-speed Internet access, Mauritius has developed a sophisticated digital infrastructure.[24] Government policy favours business facilitation and delegation of production to the private sector to a significant extent. Yet it still maintains direct or indirect control over several important public utilities, including broadcast television, energy, water, and wastewater. Under the State Trade Corporation, the government also has control over the importation of goods it sees as strategically important, including cement, rice, wheat flour, and petroleum products.[25]

In terms of its foreign relations, Mauritius has stable and friendly ties with the international community and particularly with India and the nations of southern and eastern Africa. It is a member state of several international organisations, including the United Nations (UN), the African Union (AU), the Commonwealth, the World Trade Organisation (WTO), *La Francophonie*, the Indian Ocean Commission, the Southern African Development Community (SADC), the Common Market for Eastern and Southern Africa (COMESA), and Indian Ocean Rim Association. Mauritian foreign policy is motivated by trade, adherence to democracy, historical and cultural ties, and the relatively small size of the nation.[26] Due to its political past and reliance on Western markets, the nation has developed tight ties with the

[20] US Department of Commerce International Trade Administration 'Mauritius-Country Commercial Guide' (20 October 2021) available at https://www.trade.gov/country-commercial-guides/mauritius-market-overview (accessed 20 February 2025).

[21] Subramanian and Roy (2001).

[22] Sobhee (2009), pp. 29–42.

[23] Ulriksen (2011), pp. 194–213.

[24] Kumar and Strazdins (2021), p. 17.

[25] See State Trading Corporation available at https://www.stcmu.com/products/brief-on-main-activities-of-stc (accessed 25 April 2025)

[26] See Country Studies 'Foreign relations' Mauritius available at https://countrystudies.us/mauritius/25.htm (accessed 25 April 2025).

European Union and its members, especially with France and the United Kingdom.[27] Geographically a part of Africa, Mauritius maintains cordial ties with other African nations in the region, especially with South Africa, which is by far its most important continental commercial partner.[28] Mauritius investors have progressively started investing in African markets, including the close-by states such as Mozambique and Madagascar, although the rate of investment in Madagascar has significantly slowed following the country's 2009 coup d'etat. A significant part of Mauritius' foreign policy is coordinated with the AU and the SADC.[29]

Regarding defence, it should be underlined that there is no standing military force in Mauritius. Under the direction of the Commissioner of Police, roughly 10,000 active-duty personnel perform all military, police, and security duties. Domestic law enforcement is handled by the National Police, which has 8000 members. There are just two paramilitary organisations: the Special Mobile Force (SMF), which has about 1200 members, and the National Coast Guard, which has about 740 members.[30] These groups are made up of police officers who are assigned to those services on extended rotations. The SMF actively participates in community service programmes and is structured as a ground infantry unit. Four patrol craft are used for search and rescue missions and territorial water surveillance by the Coast Guard, which is commanded by a detailee from the Indian Navy.[31] There are also 41 small craft for coastal surveillance and search and rescue operations. Three aircraft are also available to the Coast Guard (two Dornier and one Defender aircraft). A squadron of 90 police helicopters helps with search and rescue missions. The Special Supporting Unit (SSU) with around 400 members that is trained in riot control is also there.[32] The SMF, the Police Helicopter Unit, and the Coast Guard all receive military advice from the United Kingdom and India, while Mauritius police officers receive training in the United Kingdom, France, and India. Mauritian security personnel are trained by the United States in areas such as maritime law enforcement, forensics, and counterterrorism techniques and methods.

1.2 Mauritius and the Organisation of African Unity (OAU)/African Union (AU)

It is apposite to understand the degree and scope of adherence of Mauritius to the continental intergovernmental institution of the OAU/AU in order to assess the relevance of the African human rights system to Mauritius. Indeed, as Viljoen argues,

[27] Ibid.

[28] Ibid.

[29] Graham (2017), pp. 133–155.

[30] Mauritius Police Force. https://police.govmu.org/police/?page_id=96

[31] Badri-Maharaj (2016).

[32] Mauritius Police Force 'Special Support Unit'. https://police.govmu.org/police/?page_id=96

'the emergence of this system was dependent on an agreement between African states about the nature and powers of the continental political body, and its further development has been and remains closely linked to the evolving form this agreement takes'.[33] One way of gauging the degree and scope of adherence of Mauritius to the OAU is through the prism of ideological underpinning based on which the OAU was established. That ideological underpinning was the contested concept of pan-Africanism. Simply put, the primary question is to what extent Mauritius, as an independent state, had/has embraced the concept of pan-Africanism. Geiss has argued that pan-Africanism can be understood from a 'cultural' perspective which is people centred or from a 'political' perspective which is state centred.[34] Culturally, pan-Africanism is the affirmation of a shared ancestry of the members of 'the black race' with their roots or origins in Africa.[35] Politically, it is a movement which has as objective a closer unity of African states.[36]

Before answering the question set above, a brief overview of the concept of pan-Africanism as a foundational basis of the OAU is relevant and provides guidance. While the first pan-African conference was organised in London in 1900, it is the fifth one, which took place in Manchester in 1945 that is more directly relevant to Africa with the participation of stalwart pan-Africanists such as Kwame Nkrumah and Jomo Kenyatta. It represented a great source of motivation and inspiration for African politicians and liberation leaders who were combating colonial rule with the aim of acquiring independence.[37] However, the antithesis to this ideological movement was the discourse of nationalism, used domestically by African colonies to gain independence. The image of nationhood was being inevitably invoked to legitimise the new state after independence. As Pakenham contended, this concept of nation which was based on border lines created by European colonial powers and formalised at the Berlin Conference was artificial and temporary.[38] As a result, nation-building campaigns and efforts with the aim of managing competing interests of the various factions and entities forming the state failed to ensure enduring stability, cultural identity, and national development.[39]

In 1958, the First Conference of Independent African States was organised by Nkrumah which 'marked the formal launching of pan-African movement on African soil'.[40] Pan-Africanism became the guiding principle based on which independent African states would anchor their coexistence and relationships. Nkrumah was also the origin of ideas such as 'Africa must unite' so that a 'United States of Africa'

---

[33] Viljoen (2012), p. 151.

[34] Geiss (1974), p. 7.

[35] Ajala (1974), p. 93.

[36] Viljoen (2012), p. 152.

[37] Viljoen (2012), p. 152.

[38] Pakenham (1991), part III.

[39] Castellino and Allen (2003), p. 113.

[40] Ajala (1974), p. 14.

could see the day.[41] Viljoen argues that three cases challenged the growing effort of continental unity—the struggle of the Algerian National Liberation Front, the Katangese secession attempt from Congo added to the overthrow of Lumumba, and Morocco's challenge to Mauritania's claim to membership at the UN.[42] A majority of these cases and similar ones were linked to territory and existing borders which made African leaders of independent states, through the OAU, to invoke the principle of *uti possidetis* which is the respect for colonial borders no matter how arbitrarily they were drawn.[43] Furthermore, pan-Africanism was also challenged by various political aspirations of newly independent states which can be broadly identified as follows: the 'Brazzaville' group (consisting of former French colonies except Guinea) unwilling to form part of a radical unitary Africa without any ties with France on which they were dependent militarily, economically, and administratively, the 'Casablanca' group led by Ghana and Guinea which were aiming for radical transformation and integration in the name of African Unity, and the 'Monrovia' group (Ethiopia, Nigeria, and Liberia) which was aiming at a more moderate approach to African Unity by finding a compromise.[44]

Nigerian President Azikiwe summarised the growing sentiment against a political union based on a radical form of pan-Africanism when he stated that 'if for many years certain parties have fought for their sovereignty, it is unlikely that they will surrender that sovereignty to a nebulous organisation simply because we feel it necessary to work together'.[45] In addition, the inclusion of Arabs and French-speaking Africans further blurred the vision of pan-Africanism. Indeed, the version of pan-Africanism based on the 'black race' had to be revisited if Arab North African states were to be included, especially in the midst of Egyptian President Nasser vision of pan-Arabism.[46] For French-speaking African states, a more cultural version of pan-Africanism was preferred as viewed by Senegalese President Senghor in a gradualist approach. He stated that 'if we wish to succeed, we must put the stress on cultural, technical and economic co-operation, rather than on the co-operation of political parties. We must progress step by step, keeping our feet firmly on the ground'.[47] In the midst of all these divides emerged two major models as elaborated upon by Viljoen in the following terms:

> As more states gained independence and membership of the UN, the question turned to the practical manifestation of unity of the newly independent states. Two major models served as points of reference: The United States inspired the notion of a closely knit 'United States of Africa'; and the UN, provided the model for a loose association in the form of a United Africa of (independent) states.[48]

---

[41] Nkrumah (1963) p. 51.

[42] Viljoen (2012), p. 154.

[43] See OAU Doc AHG/Res 16(1), July 1964 'Borders Disputes among African States' para 2.

[44] Viljoen (2012), p. 154.

[45] See Ajala (1974), p. 23.

[46] Mazrui & Tidy (1984), pp. 51–55.

[47] Ajala (1974), p. 35.

[48] Viljoen (2012), p. 155.

On 25 May 1963, Ethiopian Prime Minister Selassie brought together the 32 independent African states to create the OAU which took the form of a loose association analogical to a 'United Africa of independent states'. The OAU Charter was firmly premised on principles such as respect of sovereignty and territorial integrity and, implicitly, on the principle of *uti possidetis*. Indeed, Somali's demand to reopen discussions about its borders that were colonially drawn to unite all Somalis was met with stern opposition. According to them, colonial borders had to be maintained 'in the interest of Africa'[49] or 'out of respect for the legacy that we have received from the colonial system'.[50] It can be argued that too much emphasis on sovereignty and territorial integrity by the OAU relegated economic development and human rights somewhat to the background and also allowed the proliferation of dictators and gross human rights violations, often overlooked by African states' negative position on non-interference in the domestic affairs of other African states.

It can be argued that Mauritius' adherence to the OAU and to the idea of pan-Africanism has been quite singular and different from the majority of African states. To some extent, it can be said that, unintentionally and not by design, Senghor's gradualist approach to pan-Africanism was followed with cultural, technical, and economic cooperation rather than cooperation from the political perspective. Indeed, the colonisation history and trajectory of Mauritius were uncommon to other African states. In addition, post-colonisation issues and challenges were equally different in comparison to newly independent African states with border tensions, ethnicity-related challenges or plaguing dictatorships. Mauritius' main challenge was primarily its economic survival. From an economic perspective, post-colonial economic ties with France and the United Kingdom were carefully nurtured for economic development, whereas sociocultural ties with India were highly privileged given that the majority of Mauritians were of Indian origin. In a sense, when Mauritius became independent in 1968, its adherence to the OAU was more of a de facto political manoeuvre rather than adherence based on a shared ancestry of members of the 'black race' with roots or origins in Africa. There was no politically motivated decision to adhere to Africa because Mauritius is part of it or it is the place of origin of some Mauritians. For primarily economic purposes, it was relevant for Mauritius to adhere to the OAU.

This has raised an important question as to whether Mauritius has genuinely wanted to be part of Africa and whether it faces an 'identity crisis' in recognising its 'Africanness'. This alleged indifference is at least partially explained by the history of the country. European influence has been profound and pervasive in Mauritius since it was first discovered by the Dutch and then colonised by the French and finally by the English. Nonetheless, Mauritius' strong Asian influence is the more obvious cause of the limited allegiance and adherence to African and its continental political system. Given that over 70% of the people are of Indian origin and that there are many connections to India, the Mauritius identity is marked by a strong

[49] Ajala (1974), p. 84.

[50] Ajala (1974), p. 85.

historical and cultural symmetry. Further complicating the unravelling of these solid ties are the island's proximity to India and the substantial diaspora.[51] India and Europe have provided the foundation for the nation's heritage. This is demonstrated by data on trade and investment, both of which show that they account for the majority of economic activity with Mauritius. It has therefore been challenging for Mauritius to develop a clear African identity. This is echoed in a statement made by Amédée Darga, chairman of the Mauritius Africa Business Club, which is as follows: 'Mauritius as a country is well embedded in Africa but a majority of the Mauritian people still do not feel the African identity. This schizophrenic state is partly due to the internal ethnic dynamics of the country'.[52] The closer ties between Mauritius and the rest of Africa reflect similar patterns in North Africa, which has likewise struggled with existential issues related to the idea of being African. Indeed, Egypt and Morocco have always been criticised for their exceptionalism and ethnic isolation from sub-Saharan Africa.

It can be argued that Mauritius' strategy towards the African continent and African states has been mostly of an economic nature. This is echoed in the following statement by Tsang Man Kin in the following terms:

> Mauritians generally have to be reminded that our economic success and prosperity, starting in the mid-1970s and for the next thirty years, were due to our membership of the ACP countries that negotiated and obtained the Lomé Convention and the Sugar Protocol. We would never have been able to achieve this without the support of the African countries of AASM (Associated African Countries, Madagascar and Mauritius), which was obtained thanks to the intervention of two Presidents, French General De Gaulle and Senegalese Leopold Sédar Senghor, who readily and positively responded to Sir Seewoosagur Ramgoolam, who had the vision and sagacity to seek their help. Mauritius is fortunate to have been anchored since then on to Africa. The result is that today our African credentials are most powerful, and unquestionable as members of the continental African Union, and its regional organisations like SADC or Comesa. Now, in order to fully take advantage of all that the African Union has to offer especially in the African Renaissance, Mauritius has to assume fully its African identity.[53]

Louw-Vaudran contends that Mauritius 'excelled when it comes to promoting regional economic integration and improved involvement of the private sector'.[54] However, an integration of the country from a political and cultural perspective is still blatantly lacking. Indeed, it has since independence, and therefore the adherence of Mauritius to the idea of pan-Africanism and its membership to the OAU/AU has not been at par with other African states. Darga highlights the lack of diplomatic presence of Mauritius in countries such as Kenya and other West African countries

[51] Gopaldas (2019) https://issafrica.org/iss-today/does-mauritius-have-an-identity-crisis

[52] Ibid.

[53] Tsang Man Kin (2015).

[54] Institute for Security Studies 'Power and Influence: Identifying champions of change in the SADC' (April 2019) https://issafrica.org/research/policy-brief/power-and-influence-identifying-champions-of-change-in-sadc

which partially explains the lack of 'Africanness' of Mauritius.[55] Albeit not within the purview of this book, a lack of political and cultural investment towards Africa and a lack of a sense of belonging towards the continent have to be underlined as critical issues deserving further academic investigation and attention. What is of concern to the current work is that the lack of pan-Africanist vision and 'Africanness' of Mauritius, for reasons explained above, has indeed had an impact on its adherence to the African human rights architecture in terms of which treaty or convention it decided to ratify or which African judicial or quasi-judicial body it decided to give access to its citizens as would be discussed later in this book. Historically, Mauritius did not consider the importance and relevance of the African human rights architecture with the same seriousness and urgency as other African countries, grappling with much more serious human rights issues compared to it, had had.[56]

1.3 The African Human Rights Architecture

The evolution of the OAU to the African Union (AU) has had a significant impact on the African human rights architecture. It is therefore relevant to firstly understand this evolution through the prism of their respective engagements with human rights before, secondly, getting acquainted with the contours and components of the African human rights architecture.

1.3.1 From the OAU to the AU

Viljoen has proposed four phases of the evolution of the OAU into the AU.[57] These are the 'foundation and stagnation' period from 1963 to 1978, the 'shaking the baobab' period from 1979 to 1989, the 'winds of change' period from 1990 to 2000, and the 'new institution for a new millennium' period from 2001 to date.[58] The first phase was characterised by the priority that the OAU Charter gave to concepts such as sovereign equality of states, respect for territorial integrity, and non-interference in the internal affairs of states.[59] While these concepts in themselves are vital to any sovereign state, the problem was that they were used to shield human rights violations that were massively occurring in several African states. For instance, the OAU did not genuinely probe into these allegations by invoking the need to respect the

[55] AFM 'We are definitely deficient in our diplomacy towards Africa' (January 2021) https://afm.media/2021/01/26/mauritius-diplomacy-deficiency-towards-africa/

[56] See generally Tinker (1977), pp. 321–338.

[57] Viljoen (2012), p. 156.

[58] Viljoen (2012), pp. 156–169.

[59] Article 3(1), 3 and 3(2) of the OAU Charter respectively.

principle of non-interference as enshrined by its Charter. Welch even described the OAU as 'a club of presidents, engaged in a tacit policy of not inquiring into each other's practices'.[60] Indeed, the OAU Charter did not expressly and unequivocally include human rights in the OAU's mandate except for its article 2(1)(e) requiring member states to have 'due regard' to the human rights provided for in the Universal Declaration on Human Rights. As a consequence, the OAU managed to address only two human rights issues during that period—the right to self-determination of 'peoples' still under colonisation[61] and rights of refugees which resulted in the adoption of the OAU Convention Governing the Specific Aspects of Refugee Problems in Africa.

The second phase or period was about 'shaking the baobab' with reference to the principle of non-interference in internal affairs of states being 'firmly rooted in African soil as an unwavering baobab'.[62] This resulted in gross human rights violations notably in Amin's Uganda, Bokassa's Central African Empire, and Nguema's Equatorial Guinea which arguably acted as a catalyst for the drafting and adoption of the African Charter, among other things.[63]The atrocities committed on Africans had an 'impact on Africa and the OAU',[64] and the alleged 'double standards' of the OAU were highlighted given their silence on the aforementioned repressive regimes while at the same time condemning apartheid in South Africa.[65] With the three 'waves of democratisation in Africa' during that period, the invasion of Uganda in 1978–1979, the use of human rights as an ideological tool by the West during the Cold War, and the adoption of the Helsinki Final Act in 1975, US President Jimmy Carter's emphases on human rights were some of the major factors that pushed the OAU to reconsider its position on the non-interference principle and respect for human rights.[66] It should be underlined that Mauritius was part of the group of African states, together with Senegal, Nigeria, and Uganda, which initiated the process of drafting the African Charter by proposing to the OAU that its Assembly adopt a resolution to start the process of adopting an African human rights instrument.[67] Viljoen has highlighted the way in which African states had attempted to derail the whole process by delaying it at every turn since they would not publicly oppose the adoption of a human rights instrument.[68] After numerous challenges, the

---

[60] Welsh (1995), p. 151.

[61] The OAU supported decolonisation of Angola and Mozambique from the repressive rule of the Portuguese and fought against apartheid in South Africa and the rule of the white minority in Rhodesia (now Zimbabwe). It is to be noted that the right to self-determination was only understood by the OAU in the context of decolonisation which meant that post-independence demands for self-determination in Biafra, Katanga, Eritrea, Shaba, and southern Sudan were rejected.

[62] Viljoen (2012), p. 158.

[63] Kannyo (1984), p. 128.

[64] Umozurike (1992), p. 3.

[65] RF Weisfelder (1984), p. 90.

[66] Viljoen (2012), p. 159.

[67] OAU DOC AHG/Dec.115 (XVI) Rev.1).

[68] Viljoen (2012), p. 160.

African Charter was adopted in 1981 but only came into force after 5 years—time for it to receive a simple majority of states to rectify it—on 21 October 1986 which showed once again that stagnation had creeped into the African human rights system after the adoption of the Charter.

The 'wind of change' period was characterised by the end of the Cold War and multiparty democratic elections all over the continent. In 1990, the Declaration on Political and Socio-Economic Situation in Africa and the Fundamental Changes Taking Place in the World, also known as the Algiers Declaration, was adopted by the OAU. A political environment which allowed for popular participation, human rights, and rule of law and an effective dispute resolution mechanism that would guarantee lasting peace and stability were the two preconditions for economic growth.[69] The OAU also adopted the African Charter on the Rights and Welfare of the Child in 1990 and the Protocol to the African Charter on Human and Peoples' Rights on the Establishment of an African Court on Human and Peoples' Rights in 1998. In 1999, Mauritius hosted an OAU Ministerial Conference on Human Rights at Grand Baie which culminated in the adoption of the Grand Baie Declaration and Plan of Action. In the same year, in Libya, the Sirte Declaration was adopted with the commitment of the African leaders to form an African Union with the aim of accelerating the implementation of the treaty establishing the African Economic Community (the Abuja Treaty 1991) with the aim to 'promote economic, social and cultural development and integration of African economies' in view of raising 'the standard of living of African peoples'.[70]

African heads of state and government decided to establish the AU to replace the OAU at the fourth extraordinary session of the OAU Assembly, held in Sirte, Libya, on 9 September 1999 with the aim of 'a new institution for a new millennium'. On 11 July 2000, the AU's Constitutive Act, which succeeded the OAU, was approved. It became effective on 26 May 2002. In sharp contrast with the OAU Charter, the AU's Constitutive Act makes extensive reference to human rights, rule of law, and good governance with explicit mention of the African Charter and the promotion and protection of human and peoples' rights.[71] Article 4(h) goes even further to provide that the AU can intervene in view of protecting human rights in the circumstances of war crimes, genocide, and crimes against humanity with the approval of the AU's Assembly. Issues such as promotion of gender equality, the promotion of social justice for economic development in a balanced way, the sanctity for human life and dignity, as well as unconstitutional changes in government are catered for by the AU's Constitutive Act.[72] Under the aegis of the AU, the New Partnership for Africa's Development (the NEPAD) was also adopted, with a pledge by African leaders to eradicate poverty and to pursue sustainable development.[73] Baimu argues

[69] Paragraph 10 and 11 of the Algier Declaration OAU Doc AHG/Dec.1 (XXVI).

[70] Article 4(1) a and c of the AEC Treaty.

[71] Art 3(h) of the AU's Constitutive Act.

[72] Art 4 of the AU's Constitutive Act.

[73] Paragraph 1 of the NEPAD Declaration.

that one of the components of the NEPAD which is democracy and political governance is most relevant to the promotion of human rights.[74] NEPAD's African Peer Review Mechanism (APRM) further provides for an expansion for its provisions connected to human rights and their protection and promotion.

1.3.2 *The African Human Rights Architecture: Salient Features*

African elites founded the Organisation of African Unity in 1963 with the goal of advancing regional cooperation and decolonisation in Africa. The OAU was founded on the principles of state sovereignty, non-interference in internal matters of states, and territorial integrity. As Viljoen and Baimu argued, human rights were sidelined and relegated to the background in the agenda of the OAU.[75] Human rights concerns were treated as problems that were solely the responsibility of nations, and anyone who championed them was viewed as subversive.[76] The OAU Charter's human rights consideration can be summed up by saying that state rights predominated over those of individuals and entire populations.[77] The political freedom and decolonisation of African states are thus one significant accomplishment of the OAU.[78] The OAU Charter needed to be amended as a result of these shortcomings and the reality of globalisation.

Although the OAU had adopted a number of human rights documents, the change from the OAU to the AU was a significant turning point in the development of human rights in Africa. The new foundation document formally and explicitly adds human rights to the AU's agenda as a major breakthrough.[79] In light of the foregoing, both normative and institutional components are a part of the African regional human rights system, often known as the 'pan-continental human rights system in Africa'.[80] African governments have adopted, ratified, and enacted a large number of human rights accords under the auspices of the OAU/AU.[81] The African human

[74] Baimu (2002), p. 302.

[75] Viljoen and Baimu (2004), p. 241.

[76] Mangu (2005), p. 381.

[77] Isanga (2013), p. 271.

[78] Maluwa (2007), p. 10.

[79] Heyns (2004), p. 681.

[80] Odinkalu (2002), p. 99.

[81] OAU Convention Governing the Specific Aspects of Refugee Problems in Africa 1969, Cultural Charter for Africa 1976, African Charter on the Rights and Welfare of the Child 1990, Protocol to the African Charter on Human and Peoples' Rights on the Establishment of the African Court on Human and Peoples' Rights 1998, the Constitutive Act of the African Union 2000, Protocol to the African Charter on Human and Peoples' Rights on the Rights of Women in Africa 2003, Convention on Prevention and Combating Corruption 2003, African Charter on Democracy, Elections and Good Governance 2007, and the AU Convention for the Protection of and Assistance of Internally

rights normative system is made of these treaties, alongside the essential soft law norms and standards. Whereas the institutional dimension of the normative system is constituted of mechanism responsible for the supervision and monitoring of state implementation of human rights treaties and standards, the normative system is composed of treaties and soft law norms. In order to monitor and encourage states to implement human rights treaty standards and to provide recourse for people whose rights under the treaties are violated by their states, state parties have established independent expert committees, quasi-judicial institutions, and full-fledged judicial institutions.

1.3.2.1 The Normative System

Ayeni has argued that the African Charter on Human and Peoples' Rights (hereafter referred to as the Charter) serves as the normative framework of the African human rights system.[82] In terms of its ratification, the latest update from the African Union shows that, with the exception of Morocco, all African states have ratified the Charter.[83] Mauritius signed the Charter on 27 February 1992 and ratified it on 19 June 1992. The ratification of the Charter, which is the main instrument for advancing and defending human rights in Africa, signalled the beginning of a concerted effort to advance and defend these rights.[84]

Boven has hailed the Charter as one that responds to 'African concerns, African traditions and African conditions',[85] whereas others have generally recognised it as a unique human rights instrument.[86] Aligned with the principle of indivisibility of human rights, the Charter provides for both first-generation rights, which are civil and political rights, and second-generation rights in the form of socio-economic rights are fully justiciable and enforceable. It has to be underlined that even the United Nations human rights system could not achieve this given that there are two separate covenants for these rights, that is, the International Covenant on Civil and Political Rights and the International Covenant on Economic, Social and Cultural Rights. The uniqueness of the Charter is further consolidated by the fact that it is the only binding human rights instrument that incorporates the concept of solidarity rights, peoples' rights or collective rights.[87] Indeed, collective and peoples' rights such as the right to equality, existence, free disposal of wealth and natural resources, the right to development, security, and peace, and the right to a generally

---

Displaced Persons 2009; Protocol to the African Charter on Human and Peoples' Rights on the Rights of Older Person, 2016.

[82] Ayeni (2011), p. 14.

[83] See African Union 'OAU/AU Treaties, Conventions, Protocols and Charters' https://au.int/en/treaties/1164

[84] Gumedze (2003), p. 119.

[85] Boven (1986), p. 186.

[86] Mutua (1995), p. 339.

[87] Kiwanuka (1988), p. 80.

satisfactory environment are all guaranteed from articles 19 to 24 of the Charter. Regarding its provisions, the African Commission on Human and Peoples' Rights (hereafter the African Commission) upheld that they cannot be derogated even in times of national emergencies.[88]

There are still some criticisms that have been levelled against the Charter that need to be highlighted. Viljoen has argued that the Charter is normatively deficient when it comes to the protection of the rights of vulnerable groups such as women, persons with disabilities, and children.[89] The existence of limitation clauses or 'claw-back clauses' in some of its articles has also been qualified as a drawback.[90] In addition, the provision of individual duty in the Charter, which is another unique feature, has been interpreted as having the potential of allowing states to detract from their obligations given the language which has been used to provide for it.[91] The need for reform of the Charter has been consequently voiced out consistently despite the fact that a number of the drawbacks have been mitigated or circumvented through a progressive interpretation of the Charter by the African Commission.[92]

As a result, two protocols to the Charter were adopted in view of remedying some of these shortcomings. On 11 July 2003, the Protocol to the African Charter on Human and Peoples' Rights on the Rights of Women in Africa was adopted in Maputo, Mozambique (hereafter the Maputo Protocol). The primary objective of the Maputo Protocol was to eliminate discrimination against women, violence against women, and harmful traditional practices to which African women are subjected.[93] By providing for the right to medical abortion and protection against domestic violence and HIV infections, the Maputo Protocol proved to be more progressive than even the UN Convention on the Elimination of All Forms of Discrimination against Women (hereafter the CEDAW). It should be highlighted that Mauritius signed the Maputo Protocol on 29 January 2005 but only ratified it on 16 June 2017, a matter to be invoked and discussed in Chap. 8. Another protocol to the Charter created was that regarding the establishment of an African Court on Human and Peoples' Rights (hereafter the African Court).[94] Mauritius signed this Protocol on 9 June 1998 and ratified it on 3 March 2003. The African Court is discussed in Chap. 12. The Charter, the Maputo Protocol, and the African Court's Protocol are often referred to as the African Charter system. As a complement to this system, there exist the African Charter on the Rights and Welfare of the Child, OAU Convention Governing Specific Aspects of Refugee Problems in Africa 1969,

---

[88] Commission nationale des droits de l'Homme et des libertés v Chad (2000) AHRLR 66 (ACHPR 1995) para 21.

[89] Viljoen (2012), p. 269.

[90] Singh (2009), p. 104.

[91] Cohen (1993).

[92] Heyns (2001), p. 157.

[93] Banda (2006), p. 72.

[94] Protocol to the African Charter on Human and Peoples' Rights on the establishment of an African Court on Human and Peoples' Rights.

AU Convention for the Protection and Assistance of Internally Displaced Persons 2009, OAU Convention on the Conservation of Nature and Natural Resources 1969, African Convention on the Conservation of Nature and Natural Resources 2003, and the African Charter on Democracy, Election and Governance 2007 which are pertinent to the protection and promotion of human rights in Africa.

The treaties creating political bodies whose duties include promoting and defending human rights in Africa are part of the normative part of the African human rights framework. Moreover, the normative framework includes 'soft law' principles. These technically 'non-binding' human rights instruments are widely used in Africa and are an essential part of the continent's human rights framework.[95] They still have significant political force, and subsequently they can 'harden' to become mandatory.[96]

1.3.2.2 Institutional Mechanisms

Specialised human rights tribunals and other AU bodies that support the advancement and defence of human rights in Africa constitute the African system for ensuring those rights. The African Commission, the African Court, and the African Committee of Experts on the Rights and Welfare of Children (African Children's Committee) are the tribunals that are generally recognised as the main instruments for enforcing and implementing human rights in Africa. Chapter 12 of this book thoroughly discusses their potential contribution to human rights law in Mauritius. The realisation of human rights in Africa is a goal shared by all of the AU's primary institutions. The duties of these bodies with regard to human rights are outlined in the African Union's (AU) Constitutive Act.[97] All AU organs work to advance, realise, and promote the AU's human rights agenda because these issues are fundamental to how the organisation functions. As a result, political bodies such as the AU Assembly, Executive Council, pan-African Parliament, AU Commission, and Peace and Security Council (PSC) carry out a variety of tasks related to the advancement and defence of human rights on the African continent. As a matter of illustration, being the top body of the AU, the Assembly is in charge of establishing and updating human rights treaties, for instance.

On certain human rights subjects like gender equality, employment, and poverty reduction, the AU Assembly also passes non-binding soft law norms including resolutions, declarations, and guiding principles. The Assembly also assists in maintaining oversight on how these soft law principles are being applied. The Executive Council is in charge of keeping track of how the AU Assembly's decisions are being

[95] Protocol relating to the Establishment of the Peace and Security Council of the African Union 2002; the Constitutive of African Union 2000; Treaty Establishing the African Economic Community 1991; statute of the Economic, Social and Cultural Council of the African Union 2004; Protocol to the Treaty Establishing the pan-African Parliament 2001.

[96] Shelton (2007).

[97] Lloyd and Murray (2004), p. 165.

carried out, including taking into account the African Union Commission's Activity Reports. The Council is in charge of overseeing African Court rulings as well. It is impossible to overstate the importance of the AU Commission's function as the 'heart' of the pan-African continental organisation. There are eight departments within the Commission. The fulfilment of human rights within the AU is greatly aided by the efforts of two of these departments, namely, the Political Affairs and Social Affairs departments. The primary institution for preserving regional peace, security, and stability in Africa is the Peace and Security Council (PSC). The PSC's aims and guiding principles accentuate the promotion and defence of human rights and fundamental freedoms.[98] The Council is expressly required to collaborate closely with the African Commission by the Protocol creating the PSC.[99] Human rights have been said to take centre stage in the African Peer Review Mechanism (APRM) process, despite the fact that it is not solely focused on protecting these rights.[100]

1.4 The Relevance and Significance of the African Human Rights Architecture to Mauritius

How Africa is important to Mauritius from a political, economic, cultural, and historical sense has always been subject to a laborious exercise of having to convince Mauritians about it, be it the common man or successive governments that the country has had. The relevance and significance of the African human rights regime and architecture to Mauritius are no different from this perception. Indeed, law and policymakers, judges, lawyers, civil society organisations, academics, students, and the ordinary citizen still need to be convinced that the African Union and its human rights mechanisms are of great importance to the country and its people. As evidence to substantiate this statement, one simply has to note the number of times African human rights treaties have been used as a foundation for a legislation or the number of times the judiciary has meaningfully and progressively utilised them when adjudicating human rights matters. Consequently, this section attempts at providing arguments as to how and why the African human rights architecture is of relevance and significance to Mauritius.

Firstly, it is argued that hard and soft laws on human rights from the African Union (and the OAU) fill in the various gaps and voids that exist in the domestic legal and normative framework on human rights. For instance, the absence of socio-economic rights and third-generation rights from the Mauritian legal system and the incomplete (despite arguably relatively decent) protection of women's, children's, sexual minorities', and elderly persons' rights can be countered by the application

[98] Article 3(f) and 4(c) of the Peace and Security Council Protocol.

[99] Rules 80 and 84 of the Rules of Procedures of the African Commission.

[100] Killander (2008), p. 41.

of the African human rights instruments in Mauritius as would be discussed in the subsequent chapters of this book. Victims and aggrieved persons could still have their rights enforced and rendered justiciable by relying on these instruments with their proper domestication in the Mauritian legal system. One has to be mindful of the following in Mauritius—while the situation concerning human rights is arguably relatively better compared to other African states, the state of affairs of human rights law and their adjudication are a cause of concern. They have numerous limitations and shortcomings that can only be addressed by a complete adherence, application, and implementation of the African human rights architecture. This remains valid despite Mauritius being a state member to the various human rights instruments at the UN level. In addition, it cannot be envisaged that domestic laws pertaining to human rights would be created or amended to cater for the various lacunas given that meaningful debates and discussions, of the most basic and preliminary form, related to critical issues such as the enshrinement of socio-economic rights in the Constitution are yet to take place 55 years after independence. The African human rights architecture therefore remains critically relevant and significant to Mauritius.

Secondly, judicial and quasi-judicial bodies such as the African Court, the African Commission, and the African Children's Committee present a unique opportunity for the protection and promotion of human rights in Mauritius. With the limited jurisdiction of the Supreme Court of Mauritius, mostly constrained to civil and political rights adjudication, as well as its rather conservative nature and its lack of judicial activism, the aforementioned bodies become very relevant and significant for human rights victims seeking remedies and justice. While institutions such as the Equal Opportunities Commission (and its ad hoc Tribunal), the National Human Rights Commission, the Independent Police Complaints Commission, and the Office of the Ombudsperson for Children are operational in Mauritius, their limited mandate and scope imply that they cannot be relied upon for a complete protection and promotion of human rights. The above named African bodies can be considered as platforms on which human rights lawyers can conduct strategic human rights litigation and public interest litigation—legal concepts and techniques that are not recognised in the Mauritian jurisdiction.

Thirdly, there is a political significance for the state of Mauritius to demonstrate complete and genuine adherence to, generally, the African Union and more specifically to the African human rights architecture. Against the backdrop of the historical context of Mauritius' adherence to the OAU/AU as discussed above, the African continental body has been of support to the various causes of the country. A recent and pertinent one has been the claim of sovereignty by Mauritius over the Chagos and the demand for the complete decolonisation of the country by the United Kingdom, its former coloniser.[101] It should be highlighted that the African Union, through its legal team, participated in the oral hearing before the International Court

[101] ICJ Legal Consequences of the Separation of the Chagos Archipelago from Mauritius in 1965 - https://www.icj-cij.org/case/169

of Justice in an effort to achieve the decolonisation of the Chagos Archipelago.[102] The AU was the sole organisation that provided legal assistance in the proceedings, and this was the first time in the AU's history that it had done so in support of one of its member states before the International Court of Justice. Based on a sense of political morality, it is relevant therefore for Mauritius to give full effect to its membership to the AU, which includes, inter alia, giving full effect to the AU's human rights architecture. In addition, it is also the primary legal obligation of Mauritius to respect the obligations it has undertaken by either signing or ratifying human rights instruments under the aegis of the OAU/AU.

Fourthly, the nature of alleged human rights violations and claims has changed and is touching matters that were not necessarily being revendicated in the past in Mauritius. For example, there are more and more claims which can be based on the right to development related to infrastructure developments and hotel construction. The right to a healthy environment is also often claimed in relation to corporate activities. Same-sex marriage and protection from criminal laws such as sodomy are also contentions that the Mauritian judiciary has been called upon to adjudicate. The extensive use of social media has often brought to the limelight the scope, limitation, and purview of the right to privacy and freedom of expression. Various policies on housing, education, health (in the context of the COVID-19 pandemic), culture, and employment have prompted social debates premised on socio-economic rights. In essence, basic rights and fundamental freedoms which were not referred to previously are now being invoked, judicially or extra-judicially. In the face of this evolution, the African human rights architecture becomes relevant and significant to Mauritians since they do provide for the legal basis on which most, if not all, of the above-mentioned claims can be based and argued before a judicial or quasi-judicial body.

1.5 Why This Book?

This chapter sets the tone and provides for the background against which this book has been contemplated. It is apposite to mention that a critical need was felt by the author to come up with a comprehensive work on the African human rights architecture and the engagement of Mauritius with it. This is motivated by the fact that there is a dearth of research and literature on this subject matter to the detriment of academics, researchers, legal practitioners, judges, lawmakers, and others who wish to engage with this human rights system. As discussed above, the African human rights system remains so relevant and significant to Mauritius which justifies the need for this piece of work. It therefore focuses on thematic issues such as civil and political rights, socio-economic rights, the right to development and environment, women's rights, children's rights, rights of elderly persons, rights of persons with

[102] African Union Press Release - https://au.int/fr/node/34827

disabilities, and minorities' rights relevant to Mauritius. Each theme is discussed in a critical manner using the African human rights architecture as a barometer in assessing the effectiveness of the domestic legal and normative framework relevant to the themes.

References

Ajala A (1974) Pan-Africanism: evolution, progress and prospects. Andre Deutsch, London
Ayeni VO (2011) Domestic impact of the African Charter on Human and Peoples' Rights and the Protocol on the Rights of Women in Africa: a case study of Nigeria. University of Pretoria, Pretoria, p 14). Unpublished LLM Dissertation
Badri-Maharaj S (2016) The Mauritius-India naval relationship: naval diplomacy 2.0. Africa Trends, April–June
Baimu E (2002) Human rights in NEPAD and its implications for the African human rights system. Afr Hum Rights Law J 2:301–302
Banda F (2006) Blazing a trail: the African protocol on women's rights comes into force. J Afr Law 50:72–84. https://doi.org/10.1017/S0021855306000076
Boven T (1986) The relations between Peoples' Rights and Human Rights in the African Charter. Hum Rights Law J 7:186
Carroll BW, Carroll T (1999) The consolidation of democracy in Mauritius. Democratization 6(1):179–197
Castellino J, Allen S (2003) Title to territory in international law: a temporal analysis. Ashgate, Aldershot
Cheke A (2001) Is the bird a dodo? The wildlife of a mid-seventeenth century drawing of Dutch Mauritius. Arch Nat Hist 28(3):347–351
Claveyrolas M (2017) 'Indo-Mauritians' and the Indian Ocean: literacy accounts and anthropological readings. J Indian Ocean Reg 13(2):174–189
Cohen R (1993) Endless teardrops: Proleg-Omena to the study of human rights in Africa. In: Cohen R, Hyden G, Nagan W (eds) Human rights and governance in Africa. University Press of Florida, Gainesville
Darga LA, Joomun GD (2005) Mauritius. S Afr J Int Aff 12(1):95–110
Geiss I (1974) The pan-african movement: a history of pan-Africanism in America, Europe, and Africa. Taylor & Francis
Graham S (2017) Drivers of the foreign policies of Southern African small states. Politikon 44(1):133–155
Gumedze S (2003) Bringing communications before the African Commission on Human and Peoples' Rights. Afr Hum Rights J 3:119
Heyns C (2001) The African Regional Human Rights System: in need of reform? Afr Hum Rights Law J 2:157
Heyns C (2004) The African Human Rights System: the African Charter. Penn State Law Rev 108:681
Hookoomsing VY (2003) Chota Bharat, Mauritius: the myth and the reality: the myth and the reality preamble. In: Culture and economy in the Indian diaspora. Routledge, pp 25–44
Houbert J (1981) Mauritius: independence and dependence. J Mod Afr Stud 19(1):75–105
ICJ Legal Consequences of the Separation of the Chagos Archipelago from Mauritius in 1965. https://www.icj-cij.org/case/169
Isanga JM (2013) The Constitutive Act of the African Union, African Courts and the Protection of Human Rights: new dispensation? Santa Clara J Int Law 1:271
Johnson D (2006) Comparing the trajectories of educational change and policy transfer in developing countries. Oxf Rev Educ 32(5):679–696

Kadima DK, Kasenally R (2005) The formation, collapse and revival of political party coalitions in Mauritius: ethnic logic and calculation at play. J Afr Elect 4(1):133–164
Kannyo E (1984) The Banjul Charter on Human and Peoples' Rights: genesis and political background. In: Welch CE, Meltzer RI (eds) Human rights and development in Africa. State University of New York, Albany
Khalid M (2013) Disputed Islands of the Indian Ocean: a potential danger to regional peace. J Indian Ocean Stud 21(2)
Kiwanuka R (1988) The meaning of peoples' rights in the African Charter on Human and Peoples' Rights. Am J Int Law 80:80
Killander, M., 2008. The African Peer Review Mechanism and human rights: the first reviews and the way forward. *Human Rights Quarterly*, 30(1), pp. 41–75.
Kumar R, Strazdins N (2021) The digital infrastructure divide in the commonwealth. Commonwealth Secretariat
Lloyd A, Murray R (2004) Institutions with responsibility for Human Rights Protection under the African Union. J Afr Law 48:165–186. https://doi.org/10.1017/S0021855304482035
Mahadew R (2015) The best loser system in Mauritius: an essential electoral tool for representing political minorities. Constitutional building in Africa
Maluwa T (2007) From the Organization of African Unity to the African Union: rethinking the framework for inter-state cooperation in Africa in the era of globalisation. University of Botswana Law Journal 5:10
Mangu AMB (2005) The changing human rights landscape in Africa: Organization of African Unity, African Union, New Partnership for Africa's development and the African Court. Neth Q Hum Rights 23:381. https://doi.org/10.1177/016934410502300304
Mathur R (1997) The republican model of Mauritius a short comparative study. Afr Rev J Afr Polit Dev Int Aff 24(1/2):180–207
Mauritius Police Force. https://police.govmu.org/police/?page_id=96
Mazrui, A.A. and Tidy, M., 1984. Nationalism and the New States in Africa: From about 1935 to the Present.
Mehta SR (1995) Power dynamics of Indian immigrants in Mauritius: a study in ethnic relations. Indian Anthropol 25(1):1–11
Miles WF (1999) The creole malaise in Mauritius. Afr Aff 98(391):211–228
Mutua M (1995) The Banjul charter and the African cultural fingerprint: an assessment of the language of duties. VA J Int Law 35:339
Nkrumah K (1963) Africa must unite. Praeger, New York
Odinkalu, C.A., 2002. Africa's regional human rights system: Recent developments and jurisprudence.
Pakenham T (1991) Scramble for Africa: 1876–1921. Random House, New York. Part III
Salverda T (2008) Maintaining an elite position: how Franco-Mauritians sustain their leading role in post-colonial Mauritius, Dilemmas of development, p 93
Shelton DL (2007) Introduction: law, non-law and the problem of soft law. In: Shelton DL (ed) Compliance and commitment: the role of non-binding norms in the international legal system. Oxford University Press, Oxford, p 1
Singh S (2009) The impact of clawback clauses on human and peoples' rights in Africa. Afr Secur Rev 18:95–104
Sobhee SK (2009) The economic success of Mauritius: lessons and policy options for Africa. J Econ Policy Reform 12(1):29–42
Subramanian A, Roy D (2001) Who can explain the Mauritian miracle: Meade, Romer, Sachs or Rodrik?
Tinker H (1977) Between Africa, Asia and Europe: Mauritius: cultural marginalism and political control. Afr Aff 76(304):321–338
Tsang Man Kin J (2015) Mauritius Times. Mauritius and the African Union. Available at http://www.mauritiustimes.com/mt/joseph-tsang-mang-kin-gosk-3/

Turner B (2014) Mauritius. In: The statesman's yearbook: the politics, cultures and economies of the world 2015, pp 847–850

Ulriksen MS (2011) Social policy development and global financial crisis in the open economies of Botswana and Mauritius. Global Soc Policy 11(2–3):194–213

Umozurike U (1992) Five years of the African Commission on Human and Peoples' Rights. Obafemi Awolowo University, Ile-Ife

Viljoen F (2012) International human rights law in Africa. OUP, Oxford

Viljoen F, Baimu E (2004) Courts for Africa: considering the co-existence of the African Court on Human and Peoples' Rights and the African Court of Justice. Neth Q Hum Rights 22:241. https://doi.org/10.1177/016934410402200205

Weisfelder RF (1984) Human rights and majority rule in Southern Africa: the mote in thy brother's eye. In: Welch CE, Meltzer RI (eds) Human rights and development in Africa. State University of New York, Albany

Welsh CE (1995) Protecting human rights in Africa: strategies and roles of non-governmental organisations. University of Pennsylvania, Philadelphia

Chapter 2
Introductory Aspects on Human Rights Law in Mauritius

Abstract It is indubitable that colonial history had a significant impact on the normative and institutional framework on human rights in Mauritius. Both French and British colonisation influenced discourses and narratives on human rights to a significant extent in Mauritius. This chapter attempts at capturing the essence of the above. It then provides for an overview of the 1968 Constitution and its cardinal principles relevant to human rights in Mauritius. Chapter 2 of the Constitution, referred to as the bill of rights, is discussed from the perspective of its enforceability and the extent of its permissible derogation. Lastly, the chapter focuses on the National Human Rights Commission as the quasi-judicial institution in Mauritius with a promotional and protective mandate regarding human rights.

2.1 A Historical Perspective

It is indubitable that colonial history had a significant impact on the normative and institutional framework on human rights in Mauritius. Both French and British colonisation influenced discourses and narratives on human rights to a significant extent in Mauritius. During the French colonisation, slaves were brought to the island in greater numbers The latter were defined by the 1723 'Code Noir' as *meubles* (movables) for legal purposes.[1] Back then, using torture to look into crimes was considered standard procedure. On a court's order, torture des brodequins was used in the Admiral Sans Ouartier case.[2] During the Napoleonic era, under Decaën's administration (1803–1810), the inflexible class and racial system were further solidified and made harsher. The majority of land ownership was held by the French colonists. The excessive use of fire for clearing land for the export of timber resulted in harm to the environment.

[1] North-Coombes (2018), p. 78.

[2] Seetulsingh (2004), p. 1309.

R. Mahadew, *Mauritius and African Human Rights Law*,
https://doi.org/10.1007/978-3-032-08832-1_2

The Code Noir and other legislation were employed by the Colonial State of Isle de France to bar non-white people from participating in mainstream social, political, and economic spheres. The enslaved population was subjected to an especially harsh regime.[3] These colonial episodes in the history of Mauritius would go on to have an impact on human rights and fundamental freedoms and liberties. The emergence of the sugar industry oligarchy and social and economic forces of predominantly French planter community yielding massive political influence and illegal slave trade on the Island had some bearing on human rights.[4]

The Isle de France witnessed several changes as a result of the French Revolution. There were elections conducted and a Colonial Assembly established. The 1789 French Declaration des Droits de L'Homme et du Citoyen was published in 1794 by the Colonial Assembly. Despite the fact that the rights it guaranteed were limited to those of white people and free multiracial people, it was a landmark in the nation's history of protecting human rights. It was to have a significant effect much later. The Supreme Court used these assurances in the 1990s to broaden the scope of the protection that the Constitution provides for an individual's human rights.[5]

In 1810, the British took control of Mauritius. Up to 12 March 1968, when it became an independent state within the Commonwealth, Mauritius was still a British colony. Articles 7 and 8 of the 1810 Treaty of Capitulation (subsequently ratified by the 1814 Treaty of Paris) permitted the locals to 'preserve their religion, laws, and customs' as permitted by the British. The conditions for the extension of slavery until 1835 and the widespread corruption of the state machinery were established by the Treaty of Capitulation, which served as the foundation for the British capture of Mauritius in 1810. The British Colonial State colluded with French and British plantation owners and merchants to engage in an illicit slave trade.[6] Whether they were French or British, the civil servants tended to be biased in favour of the landowners and slave owners. The Court was not exempt. The interests of the planters and merchant class were served by the various institutions. An ideology gained momentum in order to rationalise the current situation, and racism was a key component of that ideology. People who rebelled in any form were viewed as 'lazy, indolent or even vagrant'.[7] In the economic interest of the plantocracy, labour was expected to be attached to the plantations; any departure from this policy was interpreted and portrayed as a sign of inherent inadequacy. Slavery and the beginnings of British colonialism laid the basis for an unstable economy and racist ideology that resulted.[8]

In the early twentieth-century British colonialism, the cheap labour policy of the plantocracy and the free trade policy of the British Imperial Government both led to

[3] Report of the Truth and Justice Commission (2011), p. 64.

[4] Report of the Truth and Justice Commission (2011), p. 65.

[5] Seetulsingh (2004), p. 1310.

[6] Stanziani (2020).

[7] Report of the Truth and Justice Commission (2011), p. 70.

[8] Vaughan (1998), p. 210.

the decline in the earnings of sugar industry workers.[9] Through a taxing structure that required the working classes to contribute a larger share of their wages and salaries than other social classes, the colonial state contributed to the continued impoverishment of the working classes. In their efforts to take as much money as they could from the working classes—whether it was through taxes or labour in the sugar cane fields—the colonial state and the plantocracy shared similar practices. Between 1937 and 1943, labourers' resistance actions claimed lives.[10] A harsh, class-based, racially stratified society was created by the plantation industry and will rule Mauritius after independence.[11]

In 1886, the first elections were conducted in Mauritius. There were restrictions on the franchise, including a property requirement and an English language competency requirement.[12] Various political movements have spearheaded the fight for independence, aiming to grant adult suffrage, establish a legislature that is completely elected, and establish an accountable government. Women were permitted to vote in the 1948 legislative election, although their ability to do so was contingent upon passing a literacy test in either of the colony's recognised languages.[13] Universal suffrage did not serve as the foundation for the right to vote in general elections until 1958. However, the Supreme Court ruled in *Roussety v Attorney-General*[14] that the electoral districts incorrectly excluded the dependencies (Les Constitutions de l'Ile Maurice), depriving a portion of the colony's residents of their ability to vote. As a result, in 1967, the residents of Rodrigues, one of the dependencies, cast their first ballot in a general election.[15]

Starting from the 1940s up to independence in 1968, the British government's perspective on its colonies and their citizens underwent a significant shift. Significant reforms occurred in the domains of healthcare, housing, and education with the Colonial and Development Welfare Act of 1940 and the publishing of the Hooper Report in 1938.[16] The cornerstones of the Mauritian welfare state were also established by these rulings. The Labour Party planned to implement mandatory schooling, social security, old age pension, low-cost housing, and the growth of co-ops for small plantation owners in their 1948 manifesto.[17] Advocated were additional improvements in the fields of education and health services. The Education Act of 1941, which centralised primary, secondary, aided, and non-aided school administration, was the first major development in the field of education. The political class exerted pressure to extend primary education, which allowed almost all children to

[9] Report of the Truth and Justice Commission (2011), p. 74.
[10] Report of the Truth and Justice Commission (2011), pp. 74–76.
[11] Report of the Truth and Justice Commission (2011), p. 77.
[12] Ballhatchet (1995), p. 990.
[13] Ramtohul (2016), p. 1225.
[14] *Roussety v. Attorney-General* (1967) MR 15.
[15] Seetulsingh (2004), p. 1310.
[16] Seekings (2011), p. 157.
[17] Kasenally (2018), p. 43.

be enrolled, even if primary schools were non-existent in many areas. A common sixth standard examination was also created.[18] In addition, a new housing strategy for the impoverished was put into place after hurricane Carole, giving housing facilities to those who needed them the most.[19] The reports of economists Meade and Titmuss served as an inspiration for many of the actions implemented to uphold social justice.[20]

The dual colonisation of Mauritius has shaped the societal, economic, political, and institutional contours of the country. It has impacted significantly on the sources of law generally in Mauritius and, more specifically, on the sources of human rights law. As a point of illustration, by changing from French colonisation to British colonisation, Mauritius has also moved away from the principle of monism to that of dualism which have had an impact on the ways, and effectiveness, with which international human rights law would domestically be applicable. Additionally, the French culture of human rights is fundamentally distinct from the British one which had seen Jeremy Bentham applauding the latter to be a far more superior culture or system compared to the former.[21] While this debate does not fall under the purview of this work, it can be inferred from Bentham's essay entitled the *Anarchical Fallacies* on the Declaration of the Rights of Man and of the Citizens 1789 that these two systems are different from each other.

It can therefore be further inferred that due to the change in colonisation from French to British, the scenario of Mauritian human rights law must have arguably changed in a significant manner. As would be discussed elsewhere in the chapter, the focus shifted to a practical and substantive bill of rights (the British style) especially given that Mauritius' immediate post-colonial rule was characterised by colonial continuity instead of colonial rupture. Indeed, Gray has expanded on this point as follows:

> First, the government's maintenance of a constitution negotiated under imperialism that reinforced colonially defined community divisions and also gave successive Mauritian elites an advantage in electoral processes; second, the political elite's open allegiance to British structures of power through overt celebrations of the British monarchy and parliamentary democracy; third, the reliance of postcolonial elites on old and new legislation that reproduced the repressive conditions of the colonial period. Together these examples historicise Mauritian governance to highlight some of the lingering legacies of colonialism and how elites chose to embrace rather than reform them.[22]

[18] Rughoonundun-Chellapermal (2022), p. 210.

[19] Ballgobin (2017), p. 265.

[20] Holmberg (1962), p. 3.

[21] The discovery of the rights of man ought naturally to have taken its rise: it is we-we English, that have the better *right* to it… Our right to this precious discovery, such as it is, of the rights of man, must, I repeat it, have been prior to that of the French. It has been seen how peculiarly rich we are in materials for making it. *Right*, the substantive *right*, is the child of law: from *real* laws come *real* rights; but from *imaginary* laws, from laws of nature, fancied and invented by poets, rhetoricians, and dealers in moral and intellectual poisons, come *imaginary* rights.

[22] Gray (2023), p. 36.

This 'colonial continuity' has shaped human rights law in Mauritius in a fundamental manner. As discussed above, while the French period of colonisation has contributed to the substance of human rights law in Mauritius, the substantive and procedural aspects have been mostly impacted by British colonisation. It has to be added that over the years, the judiciary in Mauritius has developed a body of human rights jurisprudence, and the legislature has enacted various legislation pertaining to human rights directly or indirectly. It can be argued that since independence in 1968, these two arms of the government, without undermining the role of the executive in human rights promotion, have contributed in the development of a Mauritian system of human rights. Though still at its developmental stage, it is an area which is undergoing noticeable transformation as would be discussed at various stages in this book. At this point, focus is turned towards the supreme law of Mauritius, that is the Constitution, and human rights law.

2.2 The 1968 Constitution and Cardinal Principles Relevant to Human Rights

Meetarbhan has argued that modern Mauritius constitutional history can be broadly categorised in three periods: (1) **1938–1948, rise of political and trade union movements**, characterised by the creation of the new Labour Ordinance of 1938 and the new Constitution of 1948, which allowed for women to vote for the first time even though there were still requirements of property and literacy; (2) **1948–1958, foundations of democratic governance** with the 1948 election proving to be a turning point in political emancipation and the 1956 Constitutional conference in London giving birth to the new 1958 Constitution that granted universal suffrage in 1958; and (3) **1958–1968, the pre-independence period** which saw the 1961 Constitutional Review, the 1964 Constitution, the 1965 debates on the electoral system, and the August 1967 elections leading to independence in 1968.[23]

Ethnic considerations dominated public discourse on constitutional emancipation during the course of these three decades. Strong demands for quotas, proportional representation based on community membership, and separate voter registrations for each particular community were made in opposition to democracy and responsible governance. The argument centred on the election system with opposing perspectives on protecting ethnic considerations on the one hand and limiting the continuation of divisions that could impede nation-building on the other, after it became evident that the country would be heading towards independence. The governor general was granted unique powers as a result of the protections eventually outlined in the Constitution and the independence of institutions.[24] In these

[23] Meetarbhan (2015), pp. vii–ix.

[24] Meetarbhan (2015), p. viii.

circumstances, one can argue that the place of human rights in the Constitution was neglected or at least not sufficiently accentuated upon.

This should not come as a surprise given that the Constitution of Mauritius was merely granted by the United Kingdom and it never emanated from the people of Mauritius or their representatives. Even if the British colonial power had consultations with political parties in Mauritius as well as in London during the Lancaster House Constitutional Conference, there was never any constituent assembly appointed to adopt the Constitution with the participation of all stakeholders as was the case in India and South Africa, to name a few. Even during the September 1965 Lancaster House Constitutional Conference, the emphasis was acutely on independence or not and not one human rights and the Constitution.[25] Indeed, Sir Seewoosagur Ramgoolam of the Mauritius Labour Party stated in its opening remarks that his party 'wants independence of Mauritius within the Commonwealth', whereas Jules Koenig of the Parti Mauricien made the following remarks:

> If we contend that decolonisation there must be, we discard independence as being fatal to the prosperity and the peaceful and harmonious development of Mauritius as part of the free world. We claim that it is the general wish of the people of Mauritius that as a substitute for independence, close constitutional associations with Great Britain should be maintained within the framework of a new pattern.[26]

In spite of the fact that the Constitution of Mauritius had been granted by Great Britain without much participation of Mauritians in its drafting, it did come with several cardinal principles such as the notion of democracy, rule of law, supremacy of the Constitution, and separation of powers that have helped in shaping the face of human rights in Mauritius. These principles are essential for human rights to be effectively protected, promoted, respected, and fulfilled. Linking democracy to human rights, De Mesquita et al. argued that political participation in multiparty competition reduces human rights abuses. Full democracy is crucial for respecting integrity rights, while limited accountability hinders progress. Only states with high levels of democracy show better human rights practices.[27] The importance of the rule of law to human rights is underlined by Apodaca who argued that 'functioning, independent judiciaries under the rule of law can end impunity, preferential treatment, and political protection of the perpetrators of human rights violations—without them, human rights and humanitarian guarantees are fragile and social justice merely a dream'.[28] The Supreme Court of Mauritius has played a crucial role in upholding these doctrines and notions and merits a brief discussion here from a case law perspective.

The Constitution of Mauritius is neither ideological nor programmatic given that it does not mention that the state of Mauritius shall be 'socialist' or 'secular'. However, it does explicitly provide that Mauritius shall be a democratic state in its

---

[25] Mauritius Constitutional Conference Report (1965) para 6.

[26] Meetarbhan (2015), p. 1.

[27] De Mesquita et al. (2005), p. 439.

[28] Apodaca (2003), p. 292.

section 1. Furthermore, this section is entrenched and can only be altered if at least three quarters of the population approves such alteration through referendum and all members of the National Assembly vote for such an alteration.[29] This special status given to section 1 has been qualified as 'an exceptional degree of entrenchment' by the Judicial Committee of the Judicial Committee of the Privy Council (JCPC).[30] Earlier interpretations of section 1 reduced it to a 'mere preamble, the content of which are only defined by other provisions of the Constitution'[31] dealing with fundamental rights and freedoms, the executive, the legislature, the electoral system, the National Assembly, and the judiciary.[32] This interpretation changed when the JCPC stated that:

> It is not simply a guide to interpretation. In this respect it is to be distinguished from many other constitutional provisions. It is of the first importance that the provision that Mauritius 'shall be…a democratic state' is an operative and binding provision.[33]

In Ahnee v Director of Public Prosecutions, the JCPC stated that 'from these provisions, the following propositions can be deduced. First, Mauritius is a democratic state constitutionally based on the rule of law. Second, subject to its specific provisions, the Constitution entrenches the principle of separation of powers between the legislature, the executive and the judiciary'.[34] It also mentioned that 'the democratic nature of the sovereign state of Mauritius is an important matter to be taken into account in the construction of any part of the Constitution and in particular its guarantees of fundamental rights and freedoms'.[35] It further noted that 'the idea of democracy involves a number of different concepts…there is the principle that fundamental rights should be protected by an impartial and independent judiciary'.[36] The Supreme Court of Mauritius underlined that 'the whole of our Constitution clearly rests on two fundamental tenets, the rule of law and the juxtaposition (or separation as it is more often called) of powers'.[37] It further stated that 'it is not in accord with the letter or spirit of the Constitution, as it presently stands, to legislate so as to enable the Executive to overstep or bypass the Judiciary in its essential roles, namely those of affording to the citizen the protection of the law and, as guardian of the Constitution, to ensure that no persons human rights or fundamental freedoms are placed in jeopardy'.[38]

---

[29] Section 47(3) Constitution of Mauritius.

[30] State v Khoyratty (2004) PRV 59.

[31] Meetarbhan (2015), p. 5; Lincoln & Ors v Governor General & Ors (1974) MR 112; U.D.M & Anor v The Governor General & Anor (1990) SCJ 171.

[32] See Vallet V Ramgoolam (1973) MR 29.

[33] State v Khoyratty (2006) UKPC 13.

[34] (1999) 2 AC 294.

[35] Matadeen v Pointu (1998) MR 172.

[36] State v Khoyratty (2006) UKPC 13.

[37] Noordally v Attorney-General (1986) MR 204.

[38] Noordally v Attorney-General (1986) MR 204.

The Supreme Court and the JCPC confirmed that a constitutional amendment adopted with the prescribed majority could still be deemed unconstitutional if it is inconsistent with the principles of a democratic state as established by section 1 of the Constitution. More specifically, the JCPC stated that 'the Constitution deliberately places certain rights out of the realm of being overridden even by majority decision and confers upon the courts the power to decide whether the protected right has been infringed. The Constitution of Mauritius clearly follows this pattern'.[39] Reconciling the notion of sovereignty of Parliament and supremacy of the Constitution, the Supreme Court stated that 'where Parliament exercises sovereign powers under the Constitution and the courts are empowered to exercise a particular jurisdiction which itself requires an enquiry into the exercise of those powers by Parliament, then the jurisdiction of the courts must be exercised to the appropriate extent in order to enable it to determine the particular question that is before it. It would be misleading, in those circumstances, to invoke the sovereignty of the National Assembly which would have the effect of paralysing—the effective exercise of the constitutional jurisdiction of the Court'.[40] The Supreme Court has maintained that Parliament is 'supreme as long as it legislates within the framework of the Constitution'.[41]

Regarding the interpretation of the Constitution, and specifically the bill of rights within, the Supreme Court has adjudicated that 'a Constitution, more particularly that part of it which embodies fundamental rights, should be interpreted in the light of its history, its sources and, wherever applicable, pronouncements on provisions similar to ours either by national courts or by international institutions. These rights are not confined to any particular territory but have become a global and universal concept. They are almost invariably linked to economic development, economic aid, the establishment of diplomatic relationships and are often used as a mode of pressure on certain countries whose track record in the field of human rights is sorely lacking'.[42]

It can be noted from the above discussion that the judiciary in Mauritius has played a key role in not only interpreting but also upholding firmly and vehemently key doctrines and concepts through the post-independence history of Mauritius. This inevitably had a positive impact in the promotion, protection, and respect of human rights which cannot thrive if the above-mentioned principles are not afforded any constitutional importance.

---

[39] Matadeen v Pointu (1998) MR 172.

[40] Attorney General v Ramgoolam (1993) MR 81.

[41] Motee v R (1969) MR 34.

[42] M G C Pointu v The Minister of Education and Science & Anor (1995) SCJ 359.

2.3 The Bill of Rights

The bill of rights (BoR) is enshrined in Chapter 2 of the Constitution of Mauritius as it is essentially composed of civil and political rights. The discussion on each of the civil and political rights as well as on the absence of socio-economic rights is carried out in subsequent chapters of this book. For now, the focus would be on section 3 of the BoR which introduces the latter. Section 3, entitled fundamental rights and freedoms of the individual, reads as follows:

It is hereby recognised and declared that in Mauritius there have existed and shall continue to exist without discrimination by reason of race, place of origin, political opinions, colour, creed or sex, but subject to respect for the rights and freedoms of others and for the public interest, each and all of the following human rights and fundamental freedoms

(a) the right of the individual to life, liberty, security of the person and the protection of the law;
(b) freedom of conscience, of expression, of assembly and association and freedom to establish schools, and (c) the right of the individual to protection for the privacy of his home and other property and from deprivation of property without compensation, and the provisions of this chapter shall have effect for the purpose of affording protection to those rights and freedoms subject to such limitations of that protection as are contained in those provisions, being limitations designed to ensure that the enjoyment of those rights and freedoms by any individual does not prejudice the rights and freedoms of others or the public interest.

It is noteworthy that this section emphasises on the fact that fundamental rights and freedoms have existed in Mauritius even before the advent of the Constitution. Indeed, the Supreme Court had made reference to a Colonial Assembly Declaration of August 1794 which proclaimed that the citizens of the colony shall enjoy their natural rights which are imprescriptible.[43] Meetarbhan has noted that 'well before the adoption of the Constitution, article 12 of the Mauritius Civil Code provided that all Mauritians shall have civil rights'.[44] However, the difference with the provisions of the Mauritius Civil Code on human rights and that of the Constitution is related to their degree of entrenchment, with the latter's provisions alterable only by a super majority. During the 1965 Constitutional Conference, provisions were made for a chapter dealing with fundamental rights as evidenced by the framework for the Constitution annexed to the proceedings. Citing the same, the Supreme Court remarked that 'among the annexes to the report of the Conference of 1965, there is Annex D which deals with the framework of the proposed Constitution. One of the items dealt with under the heading fundamental rights says that the Constitution

[43] Peerbocus v R (1991) MR 90.

[44] Meetarbhan (2015) 24.

will include a chapter providing for the fundamental rights and freedoms of the individual which will closely follow Chapter 1 of the existing Constitution of 1964'.[45]

A comparative study would reveal that a number of the provisions of the BoR have close similarity with the European Convention on Human Rights. After ratifying the said Convention in 1951, the United Kingdom extended its application to its colonies, including Mauritius.[46] The Mauritian Judiciary, however, made it clear that this does not compel it to follow decisions of the European Court. It stated that 'while the court will willingly turn to the Convention and the decisions of the European Court of Human Rights for guidance when it has to determine the meaning and scope of the fundamental rights and freedoms embodied in our Constitution, it could plainly not see in the Convention some kind of supra-national law to which the municipal law of this country is subordinate unless and until our municipal law itself made provision for its overriding by the Convention'.[47] Despite this proposition, one can argue that the interpretation of the BoR has historically been dominated by European jurisprudence, sometimes to the detriment of jurisprudence from the African supranational and national judicial bodies. This is evidenced by the Supreme Court stance in a case where it stated that 'the Strasbourg jurisprudence therefore gives persuasive guidance on the contents of the fundamental rights embodied in Chapter II of our Constitution respect of those rights which are couched in terms which bear very close resemblance to the corresponding articles of the European Convention'.[48] It is argued that there is no reason as to why the judiciary should not look towards jurisprudence of the African Commission, the African Court, and judiciaries such as the South African one for the interpretation of the BoR given that the Supreme Court itself had noted that 'there are also significant differences in language and structure and it cannot be assumed that particular sections were necessarily intended to have the same meanings'.[49]

Regarding limitations or exceptions to the fundamental rights enshrined in the BoR, the test is premised on whether the limitation or the exception is reasonably justifiable in a democratic society. The Supreme Court drew inspiration from the European Court of Human Rights' case of S and Marper v UK which stated that 'an interference will be considered necessary in a democratic society for a legitimate aim if it answers a pressing social need and, in particular, if it is proportionate to the legitimate aim pursued and if the reason adduced by the national authorities to justify it are relevant and sufficient'.[50] In DPP v Boodhoo, the Supreme Court further added that 'the necessity of any constitutionally permissible limitations must, like

[45] Bhewa and Alladeen v Government of Mauritius and DPP (1990) MR 79.

[46] Council of Europe (1953).

[47] Lincoln & Ors v Governor General & Ors (1974) MR 112.

[48] Madhewoo M v The State (2015) SCJ 177.

[49] Matadeen v Pointu (1998) MR 172.

[50] Madhewoo M v The State (2015) SCJ 177 citing the case of S and Marper v UK (2008) ECHR 1581 and the case of Sahin v Turkey (2005) 41 E.H.R.R.8.

all derogations, be narrowly construed and must respond to what has generally been understood to be a pressing social need'.[51]

2.4 Enforceability of the Bill of Rights

Section 17 of the Constitution provides for effective remedy for the violation of the rights contained in the BoR. The scope of application of section 17 is well defined, and, for example, redress for a potential violation of section 1 of the Constitution cannot be sought under section 17 which seems strictly reserved for the BoR as highlighted in the case of Pointu v Minister of Education and Science and Anor.[52] It is important that subsection 1 explicitly indicates that the enforcement measures apply to accusations of violations of any of the BoR's sections 3 through 16 in light of the previous discussion regarding the real status of section 3. Furthermore, according to subsection 2, the Supreme Court has the original authority to hear and decide on any application filed under subsection 1 and may issue writs, orders, and directives pertaining to any of the BoR's sections 3 through 16. This makes it clear that section 3 was meant to be a justiciable provision and that the Supreme Court has the authority to offer remedies to the victims. It should be noted that the Supreme Court is prohibited from using its authority under the proviso to subsection 2 if it determines that the aggrieved party has or has had access to adequate methods of remedies for the claimed violation under any other legislation. The individual must not only have truly used up all of his other available legal options, but he also cannot use section 17 of the Constitution to seek redress if he was allowed to use these options but chose not to do so. The proviso may represent a significant restriction on section 17's applicability.

Redress under section 17 shall not be regarded as an extra level of jurisdiction simply because all other legal remedies have been exhausted. The Supreme Court has ruled that a convicted person who has been granted a fair trial pursuant to section 10(1) of the Constitution and who has used every available option to contest his conviction is not eligible to do so under section 17 of the Constitution.[53] There has been a contention that the Constitution's section 81 right of appeal to the JCPC is insufficient as a remedy under any other statute. The Supreme Court affirmed that the Constitution is a law and cited multiple judgments to support its ruling that there cannot be concurrent processes that allow for the availability of both a section 17 claim for redress and an appeal to a higher court for the same decision.[54]

Regarding the issue of locus standi, according to subsection 1, a person who feels wronged and believes that any of the sections 3 through 16 are being violated or are

[51] DPP v Boodhoo (1992) MR 284.

[52] M G C Pointu v The Minister of Education and Science & Anor (1995) SCJ 359.

[53] Luk Tung v Commissioner of Police and ors (1997) MR 253.

[54] Chady S B v Habib Bank Ltd. (2015) SCJ 431.

likely to be violated in connection to him may file an application for redress. Section 83 allows anybody to request a declaration or redress if they believe that a provision of this Constitution has been violated and that the violation is affecting or likely to affect their interests. In the case of Beeharry v The State of Mauritius and Ors, the plaintiff failed to show a sufficient relationship between himself and the specifics of the alleged constitutional violation, and as a result, the Supreme Court rejected his action and upheld the defendants' objection.[55] In Tengur v Ministry of Education, the plaintiff attempted to contest the decision of the government to permit certain schools sponsored by public funds to reserve 50% of seats to pupils of a particular religious denomination as a taxpayer under section 17 of the Constitution. The plaintiff's failure to show a relationship between himself and the specific nature of the alleged constitutional violation, and consequently his standing, was deemed by the Supreme Court. The Supreme Court also stated that by filing a plaint, the plaintiff is essentially attempting to bring an action to court to litigate a topic of wide public interest, even though public interest litigation is outside the purview of our court.[56] It can be stated that the threshold is quite high when it comes to locus standi before the Supreme Court as revealed by several of its decisions.[57]

2.5 Derogation from Fundamental Rights and Freedoms under Emergency Powers

Section 18 of the Mauritius Constitution allows for deviations from basic freedoms and rights in the event of an emergency. It is necessary to define what constitutes an emergency in terms of fundamental freedoms and human rights before delving into this section. Accordingly, a period of emergency is defined by section 19(7) of the Constitution as any time that (1) Mauritius is involved in a war; (2) the President issues a proclamation declaring the existence of a state of public emergency; or (3) the Assembly adopts a resolution, backed by the votes of a majority of its members, stating that subversion poses a threat to Mauritius' democratic institutions. Section 19(8) states that a proclamation issued by the President pursuant to section 19(7) shall (a) expire when the Assembly is in session or when plans have been made for it to convene within 7 days of the date of the proclamation, unless the Assembly, by resolution, approves the proclamation within that 7-day period and (b) will expire if the Assembly does not meet and no plans are made for it to reconvene within 7 days, unless it meets and accepts the proclamation by resolution within 21 days. (c) The

55 Beeharry v The State of Mauritiuss & Ors (2008) SCJ 241.

56 Tengur v Ministry of Education (2002) SCJ 48.

57 Hurnam v State & Ors (2007) SCJ 140; Jaulim v DPP (1976) MR 96; Ius Ad Vitam Association v The State of Mauritius & Ors (2017) SCJ 1; Quedou v State of Mauritius (2005) SCJ 70; Betsy v Bank of Mauritius (1992) MR 231; Association of Campement Owners and Users v State of Mauritius & Anor (2007) MR 1; Duval v Seetrame and Attorney General (1991) MR 21; Valayden & Ors v President of the Republic of Mauritius (1995) SCJ 16.

proclamation may be withdrawn at any time by the President or the Assembly through resolution.

Section 19(9) outlines the maximum duration of the emergency that can be declared. It states that a resolution passed by the Assembly in support of section 19(7) will (a) stay in effect for the period that the Assembly may specify in the resolution, not to exceed 12 months; (b) be extended for additional periods, not to exceed 12 months at a time, by a subsequent resolution that is supported by the votes of a majority of all Assembly members; and (c) be revoked at any time by an Assembly resolution. Section 18, which deals with the derogations from fundamental rights and freedoms under emergency powers, states that nothing done or contained in a law shall be deemed to be in conflict with or in violation of any applicable sections to the extent that the law permits the taking of reasonable measures to address the situation that exists in Mauritius during any public emergency. The Supreme Court of Mauritius provided clarity on a crucial issue: could the Court declare that a state of emergency should end if it was satisfied that the conditions that initially warranted the declaration of a state of emergency were no longer present? The Supreme Court took this important issue into consideration in the case of Mathoorasing v Governor-General and declared that it possesses no such authority at all in the following terms:

> There would seem to be a short answer to this contention, which is that the Constitution has prescribed only two modes of terminating a period of emergency proclaimed by the governor general, namely, by revocation of the proclamation by the governor general himself on the one hand or by the Assembly on the other. Neither mode has been made to depend on prevalent conditions so that the advisability of revoking a proclamation remains a matter entirely for the responsible authority. We think that we would be arrogating to ourselves a power entrusted exclusively to others if we were to laugh upon an inquiry into those conditions and to interpose in the way desired by counsel and declare the emergency to be over.[58]

Meetarbhan stated that a claim that the declaration of a state of emergency was void and had lost its justification would not be taken into consideration by the Supreme Court.[59] It should be emphasised that since no states of emergency have been proclaimed since 1973, the Supreme Court has not had the chance to rule on any cases involving states of emergency. The Siracusa Principles unequivocally declare that a public emergency arises when a country's life is under danger.[60] It goes on to clarify that a threat to a nation's life is defined as one that impacts the entire population as well as all or a portion of the state's territory. It also includes threats to the population's physical integrity, the state's political independence, its territorial integrity, or the continued existence and proper operation of institutions that are essential to upholding and advancing the rights outlined in the Covenant.[61]

---

[58] Mathoorasing v Governor-General 1973 SCJ 156.

[59] Meetarbhan (2015), pp. 139–140.

[60] United Nations, Economic and Social Council, Siracusa Principles on the Limitation and Derogation Provisions in the International Covenant on Civil and Political Rights, U.N. Doc. E/CN.4/1985/4, Annex (1985).

[61] Siracusa Principles (1985) para 39.

It is important to stress that provision 19(7) of the Constitution, which was previously mentioned, may not be in accordance with the Siracusa Principles. It is true that there are no definitions or illustrative notes for several public emergency-related terms, including the term 'public emergency'. In the case of ending a public emergency, for example, paragraph 48 of the Siracusa Principles stipulates unequivocally that the public emergency must be ended as soon as possible in order to prevent it from endangering the lives of citizens. But neither the Constitution's section 19(7) nor Supreme Court case law has emphasised how important it is that the government terminate a state of emergency as quickly as feasible. Instead, it appears that the Supreme Court will refrain from interfering with the executive's decision about the length of a state of emergency in the Mathoorasing v Governor-General case because it will be satisfied if the constitutional provisions are followed, even though section 19(7)(b) appears to give the executive unlimited authority to extend a period of emergency indefinitely.[62]

Section 18 permits the government to suspend the bill of rights in times of public emergency based on a standard of 'reasonably justified', with regard to violations of constitutionally guaranteed rights during such time. The Siracusa Principles' barrier, which is based on being 'strictly required by the exigencies of the situation', is, in fact, significantly below this. Furthermore, as stated in paragraph 55 of the Siracusa Principles, the Constitution does not expressly mention the possibility of 'prompt and periodic independent review by the legislature of the necessity for derogation measures'. In addition, it appears that there are no meaningful constitutional remedies available to those who argue that derogatory actions against them are not absolutely necessary given the circumstances, in contrast to what paragraph 56 of the Siracusa Principles stipulates. This view is further undermined by the Supreme Court's lack of judicial activism and its conservative and limiting inclination to uphold what the Constitution says—or does not say—so far.[63]

2.6 The National Human Rights Commission

There is a significant number of human rights institutions in Mauritius such as the Equal Opportunities Commission, the Ombudsperson for Children, the Independent Police Complaints Commission, and the Human Rights Division operating directly in the field of human rights. They would be discussed in subsequent chapters of this book. For now, there is a need to focus on the National Human Rights Commission (NHRC) given that it is a quasi-judicial body which has the mandate to protect and promote all human rights of Mauritius in a general sense. Ideally, the NHRC is supposed to complement the judiciary in ensuring the respect, protection, and promotion of human rights in Mauritius. But how far has it succeeded?

[62] Mathoorasing v Governor-General 1973 SCJ 156.

[63] Mahadew (2018), pp. 189–204.

The NHRC was established under the Protection of Human Rights Act 1998 (PHRA 1998) with the primary objectives of promotion and protection of human rights. According to section 3A of the PHRA 1998, the NHRC is mandated to:

> promote and protect human rights; review the safeguard provided by or under any enactment for the protection of human rights; review the factors or difficulties that inhibit the enjoyment of human rights; submit to the Minister any opinion, recommendation, proposal or report on any matter concerning the promotion and protection of human rights; prepare reports on the national situation with regard to human rights in general, and on more specific matters; inform the Minister of situations of violation of human rights and advise on ways in which such situations can be ended; promote and ensure the harmonisation of national legislation and practices with the international human rights instruments to which Mauritius is a party, and their effective implementation; encourage ratification or accession to the instruments referred to in paragraph (g), and ensure their implementation; contribute to the reports which Mauritius is required to submit to United Nations bodies and committees, and to regional institutions, pursuant to its treaty obligations and, where necessary, to express an opinion on the subject, with due respect for its independence; cooperate with the United Nations and any other organisation in the United Nations system, the regional institutions and the national institutions of other countries that are competent in the areas of the protection and promotion of human rights; assist in the formulation of programmes for the teaching of, and research into, human rights and take part in their execution in schools, universities and professional circles; publicise human rights and efforts to combat all forms of discrimination by increasing public awareness, especially through information and education and by making use of all press organs and exercise such other functions as it may consider to be conducive to the promotion and protection of human rights.

The NHRC is accredited with 'A' status by the Global Alliance of National Human Rights Institutions (GANHRI), which was founded under the Office of the High Commissioner for Human Rights in Geneva, and it arguably functions in compliance with the Paris Principles. It is also a member of the following organisations: The Global Alliance of National Human Rights Institutions (GANHRI) based in Geneva, the regional Network of African National Human Rights Institutions (NANHRI) based in Nairobi, the Association Francophone des Commissions Nationales des Droits de L'Homme (AFCNDH) based in Paris, and the Commonwealth Forum of National Human Rights Institutions (CFNHRI).[64] It has also witnessed a number of structural changes. In 2003, Following the passage of the Sex Discrimination Act of 2002, the NHRC formed a Sex Discrimination Division to look into allegations of sex discrimination and sexual harassment. However, since the Equal Opportunities Act of 2008 was passed replacing the Sex Discrimination Act 2002, the said Division was dismantled. In 2012, the NHRC underwent substantial structural modifications that have led to the creation of three distinct divisions: the National Preventive Mechanism Division (NPMD), the Police Complaints Division, and the Human Rights Division (HRD). As of 2018, the National Preventive Mechanism Division and the Human Rights Division are the two divisions that make up the National Human Rights Commission currently.

[64] NHRC Website (2024).

Since the Independent Police Complaints Commission (IPCC) was founded in 2018, the NHRC's Police Complaint Division is no longer in existence.[65]

Allegations of rights abuses mentioned in Chapter II of the Constitution are to be investigated by the HRD.[66] Section 4 of the Protection of Human Rights Act 1998 states that the HRD may investigate any written complaint from any individual claiming that his or her human rights have been, are being, or are likely to be infringed by the act or omission of any other person acting in the discharge of a public function provided by any law, or otherwise in the fulfilment of the duties of any public office or public body,[67] without prejudice to the authority of the Courts, the powers granted on the Director of Public Prosecutions, or the relevant Service Commission. Section 4(2)(a) imposes a time limit of 2 years for the complaint to be made since the act of commission or omission forming the basis of the complaint took place. In cases where the Human Rights Division is unable to reach a resolution through conciliation, it will, upon completion of its investigation, (a) refer the matter to (i) the Director of Public Prosecutions if it appears that an offence may have been committed; (ii) the appropriate Service Commission if it appears that disciplinary procedures may be warranted; (iii) the Chief Executive Officer of the appropriate public body if it appears that disciplinary action is warranted against an employee of a public body who is not under the purview of a Service Commission and (b) recommend that the complainant be granted such relief or to such.[68]

Since 2013, when the Criminal Appeal Act was amended, the HRD has the authority to request that convictions be reviewed by the Supreme Court in cases when convicted parties provide new and convincing evidence to refute their convictions. A convicted person or his representative may apply to the HRD under section 4A in the format that may be prescribed, asking for an investigation into whether there is enough new and convincing evidence to persuade the HRD to refer a case under section 19A(4) of the Criminal Appeal Act. Upon receiving an application, the HRD will (a) carry out any preliminary inquiry that it deems necessary; (b) determine whether to look into the case within 30 days of receiving the application; and (c) notify the convicted party or his agent of the decision.[69]

Mauritius became a state party to the Convention Against Torture (C.A.T.) on 21 June 2005 and also became a member of the Optional Protocol to the Convention Against Torture and other Cruel, Inhuman or Degrading Treatment or Punishment (O.P.C.A.T.). Consequently, the National Preventive Mechanism (NPM) function was taken over by the National Human Rights Commission (NHRC) in Mauritius. The National Preventive Mechanism Act 2012 (NPMA 2012), which was passed on

[65] NHRC Website (2024).

[66] Section 4(1) PHRA 1998.

[67] Section 2 PHRA 1998—Public body means a ministry or government department, a local authority, a statutory corporation, or any other company, partnership, or other entity of which the government or an agency of the government is, by the holding of shares or some other financial input or in any other manner, in a position to influence the policy or decisions.

[68] Section 4(4) PHRA 1998.

[69] Section 4A PHRA 1998.

3 August 2012, gave rise to the NPM Division (NPMD) in 2014. The NPMD has been one of the two Divisions of the NHRC since its founding. According to the NPMA 2012, the NPMD is in charge of making sure public bodies and authorities uphold the fundamental human rights of prisoners as outlined in the Nelson Mandela Rules, or UN Standard Minimum Rules for the Treatment of Prisoners, which were approved by the UN General Assembly on 17 December 2015.[70] Section 4 of the NPMA 2012 imposes an obligation on the NPMD to regularly visit detention facilities to inspect the treatment of individuals detained in order to guarantee their safety from torture and cruel or degrading treatment or punishment, to look into any complaints that a detainee might make and, upon request, look into the complaint in secret, to provide suggestions to the Minister concerning the enhancement of the circumstances and treatment of those deprived of their freedom in detention facilities, while considering pertinent United Nations standards, to provide recommendations and comments regarding legislation pertaining to detention facilities and the treatment of individuals deprived of their freedom to the Minister and other pertinent authorities, and to carry out any of its duties under this Act and the Optional Protocol in cooperation or consultation, as appropriate, with any person or body, whether public or private.

The promotion of human rights mandate of the NHRC is generally characterised by workshops, sensitisation, and educational campaigns and training given to relevant stakeholders. For instance, for the year 2023, the NHRC focused on drugs issues, gender-based violence, delays in police enquiries, prisons, prevention of torture, business and human rights, women's sexual and reproductive health rights, sexual minorities rights, rights of older persons, rights of persons with disabilities, children's rights, climate change, mental health, and human rights and human trafficking.[71] The Annual Reports also contain information about the various workshops, seminars, and webinars organised by the NHRC or in which it participated in a heavily descriptive manner.[72] While the promotion of human rights is an important aspect of the work of the NHRC, it seems that this is all that is done or focused on by the NHRC. The NHRC does not sufficiently and critically engage in discussion of key issues on human rights. None of its recent reports since 2020 provide evidence of its duty of encouraging the government to ratify or accede to human rights treaties and conventions that are relevant to Mauritius. It is silent on the need for domestication of treaties and conventions that have already been ratified and does not deal with the issue of harmonisation of domestic human rights laws with international obligations.

For instance, its Annual Reports of 2020 and 2021 covered the issue of COVID-19 and human rights in a minimum number of pages in a way that would amount to 'stating the obvious'.[73] The poor performance of the NHRC during the pandemic

[70] UNODC (2015).

[71] NHRC Annual Report (2023), pp. 5–50.

[72] NHRC Annual Report (2021), pp. 29–39 & 57–60.

[73] NHRC Annual Report (2020), pp. 5–7; NHRC Annual Report (2021), pp. 6–8.

time can easily be gauged when one finds that the South African Human Rights Commission (SAHRC) went as far as legally challenging the City of Cape Town on the issue of governmental responses to evictions during the pandemic.[74] Such a move by the NHRC is unfathomable in Mauritius. Being the most important national human rights institution in the country, the NHRC is way too dormant and inactive. While the people would level criticism against actions of the government that affect human rights of Mauritians, the NHRC would be completely silent, except for a few passing remarks in its annual reports in descriptive and well-weighed terms.[75] What explains such a position or stand of the NHRC?

There are a number of critical limitations to the way the NHRC functions which does not allow it to play a key role in its duty to promote and protect human rights. The NHRC does not have any mention in the Constitution of Mauritius as the supreme law. This is contrary to the SAHRC which is explicitly mentioned in the Constitution of South Africa as one of the 'institutions that strengthen constitutional democracy in the Republic'.[76] The Constitution of South Africa further provides that:

> These institutions are independent and subject only to the Constitution and the law, and they must be impartial and must exercise their powers and perform their functions without fear, favour, or prejudice. Other organs of state, through legislative and other measures, must assist and protect these institutions to ensure the independence, impartiality, dignity, and effectiveness of these institutions. No person or organ of state may interfere with the functioning of these institutions. These institutions are accountable to the National Assembly and must report on their activities and the performance of their functions to the Assembly at least once a year.[77]

There are no similar constitutional provisions on the NHRC that exist in the legal framework on human rights in Mauritius. Section 3(2) does provide that 'the Commission shall not, in the exercise of its functions, be subject to the direction or control of any other person or authority'. This is not comparable to the way the SAHRC has been conferred constitutional guarantee for its independence, impartiality, dignity, and effectiveness. As such, the NHRC's mandate, powers, and, other crucial components can be readily modified by a simple majority in Parliament to align with the policies of the ruling administration. The mode of appointment of the chairperson, the deputy chairpersons, and the members is questionable. The President, acting on the Prime Minister's advice, appoints the chairperson, the deputy chairperson, and the members of each division on such terms and conditions as the President deems appropriate. Furthermore, the President is required to consult with the opposition leader regarding this issue.[78] This is again in sharp contrast with the South African model. According to the South African Human Rights Commission Act 2013 (SAHRCA 2013), the President must, on the recommendation of the

---

[74] South African Human Rights Commission v City of Cape Town 2021 2 SA 565 (WCC).

[75] Mahadew (2022), pp. 255–281.

[76] Section 181(1) Constitution of South Africa.

[77] Section 181(2), (3), (4) & (5) Constitution of South Africa.

[78] Section 8 PHRA 1998.

National Assembly, appoint a chairperson and deputy chairperson of the commission, respectively.[79] As for the commissioners (the equivalent of members of the NHRC in Mauritius), the South African National Assembly must recommend individuals nominated by the National Assembly committee that is proportionally made up of members of all parties represented in the Assembly and approved by the Assembly by a resolution adopted with the support of a majority of the members of the Assembly.[80] Section 59(1)(a) of the Constitution of South Africa provides for the participation of civil society in the recommendation process.

In Mauritius, the chairperson, the deputy chairpersons and the members are de facto nominated by the Prime Minister despite the procedural requirement of section 8 of the PHRA 1998 and approved by the Cabinet of Ministers headed by the Prime Minister himself. According to this appointment process, the Prime Minister would often select candidates that he/she is confident will not cause problems. A fervent advocate for human rights, for example, would probably not be the best choice since they may disagree with the current government's actions regarding national human rights and insist that it be held responsible and liable. The UN HRC has raised concern regarding the appointment of the members of the NHRC, qualifying it as 'not sufficiently transparent and participative'.[81] There is a contention that the selection of NHRC members is purely a political process and that the appointment process is likely to favour people who are 'well liked' by the administration. This has a detrimental effect on the NHRC's independence since it raises the potential that it will not be willing to look into or report on human rights incidents that damage the government's reputation. At the NHRC, these high-level positions are chosen and appointed without a democratic selection process or open, public advertisement.

Section 3 of the Protection of Human Rights Act stipulates that the chairman must have served as a judge, magistrate, or legal practitioner for a minimum of 10 years in order to qualify as the chairwoman or deputy chairperson. It is mandatory for the deputy chairperson to have practiced law for a minimum of 5 years. Human rights issues are not limited to those who have practiced law, even if it is crucial that those appointed at that level have a strong legal experience. Furthermore, there is no rational basis for requiring legal experience for both the chairman and deputy chairpersons. The requirements for qualification, particularly for deputy chairpersons, should have been more accommodating to those with credentials in social work, sociology, and similar subjects. This would have provided the NHRC with a multidisciplinary focus, which would have ultimately produced better, more productive outcomes.

Undoubtedly, much more is required by the NHRC for a genuine promotion and protection of human rights in Mauritius. While the contribution of the HRD with its

[79] Section 6(1) of the SAHRCA 2013.

[80] Section 193(5) Constitution of South Africa.

[81] UN HRC, Concluding Observations on the Fifth Periodic Report of Mauritius, UN Doc CCPR/C/MUS/CO/5 (9 November 2017), paragraph 7.

42 hearings completed out of 193 complaints[82] and that of the NPMD with 117 complaints on conditions of detention and others[83] are notable, it is required to do much by law. Its perceived lack of independence and autonomy and a lack of genuine willingness from the people who have headed it since its creation have posed impediments to its effective functioning. There is a crucial need for legal amendments to be brought to its structure and mode of appointment as well as confer a degree of constitutional protection to it.

References

Apodaca C (2003) The rule of law and human rights. Judicature 87:292

Ballgobin VD (2017) Cyclones (1960–1980) and housing policy: toward an internally controlled migration? Revue Historique de l'Océan Indien 14:260–277

Ballhatchet K (1995) The structure of British official attitudes: colonial Mauritius, 1883–1968. Hist J 38(4):989–1011

Council of Europe (23 October 1953) Declaration from the Permanent Representative of the UK

De Mesquita BB, Downs GW, Smith A, Cherif FM (2005) Thinking inside the box: a closer look at democracy and human rights. Int Stud Q 49(3):439–457

Gray S (2023) Colonial continuities in independent Mauritius: parliamentary democracy, the British Crown, and state repression. J Indian Ocean World Stud 7(1):36–58

Holmberg L (1962) Mauritius. A study in disaster. Econ Hist 5(1):3–29

Kasenally R (2018) Political leadership in Mauritius, The Mauritian paradox: fifty years of development, diversity and democracy, p 43

Mahadew R (2018) Does the Mauritian Constitution protect the right to privacy? An insight from Madhewoo v The State of Mauritius. Afr Hum Rights Law J 18(1):189–204

Mahadew R (2022) The constitutionality of legal measures taken by the Government of Mauritius in the context of the Covid-19 pandemic. In: Constitutional resilience and the COVID-19 pandemic: perspectives from Sub-Saharan Africa. Springer International Publishing, Cham, pp 255–281

Meetarbhan M (2015) Constitutional law of Mauritius: constitution of Mauritius with commentaries. Precigraph Mauritius

National Human Rights Commission (2020) Annual Report Available at nhrc.govmu.org Accessed 20 May 2025.

National Human Rights Commission (2021) Annual Report Available at nhrc.govmu.org Accessed 20 May 2025.

National Human Rights Commission (2023) Annual Report Available at nhrc.govmu.org Accessed 20 May 2025.

National Human Rights Commission Website (2024) Home. Available at https://nhrc.govmu.org/Pages/index.aspx. Accessed 20 May 2025

North-Coombes MD (2018) From slavery to indenture: forced labour in the political economy of Mauritius 1834-1867. In: Indentured labour in the British Empire, 1834–1920. Routledge, pp 78–125

Ramtohul R (2016) Contested terrain: identity and women's suffrage in Mauritius. J South Afr Stud 42(6):1225–1239

Report of the Mauritius Constitutional Conference September 1965' Sessional Paper No. 6 of 1965

---

[82] NHRC Annual Report (2023), pp. 53–58.

[83] NHRC Annual Report (2023), pp. 110–115.

Rughoonundun-Chellapermal N (2022) Pluralism without inclusion: the case of Mauritius, a linguistically diverse diasporic small Island developing state (sids). In: Handbook of language policy and education in countries of the Southern African Development Community (SADC). Brill, pp 199–221

Seekings J (2011) British colonial policy, local politics, and the origins of the Mauritian welfare state, 1936–50. J Afr Hist 52(2):157–177

Seetulsingh DB (2004) Mauritius. Hum Rights Law Afr Online 2(1):1309–1330

Stanziani A (2020) Slavery and post-slavery in the Indian Ocean world. In: Oxford research encyclopedia of African history

Truth and Justice Commission (Mauritius) (2011) Report of the truth and justice commission (Vol 1)

UNODC (2015) The United Nations Standard Minimum Rules for the Treatment of Prisoners (the Nelson Mandela Rules). Available at https://www.unodc.org/documents/justice-and-prison-reform/Nelson_Mandela_Rules-E-ebook.pdf. Accessed 20 May 2025

Vaughan M (1998) Slavery and colonial identity in eighteenth-century Mauritius. Trans R Hist Soc 8:189–214

Chapter 3
The Role and Impact of African Regionalism on the Protection and Promotion of Human Rights in Mauritius

Abstract The impacts and effects of African regionalism on Mauritius' human rights situation are examined in this chapter. It is divided into four sections. Determining the unique relevance of regionalism to small nations and small island economies is the first step. After introducing African regionalism, it highlights recent advancements and developments while providing a summary of its origins and traits. The impact of African regionalism on human rights in Mauritius is discussed in the third section. It pulls from two recent events to demonstrate the African Union's increasing influence in advancing Mauritius' human rights interests, in addition to stressing the prospects presented as a regional system of human rights protection and as a norm builder. The chapter concludes by outlining prospective collaboration paths and discussing the unrealised significance of Mauritius' engagement with the African supranational order in terms of the realisation and advancement of human rights.

3.1 Introduction

Regionalism, the process of deepened regional cooperation and integration and the partial transfer of decision and norm making to supranational institutions in view of managing international interdependence,[1] has progressed incrementally in Africa. Pan-Africanism may have held sway in the post-colonial era, yet the implied erosion of Westphalian sovereignty and incursions to the sustainability of a neo-patrimonial state system have unabatedly met with significant resistance from African states.[2] The phenomenon gained ground with the creation of the African

[1] For definitions and characteristics of regionalism, see notably Fawcett (2004), Hettne (2005), Mansfield and Solingen (2010), and Söderbaum (2013). For the practice of regionalism in a comparative and the African context, see Börzel and Risse (2016), Fawcett and Gandois (2010), and Iroulo and Lenz (2022).

[2] See notably Gibb (2009), Fagbayibo (2013) and Aniche (2020).

R. Mahadew, *Mauritius and African Human Rights Law*,
https://doi.org/10.1007/978-3-032-08832-1_3

Union[3] in 2000 which paved the way for accelerating African regional integration, bolstered by the adoption of the African Union Agenda 2063[4] in 2013 and more recently by the establishment of the African Continental Free Trade Area[5] coupled with the adoption of the African Union Protocol on Free Movement[6] in 2018. Enhanced regional integration presents multiple benefits for states, both economic, political, and social, and even more profoundly for small nations, typically disadvantaged by their marginality along with their relatively low bargaining power and high negotiation costs in the international arena.[7]

For Small Island Developing States (SIDS)[8] such as Mauritius, in particular, regional cooperation and integration are vital, given their small size, remoteness, exposure to external shocks, vulnerability to natural disasters and climate change, dependence on international trade, economic volatility, and limited resources and capacity.[9] Significantly, the impacts of these adverse factors are felt first by local communities.[10] This has been prominently recognized in the post-2015 development agenda of SIDS, which stresses the urgent need to scale up cooperation at the national, regional, and international levels to address the distinct challenges and vulnerabilities of Small Island Developing States in favour of their sustainable development[11] while underlining the intimate interdependency of human rights and

[3] African Union Constitutive Act (AU Constitutive Act), adopted by the 36th Ordinary Session of the Assembly of Heads of State and Government of the Organisation of African Unity (OAU), 11 July 2000, Lomé, Togo, OAU Doc CAB/LEG/23.15.

[4] African Union Commission (AUC), *African Union Agenda 2063: A Shared Strategic Framework for Inclusive Growth and Sustainable Development,* Addis Ababa, Ethiopia (January 2013).

[5] Agreement Establishing the African Continental Free Trade Area, adopted by the tenth Extraordinary Summit of the Heads of State and Government of the African Union, 21 March 2018, Kigali, Rwanda, 58 ILM 1028.

[6] Protocol to the Treaty Establishing the African Economic Community Relating to Free Movement of Persons, Right of Residence and Right of Establishment, adopted by the 13th Ordinary Session of the Heads of State and Government of the African Union, 29 January 2018, Addis Ababa, Ethiopia, available at https://au.int/en/treaties/protocol-treaty-establishing-african-economic-community-relating-free-movement-persons

[7] African Union Commission (2021) African Integration Report 2021: Putting Free Movement of Persons at the Centre of Continental Integration, available at https://au.int/en/documents/african-integration-report-2021 Accessed 20 December 2022, p. 10.

[8] SIDS are a distinct group of developing countries, first recognised at the United Nations Conference on Environment and Development (UNCED) in 1992, to share specific social, economic, and environmental challenges and vulnerabilities. SIDS comprise 38 UN Member States and 20 non-UN members/Associate Members of Regional Commissions.

[9] Bishop et al. (2021).

[10] United Nations Economic Commission for Africa (2014), Climate Change in the African Small Island Developing States: From Vulnerability to Resilience—The Paradox of the Small, available at https://repository.uneca.org/handle/10855/22515 Accessed 20 December 2022, p. v.

[11] Small Island Developing States Accelerated Modalities of Action (SAMOA Pathway) adopted by UN General Assembly Resolution 69/15 ‘Small Island Developing States Accelerated Modalities of Action (SAMOA Pathway)’ Samoa, 14 November 2014, para 21.

development in SIDS.[12] The critical reliance of SIDS on reinforced regional cooperation and integration for advancing their effective economic and social development has called for better harmonisation and coordination across relevant mechanisms.[13] In the African context notably, the African Union has underscored the sustainable development of island states as an inextricable component of the continent's socio-economic progress.[14]

The economic paybacks of regional integration for Mauritius have attracted steady scholarly interest from the fields of trade and economics.[15] Conversely, the equally crucial influence of the continental framework as impetus towards sustainable, inclusive, and human-centred development and the fulfilment and promotion of human rights in Mauritius has benefitted from considerably less academic insight.[16] Although Mauritius is a member of regional and subregional structures, it has not developed a comprehensive regional integration strategy, which would provide the basis for coordinating cooperation on sustainable development and human rights. A better-defined agenda would potentially also enhance peer learning and knowledge transfer.

This chapter examines the role and impact of African regionalism in the sphere of human rights in Mauritius. It is structured in four parts. It begins with defining the special pertinence of regionalism to small states and small island economies. Then it introduces African regionalism, through an overview of its conception and characteristics while highlighting recent progress and developments. The third section articulates the role of African regionalism in human rights in Mauritius. Aside from highlighting the opportunities proffered as a regional system of human rights protection and as a norm creator, it also draws from two contemporary developments to illustrate the growing impact of the African Union in furthering the interests of Mauritius in the realm of human rights. The chapter ends with concluding remarks on the untapped relevance of the relationship between Mauritius and the African supranational order towards the realisation and promotion of human rights while defining trajectories for future cooperation.

---

[12] Ibid, para. 7.

[13] Harris and Khonje (2011), p. 80.

[14] Declaration in Support of Small Island Developing States ahead of the Third International Conference on Small Island Developing States to be held in Samoa from 1 to 4 September 2014, adopted by the 23rd Ordinary Session of the Assembly of Heads of State and Government of the African Union, 26–27 June 2014, Malabo, Equatorial Guinea, Assembly/AU/Decl.3 (XXIII).

[15] See notably Tandrayen-Ragoobur (2019); Tandrayen-Ragoobur, Tengur and Seewooruttun (2021); Gowreesunkar (2019) and Tsakok (2021).

[16] See notably Techane (2011).

3.2 SIDS and Regionalism

Small states are demonstrated to face unique structural constraints to their development, as a result of their innate vulnerability and dependency, while exposing power asymmetries found in the relative size of polities within the international political economy.[17] Small states employ a spectrum of strategies in the pursuit of better economic, social, and political positions. Kurecic identifies a few responses in this view, including bandwagoning, balancing, protection by larger states, neutrality, non-interference, cooperation with other smaller states, and integration,[18] which he notes differ subject to the regional position, history, and economy of small states.[19] Strikingly, Baldacchino and Wivel underline that the influence of small states on the international plane is negotiated and maximized in institutions, which act as shelters from external shocks and platforms for influence.[20] It has been found that small states benefit the most from international institutions.[21] By setting standards, monitoring compliance, and prescribing sanctions, multilateral institutions attenuate power divergences based on territorial size and facilitate reciprocity.[22] They also reduce the transaction costs of diplomacy, by bringing together actors. Given their diplomatic resource limitations, small states stand more to profit in this regard, particularly in access to information, learning best practices and forging relationships.[23] Small states also have more to benefit from the security gains brought about by international institutions.[24]

The framing of the interests of small island states within the international community has evolved over time since the emergence of newly independent states after decolonisation, mostly shaped by the dynamics of the relationship between developed and developing countries.[25] Small island states became a distinct developing country category in the international arena under the United Nations Conference on Trade and Development (UNCTAD) III, characterised by their smallness, remoteness from main shipping routes and world markets, and exposure to natural disasters.[26] The first report on small island states shed light on three singular issues.[27] First, their highly specialized and often externally controlled economies and resulting economic dependence were underlined. Second, it pointed to the limited skilled

[17] Baldacchino and Wivel (2020).

[18] Kurecic (2017a), p. 280.

[19] Kurecic (2017b), p. 343.

[20] Baldacchino and Wivel (2020), p. 13.

[21] Neumann and Gstöhl (2006).

[22] Thorhallsson and Steinsson (2017).

[23] Ibid.

[24] Ibid.

[25] Grote (2010).

[26] Report of the Sixth Committee, Proceedings of the United Nations Conference on Trade and Development, Third Session, Santiago de Chile. 13 April–21 May 1972. TD/180, Vol. I, p. 288.

[27] Developing Island Countries. Report of the Panel of Experts, TD/B/443/Rev. 1, New York 1974.

manpower, growing unemployment, and migration. The third challenge identified was their sustainability in light of the multiple constraints they are confronted with. Importantly, on all three fronts, the report recommended regionalism as a compelling remedy. Concerning economic dependence, it underscored the relevance of regional integration for enhancing the bargaining power of small island states in the face of limited local markets and resources. It also advanced regional capacity building initiatives, service institutions, and labour markets for offsetting skills gap. In addition, it was asserted that efforts should be focused, especially regionally, in supporting small island states.

Subsequent studies and policy instruments on the needs and solutions to the problems of small island states continued to stress upon the credence of cooperation arrangements and integration schemes.[28] Notably, regional cooperation and integration have featured prominently in seminal international policy initiatives on the sustainable development of small island states. The 1994 Barbados Programme of Action[29] identifies necessary actions across various cross-sectoral priority areas at the national, regional, and international levels. It also singles out regional institutions as a specific area.[30] It lays emphasis on the need to gather resources through regional cooperation and institutions, to tap into the programming, administrative, and implementation capacities of regional bodies, in view of ensuring complementarity of action.[31] It refers more specifically to research, training, the development and transfer of technology as well as technical assistance in the areas of environmental law. The 2005 Mauritius Strategy[32] accentuates the role of strengthening regional intergovernmental institutions by providing economies of scale and expertise, in supporting the implementation of the Programme of Action.[33] The SIDS Accelerated Modalities of Action (SAMOA) Pathway, the outcome of the Third International Conference on Small Island Developing States in 2014, also underlines the importance of regional initiatives in a broad set of areas key to the development of small island states.

Although small states engage in multiple partnerships concurrently, regional affiliations presumably offer the most effective avenues for maximising influence and advancing interests. The diversity of small states manifests the precedence of regional approaches on the basis of factors other than size or insularity only.[34] This

[28] See Grote (n 25).

[29] Established by UN General Assembly Resolution 47/189, at the UN Global Conference on the Sustainable Development of SIDS, Barbados, 25 April–6 May 1994.

[30] Annex II, Report of the Global Conference on the Sustainable Development of SIDS, UN General Assembly A/CONF. 167/9, October 1994, Chapter XI.

[31] Ibid.

[32] Mauritius Strategy for the Further Implementation of the Programme of Action for the Sustainable Development of Small Island Developing States, UN Doc. A/CONF.207CRP.7, January 2005.

[33] Ibid, p. 8.

[34] Súilleabháin (2014), p. 7.

proposition becomes more forceful against the increasingly polarized character of geopolitics.[35]

3.3 African Regionalism and Human Rights

The institutional form of political and economic integration as well as that of the promotion and protection of human rights has constantly evolved in post-colonial Africa.[36] In the wake of the accession of African states to independence, the Organisation of African Unity (OAU) was founded to promote African unity and solidarity, to safeguard the sovereignty, territorial integrity, and independence of its member states, and to foster international cooperation.[37] Although inroads into the process of regional integration as well as, notably, the early development of human rights within the pan-African organisation[38] had begun since, as a hallmark of Africa's post-independence developmental strategy.[39] Its failure as a continental body is mainly attributed to its policy of non-interference in the internal affairs of member states and the polarisation among African states on the pace and scope of regional integration.[40] Despite these limitations, however, amidst the second wave of democratisation in Africa, and long-running mobilisation within the continent,[41] the first regional human rights instrument, the African Charter on Human and Peoples' Rights,[42] was adopted in 1981 and came into force in 1986. Its implementing organ, the African Commission on Human and Peoples' Rights (ACHPR), was established in 1987 and became fully operational in 1989.

The end of the Cold War heralded sturdier commitments towards economic integration. The Algiers Declaration, adopted in 1990, stressed the need to shift the primary focus of the OAU from political liberation and national building to

[35] See for instance Overseas Development Institute (2022) With Geopolitics Undermining Development in Small Island Developing States, Stronger Alliances are Needed More than Ever, available at https://odi.org/en/insights/with-geopolitics-undermining-development-in-small-island-developing-states-stronger-alliances-are-needed-more-than-ever/ Accessed 20 December 2022.

[36] See Viljoen (2012), pp. 151–212 for a comprehensive account of the evolution of the continental framework on regional integration and the protection and promotion of human rights.

[37] See Article 2 of the Charter of the Organization of African Unity (OAU Charter), adopted on 25 May 1963, 3 ILM 1116.

[38] Murray (2004) pp. 2–30.

[39] Khadiagala (2015).

[40] Kufuor (2005), p. 134.

[41] See Roberts (2023).

[42] African Charter on Human and Peoples' Rights ("Banjul Charter"), adopted by the 18th Assembly of the Heads of State and Government of the Organisation of African Unity, 27 June 1981, Nairobi, Kenya, OAU Doc CAB/LEG/67/3 rev. 5, 21 ILM 58; see also Umozurike (1983).

economic development.[43] Subscribing to a gradualist approach to economic integration, the OAU endorsed the formation of an economic community in stages. In 1991, the Treaty Establishing the African Economic Community was adopted, laying the groundwork for the creation of the African Economic Community (AEC), which would include the strengthening of the regional economic communities (RECs), the integration and harmonisation of economic sectors, and the establishment of a common African market and a pan-African economic and monetary union, among others.[44] Critical human rights instruments were also adopted in this period, including the African Charter on the Rights and Welfare of the Child[45] and the Protocol on the Establishment of an African Court on Human and Peoples' Rights.[46]

The establishment of the OAU's successor, the African Union (AU) in 2002, which was equipped with more robust administrative mechanisms and enhanced powers of intervention in member states, cemented the role of the continental body in spurring regionalism and regional integration efforts, notably in the fields of economic development, security, democratisation, and human rights.[47] Significantly, marking a clear break from the OAU, the realisation of regional integration and the promotion and protection of human rights constituted an express feature of the mandate of the AU.[48] Its objectives, as spelt out in its constitutive instrument, include the acceleration of the political and socio-economic integration of the continent, the integration of African economies, and the promotion and protection of human and peoples' rights.[49] Strikingly, the AU is also empowered to intervene in a member state pursuant to a decision of the Assembly of Heads of State and Government in respect of grave circumstances, namely, war crimes, genocide, and crimes against humanity.[50]

---

[43] Declaration on the Political and Socio-Economic Situation in Africa and the Fundamental Changes Taking Place in the World, adopted by the 26th Ordinary Session of the OAU Assembly Heads of State and Government, 9–11 July 1990, Addis Ababa, Ethiopia, OAU Doc AHG/Dec.1(XXVI).

[44] Treaty Establishing the African Economic Community, adopted by the Heads of State and Government of the Organization of African Unity, 3 June 1991, Abuja, Nigeria, 30 ILM 1241; see also Danso (1995).

[45] African Charter on the Rights and Welfare of the Child, adopted by the 26th Ordinary Session of the Heads of State and Government of the Organisation of African Unity, 11 July 1990, Addis Ababa, Ethiopia, CAB/LEG/24.9/49 (1990); see also Olowu (2002).

[46] Protocol to the African Charter on Human and Peoples' Rights on the Establishment of an African Court on Human and Peoples' Rights, adopted by the 34th Ordinary Session of the Assembly of Heads of State and Government of the Organisation of African Unity, 8–10 June 1998, Ouagadougou, Burkina Faso, available at https://au.int/en/treaties/protocol-african-charter-human-and-peoples-rights-establishment-african-court-human-and; see also Udombana (2000).

[47] See Packer and Rukare (2002).

[48] Nmehielle (2003).

[49] Article 3(c), (j) and (h) respectively of the AU Constitutive Act (third reference).

[50] Article 4(h) of the AU Constitutive Act (third reference).

Among the intricate institutional framework of the newly formed AU, a multiplicity of organs were established to consolidate the advancement of regional integration.[51] The African Peace and Security Architecture (APSA), including notably the AU Peace and Security Council, was created for fostering a long-term regional security and early-warning arrangement for decision-making for the prevention, management, and resolution of conflicts.[52] The New Partnership for Africa's Development (NEPAD), the AU's strategic framework for socio-economic development, focuses on regional integration as one of its priorities.[53] The African Peer Review Mechanism (APRM), established by the NEPAD Heads of State and Government Implementation Committee and later integrated into the AU,[54] is a monitoring mechanism geared to the adoption of policies and practices relating to sustainable development and regional integration.[55] The Pan-African Parliament (PAP) was set up with advisory and consultative functions, to ensure the participation of the African people in development and continental integration.[56] The African Governance Architecture was also established in view of promoting good governance and strengthening democracy in Africa.[57]

The advent of the AU also saw further development of human rights norms, including the adoption of the Protocol to the African Charter on the Rights of Women in Africa,[58] the AU Convention on Prevention and Combating Corruption

---

[51] See Maluwa (2003).

[52] Protocol Relating to the Establishment of the Peace and Security Council of the African Union, adopted by the first Ordinary Session of the Assembly of the African Union, 9 July 2002 in Durban, South Africa, AU Doc. 9/7/2002; see also Kindiki (2003).

[53] NEPAD was adopted by the 37th Ordinary Session of the Heads of State and Government of the Organisation of African Unity in July 2001 in Lusaka, Zambia. Declaration on the Implementation of the New Partnership for Africa's Development Ass/AU/Decl.1 (I), adopted by the Inaugural Session of the Assembly of the African Union, July 2002, Durban, South Africa, available at https://archives.au.int/handle/123456789/334; see also Baimu (2002) and Appiagyei-Atua (2006).

[54] Decision on the Integration of the APRM into the African Union, adopted by the 23rd Ordinary Session of the Assembly of Heads of State and Government of the African Union, 26–27 June 2014, Malabo, Equatorial Guinea, Doc Assembly AU Dec 527 (XXIII).

[55] The New Partnership for Africa's Development: The African Peer Review Mechanism (APRM Base Document) adopted by the 38th Ordinary Session of the Organisation of African Unity, 8 July 2002, Durban, South Africa, AHG/235 (XXXVIII) Annex II; see also Kanbur (2004).

[56] Article 14 of the Treaty Establishing an African Economic Community (twentieth reference); Articles 5 and 17 of the AU Constitutive Act (third reference); Protocol to the Constitutive Act of the African Union Relating to the Pan-African Parliament, adopted by the 23rd Ordinary Session of the Assembly of Heads of State and Government of the African Union, 27 June 2014, Malabo, Equatorial Guinea, available at https://au.int/sites/default/files/treaties/7806-treaty-0047_-_protocol_to_the_constitutive_act_of_the_african_union_relating_to_the_pan-african_parliament_e.pdf; see also Magliveras and Naldi (2003).

[57] Decision on the Theme, Date and Venue of the Sixteenth Ordinary Session of the Assembly of the African Union, adopted by the 15th Ordinary Session of the Assembly of Heads of State and Government of the African Union, 25–27 July 2010, Kampala, Uganda, Doc Assembly/AU/Dec.304(XV); see also Kariseb and Okoloise (2019).

[58] Protocol to the African Charter on Human and People's Rights on the Rights of Women in Africa, adopted by the second Ordinary Session of the Assembly of Heads of State and Government of the

and related offences,[59] the African Charter on Democracy, Elections and Governance,[60] and the AU Convention for the Protection and Assistance of Internally Displaced Persons in Africa.[61] The Protocol on the Establishment of an African Court on Human and Peoples' Rights also came into force. Significantly, the growing plethora of treaties, resolutions, and decisions of the AU over the years on far-reaching issues affecting the continent has prompted recognition of the emergence of an African Union legal order, with considerable impact on domestic law, importantly in the areas of human rights, the rule of law, and constitutional law.[62]

On the 50th anniversary of the continental body, the AU adopted Agenda 2063, its long-term strategic framework for the development of the continent.[63] It also launched the Common African Position on the post-2015 development Agenda which notably highlights the need for enhancing the implementation and impact of extant mechanisms such as the APRM, NEPAD, and the African Governance Architecture, as well as for enhancing the protection of human rights and accountability.[64] A revised Protocol on the Pan-African Parliament, designating the Pan-African Parliament as the legislative organ of the AU, was adopted.[65] It has however yet to come into force. A series of institutional and financial reforms in the face of the AU's challenges in spearheading socio-economic and political integration were also initiated.[66] The Kagame Report identified 21 recommendations cutting across 6

African Union, 11 July 2003, Maputo, Mozambique, available at https://au.int/en/treaties/protocol-african-charter-human-and-peoples-rights-rights-women-africa; see also Viljoen (2009).

[59] African Union Convention on Prevention and Combating Corruption and related offences, adopted by the second Ordinary Session of the Assembly of the Heads of State and Government of the African Union, 11 July 2003, Maputo, Mozambique, available at https://au.int/sites/default/files/treaties/36382-treaty-0028_-_african_union_convention_on_preventing_and_combating_corruption_e.pdf; see also Olaniyan (2004).

[60] African Charter on Democracy, Elections and Governance, adopted by the eighth Ordinary Session of the Assembly of the Heads of State and Government of the African Union, 30 January 2007, Addis Ababa, Ethiopia, available at https://au.int/en/treaties/african-charter-democracy-elections-and-governance; see also Wiebusch et al. (2019).

[61] African Union Convention for the Protection and Assistance of Internally Displaced Persons in Africa, adopted by the Special Summit of the African Union, 23 October 2009, Kampala, Uganda, available at https://au.int/en/treaties/african-union-convention-protection-and-assistance-internally-displaced-persons-africa; see also Abebe (2010).

[62] See Amao et al. (2021); Olivier (2015) and Lubbe and Spijkers (2021).

[63] African Union Commission, African *Union Agenda 2063: A Shared Strategic Framework for Inclusive Growth and Sustainable Development* (2013) Addis Ababa, Ethiopia; see also Vickers (2017).

[64] Common African Position on the post-2015 Development Agenda, adopted by the 22nd Ordinary Session of the Heads of State and Government of the African Union, 30–31 January 2014, Addis Ababa, Ethiopia, Doc Assembly/AU/Dec.503(XXII).

[65] Protocol to the Constitutive Act of the African Union Relating to the Pan-African Parliament, adopted by the 23rd Ordinary Session of the Assembly of the Heads of State and Government of the African Union, 27th June 2014, Malabo, Equatorial Guinea.

[66] Decision on the Institutional Reform of the African Union, adopted by the 27th Ordinary Session of the Assembly of Heads of State and Government of the African Union, 17–18 July 2016, Kigali, Rwanda, Doc Assembly/AU/Dec.606(XXVII).

reform areas, including the implementation of the Kigali Financing Decision and better coordination between the AU, RECs, member states, and other continental institutions.[67] Pursuant to the recommendations, the mandate of the APRM was expanded to include tracking and monitoring the implementation of Agenda 2063 and UN SDGs and to cover governance issues across all African states, beyond APRM members.[68]

Most recently, the African Continental Free Trade Area Agreement was adopted, providing for the creation of a single market for goods and services, facilitated by the free movement of persons, and geared towards, among others, the promotion of sustainable and inclusive socio-economic development, gender equality, and structural transformation of state parties.[69] The Protocol on the Free Movement of Persons was also adopted, establishing the progressive realisation of the free movement of persons in phases.[70]

3.4 Role and Impact of Regionalism in the Protection and Promotion of Human Rights in Mauritius

3.4.1 Mauritius and Regionalism

Mauritius joined the OAU after its accession to independence in 1968. It is also a member of Regional Economic Communities such as the Common Market for Eastern and Southern Africa (COMESA) since 1981 and the Southern African Development Community (SADC) since 1995. Its membership to COMESA and SADC grants Mauritius preferential market access to 25 African countries. It benefits from a 5% preferential tariff within COMESA and a 4% preferential tariff within SADC. Mauritius is also a member of the COMESA-EAC-SADC Tripartite Free Trade Area, which aims at harmonising trade policies across the member states

[67] Kagame P, 'The Imperative to Strengthen our Union: Report on the Proposed Recommendations for the Institutional Reform of the African Union', 29 January 2017, p. 3, https://au.int/sites/default/files/pages/34915-file-report-20institutional20reform20of20the20au-2.pdf Accessed 20 January 2023.

[68] Decision on the Revitalisation of the African Peer Review Mechanism, adopted by the 28th Ordinary Session of the Assembly of the Heads of State and Government of the African Union, 30–31 January 2017, Addis Ababa, Ethiopia, Doc Assembly/AU/Dec.631(XXVIII).

[69] Agreement Establishing the African Continental Free Trade Area (AfCFTA), adopted by the tenth Extraordinary Session of the Assembly of Heads of State and Government of the African Union, 21 March 2018, Kigali, Rwanda, available at https://au.int/en/treaties/agreement-establishing-african-continental-free-trade-area Accessed 20 January 2023.

[70] Protocol to the Treaty Establishing the African Economic Community Relating to Free Movement of Persons, Right of Residence and Right of Establishment, adopted by the 13th Ordinary Session of the Assembly of Heads of State and Government of the African Union, 29 January 2018, Addis Ababa, Ethiopia, available at https://au.int/en/treaties/protocol-treaty-establishing-african-economic-community-relating-free-movement-persons Accessed 20 January 2023.

of the three trading blocs. After Europe, Mauritius exports most to Africa, representing 25% of total exports, mainly to South Africa, Madagascar, and Kenya.[71] Approximately 14% of Mauritian imports originate from Africa, mostly from South Africa, Seychelles, Madagascar, Kenya, and Egypt.[72] Although trade was earlier deplored as being concentrated in a few countries only,[73] Mauritius' trading links with Africa have widely diversified in recent years.[74] Yet, similar to other African countries, intra-regional trade still remains underexploited as a result of limited shipping lines, poor infrastructure, and high freight costs.[75] Mauritius became a member of the AfCFTA on 7 October 2019. The latter brings about significant opportunities for Mauritius, given its low endowment of natural resources and its dependence on international trade as a small export-oriented economy, to position itself as a regional trade gateway, in line with the Mauritius-Africa Strategy.[76] Mauritius launched the AfCFTA National Strategy Response which aims to improve its readiness for intra-African trade. Notably it focuses on guidance on further economic diversification, increasing investment potential, addressing intellectual property rights, competition policy, and e-commerce, and mainstreaming gender, climate change mitigation, and digital technologies in pursuing necessary trade reforms.

The continental development agenda focuses on salient SIDS development priorities. Notably, Agenda 2063 stresses the links between the environment, climate, and long-term development. It defines environmentally sustainable and climate-resilient economies and communities as a goal, including priority areas such as sustainable natural resource management, biodiversity conservation, climate resilience and natural disasters preparedness and prevention, water security, and renewable energy. Additionally, the first AU Climate Change Strategy provides the continental framework for climate action and cooperation, centred around the principles of the green economy, sustainable development, and poverty reduction.[77] Agenda 2063 also points to the blue/ocean economy as another goal and catalyst for economic growth. The blue economy has also been increasingly identified as an important policy area for sustainable development in the Mauritian context. Mauritius is among the first countries on the continent, followed by Seychelles and South Africa, to have advanced blue economy policies and institutional frameworks.

---

[71] Tandrayen-Ragoobur (2019).

[72] Same as above.

[73] See the African Peer Review Mechanism, Mauritius Country Review Report (July 2010), available at https://www.aprm-au.org/wp-content/uploads/2014/11/admin_pdfFiles_CRR_No13-Mauritius_EN.pdf Accessed 20 January 2023, p 18.

[74] Tandrayen-Ragoobur (n 50).

[75] United Nations Economic Commission for Africa, The Mauritian Strategy to Leverage Opportunities in the African Continental Free Trade Area (2022), p. 14, available at https://repository.uneca.org/handle/10855/49336. Accessed 20 January 2022.

[76] Tsakok (2021).

[77] African Union AU Climate Change and Resilient Development Strategy and Action Plan 2022–2032, available at https://au.int/sites/default/files/documents/42276-doc-CC_Strategy_and_Action_Plan_2022-2032_23_06_22_ENGLISH-compressed.pdf. Accessed 20 January 2023.

Since the early 2010s, Mauritius has had a dedicated blue economy ministry and a consultative entity, the National Ocean Council. It has committed to boost the contribution of the blue economy to its GDP by 2025, focusing on fisheries, information and communications technology in maritime ports, marine energy, a seafood hub, sustainable aquaculture, and lagoon ecosystem management. The African Union's Department of Agriculture, Rural Development, Blue Economy, and Sustainable Environment (ARBE) is responsible for implementing the blue economy and sustainable environment policies, programmes, and strategies of the African Union Commission. The AU Africa Blue Economy Strategy adopted in 2019 highlights its significance in reducing poverty, creating employment, and providing food and energy security, within the continent, guiding member states in exploiting potential in blue economy sectors namely port and shipping, fishery, aquaculture, sustainable blue energy, ocean mining, oil and gas, coastal tourism, blue carbon and ecosystem services, and research and education.[78]

Whereas Mauritius has consistently ranked high in continental indexes on governance, a decline across various sectors such as public administration, rule of law, and corruption has been reported more recently.[79] These challenges have been recognized in Vision 2030, which highlights the need to improve transparency, effectiveness, and efficiency in the delivery of public services.[80] It has also receded in rankings on transparency and corruption.[81] Mauritius does not meet the commitment of SADC members to the 30% quota of women in government, Parliament, and political parties. The AU's commitment to the advancement of good governance is manifest in various instruments such as the Charter on Democracy, Elections and Governance (ACDEG), the OAU/AU Declaration on Principles Governing Democratic Elections, the New Partnership for Africa's Development (NEPAD) Declaration on Democracy, Political, Economic and Corporate Governance, the (Algiers and Lomé) Declarations on Unconstitutional Changes of Government, and the African Union Convention on Preventing and Combating Corruption.

The current Mauritian national development plan, *Vision 2030—Transforming Our Future for the Better*, identifies the enhancement of regional integration as a priority growth enabler, alongside good governance, infrastructure, transition to and storage of green energy, and human capital development.[82] Recently, the Mauritian

---

[78] African Union Africa Blue Economy Strategy (2019), available at https://www.au-ibar.org/sites/default/files/2020-10/sd_20200313_africa_blue_economy_strategy_en.pdf. Accessed 20 January 2023.

[79] See 2022 Ibrahim Index of African Governance, available at https://mo.ibrahim.foundation/sites/default/files/2023-01/2022-index-report.pdf. Accessed 20 January 2023.

[80] Vision 2030 (n 48).

[81] See 2022 Transparency International Corruption Perceptions Index, available at https://www.transparency.org/en/cpi/2022/index/mus Accessed 20 January 2023.

[82] Mauritius Vision 2030, available at https://www.foreignaffairs.com/sites/default/files/mauritius_jan-feb_2017_reprint_compr.pdf Accessed 20 January 2023.

experience during the COVID-19 pandemic demonstrated the need for a strengthened commitment to regional integration.[83]

3.4.2 *Gains for the Protection and Promotion of Human Rights: Norm Setting, Redress, and Oversight*

3.4.2.1 Norm Setting

As a member state of the African Union, Mauritius benefits from participating in the generation and diffusion of human rights legal standards within Africa and globally. The process of standard setting and norm creation on the global scale is typically thwarted with painstaking and complex negotiation and consensus building. It often eludes the democratic and equitable participation of actors, particularly marginalising partake and ownership by the Global South, smaller or poorer states, and their populations.[84] In this view, the African system, as a tighter-knit and 'like-minded' community with shared history and challenges, opens up opportunities for Mauritius to have a stronger voice in such processes. Norm diffusion and adhesion are especially meaningful for a SIDS such as Mauritius, where it has been shown that the commitment to the international rule of law is a vital means to elevate the status and position of small island states in the hierarchy within the international community.[85]

It is well established that whereas regional human rights systems are largely complementary to the universal UN system, they have on occasion created novel and innovative standards to respond to the political, economic, legal, and cultural particularities of the region. In fact, African human rights norms have in notable instances filled lacunae in global norms, by providing for an extended definition of 'refugee' in the OAU Refugee Convention and extending and refining the protection of the environment, children, women, internally displaced persons, and older persons.[86] The African Charter also singularly recognises collective or group rights and the right to economic, social, and cultural development.[87] This body of international law in turn has an important impact on domestic law, through its incorporation in national laws. The African Commission has also distinctly produced a wealth of soft law instruments which can inform and guide the interpretation and application of human rights law.[88] Mauritius ratified the African Charter on Human and Peoples'

[83] See notably COMESA 'Regional-Wide Post-COVID-19 Recovery Plan is a Top Priority' 27 September 2020, available at https://www.comesa.int/comesa-mauritius-considers-post-covid-19-regional-recovery-plan-as-priority/ Accessed 20 January 2023.

[84] Mutua (2007), pp. 557–578.

[85] See Slade (2003); Menon (2020).

[86] Viljoen (2001).

[87] Mutua (1995).

[88] Long and Murray (2016).

Rights[89] and the African Charter on the Rights and Welfare of the Child[90] in 1992. It signed the Maputo Protocol[91] with reservations in 2005, which it ratified in 2017. While it signed the African Charter on Democracy, Elections and Governance[92] in 2007, it has not ratified the latter yet. Similarly, it has signed but not ratified the OAU Convention Governing the Specific Aspects of Refugee Problems in Africa in 1972 and has not signed the AU Convention for the Protection and Assistance of Internally Displaced Persons in Africa. It should be noted from the above that in the absence of a designated office responsible for treaty monitoring and follow-up until recently, the ratification and domestication of African human rights instruments have been delayed and wanting in Mauritius.[93] The Mauritian Bill of Rights does not correspond with the African Charter in most part, thereby precluding 'indirect domestication'.[94] Constitutional and legal reforms in the last few years, despite deriving inspiration from the growing body of international human rights law, have been demonstrated not to have been influenced by the African human rights instruments but informed rather by instruments from the United Nations, the European system, or instruments from other jurisdictions.[95]

3.4.2.2 Redress

The African Commission, as a quasi-judicial mechanism, provides avenues for enforcing human rights. Under its protection mandate, it considers interstate and individual communications alleging violations of human and peoples' rights, in view of handing down recommendations for remedies. Significantly, standing as well as admissibility before the African Commission has been construed broadly. It has held that a communication ought to establish prima facie evidence of a violation without needing to be founded in a series of serious or massive violations of human rights.[96] In considering the exhaustion of local remedies, it has specified that local

[89] Ratification table: African Charter on Human and Peoples' Rights, available at https://achpr.au.int/en/charter/african-charter-human-and-peoples-rights Accessed 20 January 2023.

[90] Status List: African Charter on the Rights and Welfare of the Child, available at https://au.int/sites/default/files/treaties/36804-sl-AFRICAN_CHARTER_ON_THE_RIGHTS_AND_WELFARE_OF_THE_CHILD.pdf Accessed 20 January 2023.

[91] Status List: Protocol to the African Charter on Human and Peoples' Rights on the Rights of Women in Africa, available at https://au.int/sites/default/files/treaties/37077-sl-PROTOCOL_TO_THE_AFRICAN_CHARTER_ON_HUMAN_AND_PEOPLES_RIGHTS_ON_THE_RIGHTS_OF_WOMEN_IN_AFRICA.pdf Accessed 20 January 2023.

[92] Status List: African Charter on Democracy, Elections and Governance, available at https://au.int/sites/default/files/treaties/36384-sl-AFRICAN_CHARTER_ON_DEMOCRACY_ELECTIONS_AND_GOVERNANCE_0.pdf Accessed 20 January 2023.

[93] Techane and Mahadew (2016), pp. 168–173.

[94] Techane (n 16), pp. 13–15.

[95] Techane and Mahadew (n 74), p 172.

[96] *Sir Dawda K. Jawara v The Gambia*, Communication 147/95 and 149/96, 13th Activity Report, (2000) AHRLR 107, para 42.

remedies must be 'available, effective and sufficient'[97] as well as 'realistic' or 'sufficiently certain' not only in theory but also in practice.[98] Further, the African Commission found that where the jurisdiction of courts had been excluded by incontestable decrees, local remedies were unavailable and non-existent.[99] Also, complainants who are unable to engage domestic remedies for fear of persecution would be deemed to have exhausted local remedies.[100] Additionally, whereas the rights allegedly violated need to be contained in the African Charter, the Commission is required to draw from a range of international and regional human rights instruments as provided in article 60 of the Charter. The African Commission has had an expansive reading of the Charter rights, widening the protection of human rights.[101] It has eminently done so in recognising an implied right to housing and food into the Charter.[102] Furthermore, while it has initially emphasized dialogue for the amicable resolution of disputes, its recommendations have become significantly wide ranging and precise with the years, notably including rescission of deportation orders, restitution of property, abolition of corporal punishments, and just and equitable compensation.[103] The African Commission can also issue provisional measures to prevent irreparable harm to the victim.[104] The African Court complements the protective mandate of the African Commission by providing legally binding decisions since the Court became operational in 2006.

Mauritius has ratified the Protocol on the establishment of the African Court though it has not made the requisite declaration for direct access by individuals and NGOs to the Court. The Commission and the Court can serve as an important recourse for the provision of redress for violations and for the implementation of human rights. This may be particularly relevant in the Mauritian case, given the domestic judicial aversion to public interest litigation, limiting constitutional redress coupled with the dearth of domestication of international human rights law. Two complaints brought before the African Commission against Mauritius, *Digbeejaye Koonjul v The Republic of Mauritius*[105] and *Romy Goornah (Represented by Dev*

---

[97] Ibid, paras 31 and 35.

[98] *Purohit and Moore v The Gambia*, Communication 241/01, 16th Activity Report, (2003) AHRLR 96, paras 37 and 38.

[99] *Sir Dawda K. Jawara v The Gambia* (n 97), para 31.

[100] *Alhassan Abubakar v Ghana*, Communication 103/93, tenth Annual Activity Report, (2000) AHRLR 124, para 6.

[101] See for instance Kamga and Fombad (2013).

[102] *Social and Economic Rights Action Centre and the Centre for Economic and Social Rights v Nigeria*, (*SERAC v Nigeria*), Communication 155/96, 15th Annual Activity Report, 2001; (2001) AHRLR 60 paras, 60, 64–67.

[103] See Ssenyonjo (2018), pp. 12–18.

[104] Rules of Procedure of the African Commission on Human and Peoples' Rights, adopted by the African Commission on Human and Peoples' Rights during its 27th Extraordinary Session held in Banjul, 19 February–4 March 2020, Rule 100.

[105] *Digbeejaye Koonjul v The Republic of Mauritius*, Communication 569/15 (2020).

Hurnam) v Republic of Mauritius,[106] failed the admissibility test for not being submitted in reasonable time.

3.4.2.3 Oversight

The African Commission also undertakes various activities further to its promotional mandate.[107] Notably it considers state reports on measures taken to give effect to the Charter and adopts concluding observations.[108] The state reporting procedure is critical in treaty monitoring, enabling constructive engagement with the African Commission in identifying and acting upon bottlenecks in the implementation of and compliance with human rights instruments. The African Commission also appoints special rapporteurs and constitutes working groups on thematic human rights issues which examine developments relating to the areas of mandate and make recommendations for the improvement of human rights in their fields.

3.4.3 Gains for the Protection and Promotion of Human Rights: Recent Examples in Global Governance

3.4.3.1 Decolonisation of Chagos

The AU has emerged as an important actor in the Mauritian claim to sovereignty to the Chagos Archipelago, administered by the United Kingdom and leased to the United States as a military base, in exchange for Mauritian independence and at the expense of the indigenous rights of the exiled Chagossians. The AU called for 'ending the unlawful occupation of the Chagos Archipelago' in the Solemn Declaration on the 50th anniversary of the OAU/AU in 2013[109] and its 'return to the full control of Mauritius' in AU Assembly Resolution 1/(XXV) in 2015 amidst the Chagos Marine Protected Area Arbitration (Mauritius vs United Kingdom)[110] and expressed its support for the actions taken by Mauritius in the completion of its

[106] *Romy Goornah (Represented by Dev Hurnam) v Republic of Mauritius*, Communication 596/16 (2018).

[107] African Charter, Article 45.

[108] African Charter, Article 62.

[109] Adopted by the 21st Ordinary session of the Assembly of Heads of State and Government of the African Union, at Addis Ababa, on 26 May 2013, available at https://archives.au.int/bitstream/handle/123456789/320/Assembly%20AU%20Decl%203%20%28XXI%29%20_E.pdf?sequence=1&isAllowed=y Accessed 20 January 2023.

[110] AU Assembly Resolution on Chagos Archipelago, Assembly/AU/Res.1/(XXV) of June 2015, available at https://www.saflii.org/au/AURESOLUTIONS/2015/1.pdf Accessed 20 January 2023.

decolonisation in AU Assembly Resolution 1 (XXVIII) in 2017.[111] Resolution 71/292 requesting for the advisory opinion on the separation of Chagos was introduced by the Republic of the Congo on behalf of the member states of the UN that are members of the Group of African States. It notably mobilised further support by calling upon all member states and AU partners to make written submissions to the ICJ.[112] For the first time since its creation, the AU intervened before the International Court of Justice. In its submission, it relied on the doctrine of specially affected states and highlighted the significance of the case with regard to its own priorities, that is, the commitment to the protection of the right to self-determination of African peoples.[113] Post the ICJ's advisory opinion and the United Kingdom's lack of compliance, the AU has continued to press for the United Kingdom to surrender sovereignty of the islands. The AU's intervention and its emphasis on the decolonisation agenda help to draw the Court's attention to the effects of power on legal outcomes, pointing to the discourse on incursions to permanent sovereignty over wealth and resources by extractive initiatives.[114]

3.4.3.2 Climate Justice and Finance

The AU has also played a critical part in raising the profile of the needs and interests of SIDS within international negotiations for climate change, notably in climate justice and finance. The African Ministerial Conference on the Environment (AMCEN) plays a central role in Africa's approach to climate change, serving as the primary platform for environmental discussions on the continent. Complementing this, the AU has established the Committee of African Heads of State and Government on Climate Change (CAHOSCC). Together with AMCEN, CAHOSCC guides the African Group of Negotiators (AGN) within the AU framework for global environmental negotiations. The AU has issued numerous decisions on climate change, whereby it has highlighted its impacts on SIDS. In its Decision on Africa's Engagements at COP25, it supported the need for expediting the operationalisation of the Climate Commission for Island States and Ocean Economies.[115] It has also

---

[111] AU Assembly Resolution on Chagos Archipelago, Assembly/AU/Res.1 (XXVIII) of January 2017, available at https://au.int/sites/default/files/decisions/32520-sc19553_e_original_-_assembly_decisions_621-641_-_xxviii.pdf Accessed 20 January 2023.

[112] Decision on Chagos Archipelago, Assembly/AU/Dec.684(XXX), adopted by the 30th Ordinary session of the Assembly of Heads of State and Government of the African Union, at Addis Ababa, on 28–29 January 2018, available at https://au.int/sites/default/files/decisions/33908-assembly_decisions_665_-_689_e.pdf Accessed 20 January 2023.

[113] Written Statement of the African Union, Request for Advisory Opinion, 1 March 2018, https://www.icj-cij.org/sites/default/files/case-related/169/169-20180301-WRI-07-00-EN.pdf Accessed 20 January 2023, paras 10–29.

[114] Bhatt (2018) 91.

[115] Decision on The Katowice Climate Conference (UNFCC COP 24) and Africa's Engagements at the Global Climate Change Conference at COP25/CMP15, Doc. Assembly/AU/10(XXXII) adopted by the 32nd Ordinary Session of the Heads of State and Government of the African Union, at Addis Ababa, on 10–11 February 2019, available at https://au.int/sites/default/files/decisions/36461-assembly_au_dec_713_-_748_xxxii_e.pdf. Accessed 20 January 2023.

drawn attention to the need for developed countries to scale up climate finance and support for loss and damage.

3.5 Conclusion

In conclusion, this chapter has delved into the intricate interplay between African regionalism and the Mauritian context, particularly focusing on the crucial role and impact within the realm of human rights. By establishing the inherent relevance of regionalism to the socio-economic development of small island states, with a spotlight on Mauritius, it has explored the foundations of African regionalism in the context of the African Union's creation and the emergence of African Union law. Throughout the discussion, it has assessed the instrumental role of regionalism in advancing human rights in Mauritius, extending beyond the mere adoption and promotion of human rights treaties. The examination further delved into the strategic partnership between Mauritius and the African Union, exemplified by two contemporary developments. The African Union's active support for the decolonisation of the Chagos Archipelago, demonstrated notably during the Chagos Advisory Opinion proceedings in 2019, highlights a robust alliance in advancing Mauritius' causes on the international stage. Moreover, from scrutinising the African Common Position in international climate negotiations to emphasising its profound implications particularly in the realm of loss and damage—a critical concern for Mauritius as a climate-vulnerable state—the strategic partnership between Mauritius and the African Union can be illustrated further. These instances underscore the multifaceted and strategic role that African regionalism assumes in addressing complex challenges that resonate with the developmental and security priorities of Mauritius. In essence, the chapter has sought to bring to bear the dynamic and evolving nature of African regionalism and its tangible impact on the human rights landscape in Mauritius. As the intricate relationship between regionalism and state-specific concerns continues to unfold, this analysis serves as a testament to the significance of collaborative efforts in navigating contemporary global issues.

References

Abebe AM (2010) The African Union Convention on Internally Displaced Persons: its codification background, scope and enforcement challenges. Refug Surv Q 29(3):28–57

Amao O et al (eds) (2021) The Emergent African Union Law: conceptualization, delimitation, and application. Oxford University Press, New York

Aniche ET (2020) From pan-Africanism to African regionalism: a chronicle. Afr Stud 70(1):70–87

Appiagyei-Atua K (2006) Bumps on the road: a critique of how Africa got to NEPAD. Afr Hum Rights Law J 6(2):524–548

Baimu E (2002) Human rights in NEPAD and its implications for the African Human Rights System. Afr Hum Rights Law J 2:301–319

Baldacchino G, Wivel A (2020) Handbook on the politics of small states. Edward Elgar, Cheltenham

Bhatt K (2018) Chagos: a chance for the ICJ to do more for advancing human rights through the rule of law? Quest Int Law 55:85–92

Bishop M et al (2021) Towards sustained development in small island developing states: why we need to reshape global governance. Overseas Development Institute Working Paper. https://cdn.odi.org/media/documents/SIDS_sustained_development_WP_jr.pdf. Accessed 25 June 2025

Borzel TA, Risse T (2016) The Oxford handbook of comparative regionalism, 1st edn. Oxford University Press

Danso K (1995) The African economic community: problems and prospects. Afr Today 42(4):31–55

Fagbayibo B (2013) Common problems affecting supranational attempts in Africa: an analytical overview. Potchefstroom Electron Law J 16(1):32–69

Fawcett L (2004) Exploring regional domains: a comparative history of regionalism. Int Aff 80(3):429–446

Fawcett L, Gandois H (2010) Regionalism in Africa and the Middle East: implications for EU studies. J Eur Integr 32(6):617–636

Gibb R (2009) Regional integration and Africa's development trajectory: metatheories, expectations and reality. Third World Q 30(4):701–720

Gowreesunkur V (2019) African Union (AU) agenda 2063 and tourism development in Africa: contribution, contradiction and implications. Int J Tour Cities 5(2):288–300

Grote J (2010) The changing tides of small island states discourse—a historical overview of the appearance of small island states in the international arena. Verfassung und Recht in Übersee 43(2):164–191

Harris M, Khonje WH (2011) Regional approaches in sustainable development. In: Vigilance C, Roberts JL (eds) Tools for mainstreaming sustainable development in small states. Commonwealth Secretariat, London, pp 64–83

Iroulo LC, Lenz T (2022) Global theories of regionalism. In: Rüland J, Carrapatoso A (eds) Handbook on global governance and regionalism. Edward Elgar, Cheltenham, pp 36–51

Hettne B (2005) Beyond the 'new' regionalism. New Polit Econ 10(4):543–571

Kamga SAD, Fombad CM (2013) A critical review of the jurisprudence of the African Commission on the Right to Development. J Afr Law 57(2):196–214

Kanbur R (2004) The African peer review mechanism (APRM): an assessment of concept and design. South Afr J Polit Stud 31(2):157–166

Kariseb K, Okoloise C (2019) Reflections on the African governance architecture: trends, challenges and opportunities. In: Addaney M, Nyarko MG, Boshoff E (eds) Governance, human rights and political transformation in Africa. Springer, Cham, pp 41–68

Khadiagala GM (2015) Pan-Africanism and regional integration. In: Cheeseman N, Anderson D, Scheibler A (eds) Routledge handbook of African politics, 1st edn. Routledge, London, pp 375–389

Kindiki K (2003) The normative and institutional framework of the African Union relating to the protection of human rights and the maintenance of international peace and security: a critical appraisal. Afr Hum Rights Law J 3:97–117

Kufuor KO (2005) The collapse of the Organization of African Unity: lessons from economics and history. J Afr Law 49(2):132–144

Kurecic P (2017a) Small states in the multi-polar world: introduction. World Rev Polit Econ 8(3):280–294

Kurecic P (2017b) Small states and regional economic integrations in the multi-polar world: regional differences in the levels of integration and patterns of small states' vulnerability. World Rev Polit Econ 8(3):317–348

Long D, Murray R (2016) The role and use of soft law instruments in the African Human Rights System. In: Lagoutte S et al (eds) Tracing the roles of soft law in human rights. Oxford University Press, Oxford, pp 89–108

Lubbe WD, Spijkers O (2021) Taking stock of United Nations and African Union Constitutionalism. Afr J Int Comp Law 29(1):62–81

Magliveras KD, Naldi GJ (2003) The pan-African Parliament of the African Union: an overview. Afr Hum Rights Law J 3:223–234
Maluwa T (2003) The Constitutive Act of the African Union and institution-building in postcolonial Africa. Leiden J Int Law 16(1):157–170
Mansfield ED, Solingen E (2010) Regionalism. Annu Rev Polit Sci 13:145–163
Menon S (2020) The Rule of Law, the International Legal Order, and the Foreign Policy of small states. Asian J Int Law 10(1):50–67
Murray R (2004) Historical overview of human rights in the OAU/AU. In: Murray R (ed) Human rights in Africa: from the OAU to the African Union. Cambridge University Press, New York, pp 1–48
Mutua M (1995) The Banjul Charter and the African Cultural Fingerprint: an evaluation of the language of duties. VA J Int Law 35:339–380
Mutua M (2007) Standard setting in human rights: critique and prognosis. Hum Rights Q 29:547–630
Neumann I, Gstöhl S (2006) Introduction: Lilliputians in Gulliver's world? In: Ingebritsen C et al (eds) Small states in international relations. University of Washington Press, Seattle
Nmehielle VO (2003) The African Union and African Renaissance: a new era for human rights protection in Africa? Singapore J Int Comp Law 7:412–446
Olaniyan K (2004) The African Union Convention on Preventing and Combating Corruption: a critical appraisal. African Human Rights Law Journal 4(1):74–92
Olivier ME (2015) The role of African Union Law in integrating Africa. S Afr J Int Aff 22(4):513–533
Olowu D (2002) Protecting children's rights in Africa: a critique of the African Charter on the Rights and Welfare of the Child. Int J Child Rights 10:127–136
Packer CAA, Rukare D (2002) The new African Union and its constitutive act. Am J Int Law 96(2):365–379
Roberts C (2023) Foundational moments. In: Alternative approaches to human rights: the disparate historical paths of the European, Inter-American and African Regional Human Rights Systems, pp 19–94
Slade TN (2003) The making of international law: the role of small Island states. Temple Int Comp Law J 17(2):531–544
Söderbaum F (2013) Rethinking regions and regionalism. Georget J Int Aff 14(2):9–18
Ssenyonjo M (2018) Responding to human rights violations in Africa: assessing the role of the African Commission and Court on Human and Peoples' Rights (1987–2018). Int Hum Rights Law Rev 7:1–42
Suilleabhain AO (2014) Small states at the United Nations: diverse perspectives, shared opportunities. International Peace Institute. https://www.ipinst.org/wp-content/uploads/publications/ipi_e_pub_small_states_at_un.pdf. Accessed 25 June 2025
Tandrayen-Ragoobur V (2019) Can Africa serve as a trading hub for Mauritius?: an in-depth analysis. In: Seetanah B, Sannassee R, Nunkoo R (eds) Mauritius: a successful small Island developing state, 1st edn. Routledge, London
Tandrayen-Ragoobur V, Tengur ND, Seewooruttun B (2021) South-south trade: the potential for Mauritius. J Econ Dev 46(3):45–65
Techane MG (2011) Where is the African charter? Assessing the impact of the African Charter on Human and Peoples' Rights in Mauritius. Unpublished dissertation, University of Pretoria
Techane MG, Mahadew R (2016) The impact of the African Charter and the Maputo Protocol in Mauritius. In: Ayeni V (ed) The impact of the African Charter and the Maputo Protocol in selected African states. Pretoria University Law Press, Pretoria
Thorhallsson B, Steinsson S (2017) Small state foreign policy, Oxford research encyclopaedia of politics. Oxford University Press
Tsakok I (2021) The Republic of Mauritius and the African Continental Free Trade Area: opportunities and challenges in a post COVID-19 environment. Policy Center for the New South,

Policy Brief 39/21. https://www.policycenter.ma/publications/republic-mauritius-and-african-continental-free-trade-areaopportunities-and-challenges. Accessed 25 June 2025
Udombana NJ (2000) Toward the African Court on Human and Peoples' Rights: better late than never. Yale Hum Rights Dev Law J 3:45–111
Umozurike U (1983) The African Charter on Human and Peoples' Rights. Am J Int Law 77(4):902–912
Vickers B (2017) A handbook on regional integration in Africa: towards agenda 2063. Commonwealth Secretariat, London
Viljoen F (2001) Africa's contribution to the development of International Human Rights and Humanitarian Law. Afr Hum Rights Law J 1:18–39
Viljoen F (2009) An introduction to the protocol to the African Charter on Human and Peoples' Rights on the Rights of Women in Africa. Wash Lee J Civ Rights Soc Justice 16(11):11–46
Viljoen F (2012) International human rights law in Africa, 2nd edn. Oxford University Press, Oxford
Wiebusch M et al (2019) The African Charter on Democracy, Elections and Governance: past, present and future. J Afr Law 63(1):9–38

Chapter 4
Civil and Political Rights

Abstract The primary objective of this chapter is to refute the misconception that there are not any significant problems with civil and political rights in Mauritius by offering further guiding thoughts on the subject. It then shifts its focus to the Mauritian Constitution's list of rights to look at how these rights have been interpreted thus far and how they have been granted judicial protection. The African Charter and other civil and political rights instruments under the African human rights framework are then contrasted with them. The goal is to draw attention to how and when these tools should be used to further the civil and political rights agenda at home.

4.1 Introduction

Civil and political rights are the only constitutional category of human rights that are enforceable and justiciable currently in Mauritius. It means that since independence, the focus of stakeholders such as the judiciary, the executive, the policymakers, and civil society organisations has been on civil and political rights. One good effect of this has been the relatively strong framework on these rights that exists in Mauritius today, and one ill effect has been the complete neglect of socio-economic and third generations rights, addressed in other chapters on this book. That said, this chapter begins by noting the contribution of the International Covenant on Civil and Political Rights (ICCPR) and its monitoring body, the Human Rights Committee (HRC). Through not sufficiently used, the provisions of the ICCPR and the mechanism of the HRC such as the communication procedures and the state reporting mechanisms have contributed towards the respect and protection of civil and political rights in Mauritius. This is not further developed here as it is outside the scope of this book. While the focus of this work is to argue the relevance of the African human rights system to civil and political rights in Mauritius, it is important to highlight that this system itself recognises, follows, and tends to harmonise itself with the global system on civil and political rights spearheaded by the ICCPR and the HRC. Indeed, the African Commission has on numerous occasions cited the rich

R. Mahadew, *Mauritius and African Human Rights Law*,
https://doi.org/10.1007/978-3-032-08832-1_4

jurisprudence of the HRC and its General Comments while interpreting the African Charter's provisions on civil and political rights. Therefore, these two systems are meant to be complementary to each other, while the African system provides for specificities and more elaborated contents on civil and political rights. This is what demarcates it from the UN system and therefore justifies its relevance to the human rights system of Mauritius.

This chapter first provides for more guiding insights on civil and political rights in Mauritius to dispel the myth that there are no major issues regarding these rights in Mauritius. It then turns towards the bill of rights of the Constitution of Mauritius to examine how these rights have been conferred judicial protection and how they have been interpreted so far. They are then compared with the African Charter and other instruments on civil and political rights under the African human rights system. The aim is to highlight the ways and manners in which these instruments should be used to advance the agenda of civil and political rights domestically.

4.2 Insights on Civil and Political Rights in Mauritius

The HRC welcomed various legislative, institutional as well as policy measures taken by the state party, including the Police Complaints Act, Criminal Appeal Act, Criminal Procedure Act, Local Government Act, Equal Opportunities Act, Protection of Human Rights (Amendment Act), International Criminal Court Act, Legal Aid and Legal Assistance Act, National Preventive Mechanism Act, Institute for Judicial and Legal Studies Act, and Combating of Trafficking in Persons Act. It also welcomes the ratification or accession to international instruments such as the Optional Protocol to the Convention on the Rights of the Child on the sale of children, child prostitution and child pornography, the Convention on the Rights of Persons with Disabilities, the Optional Protocol to the Convention on the Rights of the Child on the involvement of children in armed conflict, and the Optional Protocol to the Convention on the Elimination of All Forms of Discrimination against Women between 2008 and 2011.[1]

Conversely, there were several areas of concerns raised by the HRC on various aspects of civil and political rights. First and foremost, regarding the applicability of the ICCPR, the HRC noted that 'the Covenant has not yet been given full effect in the domestic legal order, and about the limited number of cases in which the Covenant has been referred to by courts'.[2] The HRC was also concerned about various issues regarding the National Human Rights Commission, mandated to protect and promote civil and political rights, such as (a) the lack of transparency and participation in the selection and appointment process for members of the National Human Rights Commission and its divisions; (b) the uncertainty surrounding the tenure guarantee of mandate holders; (c) potential mission overlap among the

[1] Concluding Observations (2017) para 3 and 4.

[2] Ibid para 5.

Commission's divisions; (d) the possibility that there will be conflicts of interest among the members; and (e) the lack of staff to allow the Commission to fully carry out its mandate.[3]

The HRC underlined the persistence of violence against women in Mauritius, which, in some cases, resulted in deaths, even though it did take note of the amendments made to bolster the provisions of the Protection from Domestic Violence Act of 2007 and the numerous mechanisms put in place to strengthen the framework for protection against domestic violence, particularly gender-based violence. The fact that marital rape has not yet been made a crime by the state party was also concerning to the HRC. It also stressed on the fact that women do not always report cases of violence to the police.[4] The HRC remarked that there is still no clear prohibition on corporal punishment in day care centres, prisons, and other alternative care settings.[5] It also expressed concern about the continued occurrence of trafficking in the state party, particularly involving children and migrants, for the purposes of sexual exploitation and labour exploitation and how few trafficking-related cases are presented in court.[6]

The HRC drew the state's attention to detainees who are accused of terrorist offences and denied bail. It was particularly concerning that a person suspected of committing a terrorism-related offence may be detained for up to 36 h without access to anyone, including legal representation, under section 27 of the Prevention of Terrorism Act. It underlined the absence of statistical information regarding the implementation of anti-terrorism laws, namely, regarding the quantity of arrests, detentions, inquiries, and convictions.[7] Regarding pre-detention trials, the HRC stated that 'the Committee is concerned about the high number of persons in pretrial detention, the duration of which is excessive in many instances, in particular detention on drug-related cases'.[8] The issue of provisions charge was also a subject of criticism by the HRC. Although the HRC had taken note of the information presented by Mauritius flagging its intention to remove the provisional charges from the justice system, it remains concerned that the system allowing for detention of an individual on suspicion of committing a major offence may lead to abuse and arbitrariness. The HRC expressed concern with the Mauritius Constitution's article 5, paragraph 1 (k), and article 4's non-compliance with the Covenant.[9]

The HRC highlighted the allegations that people who have been deprived of their freedom have been mistreated by security agents. It expressed regret for the absence of precise information regarding the total number of complaints filed, the type and perpetrators of the alleged actions, the results of the investigations conducted, the

[3] Ibid para 7.
[4] Ibid para 19.
[5] Ibid para 23.
[6] Ibid para 25.
[7] Ibid para 27.
[8] Ibid para 29.
[9] Ibid para 31.

convictions of those found guilty, and the compensation awarded to victims. The HRC took note of reports showing that detainees in Mauritian jails are not being adequately treated. Alleged suicides that have happened in jails and non-separation of detainees according to their custody regime were also a cause for concern.[10] The HRC was also concerned by the lack of a national legal framework for determining refugee status and safeguarding the rights of people in need of international protection. The HRC was also critical of the absence of a nationwide statelessness process. It highlighted the absence of data regarding the population of refugees, asylum seekers, and stateless people living on state party territory.[11]

Although torture and inhumane and degrading treatments and punishments are forbidden by the Constitution and the law, there has been claims of police abuse made on social media and traditional media platforms. Several observers asserted that police abuse occurrences were not properly recorded by the authorities.[12] In June 2023, the Office of the Director of Public Prosecutions received a referral from the Independent Police Complaints Commission, an official investigative body, regarding the cases of six Terre Rouge police officers from the Criminal Investigation Division who were suspected of abusing detainees in May 2022, as revealed by a video leak. Although some abusive officials were prosecuted, opposition parties and the media expressed concerns that the government did not always look into and punish abusive authorities.[13]

Arbitrary arrests have also been an issue in Mauritius. Critics claimed that some members of the political opposition were singled out by the administration for arrests or charges related to crimes. For instance, a well-known lawyer Rama Valayden was detained and charged with 'perverting the course of justice' on May 12 after he claimed on a radio broadcast that the government was prosecuting opposition sympathisers for political reasons. The chief public prosecutor, who urged the police commissioner to refrain from invariably issuing provisional charges with scant evidence and promoted increased legal communication between prosecutors and police investigators, requested that the charges be withdrawn by a court in May 2023.[14]

A few media sources saw the arrest in May of a lawyer and government critic, followed by the dismissal of charges against him over remarks he made criticising police elements on a radio talk show, as an attempt by the authorities to restrict political speech. The state broadcaster Mauritius Broadcasting Corporation was frequently attacked by opposition parties and independent media analysts for what they saw as pro-government bias and negative coverage of the opposition parties. The majority of independent media accused the ruling party and government of anti-government bias. These issues can be considered as alleged infringement of the

[10] Ibid para 33 and 35.

[11] Ibid para 37.

[12] Dewoo (2024).

[13] US Department of State (2023).

[14] Le Matinal Media (2023).

right to freedom of expression.[15] Media activists contend that a restricted media environment and weakened democracy are caused by the absence of laws pertaining to access to information, changes to broadcasting regulations that jeopardise sensitive information and restrict investigative journalism, the arbitrary detention of journalists, penalties imposed on certain private radio stations deemed to be antagonistic to the government, and the use of the police for political ends.[16] Mauritius dropped from 56th place in 2020 to 63rd place out of 180 nations in the World Press Freedom Index rankings in 2023.[17]

The media should continuously investigate and report on government mistakes and corruption, according to nearly nine out of ten Mauritians (86%). An equally sizable majority (84%) favour media freedom, with only 12% believing that the government should be able to stop items it disagrees with from being published. Nearly two-thirds (64%) of people believe that the government has little influence over the media's ability to cover and comment on news stories in the nation, while 35% disagree. Approximately 48% of Mauritians believe that information held by public authorities should be made available to the public, while 39% believe that such information should be kept confidential.[18]

The illegal drug epidemic plaguing Mauritius society has compelled the government to implement measures to combat the problem, including CCTV cameras in public spaces and the recently imposed need that all mobile phone users re-register. Civil society, however, is worried that the information might be gathered, stored, and utilised for other reasons. The UN Special Rapporteur on the right to Privacy also underlined the importance of safeguarding children's right to privacy, particularly in light of the prevalence of child trafficking, cyberbullying, sexual exploitation, and security risks involving children's personal information when they use and post on social media platforms, which disproportionately affects the most vulnerable members of Mauritius society.[19]

The issue of discrimination is also a compelling one that requires significant attention. While the majority of Mauritians claim they experienced no harassment or discrimination in the year prior, significant segments of the populace did so on the basis of their gender (16%), religion (17%), and ethnicity (9%). Compared to the average, Afro-Mauritians (31%) and Muslims (22%) are more likely to report having encountered harassment or discrimination because of their ethnicity in the preceding year. Comparably, whereas two-thirds (66%) of Mauritians claim that the government never treats members of their ethnic group unfairly, over four in ten (47%) and Muslims (42%) think that this occurs sometimes, often, or always. Religious discrimination or harassment is more common among Christians and Muslims than among Hindus, and women are more likely than males to experience

[15] US Department of State (2023).

[16] Kasenally (2022).

[17] Reporters without borders (2023).

[18] Afro Barometer (2025).

[19] OHCHR (2023).

it (11% vs. 7%).[20] Workers who identify as members of sexual minorities experience a number of detrimental effects linked to workplace discrimination (harassment and exclusion): feeling inadequate and undervalued, being viewed as a liability to the company, and being seen as challenging to manage. These detrimental effects are mostly caused by the widespread use of ostracism and mocking (harassment) in the workplace.[21]

Regarding participation in public and political life, certain Christians and Muslims persisted in asserting that the majority of Hindus in the civil service gave them an advantage in government hiring and advancement, hence keeping Christians and Muslims from rising to more senior positions within the civil service. Non-Hindus have long complained about being underrepresented in politics in general.[22] The government declared in its 2018 response to the International Convention on the Elimination of All Forms of Racial Discrimination that it would not offer any information on racial discrimination against people of African descent or disaggregated data by ethnicity pertaining to public service recruitment, as it goes against National Unity.[23]

The Law Reform Commission expressed serious concerns about the phenomena of mob justice in Mauritius in November 2023. It stated that

> in an alarming departure from its well-earned reputation for democratic stability and social equilibrium, Mauritius is witnessing a rising propensity among its populace to engage in mob justice. No longer a mere fringe phenomena, this form of vigilante justice is increasingly becoming a default response, filling a perceived vacuum left by formal legal institutions. A cursory glance at recent indictments reveals not only the frequency but also the growing public tolerance for such extrajudicial practices.[24]

From the above overview, it is evident that there exist significant issues and challenges regarding the respect and protection of civil and political rights in Mauritius. No doubt, in comparison with other countries in Africa and around the world, Mauritius does have arguably an acceptable, if not decent, record regarding civil and political rights. However, one should adopt the philosophy of 'there is still work to do' or 'there is still room for improvement' even with a few and sporadic allegations of violation of such rights. Here, one can notice that the allegations that this section described and the concerns raised by the HRC cannot be qualified as few and sporadic. The legal framework should therefore be made to respond to these situations. In this context, the following section focuses on the Constitution and its chapter two called the bill of rights.

---

[20] Afro Barometre (2018).

[21] Bhankaraully et al. (2023), p. 1122.

[22] Carroll and Carroll (2000), pp. 25–50.

[23] US Department of State (2023).

[24] Law Reform Commission (2023).

4.3 The Bill of Rights in the Constitution

Chapter 2 of this book focused on the historical aspects of the Constitution as well as its cardinal principles relevant to human rights. It also focused on section 3 on the scope of the bill of rights (BoR) and section 17 regarding the enforcement of the protective provisions of the BoR. It is therefore apposite to focus on the substantive contents as provided by section 4 to section 16. A comparative approach is adopted here with selected jurisdictions and the African Charter for a critical analysis of the provisions of the Constitution.

4.3.1 Protection of the Right to Life

Section 4 of the Constitution provides that no person shall be deprived of this life intentionally save in the execution of the sentence of a court in respect of a criminal offence of which he has been convicted. This is followed by a second paragraph which lists down instances where a person who loses his life resulting from the use of force (1) in self-defence (2) during a lawful arrest or to prevent the escape of a person lawfully arrested (3) in suppressing a riot, insurrection, or mutiny and (4) during a lawful act of war or to prevent him from committing a criminal offence. In the case of *Madhewoo v the State*,[25] it was held that 'the wording of section 4 of our Constitution makes it clear that the constitutional protection afforded is in respect of life in contradistinction from death'.

It is also noted that section 4(1) provides for the death penalty as a punishment. However, the Abolition of Death Penalty Act 1995 has abolished the death penalty. Section 2 of that Act has amended the law in three ways. Firstly, it abolished the death penalty in section 2(1). Secondly, it provided that where under any enactment a court was empowered to impose a sentence of death, it should instead impose a sentence of penal servitude for life in section 2(2). Thirdly, it provided that where any person had been sentenced to death, and the sentence had not, at the commencement of the Act, been executed, that person should be deemed to have been sentenced to penal servitude for life and should undergo that sentence in section 2(3). However, section 4 of the Constitution has not been amended to reflect the substance of the Abolition of Death Penalty Act. Given that the said Act is a simple legislation, it implies that a simple majority is required to repeal it and thus automatically reinstate the death penalty in Mauritius. That said, the Supreme Court always adopted a cautious approach to death penalties even before the advent of the Act abolishing it. In *Amasimbi v The State*,[26] the Supreme Court noted that:

> while section 4(1) of the Constitution permits Parliament to provide for the death penalty, even on a mandatory basis, it is always open to courts, no doubt pursuant to other

[25] 2015 SCJ 177.

[26] 1992 SCJ 227.

constitutional provisions regarding inhuman punishment, to determine that any form of punishment is unconstitutional in certain cases.

Focusing on the wordings of section 4, it is argued that it is too negatively drafted for a constitutional provision that is supposed to protect life. The principle which is supposed to be premised on the sanctity of life and the dignity attached to it is completely outweighed by the exceptions to the right to life. The Constitution of South Africa provides for this right in the following terms: 'Everyone has the right to life'.[27] The entire section is powerfully worded in five words—no exceptions and no room for interpretation. Section 37 even clearly states that the right to life is entirely non-derogable and derogation is not even allowed during states of emergency. The value given to the right to life is beautifully captured by the Constitutional Court of South Africa which stated that 'everyone, including the most abominable of human beings, has the right to life, and capital punishment is therefore unconstitutional'.[28] It also stated that the right to life and the right to dignity are entwined and that the right to life is the predecessor to all other rights. Accordingly, the right to life is the right to a human life and not the right to life as 'mere organic matter'.[29]

The corresponding article in the African Charter is drafted in an even more sacrosanct manner. Article 4 of the African Charter provides that 'human beings are inviolable'. Every human being shall be entitled to respect for his life and the integrity of his person. No one may be arbitrarily deprived of this right. During its 57th Ordinary Session in November 2015, the African Commission adopted CESCR's General Comment No 3 on the right to life. It described the right to life as 'the fulcrum of all other rights and the fountain through which other rights flow'[30] and that the 'African Charter envisages the protection not only of life in a narrow sense, but of dignified life'.[31] This General Comment is of great value since it provides for essential interpretative guidance on areas such as the nature of the right and of obligations of the state in respect of the right to life, the scope of the prohibition on the 'arbitrary' deprivation of life, the requirement of accountability, the abolition of the death penalty, the use of force in law enforcement, the use of force in armed conflict, state obligations with respect to persons held in custody, responsibility for violations by non-state actors, and interpreting the right to life broadly. In the case of *International Pen and Others (on behalf of Saro-Wiwa) v Nigeria*, the African Commission held that 'the protection of the right to life in article 4 also includes a duty for the states not to purposefully let a person die while in its custody. Here at least one of the victims' lives was seriously endangered by the denial of medication during detention. Thus, there are multiple violations of article 4'.[32]

---

[27] Section 11.

[28] S v Makwanyane and Another (CCT3/94) [1995] ZACC 3 para 392.

[29] Ibid para 327 and 330.

[30] Forum of Conscience v Sierra Leone (2000) AHRLR 293 (ACHPR 2000) para 19.

[31] Ibid para 3.

[32] (2000) AHRLR 212 (ACHPR 1998) para 104.

Mauritius should consider the redrafting of section 4 of the Constitution on the right to life. It is essential to move away from the colonially inspired wording of this section and to adopt a provision which resembles that of article 4 of the African Charter, ensuring the concept of dignity and inviolability of human life. Additionally, the Supreme Court can draw guidance and inspiration from the jurisprudence of the African Commission as well as soft laws such as CESCR's General Comment No 3 to interpret section 4 of the Constitution. So far the approach taken by the Supreme Court has been guided by the wordings of section 4. Any amendment to it will enlarge the scope of interpretation of this provision by the judiciary in Mauritius which can only be beneficial for citizens.

4.3.2 Right to Personal Liberty

This right is protected under section 5 of the Constitution. It starts by stating that 'no person shall be deprived of his personal liberty save as may be prescribed by law' and then provides a long list of not less than ten exceptions. It also covers the aspect of deprivation of liberty in cases of detention for criminal offence. For this matter, section 3 extensively deals with the issue of bail, reasonable suspicion, undue delay, and the right to consult a lawyer.

Regarding the scope of liberty, the Supreme Court held that 'it follows that the suspect's remaining at large is the rule: his detention on ground of suspicion is the exception and, even then, if he is not put on his trial within a reasonable time, he has to be released'.[33] It further stated that 'it follows that the burden of showing the applicability of one of the derogations to that fundamental right must fall on the person invoking that derogation'.[34] While interpreting the essence of reasonable suspicion, the Supreme Court explained that 'reasonable suspicion is no instinct, allows no guess, no sixth sense. It is scientific, It has to find support on facts, not equivocal facts but facts consistent with guilt. Reasonable suspicion, in contrast to mere suspicion, must be founded on facts.'[35] The apex court of Mauritius has also been instrumental in shedding light on the controversial concept of provisions charge. It explained that

> as everybody knows, a provisional information is entered when a suspect is arrested or is brought into custody. Its purpose is to bring the detention of the individual under judicial supervision and control so as to prevent an administrative detention and to enable a judicial authority to decide whether the detainee should be released on bail or not and, if not, for how long he should be detained. No detainee pleads to provisional information and no trial takes place. Consequently, no question arises as to whether evidence is required to be given in those proceedings. When the need arises for evidence to be given, the provisions

[33] *Noordally v Attorney General* 1986 MR 204.

[34] Dahoo S v State of Mauritius & Anor 2007 SCJ 156.

[35] Manraj D & Ors v ICAC 2003 SCJ 75.

information is simply struck out and an information is lodged to which the accused pleads and in respect of which a trial takes place.[36]

In *Gordon-Gentil Alain v State of Mauritius*, one's right to be informed of the reason of one's arrest was upheld as a guaranteed one in the following terms: 'No citizen of this country, from the more majestic to the most humble, can be subjected to an arrest by the authorities if he is not informed of the reason for his arrest, unless, of course, the reason is patent to high heaven itself'.[37] The issue of bail has also been broadly decided by the Supreme Court under section 5 of the Constitution. The JCPC held that 'the interest of an individual is of course to remain at liberty, unless or until he is convicted of a crime sufficiently serious to justify depriving him of his liberty'.[38] The Supreme Court adjudicated further that 'the fundamental proposition of our law is that bail is a judicial matter so much so that even Parliament cannot by legislation seek to encroach on the power of the judiciary to deny bail to a defendant'.[39] Regarding undue delay, the Supreme Court held that 'we are not prepared to say *in abstracto* what is a reasonable delay, a concept which must vary according to circumstances of each case. We have however no doubt that all accused parties undisputedly involved in serious hold up like this one in which the applicant was involved cannot be heard to say that a detention of three or four months prior to his trial is, in the circumstances, an unreasonable one'.[40]

The contribution of the judiciary of Mauritius has been immense in interpreting the right to personal liberty especially regarding arrest in Mauritius. Otherwise, it would have unfortunately been a situation where this fundamental right of Mauritians would be too easily infringed, politically or otherwise motivated. Yet interpreting section 5 is not a simple task given the way it is drafted. As mentioned above, one may have a sentiment of reading the Bail Act instead of section 5 of the Constitution given the extent of details it goes into. It is argued that constitutional provisions should not be drafted in a way that is too broad and restricts interpretation. Again referring to the South African example, section 12 of the Constitution of South Africa simply provides that 'Everyone has the right to freedom and security of the person, which includes the right (a) not to be deprived of freedom arbitrarily or without just cause and (b) not to be detained without trial'. Section 35(1)(f) further provides that everyone who is arrested for allegedly committing an offence has the right to be released from detention if the interests of justice permit, subject to reasonable conditions. Mauritius already has a Bail Act in which all the details could be elaborated upon.

For example, the Constitution regulated the conditions for bail regarding terrorism and drug offence in section 5(3)(A). It is more appropriate for the Prevention of Terrorism Act or the Dangerous Drugs Act to deal with conditions of bail together

[36] Director of Public Prosecutions v Indian Ocean International Bank 1989 MR 110.

[37] 1995 SCJ 118.

[38] Hurnam v The State 2005 UKPC 49.

[39] Islam v Senior District Magistrate, Grand Port District Court 2006 SCJ 282.

[40] Muntroneea v The DPP 1983 SCJ 292.

with the Bail Act rather than the Constitution. One could argue as to why only terrorism and drug offences and not other equally heinous or dangerous crimes. This leads to a never-ending debate and does allow enough freedom for the judiciary to decide how best the right to personal liberty is to be protected. Another illustration would be section 5(1)(g) which provides that no person shall be deprived of his personal liberty save as may be authorised by law for the purpose of preventing the spread of an infectious or contagious disease. It is argued that the liberty of a person is curtailed during a health pandemic by the Public Health Act or the Quarantine Act in Mauritius. What is the need for the supreme law to mention this exception? If there is a massive flood, citizens can find themselves in the situation of their liberty being deprived. But this is not mentioned in the Constitution. Thus, the argument is that enumerating the exceptions confers more importance to them rather than to the fundamental principle of liberty of a person.

In that sense, article 6 of the African Charter is of relevance and can serve as an example. It provides that every individual shall have the right to liberty and to the security of his person. It further states that no one may be deprived of his freedom except for reasons and conditions previously laid down by law and that no one may be arbitrarily arrested or detained. The focus is on the right and not on the exceptions as is particularly the case with section 5 of the Constitution of Mauritius. It guarantees the right to personal liberty rather than emphasising on the constitutionality of the exceptions as is the case for section 5 of the Constitution. The African Commission has carefully analysed the phrase 'except for reasons and conditions previously laid down by the law' which can be the subject of abuse by states. It stated that:

> However, the mere mention of the phrase "except for reasons and conditions previously laid down by the law in article 6 of the African Charter does not mean that any domestic law may justify the deprivation of such persons" freedom and neither can a state party to the African Charter avoid its responsibilities by having recourse to the limitations and claw back clauses in the African Charter. Therefore, any domestic law that purports to violate this right should conform to internationally laid down norms and standards.[41]

Against the above backdrop, it is argued that section 5 of the Constitution of Mauritius be amended and reworded to reflect the substantive content of article 6 of the African Charter. It should be inspired by the directness and generality of the article 6, allowing for the task of detailing to be done by the legislation under the judicial control of the Supreme Court regarding their constitutionality.

[41] Purohit and Another v The Gambia (2003) AHRLR 96 (ACHPR) 2003 para 64.

4.3.3 Protection Against Torture and Inhuman or Degrading Punishment or Treatment

Section 7 of the Constitution provides that no person shall be subjected to torture or inhuman or degrading punishment or other such treatment. The Supreme Court defined inhuman as 'brutal, unfeeling, barbarous' in the case of *Virahsawmy and Anor v The Commissioner of Police*.[42] In the same case, the Court was of the opinion that 'solitary confinement and the physical and mental discomfort by such confinement cannot, in the circumstances of this case, be said to constitute torture or inhuman treatment within the meaning of section 7(1) of the Constitution. Mental or physical discomfort is not necessarily caused by torture or inhuman treatment'. In *Madhub v The State*, the Court stated that 'section 7 of the Constitution which provides protection from inhuman treatment incorporates in it the principle of proportionality of the sentence provided by law with the seriousness of the offence. The test of proportionality was to be measured by reference to foreseeable hypothetical cases in which the imposition of the minimum sentence would be startlingly inappropriate and shocking'.[43]

The corresponding article in the African Charter is article 5 which provides that every individual shall have the right to the respect of the dignity inherent in a human being and to the recognition of his legal status. It further provides that all forms of exploitation and degradation of man particularly slavery, slave trade, torture, and cruel, inhuman, or degrading punishment and treatment shall be prohibited. In 2002, the African Commission issued the Resolution on Guidelines and Measures for the Prohibition and Prevention of Torture, Cruel, Inhuman or Degrading Treatment of Punishment in Africa, also known as the Robben Island Guidelines on Torture. The Guidelines focus on prohibition of torture,[44] prevention of torture,[45] and responding to the need of victims.[46] Regarding prohibition of torture, the Guidelines stress on ratification of regional and international instruments, promotion and support cooperation with international mechanisms, criminalisation of torture, non-refoulement, combating impunity, and complaints and investigation procedures.[47] In relation to prevention of torture, emphasis is on basic procedural safeguards for those deprived of their liberty, safeguards during the pretrial process, conditions of detention, mechanisms of oversight, training and empowerment, and civil society education and empowerment.[48]

The African Commission has held that 'excessive solitary confinement, shackling within a cell, extremely poor quality of food and denial of access to adequate

[42] 1972 SCJ 169.

[43] 2007 SCJ 282.

[44] Robben Island Guidelines Part 1.

[45] Ibid Part 2.

[46] Ibid Part 3.

[47] Robben Island Guidelines Part 1 A to F.

[48] Robben Island Guidelines Part 2 A to F.

medical care' contravened article 5.[49] Further in *Article 19 v Eritrea*, the African Commission made it clear that the political situation of a country is not an excuse that can justify torture since article 5 permits no restrictions or limitations.[50] It further stated that article 5 includes not only actions which cause 'serious physical or psychological suffering, but which humiliate or force the individual abasing his will or conscience'.[51] It also underlined that 'the prohibition of torture, cruel, inhuman or degrading treatment or punishment is to be interpreted as widely as possible to encompass the widest possible array of physical and mental abuses'.[52]

The Robben Island Guidelines and the jurisprudence of the African Commission on article 5 can be used as a guidance by domestic courts in Mauritius to interpret cases regarding alleged torture or inhuman, cruel, and degrading treatment or punishment.

4.3.4 Right to Property

Section 8 of the Constitution of Mauritius seems focused on protecting individuals from deprivation of property rather than protecting the right to property. The negative drafting of such an important right is evident from the starting sentence which provides that 'no property of any description shall be compulsorily taken possession of, and no interest in or right over property of any description shall be compulsorily acquired except where…', and the list of exceptions begin. One may wonder whether this provision protects only against acquisition or taking possession of or does it also include protection against destruction of one's property. Another key consideration is whether section 8 can be interpreted as including the right to shelter as had been done by the African Commission as explained below. Thus, what is the real scope of section 8 in relation to the protection of the right to property?

In the case of *Society United Docks and Others v Government of Mauritius*, the building of a Bulk Sugar Terminal which impacted negatively on the plaintiffs' business did not amount to deprivation according to the JCPC which stated that 'the Constitution does not afford protection abasing progress or provide compensation for a business which is lost as a result of technological advance…the government did not act in order to ruin the appellants but in order to preserve an efficient sugar industry in the national interest.'[53] In The Union of Campement Sites Owners & Others v Government of Mauritius, the Supreme Court held that the imposition of a tax by a law is not of itself the compulsory taking of possession or the compulsory

---

[49] Achuthan and Another (on behalf of Banda and Others) v Malawi (2000) AHRLR 144 (ACHPR) 1995 para 7.

[50] (2007) AHRLR 73 (ACHPR) 2007 para 102.

[51] Doebbler v Sudan (2003) AHRLR 153 (ACHPR 2003) para 36.

[52] Ibid para 37.

[53] 1984 UKPC 42.

acquisition of the taxpayer's property. From the above, it can be said that the judiciary has not had the opportunity to deal with critical questions on the right to property being inclusive of housing or whether property includes intellectual property. Judicial interpretation has so far been restricted mostly to what amounts to encroachment or deprivation.

Article 14 of the African Charter adopts a more positive approach by protecting the right first and then dealing with the possible limitations. Indeed, it provides that the right to property shall be guaranteed. The African Commission considered 'that a monetary compensation granted by judgment having acquired author of res judicature should be considered as an asset'.[54] It also noted that 'the disproportionate nature of an encroachment on indigenous people, therefore falling short of the test set out by the provisions of article 14 of the African Charter, is to be considered an even greater violation of article 14 when the displacement at hand was undertaken by force'.[55] In *Constitutional Rights Project v Nigeria*, the African Commission held that 'the right to property necessarily includes a right to have access to one's property and the right not to have one's property invaded or encroached upon'.[56] In *SERAC v Nigeria*, it was held that 'the corollary of the combination of the provisions protecting…the right to property…forbids the wanton destruction of shelter because when housing is destroyed, property…are adversely affected.'[57]

4.3.5 Right to Privacy

Section 9 of the Constitution provides that except with his own consent, no person shall be subjected to the search of his person or his property or the entry by others on his premises. Critiquing this section, Meetarbhan argued as follows:

> The Constitution does not expressly provide for a right to privacy as such. Section 9 only protects the right to privacy of home and other property and its scope is essentially limited to search and seizure. It does however include protection against search of one's person. The right to privacy which may include protection of one's private life and one's image, does not enjoy express constitutional protection.[58]

Section 3(c) of the Constitution, entitled fundamental rights and freedoms of the individual and discussed in Chap. 2, makes mention of 'the right to individual to protection for the privacy of his home and other property'. While interpreting this section, the Supreme Court stated that 'the language of section 3(c) of the Constitution, construed in the light of its natural and ordinary meaning, does not create or confer any right of privacy to the person and would not, in the present

[54] Bissangou v Republic of Congo (2006) AHRLR 80 (ACHPR 2006) para 76.

[55] Centre for Minority Rights Development v Kenya (2009) AHRLR 75 (ACHPR 2009) para 218.

[56] (2000) AHRLR 180 (ACHPR 1995).

[57] (2001) AHRLR 60 (ACHPR 2001) para 60.

[58] Meetarbhan (2015), p. 70.

matter, afford constitutional protection against the taking of fingerprints as prescribed under the NIC Act and Regulations'.[59] In 2025 and in a world where technological advancement allows for the most pervasive forms of intrusion to one's privacy, it is worrying, to say the least, to note that the Constitution of Mauritius does not confer a right to privacy to its citizens except for home, property, and bodily search.

Turning towards the African Charter, one notices that there is no express provision on the right to privacy. However, it has been argued that this right finds its application in two regional treaties.[60] The African Charter on the Rights and Welfare of the Child does provide for the right to privacy in its article 10. Additionally, the African Union Convention on Cyber Security and Personal Data Protection confirms the commitment of the African Union to protect 'the privacy of its citizens in their daily or professional lives, while guaranteeing the free flow of information'.[61] There is also the revised 2002 Declaration of Principles on Freedom of Expression and Access to Information in Africa which includes significant provisions on the right to privacy.[62]

4.3.6 Provisions to Secure Protection of Law

Section 10 of the Constitution deals with essential aspects such as the right to a fair hearing, the right to a fair trial within a reasonable time, presumption of innocence, substantive and procedural due process, retrospective legislation, and mandatory sentence. In the case of *Darmalingum v The State,*[63] there was a delay of 13 years between the appellant's arrest and judgement on appeal. The JCPC adjudicated that there had been a flagrant breach of the reasonable time guarantee and that 'the appellant has had the shadow of the proceedings hanging over him for about 15 years'. The appellant saw his conviction quashed, and the JCPC further explained that when delay is assessed, the time runs from the date on which the accused was arrested and not from the date on which he was charged.[64]

According to the Supreme Court, the rationale of the presumption of innocence under section 10 is a simple one: 'that it is repugnant to ordinary norms of fairness for the prosecution to access a defendant of crime and for the latter to be then required to disprove the accusation on pain of conviction and punishment if he fails

[59] Madhewoo M v The State of Mauritius and Anor 2015 SCJ 177.

[60] Singh and Power (2019), p. 207.

[61] Preamble of the AU Convention.

[62] Articles 97–100 of the Draft Declaration of Principles on Freedom of Expression and Access to Information in Africa.

[63] 2000 MR 10.

[64] See also *Boolell v The State* Privy Council Appeal no 39 of 2005; *DPP v Hurnam* Privy Council Appeal No 42 of 2005.

to do so'.[65] In *Seegobin v the Queen*, the Court made reference to the 'well-established principle which has been formulated by the courts in England and which has been applied by our courts, that, unless the language is clear, the statute ought not to be construed so as to create new disabilities or obligations or impose new duties in respect of transactions which were complete at the time when the Act came into force'.[66] In *Amasimbi v The State*, the Supreme Court stated that 'the concept of a fair trial guaranteed by section 10 of the Constitution implies fair and impartial enquiries into allegations of accused parties…with respect, we feel that, for the sake of completeness, that sentence should have been so worded as to refer to impartial enquiries into allegations of accused parties which may have a bearing on their innocence or guilt'.[67] Regarding mandatory sentences, the Supreme Court held that 'a law which denies an accused party the opportunity to seek to avoid the imposition of a substantial term of imprisonment which he may not deserve, would be incompatible with the concept of a fair hearing enshrined in section 10 of our Constitution'.[68]

It is undeniable that since independence, the Mauritian judiciary has interpreted section 10 in an extremely progressive manner which has allowed the right to a fair trial and secured the protection of law in the most appropriate manner even in difficult politically motivated or otherwise cases. It is now argued that a bit of reference to the African human rights system's framework on this cardinal right can further enhance this protection. Through article 7, the African Charter confers protection on an individual's 'right to have his cause heard'.[69] Regarding the creation of special tribunals for the prosecution of criminal offences without possibility of appeal, the African Commission stated that 'article 7(1)(d) requires the court of tribunal to be impartial. Regardless of the character of the individual members of such tribunals, its composition alone creates the appearance, if not actual lack, of impartiality. This violates article 7(1)(d)'.[70] In *Institute for Human Rights and Development in Africa v Angola*, it further explained that 'the abrupt manner in which they were arrested, detained and deported denied them of the opportunity to engage a lawyer to take their case to court to challenge the regularity and legality of their arrest, detention and deportation'. The African Commission has ruled that every individual has the right to appeal to competent national organs for violations of his/her fundamental rights, and as such, if one is detained without charge or trial and there exists no legal remedy to challenge the detention, it is a clear violation of article 7(1)(a).[71]

---

[65] *Suneechara v The State* 2007 SCJ 131.

[66] 1969 MR 1.

[67] 1992 SCJ 178.

[68] *Philibert P. & Others v The State* 2007 SCJ 274.

[69] Article 7(1) African Charter.

[70] Constitutional Rights Project (in respect of Akamu and Others) v Nigeria (2000) AHRLR 180 (ACHPR 1995) para 11.

[71] (2008) AHRLR 43 (ACHPR 2008) para 58.

Referring to article 7(2), the African Commission stated that 'this provision is a general prohibition on retroactivity. It is to ensure that citizens at all times are fully aware of the state of the law under which they are living. The Economic Crimes (Specified Offences) Decree…which was deemed to have come into force in July 1994, is therefore a serious violation of this right'.[72] In *Law Office of Ghazi Suleiman v Sudan*, the Commission 'condemns the fact that state officers carried out the publicity aimed at declaring the suspects guilty of an offence before a competent court established their guilt. Accordingly, the negative publicity by the government violates the right to be presumed innocent'.[73] In another case, it held that it 'unfortunately cannot rest total confidence in the assurance that no one and no newspaper has yet suffered under the retroactivity of Decree no 43. Potential prosecution is a serious threat. An unjust but unenforced law undermines, a s above, the sanctity in which the law should be held'.[74]

Following the appointment of a Working Group on the Right to a Fair Trial per its 199 Resolution on the Rights to a Fair Trial and Legal Assistance, the African Commission adopted the Principles and Guidelines on the Right to a Fair Trial and Legal Assistance in Africa in 2003. This Principles and Guidelines add significantly and in much detail to the substantive contents of article 7 of the African Charter. It focuses on general principles applicable to all legal proceedings with particular emphasis on fair and public hearing and impartial and independent tribunal. It recommends judicial training as to 'judicial officials have appropriate education and training and should be made aware of the ideals and ethical duties of their office'.[75] In relation to the right to an effective remedy, the Principles and Guidelines explicitly provide that 'the granting of amnesty to absolve perpetrators of human rights violations from accountability violates the right of victims to an effective remedy'.[76] It also provides that 'the cost of the public of obtaining records of judicial proceedings or decisions should be kept to a minimum and should not be so high as to amount to a denial of access'.[77]

Specifically related to Mauritius which has a very strict locus standi regarding human rights litigation as explained in Chap. 2, the Principles and Guidelines provide that 'states must ensure, through adoption of national legislation, that in regard to human rights violations, which are matters of public concern, any individual, group of individuals or non-governmental organisation is entitled to bring an issue before judicial bodies for determination'.[78] There are extensive provisions on various aspects such as access to lawyers and legal services, legal aid and legal assistance; independence of lawyers; cross border collaboration among legal professional,

[72] Jawara v The Gambia (2000) AHRLR (ACHPR 2000) para 63.

[73] (2003) AHRLR 134 (ACHPR 2003) para 56.

[74] Media Rights Agenda and Others v Nigeria (2000) AHRLR 200 (ACHPR 1998) para 60.

[75] Section B Principles and Guidelines.

[76] Section C Principles and Guidelines.

[77] Section D Principles and Guidelines.

[78] Section E Principles and Guidelines.

access to judicial services; rights of civilians not to be tried by military courts; provisions about arrest and detention; provisions applicable to proceedings relating to criminal charges; children and the right to a fair trial and victims of crime and abuse of power.

4.3.7 Protection of Freedom of Conscience

Section 11 of the Constitution of Mauritius provides that except with his own consent, no person shall be hindered in the enjoyment of his freedom of conscience, and for the purposes of this section, that freedom includes freedom of thought and of religion, freedom to change his religion or beliefs, and freedom, either alone or in community with others and both in public and in private, to manifest and propagate his religion or beliefs in worship, teaching, practice, and observance. Elaborating on this right, the Supreme Court had stated that this 'fundamental right, however, has to be exercised in a civilised society as ours in such a way as not to cause inconvenience to others. People have the undisputed right to pray but in so doing they must assume that God, however called, is not deaf and their prayers should not cause inconvenience to those who have also an undisputed right not to play or to pray to some other God'.[79]

Dealing with the concept of secular state and its nexus with the freedom of religion, the Supreme Court addressed the issue of whether personal laws related to religion must mandatorily be enacted in laws by the state. It held that 'if freedom of religion can be fully enjoyed only on the condition that all that is ordained in religion must be given effect to in the law then (a) the question of violation of a number of fundamental rights would undoubtedly arise and (b) this would be based on an insufficient understanding of the duality of religion and state in a secular system. The Secular state is not anti-religion but recognised freedom of religion in the sphere that belongs to it. As between the state and religion each has its own sphere, the former that of law-making for the public good and the latter that of religious teaching, observance and practice. To the extent that it is sought to give to religious principles and commandments the force and character of law, religion steps out of its own sphere and encroaches on that of lawmaking in the sense that is it made to coerce the state into enacting religious principles and commandments into law. That would indeed be constitutionally possible where not only one particular religion is the state religion but also the holy book of that religion is the supreme law'.[80]

The already balanced and democratic views of the Supreme Court can be further enhanced by the jurisprudence of the African Commission of the right to freedom of religion. Article 8 of the African Charter provides that freedom of conscience, the profession, and free practice of religion shall be guaranteed. While interpreting this

[79] *Aumeer v Assemblée de Dieu* 1988 SCJ 236.

[80] *Bhewa & Alladeen v Government of Mauritius & DPP* 1990 MR 79.

article, the African Commission stated that 'other allegations refer to the oppression of Christian civilians and religious leaders and the expulsion of the missionaries…These attacks on individuals on account of their religious persuasion considerably restrict their ability to freely practice the religion to which they subscribe'.[81] Furthermore, in *Prince v South Africa*, it held that 'while the right to hold religious beliefs should be absolute, the right to act on those beliefs should not. As such, the right to practice one's religion must yield to the interests of society in some instances'.[82]

4.3.8 Freedom of Expression

The right to freedom of expression is guaranteed by section 12 of the Constitution. It provides that no person shall be hindered in the enjoyment of his freedom of expression, that is to say, freedom to hold opinions and to receive and impart ideas and information, without interference, and freedom from interference with his correspondence. It is noted that there is no express mention of freedom of media in section 12. While addressing this issue through case law, the Supreme Court has held that 'in a democratic society, any attempt by the authorities to restrain the right of newspapers to publish what they like by the imposition of pre-censorship invariably gives rise to a storm of angry protests and an avalanche of slogans in which the expression "freedom of the press" occupies a prominent place'.[83] In *Bunwaree V K v La Sentinelle*, it further stated that 'no doubt the media has a very important role to play in a democratic society, one of which is to impart reliable information to the public at large and to act as a fearless watchdog. This is rightly so by scrutinising and denouncing, without fear or favour not only the acts and doings of public figures and that of the public administration, but also those of the private sector. However, this must be done in a responsible manner, not speculating or going into sensationalism and on unchecked materials gathered from various sources, reliable or not'.[84]

The African Commission adopted the Declaration of Principles on Freedom of Expression in Africa in 2002. This Declaration provides for guidance on matters such as the guarantee of freedom of expression and interference with freedom of expression.[85] It states that freedom of expression imposes an obligation on the authorities to take positive measures to promote diversity through pluralistic access to media and other means of communication for vulnerable groups and marginalised people and the promotion of the use of local languages in public affairs,

[81] *Amnesty International and Others v Sudan* (2000) AHRLR 297 (ACHPR 1999) para 76.

[82] (2004) AHRLR 105 (ACHPR 2004) para 41.

[83] *Duval v The Commissioner of Police* 1974 MR 130.

[84] 2012 SCJ 84.

[85] Articles 1 and 2.

including in courts.[86] It equally provides for guidance on private and public broadcasting as well as the print media.[87] Focusing on attacks of media practitioners, the Declaration provides that in times of conflict, states shall respect the status of media practitioners as non-combatants.[88] Additionally, article 15 of the Declaration provides that media practitioners shall not be required to reveal confidential sources of information or to disclose other material held for journalistic purposes except as prescribed the a law which is legitimate, necessary, and proportionate.

Interpreting article 9 of the African Charter which guarantees freedom of expression and information, the African Commission has stated that 'any law…which permits the wholesale ban on the press and the imprisonment of those whose views contradict those of the government's is contrary to both the spirit and the purpose of article 9'.[89] Regarding limitation on article 9, the Commission held that 'dissemination of opinions may be restricted by law. This does not however mean that national law can set aside the right to express and disseminate one's opinions guaranteed at the international level; this would make the protection of the right to express one's opinion ineffective. To permit national law to take precedence over international law would defeat the purpose of codifying certain rights in international law and indeed the whole essence of treaty making'.[90]

4.3.9 Protection of Freedom of Assembly and Association

Section 13 of the Constitution provides that no personal shall be hindered in the enjoyment of his freedom of assembly and association, that is to say, his right to assemble freely and associate with other persons and, in particular, to form or belong to trade unions or other associations for the protection of his interests. Interpreting this right in the context of peaceful protests, the Supreme Court held that police 'has the duty to balance this duty with its obligations to preserve the peace and uphold the law. In that respect, it is recognised that some limitations on this constitutional right to assemble in order to protect and assist not only the participants, prevent unrest, violence and crime, but also for the protection of the rights and freedom of others as well as to ensure security and public safety are therefore essential'.[91]

The African Charter provides for the right to freedom of association in article 10 and that of freedom of assembly in article 11. In Civil Liberties Organisation (in respect of Bar Association) v Nigeria, the African Commission held that 'freedom

[86] Article 3.

[87] Article 5, 6 and 8.

[88] Article 11.

[89] Article 19 v Eritrea (2007) AHRLR 73 (ACHPR 2007) para 105.

[90] *Constitutional Rights Project and Others v Nigeria* (2000) AHRLR 227 (ACHPR 1999) para 40.

[91] *Police v Moorba* 1971 MR 199.

of association is enunciated as an individual right and is first and foremost a duty of the state to abstain from interfering with the free formation of associations'.[92] The 'persecution of its employees and raids of its offices in an attempt to undermine its ability to function in this regard amounts to an infringement of articles 9 and 10' was the decision of the Commission in *Huri-Laws v Nigeria*.[93] It further held that 'by preventing Mr Ghazi Suleiman from gathering with others to discuss human rights and by punishing him for doing so, the respondent state had violated Mr Ghazi Suleiman's human rights to freedom of association and assembly'.[94]

4.4 Civil and Political Rights in Mauritius and the African Human Rights System

It has been discussed that the wordings of various sections of the BoR in the Constitution of Mauritius are highly problematic. They do not reflect the international standards as set by both the ICCPR and the African Charter. They do not reflect the normative and substantive contents that have the potential to effectively respect and protect civil and political rights of Mauritians in today's times and circumstances. Furthermore, it is not possible for citizens to directly invoke and use the provisions from the ICCPR and the African Charter since these cardinal instruments have not been domesticated in Mauritian laws. Consequently, the first effort that must be made is pushing for the domestication of these instruments.

In the absence of domestication, the judiciary has a key role to play. It should be said that with its numerous judgements on matters concerning civil and political rights of Mauritians since independence, the judiciary has contributed massively in upholding these rights especially when the Constitution, through its wordings or scope, did not expressly confer adequate protection to some of them. The Supreme Court stepped in and, for decades, has tried its best to interpret these rights in accordance with international instruments. However, one constructive criticism against it is that it has almost always done so by referring to the European Convention on Human Rights and, to a lesser extent, the ICCPR. The African Charter has been scantily and extremely insufficiently used to interpret the BoR of the Constitution of Mauritius. This has to change. This is so because, as discussed above, the African Charter has more to provide in comparison with the ICCPR or the European Convention in terms of the substantive contents of civil and political rights. Additionally, the African Commission has come up with a number of resolutions, which address African realities, in a more specific and holistic manner. This is topped up by the highly instructive and guiding jurisprudence of the African Commission resulting from the interpretation of the African Charter. Therefore, it is

---

92 (2000) AHRLR 186 (ACHPR 1995) para 14.

93 (2000) AHRLR 273 (ACHPR 2000) para 47.

94 Law Office of Ghazi Suleiman v Sudan (II) (2003) AHRLR 144 (ACHPR 2003) para 56.

essential for the judiciary to find guidance and to use these instruments and judgements to interpret the BoR and to highlight the need for lawmakers to contemplate revisiting the BoR, especially its wordings and contents.

The civil society organisations also have a sacred duty to use mechanisms such as shadow reporting and communication procedures of the African Commission to bring complaints and issues to the attention of the Commission so that the latter can apply and enforce the provisions on civil and political rights against Mauritius, something that can be supranational done, being impossible domestically. Researchers and academics in the field of human rights must also engage with the African Charter through research and publication to bring to the attention of the legislature, the executive, and the judiciary the existence, efficiency, and relevance of the African human rights system in respecting and promoting civil and political rights of Mauritians.

References

African Union Convention on Cyber Security and Personal Data Protection

Afro Barometer (03 August 2018) Mauritius strong—but far from perfect—on gender equality and social tolerance. https://www.afrobarometer.org/wp-content/uploads/2022/02/ab_r7_dispatchno225_tolerance_and_equality_in_mauritius.pdf. Accessed 1 July 2025

Afro Barometer (29 April 2025) Mauritians strongly endorse media freedom and public access to government information. https://www.afrobarometer.org/wp-content/uploads/2024/04/AD799-Mauritians-endorse-media-freedom-and-public-access-to-government-information-Afrobarometer-28apr24.pdf. Accessed 1 July 2025

Bhankaraully S, Goyer M, Aroles J (2023) Workplace discrimination against LGBT employees in Mauritius: a sociological perspective. Econ Ind Democr 44(4):1105–1126

Carroll BW, Carroll T (2000) Trouble in paradise: ethnic conflict in Mauritius. J Commonw Comp Polit 38(2):25–50

Dewoo MT (2024) The democracy illusion in Mauritius. African Books Collective

Kasenally R (2022) Is digitalisation endangering democracy in Mauritius. https://www.ned.org/wp-content/uploads/2022/12/Roukaya-Kasenally_Is-Digitalization-Endangering-Democracy-in-Mauritius.pdf. Accessed 1 July 2025

Law Reform Commission (November 2023) Issue paper on autonomous criminalisation of mob justice. https://lrc.govmu.org/lrc/?p=4061. Accessed 1 July 2025

Le Matinal (17 May 2023) Rama Valayden's arrest: case adjourned to 23 May. https://english.lematinal.media/rama-valaydens-arrest-case-adjourned-to-23-may/. Accessed 1 July 2025

Meetarbhan M Constitutional law of Mauritius: Constitution of Mauritius with commentaries (2015) Precigraph Mauritius.

OHCHR (07 December 2023) UN expert says Mauritius leads on privacy in the region, but challenges remain. https://www.ohchr.org/en/press-releases/2023/12/un-expert-says-mauritius-leads-privacy-region-challenges-remain. Accessed 1 July 2025

Reporters without Borders (2023) RSF condemns harsh penalties for online content in Mauritius. https://rsf.org/en/index. Accessed 1 July 2025

Singh A, Power M (2019) The privacy awakening: the urgent need to harmonise the right to privacy in Africa. Afr Hum Rights Yearb 3:202–220

US Department of State (2023) 2023 country reports on human rights practices: Mauritius. https://www.state.gov/reports/2023-country-reports-on-human-rights-practices/mauritius/. Accessed 1 July 2025

Chapter 5
Economic, Social, and Cultural Rights

Abstract Mauritius lacks constitutionally protected socio-economic rights, including the right to education and health, housing, and workers' rights. The Constitution, inspired by the European Convention on Human Rights, does not protect these rights. Pro-independence political parties like the Mauritian Labour Party and the Independent Forward Bloc proposed including these rights in the Constitution, but colonial drafters rejected it. Professor Stanley Alexander de Smith suggested justiciable sets of fundamental rights based on the European Convention on Human Rights and fundamental freedoms. Against this backdrop, this chapter discusses the concept of welfare state as applied in Mauritius and the absence of socio-economic rights from the legal and normative framework pertaining to human rights in Mauritius. It critically engages with the relevance of the African Charter pertaining to socio-economic rights of Mauritians.

5.1 Introduction

It is imperative to start by mentioning that economic, social, and cultural rights (socio-economic rights) in Mauritius do not have any constitutional grounding. One may not be faulted for arguing that socio-economic rights do not even exist in Mauritius. Surprising as it may sound, especially given that socio-economic development and standard of life have been relatively high in Mauritius in comparison with other African countries, Mauritius arguably is more a state with socio-economic privileges through the welfare state system than enforceable and justiciable socio-economic rights. A human right is primarily characterised by its enforceability in a court of law and the extent to which it can be rendered justiciable. While these ideas and propositions will be discussed thoroughly in this chapter, it is apposite to provide for an illustration at this stage. To what extent can it be said that a Mauritian has the right to education in Mauritius? This question may surprise many who would believe that the right to education undoubtedly exists in Mauritius given that education, from the pre-primary till the tertiary level (first degree), is free of cost. However, delving deeper in the subject reveals a different reality. First, the

R. Mahadew, *Mauritius and African Human Rights Law*,
https://doi.org/10.1007/978-3-032-08832-1_5

Constitution does not provide for the right to education. Second, legislation such as the Education Act 1957 and its related regulations do not make any reference to the right to education. Third, the various international human rights conventions and treaties providing for the right to education have not been domesticated. While scores of government policies, reports, and documents would mention that all Mauritians have the right to education, some referring to it as an acquired right, this remains a fallacy.

It implies that if a citizen believes that any policy or decision taken by authorities concerned affects her or his right to education, there is no possibility for a legal challenge on the basis of this right. No doubt, he or she can proceed by way of a judicial review of the decision, or the aggrieved person may base his or her case on other available rights such as protection against discrimination or the right to equality but not on the right to education. This right is not enforceable and justiciable in Mauritius similar to the majority of the other socio-economic rights. In essence, there is free healthcare services in Mauritius but not the right to health. There are housing policies and programmes by the government for the deprived Mauritian but not the right to housing.[1] While there exists a plethora of workers' rights under the Workers' Rights Act 2019, there is no right to work in Mauritius. This reality has often been eclipsed by the relatively strong welfare state system of Mauritius. This chapter argues that it is one thing to have socio-economic privileges and an altogether different matter to have constitutionally protected socio-economic rights which are fully enforceable and justiciable.

As discussed in Chap. 2, the Constitution of Mauritius was inspired by the European Convention on Human Rights which does not protect socio-economic rights. Historically, it should be noted that pro-independence political parties such as the Mauritian Labour Party and the Independent Forward Bloc (IFB) had proposed the inclusion of socio-economic rights in the Constitution.[2] They proposed that 'the constitution should include a declaration of human rights modeled on the United Nations declaration of human rights. It must make provision regarding the life and liberty of the subject, the administration of justice, social and religious freedom and discrimination on any ground whatsoever, and the supreme court should have special jurisdiction to provide redress against any infringement of such rights'.[3] However, the colonial drafters of the Constitution rejected such a proposition in the 1965 Constitutional Conference.[4] Professor Stanley Alexander de Smith, a member of the Constitutional Office on the drafting of the Constitution of Mauritius, was hostile to the idea of the enshrinement of socio-economic rights in the supreme law of the country. He had argued that 'article 21 of the Indian Constitution, providing that "no person shall be deprived of his life or personal liberty except according to procedure established by law", is no more impressive

[1] Mahadew (2018), pp. 9–12.

[2] Houbert (1981), pp. 75–105.

[3] Memorandum to the Legislative Council (1961).

[4] Colom (2019), p. 85.

than the preamble to the French Constitution of 1946 guaranteeing the right to strike 'within the framework of the laws that govern it'.[5]

He had further added that 'for a constitution is primarily a legal document; rights ought not to be guaranteed in it unless they can be judicially enforced, and a "right" to social security manifestly cannot'.[6] He was also of the view that 'the least controversial safeguard would probably be a justiciable set of fundamental rights based on the terms of the European Convention on Human Rights and fundamental freedoms. Provision along these lines has already been made in the constitutions of Nigeria, Sierra Leone and Kenya…the main dangers of fundamental rights provisions are that they may throw a heart burden on the judiciary and bring up expectations that cannot be fulfilled'.[7] Colom has underlined the 'anglicisation' of the supreme law of the country which resulted in the absence of socio-economic rights from the Constitution since 1965 till date.[8] There is little doubt today that de Smith perceptions of socio-economic rights are obsolete and contrary to international human rights law. It is almost inconceivable that in 2024, the Constitution of Mauritius is still devoid of socio-economic rights. Yet various governments which the country has known have justified this absence by the welfare state system of Mauritius. This merits some attention in the following section.

5.2 Mauritius as a Welfare State

A historical insight to the adoption of the welfare state system by Mauritius would be useful here. Chan Low has argued that the welfare state was the cornerstone of the Mauritian system and was further consolidated under pressure from the streets, from Mouvement Militant Mauricien (MMM) political party's activists. But by providing a safety net to the poor, it has helped preserve social stability and reduce the possibility of political violence.[9] The welfare state was so anchored in the Mauritian system that even during the period of structural readjustment of the International Monetary Fund (IMF), it was not called into question.[10] The technocrats of the IMF and the World Bank understood, especially after the defeat of SSR in 1982, that any questioning of the welfare state would lead to the fall of the government. Sustaining the welfare state system has not been easy to say the least. When Mauritius gained its freedom, about 90% of the exports were made up of sugar. And turmoil kept growing at an increasing rate. It was necessary to grow other sectors. Industrialisation began in the 1960s, but the local market was small and the 'import substitution' paradigm applied. This is the

[5] de Smith (1964), p. 168.
[6] de Smith (1964), p. 185.
[7] de Smith (1964), p. 170.
[8] Colom (2019), p. 96.
[9] Chan Low (2019), p. 302.
[10] Phaala (2010), p. 79.

'Zone Franche'—an export-oriented industrialisation model—that visionaries like Jose Poncini and Professor Lim Fat envisioned, since both labour and capital were present. We are aware of the significance of the textile sector to Mauritius' economic growth. That being said, the market question was crucial. And the state would act as an intermediary through its bureaucracy.

The importance of the welfare state system of Mauritius cannot be minimised and understated. Among the various African nations, Mauritius is unique in that it has a comprehensive social welfare system to which all Mauritians have access. Although this system has its roots in British colonial authority, it was developed, refined, and implemented regularly after the island attained independence. Free healthcare, education, and transportation are among the social benefits that Mauritian citizens receive, along with a pension upon retirement. Additionally, cash transfers and subsidised housing schemes aid vulnerable groups such as persons with disabilities, orphans, and those at the bottom of the social ladder. About 27% of the government's total spending (MUR 48.7 billion) for social security and welfare was set aside for the 2020–2021 fiscal year, of which MUR 36.6 billion constituted the old age pension. According to a pre-election pledge, the basic retirement pension for all Mauritians 60 and older was raised by 45% in late 2019, increasing pension spending as a proportion of GDP by 2%. In addition, an additional 50% increase for all Mauritian citizens 65 and older is projected for FY 2023/2024. This will result in a notable increase in pension spending, which is expected to rise from 4.5% of GDP in FY 2018/2019 to over 8% of GDP by FY 2023/2024, far exceeding the revenue of the pension system.[11]

In order to ensure a monthly income to retired citizens over 65 as of July 2023, pension money will be created through the introduction of a new scheme known as contribution sociale généralisée (CSG), comprising limitless pension payments from employers and employees. By virtue of the CSG, a retiree may be entitled to benefits in excess of their base retirement income.[12] Significant controversy has resulted from concerns over the CSG's sustainability, with donations being seen as a kind of taxation in disguise. The system of public health in Mauritius is now much better than it was. There has been an increase in life expectancy to 70.8 years for males and 77.7 years for women from an average of 59 years in 1968.[13] Over the past 50 years, spending on public health has cost MUR 175 billion or 9% of total spending. After the outbreak of the COVID-19 in March 2020, a significant effect on the healthcare delivery system was noted. In 2020–2021, health expenditures amounted to about MUR 14 billion.[14]

Equal opportunity continues to be a challenge in Mauritius, despite the country's long and firmly established social protection system for its citizens. Poverty and social inequality primarily affect the Creole community (Afro-Mauritians) and

---

[11] Bertelsmann Stiftung's Transformation Index (2024), pp. 24–25.

[12] Mauritius Revenue Authority (2024).

[13] Ministry of Health and Wellness (2022).

[14] Ibid.

households led by women whose primary earner has a low level of education.[15] Despite making up about 30% of the population, Creoles—along with Hindus, Muslims, and Chinese—are the only significant community in Mauritius that does not have explicit recognition in the Constitution. Creoles experience notably high levels of socio-economic and political marginalisation in the nation, despite the official multiculturalism policy that has been in place for a long time.[16] Statistics Mauritius shows a gender gap in 2021 demonstrated by statistics such as 10.4% of employed women holding company leaders, 22.1% having tertiary qualifications, and merely 3 out of 21 ministers being women. Only 37.8% held senior government posts and Mauritius secured a meagre rank of 105 out of 146 countries in the World Economic Forum's 2022 Global Gender Gap Index. In 2011, the percentage of people in the 10+ age group who were literate was 90.1%; by 2011, it had risen to 91.9%. The gain was greater in females than in males, and as a result, the gender disparity in literacy shrank from 4.8 to 3.3 percentage points.[17]

Despite the limitations of the welfare state system, successive governments have used it to justify the absence of socio-economic rights in the Constitution of Mauritius and their inaction to include them for now. The absence of socio-economic rights in the Mauritius Constitution and the state's intention to incorporate these rights into the bill of rights have been brought to the attention of Mauritius by the United Nations Committee on Economic, Social and Cultural Rights (UN CECSR).[18] The Mauritian Mission responded as follows:

> Mauritius fully subscribes to the view that all human rights are indivisible, interdependent and interrelated. In this regard, side by side with the strengthening of the protection of civil and political rights, Mauritius has spared no efforts to advance the realisation of economic, social and cultural rights for its citizens through, inter alia, measures to combat poverty and enhance social enlistment. Mauritius is a welfare state offering free education, free health services, universal old age pensions, social security aid and benefits for widows, orphans and persons with disabilities, free public transport for students and old-aged persons and other financial assistance schemes to the needy.[19]

What is often neglected by the state is that the welfare state system has limitations and faces considerable challenges which in turn affect human rights in general and socio-economic rights in particular. The welfare system faces challenges due to its top-down, collectivised nature and lack of citizen engagement.[20] This system tends to give priority to hierarchy, discipline, and efficiency, unlike other sectors. There is a tendency to emphasise individual needs, choice, and mistrust of specialists which arguably results in a disconnect between the provision of the service and the preferences of recipients.[21] Precarious workers often encounter challenges to qualify for

---

[15] Maudarbux (2016), pp.459–481.

[16] Maurer (2014), p. 97.

[17] See Statistics Mauritius (2020).

[18] UN CESCR (2010b).

[19] UN CESCR (2010b).

[20] Gamble (2016).

[21] Page (2012), p. 106.

social protection aid which creates a situation of loss of faith in the welfare system.[22] Conversely, people affected by unstable employment, student loan debt, as well as expensive housing may naturally be in support of higher state assistance levels which ultimately make them favour the welfare state. The debate on whether the welfare state offers incentives for workforce leave remains ongoing.[23] Climate change may result in an increase in social expenditure on housing, insurance, flood protection, and disaster management. This may potentially replace traditional social justice concerns as well as social policy issues. Climate change may challenge states' reliance on economic growth, thus putting in question the 'golden age' of the welfare state. While some believe that alternative technologies can boost production and consumption and at the same time reduce carbon emissions, others interrogate how the West can continue growing in a low-carbon world.[24] Reducing Western growth can result in income loss in wealthier countries and change welfare states, while climate change might cause more people to migrate out of impacted nations.[25]

Since immigrants are not often seen as net contributors, immigration has already placed strain on welfare governments in a number of nations.[26] Large-scale immigration may make individuals less inclined to accept welfare benefits as universal and to pay for the services that underprivileged minorities need.[27] This is particularly relevant in instances where immigrants are not well integrated in society. Given examples such as the rise in terrorist attacks, Russia's annexation of Crimea, and the ongoing war in Ukraine, other budget categories such as defence spending in Europe may need additional funding. In view of advancing up the value chain and creating new goods and services, more resources must be allocated to education and training.[28] It has been argued that the low rates of ownership of houses by younger people could impact on their future housing expenses and pension requirements.[29] A greater reluctance to provide benefits to underprivileged minorities may also exist among immigrants who are from Middle Eastern nations, have lower levels of education than native-born people, and live in more segregated neighbourhoods. Due to the absence of strong international banking regulations, financial crises may occur more frequently, posing greater financial difficulties for welfare states.[30]

It is evident that Mauritius cannot continue to rely on the welfare state system for the protection and promotion of socio-economic rights of its citizens. The COVID-19 pandemic has shown that any country's economy can take serious and unpredicted blows which eventually affect the welfare state system and the government's

[22] Van Kersbergen & Vis (2014).
[23] Van Oorschot et al. (2017).
[24] Wurzel (2012).
[25] Gough & Therborn (2010).
[26] Glennerster (2007).
[27] Alesina et al. (2019).
[28] Gamble (2016).
[29] Stebbing & Spies-Butcher (2016).
[30] Gough & Therborn (2010).

capacity to provide for socio-economic benefits and privileges.[31] Constitutionalisation of socio-economic rights in an enforceable and justiciable manner is imperative even though a dose of state welfarism would still be required to effectively and efficiently guarantee socio-economic rights of Mauritians. Indeed, De Schutter has proposed the idea of the rights-based welfare state[32] which is what Mauritius should be aiming for.

5.3 Absence of Socio-Economic Rights from Legal and Normative Framework in Mauritius

5.3.1 The Constitution and Socio-Economic Rights

The absence of socio-economic rights from the Constitution has been noted with concern by various human rights treaty-based bodies. In 2019, while considering the fifth periodic report of Mauritius, UN CESCR noted the following in its Concluding Observations:

> The Committee notes that the process of amending the Constitution to enshrine the economic, social and cultural rights of the Covenant on an equal footing with other constitutional rights has not been completed. It reiterates its concern that the rights contained in the Covenant have not been incorporated into the domestic legal order and thus cannot be directly invoked by individuals before national courts. It notes with concern the intention of the State party, expressed in paragraph 23 of its National Human Rights Action Plan (2012–2020), to select for inclusion in the Protection of Human Rights Act only those provisions of the Covenant that it considers to lend themselves to being domestically enforced by the courts.[33]

Similar concerns were expressed by the same committee in 2010 while considering the combined second to fourth periodic reports of Mauritius. The Committee expressed concern that although certain individual rights declared in the Constitution are relevant to this category of rights, economic, social, and cultural rights are not primarily protected by and in the Constitution. The Committee expressed concern regarding the lack of incorporation of the provisions of the ICESCR in domestic law and the inability of persons to directly invoke them before national courts. It observed that the extent to which courts, the National Human Rights Commission, and the Ombudsman's Office were able to exercise their institutional safeguards of human rights is critically limited by this scenario.[34]

It was also recommended by the UN CESCR that the state party grant the Covenant a legal status that would for its provisions to be directly invoked and

[31] Ebbinghaus et al. (2022), pp. 297–311.

[32] See De Schutter (2018).

[33] UN CESCR Concluding Observations (2019) para 5.

[34] UN CESCR Concluding Observations (2010a) para 7.

applied in the local legal system. Additionally, the Committee suggested that the state party enhance the education of judges, attorneys, and public servants with the terms of the Covenant and their applicability to court cases.[35] In 2010, the UN CESCR made a similar recommendation and encouraged Mauritius to 'complete the planned amendment of the Constitution with a view to enshrining economic, social and cultural rights on an equal footing with other constitutional rights'.[36] In March 2024, Mauritius submitted its Sixth Periodic Report to the UN CECSR. The report does not mention anything done in line with the recommendation of the UN CESCR in granting legal status to socio-economic rights in Mauritius. This is simply because there has been nothing done concretely with regard to the constitutionalisation of socio-economic rights since 2010 (14 years after) when the first concern on this subject was raised by the UN CECSR.

It implies that no socio-economic rights of Mauritians are enforceable in a court of law domestically. Practically, any policy or decision taken by any government authority that affects the rights to education, health, food, water, housing, and others cannot be challenged before the Supreme Court of Mauritius because of a lack of legal basis. As noted in Chap. 2, there is little chance, and expectation, for the judiciary to exercise judicial activism or to apply techniques such as the implied rights theory for an indirect protection of socio-economic rights in Mauritius. In addition, as a number of case law discussed in Chap. 2 have shown, the judiciary cannot adjudicate on matters concerning socio-economic rights because of a lack of domestication of the provisions of the ICECSR. The state has admitted the impossibility of using the ICECSR before domestic courts by mentioning that 'there is no recent case where the Covenant has been invoked before our Courts'.[37] The JCPC noted in its 2004 decision in the case of Bishop of Roman Catholic Diocese of Port Louis & Ors v. Suttyhudeo Tengur & Ors that the Supreme Court closely examined the UN International Covenant on Economic, Social, and Cultural Rights and the UNESCO Convention against Discrimination in Education in addition to the Constitution when coming to its justification (on the alleged discriminatory admissions policy). However, this is merely on the basis of persuasive value, and it is inadequate and insufficient to confer the required degree of protection and promotion of socio-economic rights in Mauritius.

[35] UN CESCR Concluding Observations (2019) para 6.

[36] UN CESCR Concluding Observations (2010a) para 7.

[37] UN CESCR 'Replies of Mauritius to the list of issues' (2018) para 1.

5.3.2 The National Human Rights Commission and Socio-Economic Rights

The NHRC does not have an explicit mandate to protect and promote socio-economic rights in Mauritius. Responding to a question of the UN CESCR on the expansion of the NHRC's mandate to include the provisions of the ICECSR, the state responded as follows:

> The mandate of the National Human Rights Commission currently does not include the rights enshrined in the International Covenant on Economic, Social and Cultural Rights. This is not envisaged for the time being. The Economic and Social Rights are not enshrined in Chapter II of our Constitution. However, Economic Social rights are enshrined in our laws and they are ensured through the existence of a welfare state. Mauritius provides free education, free access to health services, social aid to vulnerable groups and pension benefits to elderly. Cultural rights are also protected through the guarantee of the rights to freedom of expression, freedom to establish schools of religious denomination, freedom of religion as well as protection from discrimination amongst others.[38]

One can again notice the over-reliance of Mauritius on the welfare state system to protect and promote socio-economic rights as discussed in the previous section in the current chapter. The above justification was arguably not accepted by the UN CESCR since it noted that:

> The National Human Rights Commission was granted A status by the Subcommittee on Accreditation of the Global Alliance of National Human Rights Institutions in 2014, with a number of recommendations for further strengthening its independence and effective functioning. Like the Subcommittee on Accreditation, however, the Committee is concerned that the Commission does not have an explicit mandate to protect and promote economic, social and cultural rights.[39]

In 2010, the UN CESCR recommended that Mauritius 'amend the Protection of Human Rights Act of 1998 in order to give the National Human Rights Commission a specific mandate to deal with economic, social and cultural rights'.[40] It was also recommended in 2019 that the state party give the National Human Rights Commission a clear mandate to safeguard and advance social, cultural, and economic rights. It further stated that the state party should fully implement the recommendations made by the Global Alliance of National Human Rights Institutions and the commitment outlined in paragraph 68 of the National Human Rights Action Plan (2012–2020) in order to further strengthen the independence and efficient operation of the Commission in accordance with the principles relating to the status of national institutions for the promotion and protection of human rights (the Paris Principles).[41] In the Sixth Periodic Report submitted in March 2024, Mauritius remained silent over the issue of expansion of the mandate of the NHRC to include

[38] UN CESCR 'Replies of Mauritius to the list of issues' (2018) para 3.

[39] UN CESCR Concluding Observations (2019) para 7.

[40] UN CESCR Concluding Observations (2010a) para 9.

[41] UN CESCR Concluding Observations (2019) para 8.

socio-economic rights. Once again, a recommendation made 14 years ago and recently reiterated has met with inaction on behalf of the state.

5.3.3 The Optional Protocol to the ICECSR

In addition to the absence of socio-economic rights in the Constitution as well as in the mandate of the NHRC, another hurdle towards an effective protection and promotion of this category of rights in Mauritius is the fact that the state has not ratified the Optional Protocol to the ICESCR (OP ICESCR). Its article 1 stipulates that a 'State Party to the Covenant that becomes a Party to the present Protocol recognises the competence of the Committee to receive and consider communications as provided for by the provisions of the present Protocol'. The non-ratification of it means that no Mauritian can submit a complaint to the UN CESCR for any alleged violation of his or her socio-economic rights. Responding to a questionnaire in relation to General Assembly resolution 68/268 on 'Strengthening and enhancing the effective functioning of the human rights treaty body system' in 2014, the Human Rights Division of the Ministry of Ministry of Foreign Affairs stated the following:

> The accession to the Optional Protocol to the International Covenant on Economic, Social and Cultural Rights is presently not on the agenda of Mauritius. Adequate avenues of redress already exist in our legal system. A person may have recourse to the provisions of Chapter II of the Constitution, enter civil actions for damages in Courts, or make complaints to the various National Human Rights institutions and the Police as well as address minor petitions to the Attorney General.[42]

The above statement is laden with inaccuracies, to say the least, and adequate avenues of redress cannot exist in the Chapter II of the Constitution where socio-economic rights do not exist and when the various NHRIs do not have any explicit mandate on socio-economic rights. This is either a lack of human rights knowledge on behalf of those producing such replies or a typical case of responding to simply say anything without any validity. In a meeting of the National Mechanism for Reporting and Follow-Up (NMRF) on 08 November 2023, the Human Rights Division was informed that 'the State of Mauritius is not envisaging to ratify the OP ICECSR for the time being'.[43] In 2010, the UN CESCR called upon the state to sign and ratify the OP ICESCR,[44] and this was reiterated in 2019[45] which clearly shows that the argument by the State that '**adequate** avenues for redress already exist in our legal system' was not accepted. The state has shown inaction towards the ratification of the OP ICESCR.

[42] Human Rights Division (2014), p. 2.

[43] NMRF (2023), p. 3.

[44] UN CESCR Concluding Observations (2010a) para 32.

[45] UN CESCR Concluding Observations (2019) para 63.

5.3.4 *Misconceptions on Socio-Economic Rights*

After discussing socio-economic rights with policymakers in Mauritius, one easily gets the impression that there are serious misconceptions about the nature and scope of these rights. For instance, there is a tendency to believe that providing for the right to housing in the Constitution will open a floodgate of litigations or will force the state to cater for individual entitlements vis-a-vis each of these rights. Another misconception is with regard to the fact that these rights require a lot of resources, especially financial, and the state may not be capable of meeting the demands. In essence, the state perhaps believes that it will be too much of a burden to provide for socio-economic rights in the Constitution, and it may be better to continue with the welfare state system. There is therefore a lack of understanding and literacy about socio-economic rights and specifically the obligations that they create for states as per article 2(1) of the ICESCR.

According to this article, each state party to the present Covenant undertakes to take steps, individually and through international assistance and cooperation, especially economic and technical, to the maximum of its available resources, with a view to achieving progressively the full realisation of the rights recognised in the present Covenant by all appropriate means, including particularly the adoption of legislative measures. It is clear from this provision of the law that socio-economic rights are to be realised progressively and by utilising a maximum of resources that are available, after having sought assistance of a financial and technical nature internationally if need be. It is not an overnight or immediate realisation of these rights with a compulsion of putting all the resources only for the realisation of socio-economic rights which is not realistic, and, had it been true, no country would have arguably ratified the ICECSR and taken up such a burden. Therefore, the understanding of the obligations of states pertaining to socio-economic rights needs to be more accurate, as proposed below, in order to compel policymakers to reconsider, or start considering, its constitutionalisation.

Article 2 of the Covenant lays down the legal obligations of conduct and results of state parties. While there are differences between this provision and the corresponding one of the ICCPR, there are also significant similarities. The Covenant acknowledges resource constraints and imposes immediate obligations, including the undertaking by states to guarantee the exercise of relevant rights in a fully non-discriminatory way.[46] Article 2 (1) of the Covenant requires states to take steps to realise the socio-economic rights of their citizens. These steps to be taken have to be deliberate, concrete, and clearly targeting the fulfilment of the obligations spelt out in the Covenant, guaranteeing the full realisation of the rights.[47] Article 2 (1) states that all appropriate means, including legislative measures, should be used to fulfil the obligation to take steps, including in combating discrimination, health, child protection, education, and matters covered in articles 6–9, to ensure effective

[46] CESCR's General Comment No 3 (1990) para 1.

[47] CESCR's General Comment No 3 (1990) para 2.

implementation.[48] The UN CESCR stresses the need for state parties to adopt legislative measures by all appropriate means, considering the circumstances and the chosen means. It has indeed invited state parties to include details of such measures in their periodic reports on the basis of which the Committee determines if all appropriate measures have been taken. This approach ensures that state parties are responsible for their own actions.[49]

The UN CESCR has suggested that judicial remedies for rights that can be justiciable in a national legal system can be considered to be an appropriate measure. State parties to the ICCPR are already required to ensure adequate and effective remedies to individuals whose rights are infringed. Other provisions in the ICESCR can be immediately applied by judicial and other national legal systems.[50] The UN CESCR seeks information on legislative policies aimed at resolving contraventions of socio-economic rights. It also requires updates on constitutional recognition of economic, social, and cultural rights as well as any regressively amended constitutional provisions. Other appropriate measures include administrative, financial, educational, and social measures.[51] The UN CESCR has affirmed that the principles of the ICESCR can be applied to various political and economic systems, provided the democratic and respectable form of government or economic system is employed and practiced. It has also stressed on the relevance of other human rights, particularly the right to development, in the context of these systems, as long as the interdependence and indivisibility of these rights are recognised.[52]

Article 2(1) of the ICESCR spells out the obligation to progressively achieve the full realisation of economic, social, and cultural rights. This principle, known as progressive realisation, recognises that full realisation may not be possible and realistic in a short time. This diverges from the immediate obligation in article 2 of the ICCPR. It should be noted that the ICESCR's overall objective is to establish clear obligations for state parties, requiring expeditious and effective progress towards this goal.[53] The UN CESCR is of the view that every state party has a minimum core obligation to guarantee the provision of essential levels of each right. If a state party fails to provide essential foodstuffs, healthcare, shelter, housing, or education, it is not fulfilling and respecting its obligations under the Covenant. The assessment of a state's minimum core obligation is conducted by taking into account resource constraints within the country. To attribute the failure to respect minimum core obligations to lack of resources, a state party must first demonstrate its genuine efforts to use available resources.[54] The UN CESCR has emphasised that even with limited resources, a state party has the duty to ensure the widest possible enjoyment of

[48] CESCR's General Comment No 3 (1990) para 3.
[49] CESCR's General Comment No 3 (1990) para 4.
[50] CESCR's General Comment No 3 (1990) para 5.
[51] CESCR's General Comment No 3 (1990) paras 6 and 7.
[52] CESCR's General Comment No 3 (1990) para 8.
[53] CESCR's General Comment No 3 (1990) para 9.
[54] CESCR's General Comment No 3 (1990) para 10.

relevant rights and monitor the realisation or non-realisation of these rights. It has equally emphasised that vulnerable individuals and communities of a society should be protected through low-cost targeted programmes, even during times of severe constraints.[55]

Article 2(1) of the Covenant requires all states to take steps individually and through international assistance and cooperation, particularly in economic and technical aspects. The phrase 'to the maximum of its available resources' refers to both internal and international resources. Articles 11, 15, 22, and 23 of the ICESCR emphasise the necessity of cooperation in assisting the realisation of rights which consists of technical assistance and others. It emphasises the importance of the Declaration on the Right to Development and the need for active international assistance and cooperation to achieve full realisation of these rights.[56] The South African Constitutional Court has laid emphasis on 'reasonableness' of measures by the government to be aligned with socio-economic rights provided by the South African Constitution. The Constitutional Court had held that:

> To be reasonable, measures cannot leave out of account the degree and extent of the denial of the right they endeavour to realise. Those whose needs are the most urgent and whose ability to enjoy all rights therefore is most in peril, must not be ignored by the measures aimed at achieving realisation of the right.... If the measures, though statistically successful, fail to respond to the needs of those most desperate, they may not pass the test.[57]

The Constitutional Court was discussing the government's commendable efforts to build affordable housing; thus this remark was important. However, because of the backlog, the Grootboom group and many others were unable to get such housing for years. The government only needed to enact legislation to support the destitute. The Constitutional Court further added:

> The nationwide housing programme falls short of obligations imposed upon the national government to the extent that it fails to recognise that the State must provide relief for those in desperate need. They are not to be ignored in the interests of an overall programme focussed on medium and long-term objectives [rather than short term objectives]. It is essential that a reasonable part of the national housing budget be devoted to this, but the precise allocation is for the national government to decide in the first instance.[58]

The Grootboom case shows that a constitution's inclusion of socio-economic rights does not automatically mean that 'every individual is entitled to assistance on demand'.[59] Rather, the Court examined the reasonableness of the government's entire programme. The South Africa case of Soobramoney v Minister of Health[60] is one that also demonstrates that constitutionalisation and adjudication of socio-economic rights do not breach the doctrine of separation of powers and the execu-

---

[55] CESCR's General Comment No 3 (1990) paras 11 and 12.

[56] CESCR's General Comment No 3 (1990) para 13 and 14.

[57] Grootboom v Republic of South Africa 2000 (11) BCLR 1169 (CC) para 44.

[58] Grootboom v Republic of South Africa 2000 (11) BCLR 1169 (CC) para 66.

[59] Kende (2003), p. 145.

[60] Soobramoney v Minister of Health 1997 (12) BCLR 1696 (CC).

tive still decides on socio-economic policies independently, though they need to be aligned with constitutional guarantees conferred to socio-economic rights through the BoR. In Soobramoney, the question was whether it was unconstitutional for a public hospital to deny a terminally ill man with diabetes, ischemic heart disease, and cerebrovascular illness access to renal dialysis services. The hospital presented proof that, due to a lack of dialysis supplies, it gave non-terminal patients' treatment priority. Soobramoney filed a lawsuit, arguing that his right to emergency medical treatment and healthcare under chapter 2, section 27 of the South African Constitution had been violated by the hospital's reluctance to treat him.

The hospital had a reasonable policy for providing access to a limited resource, hence the Constitutional Court rejected the claimant's contention that the hospital had breached his right to healthcare.[61] In the lack of a prioritising scheme, the Court claimed that the dialysis programme would fail and 'no one would benefit'.[62] The Constitutional Court added that:

> These choices involve difficult decisions to be taken at the political level in fixing the health budget, and at the functional level in deciding upon the priorities to be met. A court will be slow to interfere with rational decisions taken in good faith by the political organs and medical authorities whose responsibility it is to deal with such matters.[63]

In the case of Minister of Health and Treatment Action Campaign,[64] the Constitutional Court shed light on its standard of review when dealing with socio-economic rights in the following terms:

> Courts are ill-suited to adjudicate upon issues where court orders could have multiple social and economic consequences for the community. The Constitution contemplates rather a restrained and focused role for the courts, namely, to require the State to take measures to meet its constitutional obligations and to subject the reasonableness of these measures to evaluation. Such determinations of reasonableness may in fact have budgetary implications, but are not in themselves directed at rearranging budgets. In this way the judicial, legislative and executive functions achieve appropriate constitutional balance.[65]

In essence, the UN General Comments No 3, as discussed above, and jurisprudence, especially from the South African Constitutional Court, provide for adequate and accurate guidance as to the implementation and application of socio-economic rights. They shed light on key aspects such as progressive realisation, minimum core obligations, and maximum available resources and, at the same time, guarantee the respect for separation of powers and legislative competence of Parliament. This should be sufficient enough to dispel any myth that the state of Mauritius has on the constitutionalisation of socio-economic rights, incomplete since independence in 1968, unless there is simply no political will to genuinely protect, promote, fulfil, and respect socio-economic rights of Mauritians.

---

[61] Soobramoney (1997) para 25.

[62] Soobramoney (1997) para 26.

[63] Soobramoney (1997) para 29.

[64] Minister of Health v. Treatment Action Campaign, 2002 (10) BCLR 1033 (CC).

[65] Treatment Action Campaign (2002) para 38.

5.4 Socio-Economic Rights and the African Charter

5.4.1 Background

Understanding the rationale behind the inclusion of socio-economic rights in the African Charter requires an understanding of the ideological and historical developments that preceded the document's adoption. Following Africa's liberation from colonial authority in the early 1960s, it was widely agreed that the 'independent state' should be in charge of promoting swift political, social, and economic reforms.[66] Massive natural resource exploitation had occurred during the exploitative colonial regime but nothing in the way of socio-economic advancement had been given back to the African people.[67] Oliver and Atmore claim that the colonial state believed that upholding law and order in Africa was its primary responsibility and that it should do so at no cost to European taxpayers.[68] They use education as an example, which was left to church missions' commercial endeavours. The colonial authority believed that in order to preserve peace and order, harsh laws that interfered with every element of African life had to be adopted. It follows that the state's widespread violations of civil and political rights are not shocking.[69]

Without doubt, colonialism accelerated Africa's economic integration into the world economy. However, as Mamdani contended, this integration was unbalanced and external, with the economies developed as crop exporters and necessities importers, resulting in dependency.[70] Mamdani also shows how the colonial economy prevented Africans from being self-sufficient and instead made them reliant on it, which came with a number of restrictions that rendered the continent's citizens further poor.[71] African states with their inherited weak economy believed their main goal was to overcome poverty, sickness, starvation, illiteracy, and so on.[72] Human rights have long been opposed by post-colonial African leaders as a means of promoting human development. They contend that sensible economic policies that are carried out without being compromised by ideas of human rights are what Africa needs. However, self-sustenance has not been achieved on the continent despite the implementation of multiple economic measures. The issue facing the independent African state is that it has perpetuated and utilised in the same way the submissive connection that colonialism engendered between itself and the state, as stated by Mbembe.[73]

---

[66] Young (1999), pp. 15–38.

[67] Oloka-Onyango (2006).

[68] Oliver & Atmore (1994), p. 124.

[69] Nmehielle (2001), pp. 17–29.

[70] Mamdani (1996), p. 145.

[71] Mamdani (1996), pp. 146–147.

[72] Ankumah (1996), p. 5.

[73] Mbembe (2001), p. 34.

Mbazira has accurately argued that 'unless economic policies integrate the African individual in its making, give him or her a voice and improve his or her socio-economic wellbeing, the policies remain tools of white collar debate'.[74] He further argued that human rights norms must empower the African peasantry before they can take part in this discussion and sway its outcome in their favour. In white collar arguments, the emphasis on public well-being has a tendency to distance the person and his needs; therefore, it is important to strike a fair balance between the demands of the public good and individual rights. This can be achieved by including laws that safeguard socio-economic rights, both individual and collective, and include them into the development and application of policy.[75]

5.4.2 Towards the African Charter

Two 1978 colloquiums on human rights and development, the Butare Colloquium[76] and the Dakar Colloquium,[77] made explicit allusions to the need to safeguard socio-economics. After debating the connection between human rights and development, the Butare Colloquium attendees came to the conclusion that socio-economic and civil-political rights should not be violated because of a lack of resources in many African nations. It was determined at the Dakar Colloquium that socio-economic rights required special consideration because they were interrelated with civil and political rights and that human rights could not be limited to only these.[78] The failure of later attempts to construct a human rights system for Africa, mostly spearheaded by the United Nations (UN) Commission on Human Rights, was primarily attributed to African leaders' unwillingness to yield their sovereignty to a human rights framework.[79]

But tragic events, particularly those that occurred in the 1970s and resulted in the establishment of dictatorships in certain African nations, forced the Organisation of African Unity (OAU), which is now the African Union (AU), to acknowledge the necessity of defending human rights throughout the continent. The OAU Assembly of Heads of State and Government reaffirmed its commitment to defending human and peoples' rights, especially the right to development, at its 16th ordinary session,

---

[74] Mbazira (2006), p. 336.

[75] Mbazira (2006), p. 337.

[76] Human Rights and Economic Development in Francophone Africa, a colloquium organised by the Institute of International Law and Economic Development (Washington DC) and the Faculty of Law of the National University of Rwanda 3–7 July 1978.

[77] Organised by Association Se´ne´galaise d'Etudes et de Recherches Juridiques and by the International Commission of Jurists, September 1978.

[78] Ouguergouz (2003), p. 24.

[79] Ouguergouz (2003), p. 25.

which took place from 16 to 20 July 1979.[80] Mbazira contended that it was unclear why the right to development was given special attention; however, it is reasonable to assume that this was due to the high rates of underdevelopment that are common throughout the continent. The leaders of Africa may have aimed to convert the political responsibilities taken on by the sovereign state to promote development into legally mandated commitments grounded in human rights.[81] Though this may have been done unintentionally at the time, the OAU was going beyond just civil and political rights when it placed emphasis on the right to development. Another argument for the emphasis on the right to development is that it was necessary to build a kind of wall to counteract past colonial powers' ongoing economic exploitation and to make up for any exploitation that had already occurred.[82] Speaking to a group of specialists gathered in Dakar to map out the future of an African human rights instrument, President Senghor of Senegal said that since the right to development encompasses all socio-economic rights in addition to civil and political rights, it should be given special consideration. The African Charter was drafted with this call in mind.[83]

Despite being ratified during the height of the Cold War, the African Charter managed to overcome the ideological disagreements that had sentenced socio-economic rights to a lower position.[84] Indeed, while the initial draft of the Charter made a significant difference between civil and political and socio-economic rights especially from the implementation perspective, the final draft did away with this distinction and placed obligations on state parties to not only respect and protect but also to fulfil rights such as education and health.[85] The indivisible nature of civil and political rights as well as socio-economic rights was declared by the African Charter. Murray stated that this portrayed Africa as providing 'ripe ground for challenging the universality of international law principles'.[86] The Eighteenth Assembly of Heads of State and Government convened in Nairobi from 24 to 28 June 1981 adopted the Charter, and socio-economic rights were recognised equally with civil and political rights. Paragraph 8 of the Preamble of the African Charter proclaimed that:

> It is essential to pay particular attention to the right to development and that civil and political rights cannot be dissociated from economic, social and cultural rights in their conception

[80] AHG/Dec 115 (XVI) Rev. 1 'Decision on Human and Peoples' Rights in Africa', 16th ordinary session of the OAU Assembly of Heads of State and Government, Monrovia, Liberia 16–20 July 1979. In order to develop an initial draft of the African Charter, the resolution directed the OAU Secretary-General to set up a closed meeting of highly qualified specialists as soon as feasible.

[81] Mbazira (2006), p. 338.

[82] Mbazira (2006), p. 338.

[83] Address delivered by Mr. Leopold Sedar Senghor, President of Senegal, OAU DOC CAB/LEG/67/5.

[84] Odinkalu (2002), p. 181.

[85] Viljoen (2015), p. 215.

[86] Murray (2000), p. 11.

> as well as universality…that the satisfaction of economic, social and cultural rights is a guarantee for the enjoyment of civil and political rights.

Mbazura has remarked that this was a radical break from the ideologies that declared socio-economic rights to be subordinate and civil and political rights to be pure. Without a rebuttal, the preamble could be taken literally as implying that socio-economic rights were a prerequisite for civil and political rights.[87] The relationship between socio-economic rights and civil and political rights is mutually dependent. Despite this, socio-economic rights are still subordinated to civil and political rights. Both categories of rights should be upheld in the African setting, as the right to vote may be just as vital to an impoverished African as the right to healthcare. For example, the vote might be used to sway choices about the health system. At the UN level, a separate covenant was adopted to protect socio-economic rights, the ICESCR, and the International Covenant on Civil and Political Rights (ICCPR), in response to the split of human rights, which went against the spirit of the Universal Declaration of Human Rights.

Scott and Macklem claim that the idea that socio-economic rights are somehow less important than civil and political rights did not have any bearing on this split. They argued that 'social rights were not viewed as justiciable because courts, or court-like bodies, were not thought to be competent bodies to deal with them'.[88] Arambulo further argued that the best method for enforcing socio-economic rights was thought to be a reporting mechanism rather than a complaints procedure.[89] Some had even questioned the 'fabric of socio-economic rights as rights'.[90] These reasonings and perceptions are erroneous, though. Similar to how civil and political rights result in positive obligations, socio-economic rights do the same.[91] It is also true that, like socio-economic rights, civic and political rights must be implemented with resources.

5.4.3 Normative Content of the African Charter

A considerable range of socio-economic rights are guaranteed by the African Charter. While the ICESCR and the Charter share many similarities, they differ significantly from one another. The African Charter does not mandate 'progressive realisation subject to maximum availability of resources' contrary to the ICESCR. Spelling out the nature of states' obligations under the African Charter in a definitive manner, article 1 states that:

---

[87] Mbazira (2006), p. 339.

[88] Scott and Macklem (1992), p. 89.

[89] Arambulo (1999), p. 26.

[90] Cranston (1973).

[91] Sepulveda (2003), p. 125–126.

> The member states of the African Union parties to the present Charter shall recognise the rights, duties and freedoms enshrined in this Charter and shall undertake to adopt legislative and other measures to give effect to them.

When taken literally, it seems to support the idea that there are no restrictions on the realisation of any of the rights outlined in the African Charter, including socio-economic rights. In fact, the provision has caused some observers to claim that the responsibilities for other socio-economic rights are stated as being immediate, with the exception of the right to health.[92] According to Mbazira, this stance looks very appealing in response to the idea that socio-economic rights are not human rights.[93] In fact, the Commission itself seems to have been tempted to take this position when it declared that all rights must be implemented right away, despite its awareness of Africa's economic struggles.[94] The idea that the rights outlined in the African Charter are immediate, however, begs the question: given the continent's economic conditions, is it realistic to expect full realisation of all socio-economic rights right away? The answer is no.

The realisation of certain obligations, such as respect, may happen immediately, but significant resources are needed for the fulfilment, promotion, and protection of socio-economic rights. Numerous African nations, if not all of them, have extremely weak economies marred by corruption, weak planning, and little to no influence on the world economy except from that of consumers.[95] Such economies find it difficult to mobilise the resources required to meet all socio-economic requirements right away and to swiftly address their structural issues.[96] Human rights commitments should, at the very least, obligate African governments to take reasonable steps to enhance the resources required for the realisation of socio-economic rights and to make the most use of the resources already in place. However, Viljoen has warned that 'the qualification of available resources' should not be applied to the 'unqualified' right to education[97] even though the African Commission did apply it with regard to the qualified right to health in the case of Purohit and another v The Gambia.[98] He further argued that the idea of importing the concept of 'available resources' and the 'core obligation to take concrete, targeted and non-discriminatory steps' by the African Commission in the Purohit case 'is influenced by the wording of article 16, which provides for the "best attainable" state of health and "necessary measure", and is therefore not a general statement about the duty to "fulfil" right'.[99]

[92] Odinkalu (2002), p. 196.

[93] Mbazira (2006), p. 340.

[94] Presentation of the Third Annual Activity Report by Prof Umozurike, Chairperson of the African Commission to the 26th Assembly of Heads of State and Government of the OAU, 9–11 July 1990.

[95] Mills (2012).

[96] Cheru (1992), pp. 497–512.

[97] Viljoen (2015), p. 217.

[98] Purohit and another v The Gambia (2003) AHRLR 96 (ACHPR 2003).

[99] Viljoen (2015), p. 217.

Although resources are needed for the protection, advancement, and fulfilment of civil and political rights as well, there are typically large disparities in the amounts of resources needed for the two types of rights. Therefore, it should not be surprising that nations with abundant financial resources have consistently argued for the protection of their riches and have not yet achieved socio-economic rights. According to Nmehielle, 'the debate on the justiciability of socio-economic rights under the Charter should not assume an extreme posture'.[100] Given the underdevelopment of the majority of African nations, it is imperative that the socio-economic rights enshrined in the African Charter be realised gradually, even though states must act immediately. Apart from Africa's underdevelopment, it is crucial that socio-economic rights are gradually realised because the requirements for their complete realisation are dynamic since they are determined by shifting socio-economic conditions and setting new benchmarks. This is due to the need for constant improvement in people's standards.[101]

The rights protected by the African Charter are the right to work, the right to health, the right to education, the right to protection of the family, the right to self-determination, the right to dispose of wealth and natural resources, the right to economic, social, and cultural development, the right to peace, and the right to a satisfactory and favourable environment.[102] The mentioned collective rights (the so-called third-generation rights) do have significant and direct relevance to socio-economic rights. The African Commission has also issued the 'Principles and Guidelines on the Implementation of Economic, Social and Cultural Rights in the African Charter on Human and Peoples' Rights' which provides for critical guidance on aspects such as interpretation, nature of member states' obligations, key obligations, and an elaboration on the normative content of each socio-economic right enshrined in the African Charter.

Viljoen has noted the absence of other essential rights such as the right to social security and the right to adequate standard of living, including food, clothing, and housing due to the 'minimalist approach' adopted during the drafting process.[103] However, the African Commission has held that 'there is no right in the African Charter that cannot be made effective' in the case of SERAC v Nigeria where it recognised the implied rights of shelter and food.[104] The African Charter and CESCR differ in their focus on rights like health and work, with the former aiming to create an exclusively African instrument. While African states are involved in global instruments, they also rely on global jurisprudence, which the African Commission

[100] Nmehielle (2001), p. 124.

[101] Mbazira (2006), p. 341.

[102] Article 15 to 24 of the African Charter.

[103] Viljoen (2015), p. 215.

[104] Social and Economic Rights Action Centre and another v Nigeria (2001) AHRLR 60 (ACHPR 2001).

and Court must refer to for comprehensive understanding of human rights in the African context.[105]

5.4.4 *Jurisprudence of the African Commission on Socio-Economic Rights*

Mbazira has categorised the jurisprudence of the African Commission on socio-economic rights into two stages: the redundancy stage and the progression stage.[106] During the redundancy stage, the African Commission had found states to be in violation of socio-economic rights but without any elaboration on the interpretation and understanding of these rights.[107] The progression stage is characterised by two important decisions of the African Commission, namely, the SERAC v Nigeria case and the Purohit v The Gambia case. Mbazira argued that:

> The African Commission has given normative content to some of the socio-economic rights in the African Charter. The Commission has even gone ahead to read into the Charter rights which are not expressly protected, such as rights to food and shelter. The decisions also indicate increased reliance on standards established by international human rights in the area of socio-economic rights. In remedial terms, these decisions make clear and elaborate recommendations that transcend the declaratory nature of the Commission's recommendations in previous cases.[108]

The phase of progression is marked by two major decisions, SERAC and Purohit, which differ from redundancy decisions, elaborate protection of rights, and reference to international human rights jurisprudence. The Commission also provides comprehensive recommendations for remedying rights violations, including repealing legislation, appointing an inquiry mission, and keeping the Commission updated on the decisions. The SERAC case involved the Nigerian government's exploitation of oil resources by Shell, disregarding environmental impact assessments and regulatory mechanisms. The government's brutal military force led to thousands evicted, destroyed homes, and livestock killed, causing malnutrition and starvation.[109]

The African Commission has discussed the socio-economic rights obligations outlined by the African Charter and underlined that these obligations are premised on the duties to respect, protect, promote, and fulfilment. It also highlighted that

---

[105] Mbazira (2006), p. 342.

[106] Mbazira (2006), pp. 342–347.

[107] Free Legal Assistance Group v Zaire (2000) AHRLR 74 (ACHPR 1995) dealing with the right to health and the right to education; Union Interafricaine des Droits de l'Homme and Others v Angola (2000) AHRLR 18 (ACHPR 1997) dealing with the right to water and the right to work; International Pen and Others (on behalf of Saro-Wiwa) v Nigeria (2000) AHRLR 212 (ACHPR 1998) dealing with the right to health; Malawi African Association and Others v Mauritania (2000) AHRLR 149 (ACHPR 2000) dealing with the right to health of prisoners.

[108] Mbazira (2006), p. 347.

[109] Smis and Bello (2021), pp. 454–474.

these duties involve both negative and positive obligations.[110] The African Commission has underlined the justiciability and commitment towards the enforcement of socio-economic rights. It adjudicated that the Nigerian government infringed the right to a clean and healthy environment given that it failed to take measures to prevent pollution, promote conservation, and secure ecologically sustainable development. The African Commission also made reference to article 12 of ICESCR. It found Nigeria to have violated the right to health and a clean environment which entails the obligation on the government to avoid practices that violate individual integrity.[111] The African Commission has interpreted the Charter progressively to include rights to shelter and food which are not explicitly spelt out in the African Charter. It was of the view that these rights are implicitly recognised in other rights such as life, health, and economic development which are of great relevance and importance for human dignity. The Commission ruled that the Charter implicitly recognises the right to housing or shelter, derived from provisions protecting health, property, and family rights. The destruction of houses negatively impacts people's property, health, and families.[112] The Commission recommended investigations, prosecution of violators, compensation, environmental and social impact assessments, and government updates on measures to solve the problem.[113]

The *Purohit case* involved mental health advocates from the Gambia who claimed that the Lunatic Detention Act was in violation of the provision on the right to health of the African Charter. The plaintiff argued that the Act lacked safeguards for patients suspected of being insane, was devoid of any review and appeal mechanisms, and did not provide for a remedy for erroneous detentions. The Gambia's Lunatic Detention Act was found to be discriminatory and in violation of article 16 of the African Charter protecting the right to health.[114] The Act, which used terms such as 'idiots' and 'lunatics' referring to mentally ill persons, was pronounced by the African Commission as a violation of human dignity.[115] It emphasised the importance of the right to health, stating that it requires equal access to health facilities and services without discrimination.[116] The African Commission noted that:

> Millions of people in Africa are not enjoying the right to health maximally because African countries are generally faced with problems of poverty which renders them incapable of providing the necessary amenities, infrastructure and resources that facilitate the full enjoyment of this right. Therefore, having regard to this depressing but real state of affairs, the African Commission would like to read into article 16 the obligation on the part of states party to the African Charter to take concrete and targeted steps, while taking full advantage

[110] SERAC (2001) para 44.
[111] SERAC (2001) para 52.
[112] SERAC (2001) para 65–67.
[113] SERAC (2001) para 71.
[114] Purohit case (2003) para 53.
[115] Purohit case (2003) para 59.
[116] Purohit case (2003) para 80.

> of its available resources, to ensure that the right to health is fully realised in all its aspects without discrimination of any kind.[117]

Mbazira has argued that the availability of resources is a crucial factor in determining a state's violation of socio-economic rights in the African Charter. The African Commission's approach aligns with the Committee's General Comments on the socio-economic rights, which are not significantly different from the African Charter's formulation. The Committee interprets CESCR in a way that considers the position of poor countries, requiring states to demonstrate they have used available resources to satisfy minimum obligations under CESCR.[118]

5.5 The Relevance of the African Charter Pertaining to Socio-Economic Rights of Mauritians

The absence of socio-economic rights from the Constitution, the non-domestication of the African Charter, the absence of socio-economic rights in the mandate of NHRIs notably the NHRC, and the non-ratification of the OP ICESCR clearly mean that socio-economic rights are not enforceable and justiciable in Mauritius. As discussed in this chapter, the welfare state system of Mauritius contributes towards the socio-economic well-being of Mauritians, but it cannot be over-relied upon, and it does not confer any constitutional protection to socio-economic rights of Mauritians. Against this backdrop, the African Charter and the African Commission remain highly relevant and valid as an avenue for Mauritians to enforce their socio-economic rights. As of now, the African Court cannot be included here given that Mauritius has not yet submitted Declaration 34(6) under the Court's protocol to give direct access to individuals and NGOs to submit cases. This subject matter is treated elsewhere in this book.

The normative content of socio-economic rights in the African Charter, the progressive jurisprudence of the African Commission, and the accessibility of Mauritian citizens and NGOs to the African Commission are reasons that make this quasi-judicial avenue relevant to the enforcement and justiciability of socio-economic rights of Mauritians. In fact, as matters stand, the African Commission seems to be the only avenue available to them. However, it is surprising to note that not a single complaint has been submitted before the African Commission by Mauritians on socio-economic rights issues. So far, civil society organisations have failed to establish a working relationship with the African Commission. In addition, knowledge about the African Charter and the African Commission among Mauritians is very limited. It would not be an exaggeration to say that Mauritians, including legal professionals and human rights activists, may not be aware of the relevance of the African Commission to adjudicate on socio-economic rights. Institutions such as

[117] Purohit case (2003) para 84.

[118] Mbazira (2006), p. 353.

the NHRC have failed to educate people about this regional system, or perhaps they have been directed not to tread this path and cause annoyance to the state.

Complaints from Mauritians would not only provide them with a quasi-judicial solution to potential socio-economic rights violations but can provide the African Commission with an opportunity to enhance its jurisprudence on socio-economic rights. Indeed, Mauritius, being a strong welfare state with one of the strongest economies in Africa, would likely raise defences such as progressive realisation subject to maximum availability of resources. It is agreed that so far the African Commission has drawn inspiration from the UN-originating concepts such as progressive realisation, maximum availability of resources, and taking steps and seeking international cooperation and assistance in cases such as SERAC and Purohit. However, the economic background of Mauritius may push the African Commission to undertake a literal interpretation of the African Charter on socio-economic rights which are not subject to these concepts as Viljoen has argued.[119] There is so much potential in terms of legal engineering regarding socio-economic rights for not only Mauritians but for Africans in general.

However, the African Commission equally needs to be more assertive when dealing with the subject of socio-economic rights in Mauritius. It has been noted that none of the Concluding Observations from the African Commission has raised issues pertaining to the constitutionalisation of socio-economic rights and the duties and responsibilities of the NHRC. There is no mention of socio-economic rights or any comment made by the African Commission on such issues. The status of a high-income country of Mauritius should not be a barrier for the African Commission to genuinely engage with the state of Mauritius on the issue of socio-economic rights. In essence, citizens, policymakers, legal practitioners, civil society organisations, NHRIs in Mauritius, and any other stakeholder concerned should imperative recognise their duty towards the implantation of socio-economic rights in Mauritius and fulfil their responsibilities towards it.

References

Alesina A, Murard E, Rapoport H (2019) Immigration and preferences for redistribution in Europe IZA discussion paper no. 12130. IZA—Institute of Labor Economics, Bonn

Ankumah E (1996) The African Commission on Human and Peoples' Rights: the practice and procedures. Brill

Arambulo K (1999) Strengthening the supervision of the International Covenant on Economic, Social and Cultural Rights: theoretical and procedural aspects. Intersentia

Bertelsmann Stiftung's Transformation Index (BTI) (2024) Germany. Available at https://bti--project.org/fileadmin/api/content/en/downloads/reports/country_report_2024_MUS.pdf. Accessed 1 July 2025

[119] Viljoen (2015), p. 217.

Chan Low (2019) Constitutional development in the South Western Indian Ocean States. In: Colom J, Rohfling-Dijoux S, Schulze G (eds) The 50th anniversary of Mauritius: constitutional development. Nomos
Cheru F (1992) Structural adjustment, primary resource trade and sustainable development in sub-Saharan Africa. World Dev 20(4):497–512
Colom J (2019) Equal and non-discriminatory right to health in Mauritius. In: Colom J, Rohfling-Dijoux S, Schulze G (eds) The 50th anniversary of Mauritius: constitutional development. Nomos
Cranston M (1973) What are human rights? Basic Books, New York
De Schutter O (2018) The rights-based welfare state: public budgets and economic and social rights. Friedrich Ebert Stiftung, Geneva. Available at https://library.fes.de/pdf-files/bueros/genf/14943.pdf. Accessed 1 July 2025
De Smith S (1964) A the new commonwealth and its constitutions. Stevens University of California
Ebbinghaus B, Lehner L, Naumann E (2022) Welfare state support during the COVID-19 pandemic: change and continuity in public attitudes towards social policies in Germany. Eur Policy Anal 8(3):297–311
Gamble A (2016) Can the welfare state survive? Polity Press
Glennerster H (2007) The sustainability of Western welfare states - seminar paper - originally presented at CASE seminar, November 2007. London School of Economics and Political Science
Gough I, Therborn G (2010) The global future of welfare states. In: Castles FG, Leibfried S, Lewis J, Obinger H, Pierson C (eds) The Oxford handbook of the welfare state. OUP, Oxford
Houbert J (1981) Mauritius: Independence and dependence. J Mod Afr Stud 19(1):75–105
Human Rights Division (2014) Questionnaire in relation to General Assembly resolution 68/268 Available at https://www.ohchr.org/sites/default/files/2022-02/Mauritius.docx (Accessed 20 June 2025).
Kende M (2003) The South African Constitutional Court's embrace of socio-economic rights: a comparative perspective. Chapman Law Review 6(137):138–160
Mahadew AR (2018) Economic and Social Rights as Constitutional guarantees, compared to privileges under the welfare state system: an assessment of the case of Mauritius. ESR Rev Econ Soc Rights South Afr 19(1):9–12
Mamdani M (1996) Citizen and subject: contemporary Africa and the legacy of later colonialism. Princeton University Press, New Jersey
Maudarbux MB (2016) Interreligious education: conceptualising a needs assessment framework for curriculum design in plural societies (with special reference to Mauritius). Int Rev Educ 62(4):459–481
Maurer S (2014) Post-colonialism: the so-called malaise creole in Mauritius. Cult Anthropol 87:97
Mauritius Revenue Authority (2024) Contribution Sociale Generalisee (CSG). Available at https://www.mra.mu/business/csg. Accessed 1 July 2025
Mbazira C (2006) Enforcing the economic, social and cultural rights in the African Charter on Human and Peoples' Rights: twenty years of redundancy, progression and significant strides. Afr Hum Rights Law J 6:336
Mbembe A (2001) On the post-colony. University of California Press
Memorandum submitted by the Mauritius Labour Party to the Legislative Council (1961) Office of the Secretary of State Colonies
Mills G (2012) Why Africa is poor: and what Africans can do about it. Penguin Random House
Ministry of Health and Wellness (2022) Strategy overview. Available at https://budgetmof.govmu.org/documents/V_18_012023_24Health.pdf. Accessed 1 July 2025
Murray R, and Murray RH (2000) The African Commission on Human and Peoples' Rights and International Law. Hart Publishing.
Nmehielle V (2001) The African human rights system: its laws, practice and institutions. Brill
Odinkalu C (2002) Implementing economic, social and cultural rights under the African Charter on Human and Peoples' Rights. In: Evans M, Murray R (eds) The African Charter on Human and Peoples' Rights: the system in practice. Cambridge University Press UK, pp 1986–2000

Oliver R, Atmore A (1994) Africa since 1800. Cambridge University Press
Oloka-Onyango J (2006) Beyond the rhetoric: reinvigorating the struggle for economic and social rights in Africa. University of Minnesota Human Rights Library. http://www1.umn.edu/humanrts/africa/Oloka-Onyango.html. Accessed 1 July 2025
Ouguergouz F (2003) The African Charter on Human and Peoples' Rights: a comprehensive agenda for human dignity and sustainable democracy in Africa. Brill
Page E (2012) Bureaucracy: disregarding public administration. In: Connelly J, Hayward J (eds) The withering of the welfare state: regression. Palgrave Macmillan, Basingstoke, pp 101–120
Phaala LE (2010) Development with social justice? Social democracy in Mauritius. MA Thesis Master of Arts (International Studies), Stellenbosch University
Scott C, Macklem P (1992) Constitutional ropes of sand or justiciable guarantees? Social rights in a new South African Constitution. Univ Pa Law Rev 141
Sepulveda M (2003) The nature of the obligations under the International Covenant on Economic, Social and Cultural Rights. Intersentia
Smis S, Bello O (2021) Social and Economic Rights Action Centre (SERAC) and the Centre for Economic and Social Rights (CESR) v Nigeria: two decades on-questioning the continued implementation gap. Afr Hum Rights Yearb 5:454–474
Statistics Mauritius (2020) Gender Statistics 2022. Available at https://statsmauritius.govmu.org/Pages/Statistics/ESI/Gender/Gender_Yr22.aspx#:~:text=(i)%20In%202022%2C%20the,7%20years%20longer%20than%20men. Accessed 1 July 2025
Stebbing A, Spies-Butcher B (2016) The decline of a homeowning society? Asset-based welfare, retirement and intergenerational equity in Australia. Hous Stud 31(2):190–207
UN CESCR (8 June 2010a) Concluding observations on the combined second to fourth periodic report of Mauritius. UN Doc. E/C.12/MUS/CO/4
UN CESCR (7 May 2010b) Examination of the second, third and fourth periodic reports of the implementation by Mauritius of the ICECSR
UN CESCR (19 December 2018) Replies of Mauritius to the list of issues. UN Doc. E/C.12/MUS/Q/5/Add.1
UN CESCR (5 April 2019) Concluding observations on the fifth periodic report of Mauritius. UN Doc. E/C.12/MUS/CO/5
Van Kersbergen K, Vis B (2014) Comparative welfare state politics: development, opportunities and reform. Cambridge University Press, New York
Van Oorschot W, Roosma F, Meuleman B, Reeskens T (eds) (2017) The social legitimacy of targeted welfare: new perspectives on deservingness opinions. Edward Elgar Publishing, Cheltenham
Viljoen F (2015) International human rights law in Africa. Oxford University Press
Wurzel R (2012) The environmental challenge to nation states: from limits to growth to ecological modernisation. In: Connelly J, Hayward J (eds) The withering of the welfare state: regression. Palgrave Macmillan, Basingstoke
Young C (1999) The third wave of democratization in Africa: ambiguities and contradictions. In: State, conflict, and democracy in Africa, pp 15–38

Chapter 6
The Right to Environment

Abstract A human rights-based approach (HRBA) is crucial for environmental conservation, accountability enhancement, and empowerment of those affected. It integrates the principles of human rights, such as accountability, equality, non-discrimination, and inclusivity. HRBA strengthens the relationship between duty bearers and rights holders by empowering individuals to hold duty bearers responsible and pursue remedies for violations. Uniform international environmental human rights standards, enhanced state capacity to carry out their responsibilities, more accountability, and more successful, sustainable, and legitimate outcomes are among the advantages. It is essential to support vulnerable groups, such as women, children, the elderly, people with disabilities, indigenous peoples, and those living in poverty. In view of the aforementioned, this chapter provides a summary of Mauritius' institutional and legal framework for environmental protection in order to determine whether or not it upholds the human right to a safe and healthy environment. In order to support the domestic framework that permits the state to take an HRBA approach to environmental preservation, it then focuses on the African Charter and makes the case that there is an existing right that ought to be applied in Mauritius.

6.1 Introduction

The tropical climate, insularity, and coastal erosion of Mauritius make it an exceptional and vulnerable island with serious environmental problems. Climate change-related hazards take the forms of damage to the beaches, an already precarious imbalance and threats and dangers to the endemic and protected species inhabiting the marine ecosystem of the country.[1] Given that low-lying areas and the ecological stability of rural areas are threatened by drought and rising sea levels, the island's

[1] Gösling et al. (2007), p. 67.

R. Mahadew, *Mauritius and African Human Rights Law*,
https://doi.org/10.1007/978-3-032-08832-1_6

tiny size exacerbates the issues.[2] Mauritius' economy is also in danger due to coastal erosion, which is resulting in the loss of tourism revenue and natural resources.[3] In view of stopping the destruction of the shoreline, the state has built jetties and dykes and restored mangroves and coral reefs.[4] These steps, however, are not sufficient to address the challenges and problems that climate change has brought about. Another major threat to Mauritius is pollution, which is caused, *inter alia*, by low recycling rates, which result in an excessive accumulation of waste.[5]

Through the implementation of strategic measures to move towards a climate-resilient, cleaner, low-emission, greener, environmentally sustainable, and circular economy, Mauritius has the aspiration of becoming an inclusive, wealthy, and environmentally conscious country. A 10-year policy and strategy, legislation prohibiting non-biodegradable single-use plastic products, solid waste management plans and vehicle emissions strategies have been designed and put in place by the Ministry of Environment, Solid Waste Management and Climate Change.[6] The government is funding initiatives and actions related to coastal rehabilitation and construction of drains with over $15 million USD. Mauritius has as objective the attainment of 60% renewable energy in its energy mix and aims at reducing by 40% its emission of greenhouse gas by 2030. Approximately 35% of the total financial needs, which equate to US$ 2.3 billion, are being supported by the state, with the remaining 65% depending on outside assistance.[7]

As would be discussed in Sect. 6.2 of this chapter, the legal and institutional framework on the environment, loosely termed as environmental laws, is arguably well developed and aligned with international standards prescribed by the UN. However, its implementation has been questionable because of factors such as lack of resources, especially financially, or lack of enforceability and justiciability of these laws. On the contrary, having a human right to environment may be an approach which is more effective in the protection of the environment. It accurately places obligations and duties on states to do or not to do things in view of respecting the right to environment of individuals. Therefore, it presents the potential of protecting the environment through the action of respecting the right to environment as a human right. Indeed, Shelton has argued that:

> One view sees environmental protection as a prerequisite or precondition to the exercise of fundamental human rights. Another perspective views environmental protection not as a precondition for human rights, but rather as an integral part of their enjoyment. In a more manageable interpretation, "environmental rights" refers to the reformulation and expansion of existing human rights and duties in the context of environmental protection.[8]

[2] Gray and Lalljee (2012), p. 99.

[3] Beeharry et al. (2021), p. 10702.

[4] Sunkur et al. (2023), p. 102449.

[5] Mauthoor (2017), pp. 506–513.

[6] Republic of Mauritius 'Environment Protection and Legislation available at https://govmu.org/EN/infoservices/environment/Pages/legislation.aspx (accessed 25 June 2025).

[7] UNEP (2023).

[8] Shelton (1992), p. 103.

The human right to a healthy environment has been endorsed by the UN Human Rights Council in 2021,[9] and in 2022, the UN General Assembly recognised this right by adopting a resolution.[10] This resolution's unanimous adoption demonstrates that this right, which is already recognised by 156 states, enjoys widespread support and recognition globally. A number of parties, including business entities, civil society organisations, indigenous peoples, and human rights institutions, worked together for years to advocate for and achieve the resolution.[11] The right to a healthy environment was recognised in the Stockholm Declaration on the Human Environment in 1972, which emphasised the fundamental right to freedom, equality, and adequate conditions of life. This right was later included in national constitutions, legislation, and policy documents in over 80% of UN member states before global recognition by the Human Rights Council and the General Assembly.[12]

The right to a healthy environment consists of substantive elements in the forms of clean air, stable climate, safe water, sanitation, healthy food, non-toxic environments, and healthy biodiversity. It also encompasses procedural elements such as access to information, decision-making, justice, and international cooperation for environmental action and extraterritorial jurisdiction over human rights harms.[13] The Resolution on the right to a healthy environment has as objective the enhancement of the understanding of environmental degradation and its consequences on human rights. It is also intended to positively influence the legal recognition in domestic states, raise awareness of environmental protection, strengthen implementation in already recognised countries, enhance rights holders' enjoyment and accountability, strengthen mechanisms for protecting environmental human rights defenders, increase private sector responsibilities, support for a comprehensive response to the triple planetary crisis, and promote public participation in environmental issues.[14]

In order to conserve the environment while also improving accountability and empowering people, a human rights-based approach (HRBA) is essential. It incorporates human rights precepts including responsibility, non-discrimination, equality, and inclusivity. By giving people the ability to hold duty bearers accountable and seek remedies for infractions, HRBA fortifies the bond between rights holders and duty bearers. Benefits include uniform international environmental human rights norms, increased state capacity to fulfil their duties, improved accountability, and more legitimate, sustainable, and successful results. Encouraging vulnerable

[9] UNGA, HRC, A/HRC/RES/48/13 (18 October 2021).

[10] UNGA, The human right to a clean, healthy and sustainable environment, A/RES/76/300 (28 July 2022).

[11] UN OHCHR Information Note (2022), p. 7.

[12] Boyd (2012), pp. 3–15.

[13] A/HRC/43/53 (2019).

[14] UN OHCHR Information Note (2022), pp. 10–11.

populations, including Indigenous Peoples, women, children, the elderly, people with disabilities, and those living in poverty, is crucial.[15]

In light of the above, this chapter presents an overview of the legal and institutional framework on environmental protection in Mauritius to assess whether a human right to a safe and healthy environment is enshrined therein. It then focuses on the African Charter on argue that there is such a right which is already existent and which should be implemented in Mauritius to support the domestic framework allowing for the state to adopt a HRBA towards environmental protection.

6.2 Legal and Institutional Framework

Influenced by its colonial history, Mauritius inherited from laws protecting the environment in a sector-based manner as per the needs of the French and British colonial powers.[16] Lim Tung has argued that domestic legislation on the environment in Mauritius was determined by the intention and goodwill of the colonial powers.[17] For example, the Public Health Ordinance prohibited water pollution in connection with public health, and the Rivers and Canals Ordinance forbade constructions near canals, streams, and rivers while sanctioning their pollution. There was no specific legislation on the protection of marine environment despite the vulnerability of the marine resources and ecosystems. After independence in 1968, the state embarked on enacting several laws such as the Territorial Sea Act 1970, the Continental Shelf Act 1970, and the Maritime Zones Act 1977 providing for the legal status and the boundaries of coastal and maritime zones. These acts were motivated by economic and social development necessities as well as the need to consolidate the sovereignty of the country.[18]

A 1991 Report entitled ‘State of the Environment in Mauritius’ made an inventory of the environment of Mauritius and proposals towards a more effective protection of it.[19] With the intention of the government to provide a holistic approach, the Environment Protection Act (EPA) was enacted in 1991. The EPA 1991 enshrined the Environment Impact Assessments (EIAs), pollution standards, management of coastal and marine areas, as well as the setting up of a tribunal. The EPA’s provisions (which has now been superseded by the Environment Act 2024 discussed in the next section) and any regulations enacted pursuant to this act such as any directives, orders, or notices issued or mandated by the EPA thus constitute Mauritian environmental legislation. With the aims of updating and unifying the laws pertaining to the management and conservation of wildlife, the Wildlife and National Parks

[15] Ibid 12–14.

[16] Toussaint (1971), p. 1449.

[17] Lim Tung (2011), p. 271.

[18] Lim Tung (2011), p. 271.

[19] Ministry of Environment and Quality of Life (1992).

Act was enacted in 1993. While the EPA 2002 established more detailed and broad guidelines for environmental preservation, the Fisheries and Marine Resources Act (FMRA) provided regulations for the management, conservation, and protection of fisheries and marine resources. Additionally, the Mauritius Oceanography Institute Act (MOI) has been entrusted with the responsibility of developing, carrying out, and coordinating research activities in relation to marine living and non-living resources.[20]

It should be noted that the Constitution of Mauritius does not provide for the right to environment as a human right nor does it make any reference to the environment. This is in contrast to the Constitution of Seychelles which provides that the state recognises the right of every person to live in and enjoy a clean, healthy, and ecologically balanced environment and with a view to ensuring the effective realisation of this right the state undertakes to take measures to promote the protection, preservation, and improvement of the environment; to ensure a sustainable socio-economic development of Seychelles by a judicious use and management of the resources of Seychelles; and to promote public awareness of the need to protect, preserve, and improve the environment.[21] Similarly, the Constitution of South Africa provides that everyone has the right (a) to an environment that is not harmful to their health or well-being and (b) to have the environment protected, for the benefit of present and future generations, through reasonable legislative and other measures that (i) prevent pollution and ecological degradation, (ii) promote conservation, and (iii) secure ecologically sustainable development and use of natural resources while promoting justifiable economic and social development.[22]

This implies that while the Supreme Court and the Environmental and Land Use Appeal Tribunal of Mauritius have intercepted the various provisions of environmental legislations, there have not been instances where cases have been adjudicated upon on the basis of the human right to environment. The next section will provide for an overview of some of the fundamental legislation on environment in Mauritius which do not make explicit reference to the right to environment.

6.2.1 *Legislative Framework*

There exist a significant number of acts of parliament and regulations on the use, protection, and management of the environment in Mauritius. Some key ones would be the Fisheries Act 1980, the Waste Water Authority Act 1991, the Rivers and Canals Act 1863, and so on and so forth. These acts of parliament are supported by scores of regulations on specific matters issued by relevant ministries and authorities. Since it is outside the scope of this work, it is not possible to provide for a

[20] MOI 'The Institute' (2024).

[21] Section 38 of the Constitution of Seychelles.

[22] Section 24 of the Constitution of South Africa.

critical overview of all of them. The next section therefore focuses on the most recent, overarching, and foundational legislations governing the environment and climate change in Mauritius.

6.2.1.1 The Environment Act 2024

On 24 May 2024, the new Environment Act 2024 (EA 2024) was gazetted, and it should be proclaimed and come into force imminently. It aims at repealing the Environment Protection Act 2002 (EPA 2002) and replacing it with a modern legislative framework with a view to ensuring better protection, management, and conservation of the environment. The concept of environmental stewardship is enshrined in similar words as the EPA 2002 declaring that every person shall use his or her best endeavours to preserve and enhance the quality of life by caring responsibly for the environment.[23]

Formulation of National Policies and Priorities for the Protection of the Environment

Part two of the EA 2024 focuses on the formulation of national policies and priorities for environmental protection. Accordingly, the National Environment and Sustainable Development Commission is established with the aim of setting national objectives and goals for the protection, management, and conservation of the environment. The Commission's mandate includes the establishment of setting national objectives and targets in relation to circular economy, green economy, sustainable consumption and production, and multilateral environmental agreements. The Commission also reviews progress made by public departments on environmental protection, management, and conservation projects and programmes, ensuring coordination and cooperation between public departments and other government organisations. The Minister, guided by the Commission, has the responsibility to propose policies, monitor environmental protection projects, conduct research, prepare action plans, facilitate multilateral agreements, promote environmental stewardship, enhance legal frameworks, coordinate environmental issues, respond to emergencies, appoint technical advisory committees, and publish information.[24]

Section 8 of the EA 2024 establishes the National Network for Sustainable Development in Mauritius which is a forum for discussions and consultations on sustainable development matters. This National Network is composed of the Minister, supervising officer, Director, and other members. The National Network aims at harmonising policies, promoting greening, improving environmental quality, and protecting Mauritius' environmental assets. The Department is mandated to

[23] Section 4 EA 2024.

[24] Sections 5–7 EA 2024.

develop a National Policy, Strategy and Action Plan on Sustainable Development taking into consideration human rights, cultural heritage, and gender aspects.[25]

To facilitate the implementation of Multilateral Environmental Agreements (MEAs) by competent ministries, public departments, and organisations, a Coordinating Committee for MEAs was established. The Minister, the supervising officer, the Director, the Director of the Department of Climate Change, and a representative from each of the ministries and organisations included in the Fourth Schedule make up the committee. The committee decides on national-level actions, tracks advancement, and fosters collaborations while taking into account the results of regional or global MEAs.[26] The Department of Environment is set up within the ministry, and it is managed by a public officer whose responsibilities include the day-to-day business operations and supervision of officers. The Department also has a National Environmental Laboratory which is entrusted with the task of conducting analytical testing for environmental monitoring of water and air and plastics in conformity with national environmental standards, guidelines, and regulations.[27]

The Police de L'Environnement is a unit of the Mauritius Police Force responsible for the enforcement of environmental laws.[28] The Observatoire de L'Environnement is an organisation at the ministry level which has the mandate of information dissemination, policy development, and monitoring. Both units work with a committee to ensure effective and proper functioning and governance.[29] The Observatoire is premised on a Science to Policy Platform which is meant to support a multi-sectoral dialogue on conclusive research and act as an advisory body for decision-makers on improved environmental governance. The platform will submit technical reports to the Minister, which can be approved or requested for further work. An annual report with proposed policy orientations will follow.[30] The Environment Coordination Committee promotes cooperation among agencies and public departments in environmental protection, management, and conservation. It develops policies, advises on standards, and ensures compliance with directives. It also recommends amendments and guidelines.[31]

Enforcing agencies are designated in the Fifth Schedule for environmental mediums or pollutants, with their functions and powers as specified. The Minister, supervising officer, or Director has the same powers under environmental laws. If an enforcing agency fails to prosecute an offence or issue a notice, the Minister can issue directions and give directions. If the agency fails to comply within specified

[25] Sections 8–10 EA 2024.

[26] Section 11 EA 2024.

[27] Sections 12 and 13 EA 2024.

[28] Section 14 EA 2024.

[29] Sections 15–16 EA 2024.

[30] Section 17 EA 2024.

[31] Section 18(3) EA 2024.

timeframes, the Director can perform the task, and the Minister can report the failure to the Commission chairperson.[32]

Environmentally Sensitive Areas

The Environmentally Sensitive Areas (ESAs) consist of boreholes (wells), caves, coastal freshwater marshlands, coral reefs, forests with high native content, intertidal mudflats, islets, lakes and reservoirs, mangroves, rivers and creeks, sand beaches and dunes, seagrass beds, steep slopes, and upland marshlands.[33] An ESAs Committee is set up to regulate and monitor areas which are environmentally sensitive in Mauritius. The ESAs Committee ensures the drafting and creation of policies, programmes, initiatives, standards, and requirements for the conservation and protection of ESAs. It makes recommendations to reduce degradation, maintain ecosystem integrity, devise public awareness programmes, formulate appropriate management procedures, provide guidance to avoid adverse effects on natural habitat functions and biodiversity, update ESA inventory and maps, determine enforcement measures, and share information on environmental land issues among its members.[34]

The Minister may make regulations for managing, protecting, enhancing ESAs, preventing pollution, implementing obligations under international and regional agreements, and restoring and rehabilitating ESAs. Regulations may also provide for preservation and conservation of ESAs and control and prevention of pollution. Dumping in ESAs is prohibited, and violators commit an offence. Land clearing and development on ESAs require licenses or approval, and violators commit an offence. The Minister can declare private or state land as ESAs for conserving and managing ESAs. The Minister may exercise the power of eminent domain to secure access to ESAs or acquire high ecological importance ESAs.[35]

Environmental Assessments

The PER Committee is mandated to examine applications for PER licenses. It meets on a regular basis, may co-opt officers from other departments, and may establish subcommittees.[36] The EIA/SEA Committee undertakes to examine applications for EIA or SEA licenses or approvals. It may request points of clarification from the applicant and relevant public department officers. The committee examines the application and makes recommendations to the Minister. It must submit its recom-

[32] Section 21 EA 2024.

[33] First Schedule EA 2024.

[34] Section 22 EA 2024.

[35] Sections 23–26 EA 2024.

[36] Section 27 EA 2024.

mendations within 7 days of the application being referred. The supervising officer of a ministry or department's representative is not allowed to participate in the committee's proceedings.[37] The PER/EIA/SEA Monitoring Committee follows up on progress of applications, sets up necessary programs, coordinates implementation, conducts quarterly monitoring exercises, makes recommendations for PER, EIA, or SEA completion certificates, and prepares annual progress reports.[38] Undertakings listed in the Sixth Schedule of the EA 2024 require mandatorily a PER or EIA or SEA license.[39] The Minister has the power to declare an undertaking as a public one in the interest of the country or the people for which no PER, EIA, or SEA would be required.[40]

A PER application must be open for inspection by the public either at the department's office or a local authority or any other specified location. The Director has a legal obligation to the public 14 days after receipt of the application in the Gazette and daily newspaper. The notice should provide details of the undertaking such as address and inspection place and allow public comments. The Director has the prerogative to extend the time limit to allow for public input. Additional information submitted to a PER application should be published for public consultation.[41] A similar requirement is applicable to EIA application and SEA application.[42]

Oil Spill and Environmental Emergency

The National Oil Spill Contingency Plan presents itself as a crucial tool permitting coordinated and swift responses to oil spills. It provides a structure for preparedness and response for a period of 5 years renewable and reviewable.[43] The National Oil Spill Coordination Committee is mandated to oversee the implementation of the plan and ensure cooperation among concerned and relevant public bodies. It also has an advisory role regarding policies and administrative measures relevant to oil spill contingency planning.[44] Any person storing or using liquid fuel must conduct a risk assessment and submit a contingency plan to the Director. Existing plans must be submitted within 3–12 months, while new ones must be submitted before operation. Non-compliance can result in penalties.[45]

Oil spill management and prevention fall under the purview of the National Disaster Risk Reduction and Management Centre. When there is an oil spill, owners

[37] Section 28 EA 2024.

[38] Section 29 EA 2024.

[39] Section 30 EA 2024.

[40] Section 31 EA 2024.

[41] Section 34 EA 2024.

[42] Sections 42 and 49 EA 2024.

[43] Section 57 EA 2024.

[44] Section 58 EA 2024.

[45] Section 60 EA 2024.

are required to notify the Director and Director-General within an hour, and the Director is required to report to the National Crisis Committee. The Director may take action if there is a suspicion that the owner has violated section 61(2)(c). The Minister specifies the protocols for clean-up, removal, storage, and disposal and demands volunteers' prior consent. After consulting with the National Oil Spill Coordination Committee, independent monitoring can begin.[46]

The Prime Minister is empowered to declare an environmental emergency when there is significant damage to the environment, life, or property resulting from an oil spill. He can give directives to release necessary human and financial resources, evacuations, regulating traffic and movement, and facilitating post-disaster recovery. Contingency plans and required regulations must be prepared, and the Prime Minister can solicit international relief assistance. A technical committee may be set up for management and protection of the environment. The Director may enter premises without warrant and claim damages from the spilled oil owner.[47]

National Environmental Standards

It is the responsibility of the Minister to prescribe standards related to water quality, air quality, pesticide residues, built-up environment standards, odours, noise emissions, quality control of laboratories, industrial environmental audits, and effluent limitations. The purpose of water and air quality standards is to protect public health, the environment, and welfare generally while effluent limitations set up technology for pollution control and time schedules. In view of maintaining public health and comfort, noise emission standards are necessary and prescribed by the law.

Pesticide residue standards deal with the substance's concentration in the environment, while odour standards enhance public health and the environment. Architectural harmony and aesthetic value are preserved and maintained by the built-up environment. An industrial environmental audit may provide pollution control through an inventory of waste, development and implementation of an environmental management plan, appointment of officers, and different criteria for different industrial enterprises.[48]

Coastal and Marine Zone Management

The Integrated Coastal Zone Management Committee (ICZM Committee) is established to manage and protect the coastal zone in Mauritius. The ICZM Committee has the duty to develop an integrated management plan, to coordinate regional and

[46] Sections 61–66 EA 2024.

[47] Sections 67–73 EA 2024.

[48] Sections 75–83 EA 2024.

international projects, and to recommend measures pertaining to beach erosion control. It equally advises on matters related to upgrading recreational facilities and coastal construction guidelines. Regulations are made by the Minister for the prevention of pollution, the management of the environment, and compliance with regional and international agreements. Regulations may include preserving the environment, controlling pollution from vessels, crafts, and installations, and preventing pollution from land-based sources. Dumping and discharge are prohibited in the zone, and violators commit an offence. The Minister has the legal obligation to prepare an integrated coastal zone management plan for coastal zone planning, management, and development.[49]

The National Environment and Climate Change Fund

The National Environment and Climate Change Fund has as aim to provide foreign laboratory support for environmental sample analysis, support programmes on pollution prevention, promote research and education on the environment, assist non-governmental organisations, incentivise local environmental initiatives, publish reports, and ensure the financing of climate change and adaptation undertakings and activities. The Fund also caters for expenditure incurred in operations and provides for financing to e-waste management projects and projects related to lagoons, beach, and coral reef rehabilitation. Other aspects such as asbestos removal, solid waste management, disaster risk reduction, and flood management are equally funded by it. The Fund's sources of income are generated from public activities, contributions from the private sector, international donations, and contributions from the Consolidated Fund of Mauritius.[50]

Circular Economy and Extended Producer Responsibility

The National Circular Economy Policy, Strategy and Action Plan has the objective of formulating policies, priorities, goals, and objectives in key sectors of the economy such as agri-food, consumer goods, mobility, and logistics. It emphasises a circular culture and on aspects such as product design, sustainable production, life cycle analysis, value chain, sustainable consumption, better waste management, circular business models, and innovation. The plan promotes education, training, public awareness, and the use of criteria related to the circular economy in public procurement. It is reviewed every 5 years or at a time determined by the Minister. Extended producer responsibility is required for individuals who develop, manufacture, or process products, adopt sustainable consumption and production practices, minimise waste, and ensure proper disposal. The Minister may require

[49] Sections 84–87 EA 2024.

[50] Sections 88–92 EA 2024.

manufacturers to take in the product and its container after use and regulate waste reduction measures. The Minister may identify products or classes for extended producer responsibility measures.[51]

Enforcement Measures and the Tribunal

The Act permits authorised officers to enter premises other than dwelling houses for various purposes, including lawful directions, determining compliance with environmental laws, and discharging other functions. They must obtain consent, make tests, inspect plants, machinery, equipment, or vehicles, and provide reasonable assistance. They may enter dwelling houses without a warrant if there is a contravention of an environmental law, reasonable suspicion, an environmental emergency, oil spill, or serious pollution risk. A Magistrate may issue a warrant, and obstruction is punishable by imprisonment.[52] The Director of Environmental Protection can issue a prohibition notice for serious pollution or imminent risk to the environment, if the activity contravenes environmental laws, has a license, permit, or approval or if a court orders against issuing the notice. The notice must specify serious pollution, measures to eliminate risk, and conditions for resumption. The Director can also issue a stop order if an activity is initiated without the necessary license or approval. Revocation of notices can occur if necessary measures are implemented or the license is not effective.[53]

The Minister can issue a PER, EIA, or SEA license for multiple undertakings. A person, if aggrived or likely to be caused prejudice by such undertakings can appeal against the decision to the Tribunal. or submit a statement of concern to relevant authorities. If a person has suffered damage or prejudice due to another person's breach of environmental law, they can make a claim to the Tribunal, which may award damages. The Tribunal cannot hear a complaint unless the complainant waives their right to initiate civil proceedings.[54]

6.2.1.2 The Climate Change Act 2020

The purpose of the Climate Change Act 2020 (CCA 2020) is to establish a legal framework towards making Mauritius a climate-change-resilient and low-emission country. An Inter-Ministerial Council on Climate Change was established to achieve this objective. It has functions and powers, to make climate change policies,

[51] Roadmap and Action Plan for a Circular Economy in the Republic of Mauritius (2023) available at https://circulareconomy.govmu.org/circulareconomy/wp-content/uploads/2023/08/Roadmap-and-Action-Plan-for-a-Circular-Economy-in-the-Republic-of-Mauritius-Final-report.pdf (accessed 15 July 2025).

[52] Sections 103–110 EA 2024.

[53] Sections 111–116 EA 2024.

[54] Sections 119–122 EA 2024.

monitor progress, ensure coordination, and make recommendations. The Director serves as Secretary to the Council, performing duties as assigned. The Council's functions include adaptation, mitigation, monitoring progress, and recommending directives to government departments. The Minister is responsible for developing climate change policies, coordinating and monitoring programmes, and promoting business initiatives and environmentally sound technologies. They may appoint committees to assist the Council in its functions. The Minister may request information from the Director and give general directions to the Director, ensuring compliance with the Act's public interest.[55]

Section 8 of the CCA 2020 establishes a Department of Climate Change within the Ministry of Environment, responsible for promoting adaptation and mitigation measures to address climate change in relevant sectors. It develops and coordinates policies, projects, strategies, programmes, and action plans to address the adverse effects of climate change and oversees their implementation by stakeholders. The department formulates and updates guidelines for vulnerability and risk assessments, establishes procedures to reduce greenhouse gas emissions, and maintains a climate change database system. It provides technical support and facilitates research and studies on climate change, promotes the implementation of article 6 of the UNFCCC on education, training, and public awareness, prepares reports to meet obligations, mobilises resources for climate change projects, promotes stakeholder participation, commissions studies on climate change, identifies vulnerabilities and susceptibilities, establishes links with other Small Island Developing States, and establishes a network with climate change-related institutions and organisations. The department publishes the National Inventory Report on greenhouse gas emission by sources and removal by sinks annually.[56]

A Climate Change Committee is also established under section 11 of the CCA 2020 which is responsible for the preparation of the National Inventory Report, the implementation of measures for greenhouse gas inventories, risk assessment, vulnerability assessment, and adaptation, strategic planning, and national policies related to climate change. It also recommends monitoring and controlling greenhouse gas emissions in sectors such as agriculture, aviation, energy, industry, and transport and assessing vulnerability and risk in various sectors. The committee also coordinates resources and assistance for climate change projects.[57]

The CCA 2020 also provides for the formulation of the National Climate Change Adaptation Strategy and Action Plan as well as the national Climate Change Mitigation Strategy and Action Plan. The Department of Climate Change is required to collaborate with ministries, departments, and other bodies to formulate a National Climate Change Adaptation Strategy and Action Plan. The plan must be based on vulnerabilities and risks associated with climate change and include national development priorities, policy formulation, an action plan, compliance with international

---

[55] Sections 4–7 CCA 2020.

[56] Sections 8–10 CCA 2020.

[57] Section 11 CCA 2020.

commitments, research, climate data, education, training, public awareness, and monitoring approaches.[58] The National Climate Change Mitigation Strategy and Action Plan is a comprehensive plan aimed at achieving low emissions and a green economy, incorporating development priorities, policy formulation, mitigation measures, investment programs, compliance with international commitments, research, climate data, education, public awareness, and monitoring approaches.[59]

The Director of Mauritius can issue directives to public and private institutions to carry out vulnerability and risk assessments, implement adaptation and mitigation measures, and consider climate change in their strategies. Institutions must also report on sectoral greenhouse gas emissions for the National Inventory Report and establish a unit to coordinate climate change measures. The Director may request institutions to submit data and information on climate change, including greenhouse gas emissions and carbon sinks, to fulfil its obligations under UNFCCC, the Kyoto Protocol, and the Paris Agreement. The Minister may direct the Director to provide necessary information and reports to the UNFCCC. Government departments must conduct public consultations for climate change strategies and policies.[60]

6.2.1.3 The Native Terrestrial Biodiversity and National Parks Act 2015

The purpose of the Native Terrestrial Biodiversity and National Parks Act 2015 (NTBNP 2015) is to make further and better provision for the protection, conservation, and management of native terrestrial biodiversity in Mauritius. Section 4 establishes the Native Terrestrial Biodiversity and National Parks Advisory Council has the responsibility to advise the Minister on matters related to native terrestrial biodiversity, reserved land, and conservation generally. It should also provide guidance on the assessment of the state of wildlife resources and the effect of land use and environmental activities on wildlife and wildlife habitat. It has generally the duty to make recommendations to the Minister regarding the conservation of wildlife.[61]

Section 8 of the NTBNP 2015 also provides for the National Parks and Conservation Service which consists of scientific, technical, administrative, and public officers. The Director of the Service is a public officer with administrative control and may delegate functions with approval. The Director's functions include reviewing land conservation, carrying out management operations, providing educational information, preparing and reviewing management plans, providing council information, and submitting a report on the Service's activities to the Minister every year.[62]

[58] Section 13 CCA 2020.

[59] Section 14 CCA 2020.

[60] Sections 16–19 CCA 2020.

[61] Section 4 NTBNP 2015.

[62] Section 10 NTBNP 2015.

The President of the Republic can declare any state land as a national park or special reserve if it is of natural, scenic, scientific, educational, recreational, or other importance to the state and the preservation of that land is necessary to protect, permit access to, or allow public viewing or enjoyment of the land. Closed reserves are strictly used for conservation and biodiversity protection, while open reserves are used for conservation, educational, and recreational activities. No work or development on reserved land must be approved by the Minister or permitted under a management plan.[63]

The Minister may designate private land for the protection, enhancement, or restoration of natural ecosystems and wildlife habitats or conservation of air, soil, or water. Ownership of private reserves remains vested in the owner. The Director may request the owner or occupier to maintain the reserve in a manner specified in the notice. The Minister may declare land adjoining a private reserve or a reserved land within an area of 1 km to be a buffer zone for that land. The Director shall prepare a draft management plan for every area of reserved land and buffer zone, which shall be available for inspection or purchase, come into operation upon approval, and be binding in relation to the management and use of the reserved land and any adjoining buffer zone.[64]

A Management Authority is also established in section 18 of the NTBNP 2015 for the purposes of the Convention on International Trade in Endangered Species of Wild Fauna and Flora (CITES) acceded to by Mauritius in July 1975. It is responsible for implementing and enforcing species conservation legislation in Mauritius. It communicates with the CITES Secretariat and other relevant persons, grants permits, and certificates according to CITES, maintains records of international trade, and prepares annual reports. The Authority also consults the Scientific Authority on CITES documents, trade in CITES-listed species, quota management, trade registration, rescue centres, and proposals to amend the CITES list. The Scientific Authority advises the Management Authority on CITES matters, monitors export permits, limits export permits, advises on the disposal of confiscated specimens, conducts research on endangered species, collects and distributes information on international trade, and advises the CITES Secretariat on species protection.[65]

The NTBNP caters for the protection of wildlife, flora, fauna, and freshwater biodiversity. It provides that any person who wishes to pick, pluck, gather, collect, cut, uproot, process, breed, hunt, rear, have in their possession or under their control, or obtain, plant, propagate, purchase, sell, offer, or display any protected wildlife or its derivative must submit a written application to the Director for a permit. The Director may issue permits subject to specific terms and conditions. A similar condition applies to the capture or rearing of flora and fauna qualified as protected species. Protection is also conferred to freshwater biodiversity, and any trade activity of these wildlife is prohibited unless approval obtained. There are restrictions on

[63] Sections 11–12 NTBNP 2015.

[64] Sections 12–17 NTBNP 2015.

[65] Sections 18–20 NTBNP 2015.

hunting of wildlife also, and prior approval of the authority must be sought and obtained.[66] The Invasive Alien Species Committee, established under section 30 of the NTBNP 2015, controls the introduction of exotic wildlife in Mauritius, advises the Minister on importation and policy adoption, and prepares a prohibited list of wildlife species to be prohibited.

6.2.1.4 Energy Efficiency Act 2011

The Energy Efficient Act 2011 (EEA 2011) focuses primarily on the establishment of the Energy Efficiency Management Office. The Office aims to promote energy efficiency and national awareness to reduce carbon emissions and protect the environment. Its functions are developing and implementing strategies, establishing procedures for monitoring energy efficiency, issuing guidelines, establishing energy consumption standards, collecting and maintaining data, compiling a database for energy auditors, formulating financing schemes for energy efficiency projects, designing educational courses, establishing links with regional and international institutions, encouraging project developers to apply for carbon credits, collaborating with authorities to develop minimum energy performance standards, labelling requirements, classifying energy consumers, preparing annual reports, and dealing with other matters.[67]

6.2.2 Institutional Framework

6.2.2.1 Ministry of Environment, Solid Waste Management and Climate Change

The Ministry of Environment, Solid Waste Management and Climate Change in Mauritius aims to create a cleaner, greener, and safer environment through environmental asset protection, sustainable development principles, waste management, disaster resilience, and beach rehabilitation. The Ministry has two major departments: the Department of Environment and the Department of Climate Change. The Department of Environment has key divisions such as the Coordination and Project Implementation Division (CPID), Policy and Planning Division, Environmental Assessment Division, Environmental Law and Prosecution Division, Information and Education Division, Integrated Coastal Zone Management Division, National Environmental Laboratory (NEL), Police de l'Environnement, Pollution Prevention and Control, Plastic Management Division, Sustainable Development Division, and the Department of Climate Change.[68]

[66] Sections 21–29 NTBNP 2015.

[67] Sections 4–7 EEA 2015.

[68] Ministry of Environment (2024).

The CPID oversees 72 projects under the 2nd Environment Investment Programme, while the Policy and Planning Division organises technical advisory committees, creates and evaluates environmental policies, and handles challenges like pig farming and rock quarry disposal. The Environmental Law and Prosecution Division establishes legal instruments for environmental protection and management, reviews and amends the Environment Protection Act (EPA), and develops environmental regulations. The Plastic Management Division addresses plastic pollution and is working on new guidelines for PET containers and bottles. The Sustainable Development Division coordinates projects under the National Programme on Sustainable Consumption and Production and the SWITCH Africa Green Project. The Department of Climate Change is responsible for policy development, action plan coordination, and promoting adaptation and mitigation strategies to mitigate climate change effects. The Solid Waste Management Division (SWMD) ensures effective waste management for future generations, while the Climate Change Information Centre (CCIC) manages real-time data access.[69]

6.2.2.2 The Environment and Land Use Appeal Tribunal

The Environment and Land Use Appeal Tribunal Act of 2012 established the Environment and Land Use Appeal Tribunal (ELUAT) to consider appeals pertaining to environmental and land use issues. It considers appeals against rulings made by the Town and Country Planning Act, Municipal City Councils, the Ministry of Environment, the Morcellement Board, and other pertinent authorities. Within 21 days of the cause of action, the Tribunal may begin proceedings by *proecipe* and affidavit. Its mission includes providing efficient environmental justice, advancing environmental rule of law, and guaranteeing appropriate land use and planning regulations. As for its mission, it is to ensure the equitable, consistent, and efficient resolution of environmental cases to strive for prompt case disposal, to strive for mediation of environmental and planning disputes, and to provide a channel in emergency situations and when the environment is in danger.[70]

6.2.3 *Critical Appraisal*

Except in section 10 on National Policy, Strategy and Action Plan on Sustainable Development which is supposed to take into consideration ‘human rights’, the legal framework on environment, as described above, is devoid of any reference to the human right to environment. There is no right-based approach adopted by the state in order to protect the environment. As discussed in the introduction, such an

[69] Ibid.

[70] ELUAT (2024).

approach may have its advantages and confer better and more effective protection to the environment. That said, it has to be underlined that the Supreme Court has given a number of decisions that deals with the protection of the environment.

In the case of *Eco-Sud v The Minister of Environment*,[71] the appellant argued that the ELUAT should interpret Section 54(2) of the Environment Protection Act (EPA), which provides for grounds on which an EIA license granted by the Minister can be challenged (*locus standi*) to reflect its true intent, meaning, and spirit and not restrictively as it did in previous rulings.[72] It was argued that the *locus standi* test was meant to prevent 'to frivolously challenge lawful decisions, rather than to prevent genuine ones such as the appellant from challenging unlawful ones'. It was further argued that the Climate Change Act 2020 further affirms the legislator's intention towards a green economy and therefore a more broad interpretation of *locus standi*. The Supreme Court held as follows:

> We do not believe that, in trying to restrict the right of challenge, the legislator intended to oust a body claiming to have representative standing. It would be an obstruction to good administration of justice if that were the case, namely, in important environmental issue cases. Rather we are of the view that the true intention of the legislator was to restrict frivolous challenges against projects which are highly desirable and beneficial for our economy; not to prevent challenges against unscrupulous projects with high environmental impacts on our already vulnerable island.[73]

In defining what the environment means in Mauritius in *Mesnil Investments Co Ltd v Environment Appeal Tribunal*, the Supreme Court adopted a broad interpretation by stating that 'it is clear, therefore, from the language and broad objects of the Act already mentioned, that the protection of the environment is an all-embracing concept which not only deals with environmental issues proper but also with public interest issues or issues affecting the welfare or economy of a state'.[74] In *Ricot J & Ors v Mauriplage beach Resort Ltd*, the Supreme Court reconciled development and environment in these terms: it is true that there is a weighty argument in favour of the development and its positive impact, but this has to be viewed subject to, and if permissible, reconciliation with the stringent legal provisions which the legislator has laid down in the Act for the protection of the environment.[75] Furthermore in *Seechurn & Ors v Vadamalay*, the Supreme Court stated that 'the defendant's self-interest in carrying on his business for gain must give way to a larger social interest, namely the quality of life and welfare of his neighbours and the protection of the

[71] Eco-Sud v The Minister of Environment, Solid Waste Management and Climate Change 2023 SCJ 284.

[72] Agir pour l'Environnement v The Minister of Environment, Solid Waste Management and Climate Change & Ors [ELAT 1909/19]; J.D. Sauvage & Ors v The Minister of Social Security, National Solidarity and Environment and Sustainable Development & Ors [ELAT]1746/19.

[73] Eco-Sud v The Minister of Environment p. 16.

[74] *Mesnil Investments Co. Ltd. v Environment Appeal Tribunal & Anor* 2000 SCJ 172 p. 4.

[75] *Ricot J & Ors v Mauriplage beach Resort Ltd* 2004 SCJ 329 p. 7.

environment. The law's obligation to society must prevail over an individual's self-interest'.[76]

This being said, the African Charter does impose obligations regarding the human right to a healthy environment to all African citizens. Therefore, these obligations and duties ideally apply to the state of Mauritius. The following section provides for an overview of the opportunity that the African human rights system provides for by rendering the right to environment enforceable and justiciable, something which no other global and regional human rights system have been able to achieve so far.

6.3 The Right to Environment Under the African Human Rights System

The African Charter has been lauded as the first instrument to have established a binding international human rights-based approach to the protection of the environment.[77] It uniquely provides for the right of 'all peoples' to a generally satisfactory environment which is favourable to their development in article 24. This has not prevented scholars from underlining the vagueness and ambiguity in the terms used in the article. Van der Linde and Louw contended that:

> The right as phrased in the African Charter is vague and ambiguous. No clear indication is given by the African Charter as to what the terms 'satisfactory' and 'environment' entail. This allowed for different interpretations as to the exact meaning of this right by human rights scholars and environmentalists. This lack of clarity has initiated both positive and negative aspects of the interpretation. In a positive sense, the vagueness in itself can allow for a wider and more accommodating interpretation of the right to a satisfactory environment. On the other hand, the impact also tolerates a narrower and more restricted sense of interpretation, not giving this right the full recognition it deserves.[78]

It may arguably be necessary to interpret the right to a 'general satisfactory environment' in light of article 16 of the African Charter, conferring the right to 'the best attainable state of physical and mental health' and that states shoulder a legal duty to 'take the necessary measures to protect the health of their people'. Read together, articles 16 and 24 imply that people have a right to an environment that is generally acceptable to the extent that it does not negatively affect their physical or mental well-being. Despite such an interpretation providing some guidance for an abstractive qualitative environmental rights standard, it still lacks a more targeted and comprehensive implementation.[79]

---

[76] Seechurn & Ors v. Vadamalay 1988 SCJ 433 p. 3.

[77] Van der Linde and Louw (2003), p. 169.

[78] Van der Linde and Louw (2003), p. 174.

[79] Kotze and du Plessis (2019), p. 101.

Viljoen has optimistically argued that this particular formulation pre-empts the tension between environment and development by advocating for a mode of environmental protection which favours the development of people.[80] It should be noted that the African Charter is also the first and only international instrument that provides for the right to development in a binding manner.[81] Growth and development in a sustainable manner are a key tenant in African economic integration as illustrated by the AU Constitutive Act.[82] Kotze and du Plessis has argued that:

> The wording of article 24 implies that the issue of development is an integral part of the environmental right to the extent that 'favourable development' is contingent upon a 'general satisfactory environment'. This would not only mean that the core genesis of the environmental right is entirely anthropocentric, but also that any standards set out by the environmental right must be such that it ensures the 'favourable development' of people, including to ensure their right to development under article 22.[83]

In view of combating underdevelopment and poverty in Africa, progress and development through the utilisation and exploitation of resources are considered key elements.[84] Yet, in this discourse, there is no explicit mention of the negative impact that development in Africa has on the environment and on people who are often displaced during construction of dams, railway lines, extraction sites, and mining activities.[85] Except for mentioning 'environmental protection' as a function of the Executive Council and a mandate of one specialised committee, the AU Constitutive Act is silent on the issue of environment.

On the contrary, the African Commission recognised the nexus between environmental concerns and human rights in a 2009 resolution entitled Resolution 153: Human Rights and Climate Change and the Need to Study its Impact in Africa.[86] Through the application and interpretation of article 24 of the African Charter, the African Commission has attempted to reconcile development and environment in the African context in the case of *SERAC v Nigeria.* An oil company, controlled by the Nigerian government, contaminated the air, soil, and water in Ogoniland through its activities, driven by short-term profits and development. The African Commission stated that an obligation is imposed on the state by article 22 of the African Charter to take reasonable measures 'to prevent pollution and ecological degradation, to promote conservation and to ensure an ecologically sustainable development and use of natural resources'.[87] It did not stop only at the substantive aspect of the right to environment under article 22, but it further emphasised the procedural aspects of

[80] Viljoen (2015), p. 268.

[81] Article 22 of the African Charter.

[82] Article 3(j) and 4(n).

[83] Kotze and du Plessis (2019), p. 100.

[84] NEPAD Declaration paras 1–7.

[85] Viljoen (2015), p. 268.

[86] The African Commission on Human Rights and Peoples' Rights, meeting at its Forty-sixth Ordinary Session held from 11 to 25 November in Banjul, The Gambia. <www.achpr.org/sessions/46th/resolutions/153/>.

[87] SERAC v Nigeria para 52.

this right. It added that the state had an obligation to conduct appropriate and relevant impact assessments before embarking on oil exploration projects and to ensure that communities affected by such projects are made part of the decision-making processes.[88]

The African Commission elaborated on the standards of duty and obligations, both negative and positive, states have pertaining to article 24. The first negative duty to respect entailed that 'the State should refrain from interfering in the enjoyment of all fundamental rights; it should respect right-holders, their freedoms, autonomy, resources and liberty of their action'.[89] Secondly, protecting rights holders was deemed to be a negative duty which includes the obligation imposed on states to 'take measures to protect beneficiaries of the protected rights against political, economic and social interferences'.[90] The African Commission held that for an effective protection of rights holders, it is essential that a 'framework by an effective interplay of laws and regulations so that individuals will be able to freely realise their rights and freedoms'[91] be created and maintained. Kotze and du Plessis aptly summarised these duties as follows:

> The environmental right therefore in a 'negative' way obliges governments to desist from threatening the health and environment of their citizens, and it asks governments to respect the environmental right through noninterventionist conduct. It further obliges governments not to condone practices, policies or legal measures that violate individual integrity.[92]

Focusing on positive duties emanating from article 24, the African Commission held that the promotion of the enjoyment of environmental right imposes on states a positive obligation to 'make sure that individuals are able to exercise their rights and freedoms, for example, by promoting tolerance, raising awareness, and even building infrastructures'.[93] It further held that article 24 'imposes clear obligations upon a government. It requires the State to take reasonable and other measures to prevent pollution and ecological degradation, to promote conservation and to secure an ecologically sustainable development and use of natural resources'.[94] It went on to state that for governments to abide by article 24, they must create meaningful and effective opportunities for people to be involved and their voices and opinions be heard and taken into account in the decisions relating to development that impact on their communities, as well as facilitate independent scientific monitoring of environments which are menaced, require and publish environmental and social impact assessments before any significant industrial development, conduct appropriate

[88] SERAC v Nigeria para 71.

[89] SERAC v Nigeria para 45.

[90] SERAC v Nigeria para 46.

[91] Ibid.

[92] Kotze and du Plessis (2019), p. 103.

[93] SERAC v Nigeria para 46.

[94] SERAC v Nigeria para 52.

monitoring, and provide information to communities vulnerable to hazardous materials and activities.[95]

The case of *African Commission on Human and Peoples' Rights v. the Republic of Kenya*,[96] commonly referred to as the Ogiek case and decided by the African Court on Human and Peoples' Rights, also provided for some insights on environmental standards under the African Charter. It is pertinent to note that, in the context of the African Charter, abstract qualitative environmental standards may result from the collective protection of rights other than the environmental right, such as the rights of cultural minorities and the right of access to ancestral land, even though a violation of article 24 on the environmental right has not been argued in this case. The Court's decision was premised on defending the Ogiek people's rights pertaining to their culture and means of subsistence. The Court made clear that maintaining the natural resource base provided by the Mau Forest is necessary for the protection of these rights. The Court held that:

> The most salient feature of most indigenous populations is their strong attachment with nature, particularly, land and the natural environment. Their survival in a particular way depends on unhindered access to and use of their traditional land and the natural resources thereon. In this regard, the Ogieks, as a hunter- gatherer community, have for centuries depended on the Mau Forest for their residence and as a source of their livelihood.[97]

It further added that:

> Different reports prepared by or in collaboration with the Respondent on the situation of the Mau Forest also reveal that the main causes of the environmental degradation are encroachments upon the land by other groups and government excisions for settlements and ill-advised logging concessions…the Court is of the view that the continued denial of access to and eviction from the Mau Forest of the Ogiek population cannot be necessary or proportionate to achieve the purported justification of preserving the natural ecosystem of the Mau Forest.[98]

The connection between the natural environment and the livelihoods of indigenous peoples was considered in the case of *Centre for Minority Rights Development, Minority Rights Group International and Endorois Welfare Council (on behalf of the Endorois Community) v. Kenya.*[99] The African Commission ruled that the Kenyan government failed to recognise and protect the Endorois' ancestral land rights, provide adequate compensation, or grant restitution of their land. The case also highlighted the lack of protection for their traditional way of life, non-discrimination, property, access to natural resources, religious and cultural life, and development. The commission recommended the Kenyan government ensure unrestricted access to Lake Bogoria for religious and cultural rites. The Endorois deci-

[95] SERAC v Nigeria para 53.

[96] African Commission on Human and Peoples' Rights v. the Republic of Kenya Application 006/2012.

[97] Ogiek case para 109.

[98] Ibid para 130.

[99] Centre for Minority Rights Development, Minority Rights Group International and Endorois Welfare Council (on behalf of the Endorois Community) v. Kenya Application 276/03.

sion demonstrated that procedural abstract qualitative environmental standards can be established under the African Charter. The decision made it sufficiently clear that in order to protect the right to development, which offers a wide range of qualitative standards with potential to improve human welfare, a number of sustainability interests, including those related to nature preservation and cultural heritage protection, need to be carefully balanced by the courts.[100]

It has been contended that a human rights-based approach to environment protection under the African human rights system, spearheaded by article 24 of the African Charter, is also supported by the OAU Convention of Nature and Natural Resources and the Bamako Convention. Additionally, the Treaty Establishing the African Economic Community (AEC), also known as the Abuja Treaty, has specific provisions related to the ban on import of hazardous waste across African borders.[101] Coming into force in 1969 after its adoption a year earlier, the African Convention on the Conservation of Nature and Natural Resources (African Nature Convention) focuses on wildlife and use of natural resources such as soil and water. It links environmental protection and development in its article 7 and was described as the 'most comprehensive multilateral treaty for the conservation of nature yet negotiated'[102] in 1985. Despite the fact that the African Nature Convention had no administrative mechanisms to enhance its implementation, it did stimulate useful conservation measures adopted by countries and served as a framework on which a number of national legislations in Africa were based.[103]

Following the UN 1992 Conference on Environment and Development which gave birth to the Rio Declaration on Environment and Development, the African Nature Convention was revised, and the amended text refers to article 22 (right to development) and article 24 (right to environment) of the African Charter regarding its implementation.[104] Focusing on procedural rights, it imposes an obligation on states to ensure dissemination and access to the public to environmental information, to ensure public participation in environmental matters, and to enhance access to justice regarding environmental issues and disputes through the adoption of legislative and other measures.[105] Innovative measures of the revised treaty also include the protection of environment during armed conflicts,[106] the acceptance of state liability for damages,[107] and accurately defined derogations from its provisions during declared emergency and in order to protect public health.[108]

---

[100] Kotze and du Plessis (2019), p. 108.

[101] Articles 58 and 59 of the Abuja Treaty.

[102] Lyster (1985), p. 115.

[103] Ibid.

[104] Article 3 of the Revised African Nature Convention.

[105] Article 16(1) of the Revised African Nature Convention.

[106] Article 15(1) of the Revised African Nature Convention.

[107] Article 24 of the Revised African Nature Convention.

[108] Article 25(2) of the Revised African Nature Convention.

The Bamako Convention on the Ban of the Import into Africa and the Control of Transboundary Movement and Management of Hazardous Wastes within Africa was adopted in 1991 and came into force in 1998. The Bamako Convention was created in response to the UN Basel Convention on the Control of Transboundary Movement of Hazardous Wastes and their Disposal (the Basel Convention) which did not ban but simply required the regulation and control of such movement. Distinct and not a supplement[109] to the Basel Convention, the Bamako Convention places a ban on transboundary movement of such wastes and also has a broader definition of hazardous wastes including artificially created radioactive waste.

From the above, it can be concluded that, while the recognition of the right to a healthy environment for people came only in 2022 at the UN level as discussed in the introduction, such a right was already provided for since 1981 in the African Charter in an enforceable and justifiable way. In addition, other conventions as discussed at the AU level have added to the substantive content of this right. The following section will now discuss Mauritius' engagement with article 24 of the African Charter and other conventions in view of protecting the right to environment of Mauritians as well as the environment of Mauritius.

6.4 Right to a Healthy Environment Under the African Human Rights System and Mauritius

This chapter has discussed how the legal and institutional framework on the protection of the environment is strong but without a human rights-based approach which has proven to be more effective in protecting the environment. There is no right to a healthy or safe environment in the Constitution or in any law for that matter. At the UN level, there are no legally binding treaties that provide for the right to environment. Mauritius signed the initial African Nature Convention in September 1968 but never ratified it. As for the Revised African Nature Convention, the state has not yet signed it. It became a state party to the Bamako Convention in October 1992. This implies that the African human rights system is currently the only system that recognises the right to a healthy environment. Arguably, more important than the recognition of this right is the enforceability and justiciability of it under the African system. As discussed in the chapter, the African Commission has expanded and clarified the substantive and procedural content of the right to a healthy environment through its jurisprudence.

This is a unique opportunity which has the potential of driving forward the agenda of environmental protection in Mauritius, especially as a fundamental human right. The state has a legal obligation to report on article 24 in its state reports on the African Charter submitted to the African Commission. It has to be highlighted that the state has not been diligent enough with the duty of reporting on

[109] Akinnusi (2001), p. 315.

environmental issues and respect for environmental rights guaranteed by article 24. Indeed, the African Commission remarked 'the absence of information in the Report on the measures to be taken by the Government in order to reverse the reported environmental and biodiversity loss'.[110] This trend has to be reversed so that the state aligns itself with the state reporting requirements and provides for information on the right to environment which is critical to various stakeholders. Additionally, it is the duty of civil society organisations to ensure that they submit shadow reports with the aim of guiding the African Commission on the implementation of the right to environment (or its non-implementation by the state) so that the latter can seek for clarification on the state's position regarding this key human right.

Given that the right to environment in Mauritius is non-existent and therefore not enforceable and justiciable, the African Commission's mandate on communications presents itself as a unique opportunity for citizens and civil society organisations to submit complaints to the Commission on potential cases of violation of the right to a healthy environment under article 24. Decisions of the African Commission will have the effect of guiding the state on the implementation and formulation of the right to environment in domestic laws and will also act as remedy and justice to aggrieved parties. Despite its non-binding value, the recommendations of the African Commission have significant political force which could be instrumental in compelling Mauritius to become compliant with article 24.

It is also incumbent on the state to domesticate the African Charter and, by extension, article 24 so that the right to a healthy environment can be invoked before domestic courts and the latter can interpret them in a binding manner. It should be noted that the Environment Act 2024 makes no mention at all of the African Charter and its article 24 even for the purposes of guidance in interpreting the provisions. It defeats the purpose of ratifying the African Charter without its domestication especially in view of the right to environment, enshrined only by the African system on human rights, being deprived of any effective and meaningful use by the citizens of Mauritius.

References

African Commission on Humana and Peoples' Rights 'Concluding Observations and Recommendations on 6th to 8th Combined Report of the Republic of Mauritius on the Implementation of the African Charter on Human and Peoples' Rights' (2009)

Akinnusi A (2001) The Bamako and Basel conventions on the transboundary movement and disposal of hazardous wastes: a comparative and critical analysis. Stellenbosch Law Rev 12:306

Beeharry Y, Bekaroo G, Bussoopun D, Bokhoree C, Phillips MR (2021) Perspectives of leisure operators and tourists on the environmental impacts of coastal tourism activities: a case study of Mauritius. Environ Dev Sustain 23:10702–10726

Boyd DR (2012) The constitutional right to a healthy environment. Environ Sci Policy Sustain Dev 54(4):3–15

[110] African Commission Concluding Observations (Mauritius) 2009 para 87.

Environment and Land Use Appeal Tribunal (2024) <https://eluat.govmu.org/Pages/Legislations.aspx> Accessed 01 July 2025

Gössling S, Lindén O, Helmersson J, Liljenberg J, Quarm S (2007) Diving and global environmental change: a Mauritius case study. In: New frontiers in marine tourism. Routledge, pp 67–92

Gray M, Lalljee B (2012) Climate change adaptation in Mauritius: considering the role of Institutions. Western Indian Ocean J Marine Sci 11(1):99–111

Kotze LJ, du Plessis A (2019) The African charter on human and peoples' rights and environmental rights standards. Environmental Rights: The Development of Standards, Cambridge, pp 93–115

Lyster S (1985) International wildlife law: an analysis of international treaties concerned with conservation of wildlife. Grotius Publications), Cambridge

Mauritius Oceanography Institute (2024) The Institute. <https://moi.govmu.org/about/the-institute> Accessed 01 July 2025

Mauthoor S (2017) Uncovering industrial symbiosis potentials in a small island developing state: the case study of Mauritius. J Clean Prod 147:506–513

Ministry of Environment (2024) Solid Waste Management and Climate Change <https://environment.govmu.org/Pages/Index.aspx> Accessed 01 July 2025.

Ministry of Environment and Quality of Life, Government of Mauritius 'State of the Environment in Mauritius' a report prepared for presentation at the United Nations Conference on Environment and Development, Rio de Janeiro, Brazil (1992)

Roadmap and Action Plan for a Circular Economy in the Republic of Mauritius (2023). Available at https://circulareconomy.govmu.org/circulareconomy/wp-content/uploads/2023/08/Roadmap-and-Action-Plan-for-a-Circular-Economy-in-the-Republic-of-Mauritius-Final-report.pdf. Accessed 15 July 2025

Shelton D (1992) Human rights, environmental rights, and the right to environment. Stanford J Int Law 28:103

Sunkur R, Kantamaneni K, Bokhoree C, Ravan S (2023) Mangroves' role in supporting ecosystem-based techniques to reduce disaster risk and adapt to climate change: a review. J Sea Res:102449

Toussaint A (1971) Histoire de L'île Maurice. 1449

Tung OL (2011) Development and the balancing of interests in environmental policy and law in Mauritius. The balancing of interests in environmental law in Africa PULP: Pretoria

UN OHCHR 'Information Note' (2022) <https://www.undp.org/sites/g/files/zskgke326/files/2023-01/UNDP-UNEP-UNHCHR-What-is-the-Right-to-a-Healthy-Environment.pdf> Accessed 29 June 2024

UNEP (2023) Mauritius sets goals to curb the triple planetary crisis. <https://www.unep.org/news-and-stories/story/mauritius-sets-goals-curb-triple-planetary-crisis> Accessed 01 July 2025

Van der Linde M, Louw L (2003) Considering the interpretation and implementation of Article 24 of the African Charter on Human and Peoples' Rights in the light of the SERAC Communication. Afr Human Rights Law J 3:167

Viljoen F (2015) International human rights law in Africa. Oxford University Press UK

Chapter 7
Women's Rights

Abstract Mauritius has a high rate of sexual and domestic violence. The Global Gender Gap Index places the nation 105th out of 146. Victims of domestic abuse are more likely to be women. There have been more allegations of domestic violence to the Ministry of Gender Equality and Family Welfare. Men are more likely to be murdered and subjected to other violent crimes, but women are more likely to be sexually abused and exploited. The majority of victims of sexual assault and exploitation were female. In light of the aforementioned context, this chapter emphasises on Mauritius's legal and normative framework regarding women's rights. To illustrate the significant amount of work that still needs to be done in this area, the current laws and policies are examined, and problem areas are highlighted. The potential for improved protection, promotion, respect, and fulfilment of women's rights in Mauritius is then examined in relation to the African human rights framework, with particular attention to the instruments pertaining to women's rights.

7.1 Introduction

In Mauritius, women's roles evolved during the course of the twentieth century. Throughout history, Mauritian society has upheld patriarchal power systems in a variety of contexts, including the home and workplace. The establishment of the Export Processing Zone by the Mauritius government resulted in an increase in the participation of women in the workforce.[1] 'Dual-earner' and working single-mother households increased dramatically as a result of this change. Women in Mauritius felt the effects of colonialism in the postcolonial era. Colonial laws from the 19th century declared that wives were their husbands' unalienable property. After that, the government decided to eliminate any legislation pertaining to inheritance and immigration. Over the years, there has undoubtedly been an improvement in the

[1] Hein (1984), p. 251.

R. Mahadew, *Mauritius and African Human Rights Law*,
https://doi.org/10.1007/978-3-032-08832-1_7

field of women's rights in Mauritius, both in the public and private life.[2] Among the changes in public life are the appointment of Ameena Gurib-Fakhim to the president (from 2015 to 2018) and the 2014 election of Maya Hanoomanjee to the role of first female Speaker.[3] While this is not necessarily indicative of the conditions of women in Mauritius, it factually shows the situation in Mauritius. Indeed, there is a long way to go to achieve the appropriate situations and circumstances for an effective protection and promotion of women.

The Civil Code and the Immigration and Deportation Act, which permitted the deportation of foreign spouses of Mauritius women, marked the height of women's agitation throughout the 1970s.[4] The "Code Napoleon" was amended, placing married women in the position of "a minor", as one of the most significant measures proposed to better the lot of women in Mauritius.[5] The equality of men and women was acknowledged by Code amendments. More changes made in the 1980s allowed women to open bank accounts without their husband's approval. Furthermore, in 1999, new legal revisions that were considerate of women's rights established various marital regimes.[6] Voting rights were granted in 1956, the first female member of Parliament was appointed in 1963, institutional structures like the Women's Desk were established in 1976, and laws protecting women from domestic abuse were passed in 1997, among other significant advancements towards gender equality.[7]

In 2022, Mauritius had a population of 638,462 women compared to 623,787 men, with women living longer on average.[8] Women give birth to fewer children and marry at older ages. More women enrolled in tertiary institutions but fewer in research. Only 10.4% of working women were heads of business, and 16.2% of unemployed women had tertiary qualifications.[9] Women are underrepresented in decision-making and senior government positions. Domestic violence and sexual violence are prevalent in Mauritius. The country ranks 105 out of 146 countries on the Global Gender Gap Index. Domestic abuse victims are more likely to be women.[10] Domestic abuse reports to the Ministry of Gender Equality and Family Welfare increased from 1654 in 2021 to 5381 in 2022. Domestic abuse against

---

[2] Dey (2014), pp. 989–995.

[3] EJS Center for Women and Development (2025) 'Mauritius: Progress and Challenges for Women in Politics' available at https://ejscenter.org/mauritius-progress-and-challenges-for-women-in-politics/ (accessed 10 July 2025).

[4] Mujuzi (2017), p. 225.

[5] Jansen (2005).

[6] Ramtohul (2008), pp. 8–10.

[7] Beebeejaun-Muslum (2024), pp. 9–19.

[8] 2022 Gender Statistics Mauritius available at https://www.maurice-info.mu/2023/07/21/2022-gender-statistics.html (accessed 15 July 2025).

[9] 2021 Gender Statistics Mauritius available at https://www.maurice-info.mu/wp-content/uploads/2022/07/Gender_Stats_Yr21_190722.pdf (accessed 15 July 2025).

[10] Global Gender Gap Mauritius available at https://npccmauritius.org/images/download/293.pdf (accessed 15 July 2025).

women rose from 1434 cases in 2021 to 4,420 cases in 2022.[11] Women are more likely to experience sexual abuse and exploitation, while men are more likely to be the victims of murders and other violent crimes. Approximately 50.6% of assaults and 69.0% of deliberate homicides in 2022 involved men. Women made up around 92.8% of those who were victims of sexual assault and exploitation.[12]

Against the above backdrop, this chapter focuses on the legal and normative framework on women's rights in Mauritius. The existing legislations and policies are reviewed and areas of concerns are underlined to demonstrate the important amount of work that still remains in this field. The African human rights system, with focus on the instruments on women's rights, are then discussed in terms of their potential for a better protection, promotion, respect and fulfilment of women's rights in Mauritius.

7.2 Legal and Normative Framework on Women's Rights

7.2.1 Legislation

7.2.1.1 The Constitution

Through its Bill of Rights, the Constitution of Mauritius prohibits discrimination on the ground of sex in section 3 and 16. It should be underlined that sex as a ground was only enshrined in section 16 in 1995 prior to which protection against discrimination on the ground of sex only existed under the heading 'fundamental rights and freedoms of individuals' (section 3) and not under section 16 on protection from discrimination. Generally, a number of civil and political rights of women are protected by the Bill of Rights similar to that of men in Mauritius. There is no special mention of women in the Constitution which is a notable lacuna. For instance, the Basic Law for the Federal Republic of Germany (the German Constitution) specifically mentions that 'men and women shall have equal rights' and that 'the state shall promote the actual implementation of equal rights for women and men and take steps to eliminate disadvantages that now exist'.[13]

[11] Ministry of Gender Equality and Family Welfare 'A gender approach' (2022) available at https://gender.govmu.org/Documents/Statistics/Statistics%20in%20Mauritius%20A%20Gender%20Approach%20Year%202022%20%20Final230224.pdf (accessed 15 Jay 2025).

[12] Statistics Mauritius 'Economic and social indicators' (2022) available at https://statsmauritius.govmu.org/Documents/Statistics/ESI/2023/EI1730/CJS_ESI_Yr22_300623.pdf (accessed 15 July 2025).

[13] Basic Law for the Federal Republic of Germany available at https://www.gesetze-im-internet.de/englisch_gg/englisch_gg.html (accessed 10 July 2025).

7.2.1.2 The Protection from Domestic Violence Act 1997

The Protection from Domestic Violence Act 1997 has been significantly amended in 2016. The definition and scope of domestic violence have been broadened in 2016. As a result, domestic violence includes acts against spouse, child, or another person living under the same roof, including inflicting wounds, threatening physical injury, intimidating, harassing, forcing, confining, harming, damaging property, or depriving them of resources or rent. These acts can be intentional or unintentional and can lead to physical, emotional, or financial harm. The definition of spouse has also been amended to someone who has been civilly or religiously married to, lived with, or has a common child with someone of the opposite sex. Section 8A has been amended to provide that enforcement officers can apply for a probation report on compliance with domestic violence orders issued by the Court, and the Court may direct this report. Section 11 has been amended to include the following provisions: (1) an Enforcement Officer must investigate domestic violence cases if they reasonably suspect a victim, (2) the term "aggrieved spouse" should be replaced with "victim", (3) an Officer may apply for protection, occupation, or tenancy orders with the victim's consent, and (4) an Officer may apply without the victim's consent.

The Act has been amended to include Section 11A, which outlines the duties and powers of police officers. The police must act with diligence when an offence is reported, and if a victim of domestic violence or an aggrieved spouse reports the offence, the officer in charge of the police station must investigate the circumstances. If a person is arrested and brought before a magistrate, the officer must report the incident to the nearest hospital or the Permanent Secretary for urgent medical assistance or psychological support. Section 13 of the principal Act has been amended to include penalties for domestic violence, a new paragraph stating that a person committing domestic violence will be liable for a fine of up to 50,000 rupees, imprisonment for up to two years, and imprisonment for up to five years.

7.2.1.3 National Women's Council Act 2016 and the National Women Entrepreneur Council Act 1999

Proclaimed in 2018, the objective of this act is "to make better provision for the functioning of the National Women's Council in order to further promote women's empowerment and gender equality, and for related matters".[14] The Council aims to promote women's empowerment and gender equality, encourage active participation in social, economic, and political fields and provide a platform for women to voice their needs.[15] Its functions include implementing government policies, advising on factors affecting women's empowerment, providing a net-

[14] Explanatory Memorandum of the National Women's Council Act 2016 available at https://gender.govmu.org/Documents/legislations%202020/National%20Women's%20Council%20Act%202016.pdf (accessed 10 July 2025).

[15] Ibid.

work, collaborating with similar bodies, identifying projects promoting women's participation, promoting women's rights as human rights, and determining a yearly financial and implementation program. The Council has powers to achieve its objectives and effectively discharge its functions, including developing an organisation with adequate infrastructure, receiving grants, collecting membership fees, funding Regional Committee activities, opening a bank account, purchasing or leasing goods, and submitting quarterly reports to the Minister.[16]

The National Women Entrepreneur Council aims to establish effective communication with women entrepreneur organisations, coordinate activities, promote entrepreneurial activities, evaluate needs, establish training programs, promote cooperation, develop links with other bodies, advise the Minister on women entrepreneurship development, evaluate contributions to development sectors, and study areas for strengthening women entrepreneurship development. It should be noted that neither of the legislation adopts a rights-based approach to women's social and economic empowerment and are merely of an administrative nature though their existence is relevant.

7.2.1.4 The Gender Equality Bill

The goal of the draft Gender Equality Bill, which is presently in the consultation phase, is to promote, preserve, and regulate gender equality in both the public and private domains. It is based on a strategic overview. The aim of this extensive legislation is to end discrimination based on gender. The Bill seeks to alleviate socioeconomic disparities and promote substantive equality in all spheres of society, including the social, economic, and political ones, by integrating gender equality concepts into both new and current laws. In addition, the Bill aims to provide equal opportunities for men and women by holding public and private organisations accountable for removing obstacles that support gender discrimination. Additionally, the Bill seeks to promote parity and equity for people of all genders in family responsibilities, unpaid caregiving, and career opportunities. Since its announcement in 2017, it has to be underlined that there has been much undue delay in the enactment of this Bill.

---

[16] Ibid.

7.2.2 Policies and Action Plans

7.2.2.1 National Gender Policy Framework 2022–2030

Introductory Remark

The social duties, responsibilities, identities, characteristics, and power dynamics that exist between men and women in a society are all considered aspects of gender. Social inequality is a result of patriarchal gender norms and stereotypes. Talks about gender mainstreaming in Mauritius centre on roles and responsibilities that are binary. In its 2012 report, the World Bank highlights the relationship between gender equality and development, emphasising how it can boost productivity and improve development outcomes for coming generations.[17] The financial advantages of diversity in the workplace and in company are emphasised in the "Women Matter Reports" published by the Mckinsey Global Institute.[18] The third framework for Mauritius is the National Gender Policy Framework (NGPF) 2022–2030, which is in line with the global Agenda 2030 on Sustainable Development Goals as well as the Blueprint for Mauritius Vision 2030.[19]

The National Gender Policy (NGP) is centred on how choices are made, evaluated, and carried out from a gender perspective. The term "gender" describes the characteristics and roles that come with being male or female, as well as the socially constructed connections between girls, boys, and women.[20] In the majority of civilisations, there are disparities and inequalities between men and women in terms of roles assigned, activities engaged in, resources accessed and controlled, and chances for decision-making that disadvantage the female gender.[21] The process of determining how any proposed action, including laws, regulations, or programs at all levels and in all domains, will affect both men and women is known as gender mainstreaming. This guarantees that men and women gain from political, economic, and social endeavours in an equal manner and that factors that contribute to inequality are not maintained. Gender equality entails acknowledging the diversity of

---

[17] World Bank Group 'World Development Report 2012: Gender Equality and Development' (2012) available at https://openknowledge.worldbank.org/entities/publication/51c285f6-0200-590c-97d3-95b937be3271 (accessed 10 July 2025).

[18] McKinsey and Company 'Women Matter: Time to accelerate - Ten years of insights into gender diversity' (2017) available at https://www.mckinsey.com/~/media/mckinsey/featured%20insights/women%20matter/women%20matter%20ten%20years%20of%20insights%20on%20the%20importance%20of%20gender%20diversity/women-matter-time-to-accelerate-ten-years-of-insights-into-gender-diversity.pdf (accessed 10 July 2025).

[19] Ministry of Gender Equality and Family Welfare (2022) 'National Gender Policy 2022-2030' available at https://gender.govmu.org/Documents/2022/NationalGenderPolicy2022-2030.pdf (accessed 10 July 2025).

[20] National Gender Policy (2022), p. 15.

[21] Epstein (2007), pp. 1–22.

various groups of people of both sexes and taking into account the needs, interests, and priorities of both men and women.[22]

With regard to gender equality in legislation, regulations, and administrative practices, Mauritius has achieved significant strides. Economic and Social Indicators on gender statistics are released by the Ministry of Finance, Economic Planning, and Development.[23] These indicators provide information on labour force characteristics, health, family status, education level, and demographic profiles. According to the 2019 Human Development Index (HDI) Report, Mauritius is ranked 66th out of 189 nations, with an average HDI for women of 0.804.[24] Gender inequality is more evident in political power and less so in economic power, according to the African Gender and Development Index (AGDI), which evaluates gender performance at the African level.[25] Mauritius scores highly in terms of social power, while women are underrepresented in terms of economic and decision-making power.[26]

Situational Analysis

Adopted in 2017, the Mauritius Vision 2030 agenda recognises growing inequality in the nation and strives for an inclusive growth model that considers the interests of all individuals. A revolutionary strategy for addressing gender disparities and injustices ingrained in patriarchy, culture, and religion is gender mainstreaming. The inclusion of gender mainstreaming in the development agenda across sectors has advanced significantly since the National Gender Policy 2008 (NGPF 2008). Introducing gender mainstreaming in fiscal planning, increasing gender awareness through programmes, institutionalising gender mainstreaming through gender Focal Points and Gender Cells in all Ministries, achieving gender parity in education, increasing the number of women in senior management positions in the civil service, and offering paid maternity leave for breastfeeding mothers are examples of positive measures.[27] The National Cost Gender Action Plan on Gender Mainstreaming was absent, monitoring and evaluation procedures were lacking, ministerial core work had to take precedence, implementing agencies' comprehension of the NGPF 2008 was inadequate, and human resources capacity was constrained.[28] Gender

[22] National Gender Policy (2022), p. 15.

[23] National Gender Policy (2022), p. 16.

[24] UNDP (2020) 'The Next Frontier: Human Development and the Anthropocene' available at https://www.undp.org/sites/g/files/zskgke326/files/migration/mu/HDR-2020%2D%2D-Mauritius-Country-Note.pdf (accessed 15 July 2025).

[25] UN Economic Commission for Africa 'The African Gender and Development Index' (2004) available at https://archive.uneca.org/sites/default/files/PublicationFiles/agdi_book_2004.pdf (accessed 10 July 2025).

[26] National Gender Policy (2022), p. 17.

[27] National Gender Policy (2022), p. 18.

[28] National Gender Policy (2022), p. 19.

equality and its integration into the development agenda are the goals of the National Gender Policy 2022–2030.

The Mauritian Constitution forbids discrimination on a number of grounds, including sex.[29] Equal access to job opportunities is guaranteed under the Equal Opportunities Act, which also prohibits discrimination on the basis of sexual orientation.[30] In order to guarantee representation, the Rodrigues Regional Assembly Act of 2001 stipulates that a minimum number of candidates must belong to a specific gender.[31] The Workers' Rights Act 2019 extends paternity leave to five days in a row and boosts maternity leave, but only for unmarried individuals.[32] The Government of Mauritius has enacted Local Government Act 2011 which now stipulates that at least one-third of the candidates to be fielded for elections at Local/Municipal level should be of the opposite sex.[33] The Gender Unit of the MGEFW has taken the lead in implementing the NGPF 2008 in the public sector.[34] In 2018, the National Women's Council Act of 1985 was repealed in order to enhance its ability to carry out decisions and policies pertaining to gender equality with a new National Women's Council Act 2016.[35] In order to advance gender equality and suggest recurring gender evaluations of governmental programs, the Parliamentary Gender Caucus was founded in 2017.[36]

With every child having access to free basic education up till the age of 16, Mauritius has achieved great strides in the field of education. In 2015, the nation attained the Millennium Development Goals, including universal primary education and a higher percentage of female enrolment in primary, secondary, and university education than male enrolment.[37] Equal opportunities and access to education are provided for boys and girls at all levels via education policies. Still, there are disparities in gender, with fewer women than males in STEM professions. At secondary levels, significant rates of failure, repetition, and dropout continue to exist. Since men predominate in the maritime industry, programmes to raise awareness of employment opportunities are being created to encourage young people to pursue them. Despite the lack of job opportunities, girls continue to enrol at a higher rate in the social sciences and humanities. The government is making an effort to resolve these issues and preserve gender equity for both boys' and girls' schooling.[38]

---

[29] Section 3 and 16 of the Constitution of Mauritius.

[30] Sections 2 and 5 of the Equal Opportunities Act 42 of 2008.

[31] Section 9 of the Rodrigues Regional Assembly Act of 2001.

[32] Sections 52 and 53 of the Workers' Rights Act 2019.

[33] Sections 11-13 of the Local Government Act 2011.

[34] National Gender Policy (2022), p. 21.

[35] Sections 4, 5, 8 and 10 of the National Women's Council Act 2016.

[36] Order 69(6) of the Parliament Standing Orders as amended in 2017.

[37] National Gender Policy (2022), p. 22.

[38] Ibid.

Women must actively participate in decision-making at all levels, including the home, social, political, and religious sectors, in order to achieve gender equality.[39] There are opportunities during elections to address gender disparity, advance gender responsiveness, and boost the representation of women. A third of women are now permitted to serve on municipal and district councils according to the Local Government Act. It has become more challenging for women to be elected, nevertheless, due to the First-Past-The-Post electoral system.[40] Though it has increased, the proportion of women in high leadership roles is still small when compared to men. Electoral reforms, specific measures, and investments in training and capacity building are required to attain 50/50 representation.[41]

Although sex-based discrimination in the workplace is illegal in Mauritius, the majority of women work in the public sector, with very few in the private sector.[42] There are still obstacles in the workforce, such as persistent wage and income disparities, discriminatory wages in the tea and sugar industries, lack of paid paternity leave, high rates of unemployment for both men and women in their youth, and a dearth of female entrepreneurs.[43]

The Protection from Domestic Violence Act (PDVA) and its revisions offer protection to spouses and other individuals living under their roof, including children, in the wake of the rise in gender-based violence (GBV) in recent years.[44] In January 2020, the High-Level Committee on the Elimination of GBV was founded with the goal of addressing the operational, institutional, and legislative deficiencies that currently exist.[45] The number of cases recorded in 2017 and 2019 remained high in spite of efforts to eradicate GBV. At all levels, combating GBV necessitates a multisectoral strategy that addresses issues including the culture of silence, victims abstaining from legal action, and the provision of support infrastructures like housing units, nurseries, and child care facilities.[46]

The Mental Health Care Act, the Trust Fund for Specialised Medical Care Act, the Ayurvedic and Other Traditional Medicines Act, the HIV and AIDS Act, and the Food Act are just a few of the laws that have been passed to regulate and control the health and well-being of the populace. Nonetheless, with a higher prevalence of

---

[39] Moghadam and Senftova (2005), pp. 389–412.

[40] National Gender Policy (2022), p. 23.

[41] Ibid.

[42] National Gender Policy (2022), p. 24.

[43] Ibid.

[44] End GBV 'Mauritius' (2025) available at https://endgbv.africa/mapping/mauritius/#:~:text=Subsequent%20amendments%20to%20the%20PDVA,and%20enhanced%20enforcement%20officer%20powers. (accessed 10 July 2025).

[45] United Nations Mauritius 'Breaking the Silence: Addressing Gender-Based Violence and Upholding Human Rights' (2024) available at https://mauritius.un.org/en/285513-breaking-silence-addressing-gender-based-violence-and-upholding-human-rights#:~:text=Additionally%2C%20a%20High%2DLevel%20Committee,and%20accessible%20for%20any%20age. (accessed 10 July 2025).

[46] National Gender Policy (2022), p. 25.

HIV/AIDS in males than in women, Mauritius has difficulties in combating the disease.[47] Although there are fewer new HIV diagnoses now than there were in 2006, because of the Harm Reduction Programme, injecting drug use is still the main cause of the epidemic. Since August 2017, the WHO "Test and Treat" Strategy has been in place, providing universal access to antiretroviral medication (ART) for people living with HIV.[48]

Mauritian males tend to be less concerned about their own and their spouses' health, while women are less likely to participate in unhealthy habits and experience disease.[49] 2020 saw a higher mortality toll among men than women, with diabetes mellitus responsible for 24.9% of deaths in women and 21.4% in men.[50] Major health problems that affect Mauritius women include malignancies of the breast and other female reproductive organs.[51] In order to govern, monitor, and manage the use of pesticides in agricultural produce, the Use of Pesticides Act was enacted in 2018.[52] It is imperative to address the health repercussions of drug misuse and teenage pregnancy due to their rising incidence. Although sex education is currently included in school curricula, questions have been raised over its age suitability.[53]

Although the media in Mauritius is vital to the country's education and information landscape, it frequently reinforces restrictive, stereotyped, and unrealistic views of gender roles.[54] Gender stereotypes, the division of labour between the sexes, and silenced voices are some of the issues that women face in the workplace and in the media, where they are underrepresented.[55] In order to ensure privacy and benefit the general public, the government has implemented significant reforms in the media sector to take into account the newest advancements and trends. The government's goal is to transform Mauritius into a digital society by leveraging information technology to enhance citizen access to information and better service delivery.

Gender responsive mitigation, adaptation, and environmental service delivery are necessary due to the gender-neutral effects of climate change and environmental degradation. The severe weather that Mauritius is currently facing is harming families, farmers, fishermen, infrastructure, and agriculture. In order to mitigate these detrimental effects, the government has gathered money and is now building drains,

---

[47] National Gender Policy (2022), p. 26.

[48] Ibid.

[49] Rambaree et al. (2020), p. 1774140.

[50] National Service Framework for NCDs (2023–2028) available at https://health.govmu.org/health/wp-content/uploads/2024/06/National-Service-Framework-for-NCDS-2023-2028.pdf (accessed 10 July 2025).

[51] Pat et al. (2019), p. 101616.

[52] Mauritius Chamber of Agriculture 'The Use of Pesticides Act 2018' available at https://mauritius-chamber-of-agriculture.org/wp-content/uploads/2022/12/Use-of-Pesticides-Act-2018.pdf (accessed 10 July 2025).

[53] Emambokus and Oogarah-Pratap (2019), pp. 185–195.

[54] Tandrayen-Ragoobur (2014), pp. 535–563.

[55] UN Women Africa 'Mauritius Country Profile' (2022) available at https://africa.unwomen.org/sites/default/files/2023-11/mauritius_gender_equality_profile.pdf (accessed 10 July 2025).

renovating infrastructure, and supporting green enterprises.[56] Sensitisation and awareness-building are the purview of the Information and Education Unit of the Ministry of Environment, Solid Waste Management, and Climate Change (MOESWMCC). The unit makes use of a range of media for communication, such as posters, brochures, exhibitions, movies, speeches, and PowerPoint presentations.[57]

In order to enhance education, awareness-raising, human and institutional capacity on climate change mitigation, adaptation, impact reduction, and early warning, the MOESWMCC established the Climate Change Information Centre (CCIC) and created a Climate Change Information, Education and Communication Strategy and Action Plan.[58] In order to guarantee Mauritius's low carbon future, the MOESWMCC is also carrying out a project named "Nationally Appropriate Mitigation Actions (NAMAs) for Low Carbon Island Development Strategy" with funding assistance from the Global Environment Facility.[59]

The Policy Framework

The NGP is a commitment to integrate gender into all development processes in Mauritius, focusing on Mainstreaming Gender and Empowerment of Women and Girls. The policy aims to provide guidelines for the government's commitment to gender mainstreaming in all development processes, including planning, design, implementation, monitoring, and evaluation.[60] It is based on human rights-based approaches of equality, non-discrimination, transparency, accountability, respect, dignity, and inclusivity.[61] The NGP applies to various sectors, including the public sector, statutory bodies, local governments, private sectors, civil society organisations, media, and academia.

The vision is to create an inclusive and just society free from discrimination, where men, women, boys, and girls can participate in social, economic, political, and cultural activities equitably and equally. The policy approaches include promoting gender mainstreaming and empowerment at all levels, formulating sectoral gender policies, conducting gender analysis, disaggregating statistics and data,

[56] National Gender Policy (2022), pp. 28–29.

[57] Ministry of Environment, Solid Waste Management and Climate Change 'Information and Education Unit' (2025b) available at https://environment.govmu.org/Pages/Information-and-Education-Division.aspx (accessed 10 July 2025).

[58] Ministry of Environment, Solid Waste Management and Climate Change 'Climcate Chnage Information Centre' (2025a) available at https://environment.govmu.org/Pages/CCIC.aspx (accessed 10 July 2025).

[59] National Gender Policy (2022), p. 30.

[60] Ministry of Gender Equality and Family Welfare 'National Gender Policy 2022-2030' March 2022 https://gender.govmu.org/Documents/2022/NationalGenderPolicy2022-2030.pdf (accessed 10 July 2025).

[61] National Gender Policy (2022), p. 33.

requiring non-state actors to develop their gender policies, and ensuring active male involvement in addressing gender concerns.[62]

The NGP proposes strategies to achieve gender equality in key areas, including eliminating all forms of gender-based discrimination, achieving equity in employment access, empowering women and girls, enacting the Gender Equality Bill, fulfilling international and regional treaty obligations, recognising unpaid care and domestic work, using temporary special measures, addressing working mothers' triple roles, implementing gender mainstreaming, enhancing capacity for ministries, strengthening law enforcement and judicial officers, granting women equal rights to economic resources, enhancing women's participation and leadership opportunities, adopting gender responsive budgeting, and safeguarding sexual and reproductive health and rights.[63]

Policy Objectives and Strategies

Through the removal of prejudices and the transformation of each implementing organisation's top office, the NGP seeks to revolutionise organisational procedures and practices. The broad strategies include giving men and women, girls and boys, equal access and opportunities, ensuring full participation in decision-making, creating gender policy statements and action plans at the sectoral and institutional levels, creating gender statistics and data, creating a clear framework for monitoring and evaluation, creating tools for gender mainstreaming, offering targeted training, capacity building, raising awareness, and creating sensitisation programs at all levels, encouraging the public and private sectors, the media, academic institutions, CSOs, and NGOs to participate in the implementation of the National Gender Policy 2022–2030, and bolstering the National Gender Machinery at all levels.[64]

Guaranteeing equal access to education and training prospects, fostering gender equality in laws and policies, ensuring fair representation and participation of men and women in governance, and advocating gender mainstreaming in Parliament and political party leadership are just a few of the theme-specific goals and strategies.[65] Enabling communities to support more women running for office, encouraging the private sector to hire more women and provide gender-responsive working conditions, offering mentorship programs, advocating for legal reforms, encouraging gender mainstreaming in Parliament and political party leadership, facilitating short-term training on gender equality and gender mainstreaming at the Civil Service College and other educational institutions for public officers, including policy makers, are some strategies.[66]

---

[62] Ibid.

[63] National Gender Policy (2022), p. 36.

[64] National Gender Policy (2022), p. 37.

[65] National Gender Policy (2022), p. 38.

[66] National Gender Policy (2022), p. 39.

Promoting equity and equality of access to economic opportunities in Mauritius is the goal of the national government policy. Promoting gender equality statements in annual reports, enforcing the National Code and Corporate Governance Mauritius, reviewing labour laws and practices to introduce flexible work patterns, gender employment policies, advocating for supportive environments, gathering gender-responsive statistics, promoting accessible banking services, funding mechanisms for women entrepreneurs, facilitating SMEs' access to markets, investing in social welfare services, training women to improve their labour and entrepreneurial skills, and facilitating women's access to markets and trade with the government are some strategies.[67]

The NGP objectives are to eliminate and mitigate all forms of gender-based violence, strategies include enhancing awareness on the dangers of GBV, organising targeted training for stakeholders, enhancing investment and programming to rehabilitate perpetrators, strengthening GBV evidence-based, enhancing legislative framework implementation, and developing a monitoring and evaluation-tracking tool.[68] It also aims at promoting healthy living and wellness, strategies include promoting health awareness programs, facilitating healthcare services for terminally ill patients, offering subsidies for plastic reconstructive implants, sensitising communities on preventive measures on food consumption, conducting research on sexual and reproductive health, increasing focus on sexual and reproductive health and rights programs for adolescents, setting up day care centres, and researching and documenting the causes of teenage pregnancies.[69]

The Climate Change Information Center (CCIC) seeks to improve media coverage and environmental management's sensitivity to gender. The Blue Economy Strategy and Implementation plan incorporates gender perspectives and offers integrated information on climate change by the center. Increasing awareness of gendered methods, putting the UNFCCC Gender Action Plan into practice, and encouraging gender responsiveness in renewable energy planning are some strategies.[70] By increasing women's perspectives on politics, economics, and health, as well as by providing training and capacity building, the programme also seeks to improve gender responsive reporting in the media. Developing a comprehensive ICT education strategy, streamlining legislation and gender mainstreaming plans, enhancing adult education programmes, and advancing women's ability in media technical production are some of the strategies. These initiatives seek to advance gender equality and technology-driven service delivery.[71]

[67] National Gender Policy (2022), p. 40.

[68] National Gender Policy (2022), p. 41.

[69] National Gender Policy (2022), p. 42.

[70] Ibid.

[71] National Gender Policy (2022), p. 43.

Institutional Framework for Implementation

The NGP focuses on various institutions and the roles that they should play in the implantation of the policy. The Ministry of Gender Equality and Family Welfare acts as the National Gender Machinery responsible for promoting gender equality at the Ministerial and Cabinet Level, developing the National Gender Policy, ensuring effective gender mainstreaming in public and private entities, and coordinating the implementation of the National Gender Action Plan. It also oversees the development of sector-specific policy statements and Gender Action Plans, creates and monitors Gender Technical Working Groups, reports to treaty monitoring bodies, and sets performance indicators for reporting.[72] Gender Cells at ministerial level have also been provided for. The NGP mandates every Ministry and public agency to establish a gender cell to institutionalise gender mainstreaming in all plans, programmes, and budgets. The Deputy Permanent Secretary or senior managerial officer will chair meetings and report to the Supervising Officer. The Gender Cell will include a Deputy Permanent Secretary, Senior Human Resource Officers, Finance Officers, Technical Officers, and Statisticians.[73]

A National Steering Committee on Gender Mainstreaming (NSCGM) is also set up by the NGP. The Minister will chair a meeting for Supervising Officers to report on gender mainstreaming progress in their ministries/departments. The NSCGM will monitor, evaluate, provide guidance, facilitate discussions, identify gaps, establish working groups, and promote gender responsiveness in workplaces, ensuring a culture of gender responsiveness.[74] The Inter-Ministerial Gender Technical Working Committee serves as a consultative forum for GFP, providing guidance on gender mainstreaming, collaborating with sectors, and setting agendas for the National Steering Committee on Gender Mainstreaming.[75] The Gender Focal Point in the Ministry is responsible for addressing gender issues, reporting progress to the Supervising Officer, attending consultative meetings, overseeing gender mainstreaming in policies, collecting and disseminating gender statistics, establishing links with non-state actors, coordinating gender training, and monitoring progress made by the Gender Cell on projects and programmes.[76]

The National Women's Council and National Women Entrepreneur Council are responsible for implementing women's empowerment programs and promoting gender equality. They ensure accountability, establish effective communication with the MGEFW, and promote active participation in social and political fields. The National Women Entrepreneur Council coordinates activities of women entrepreneur associations, evaluates women's needs, establishes training programs, promotes cooperation and research on women entrepreneurship development, and

---

[72] National Gender Policy (2022), p. 44.

[73] National Gender Policy (2022), p. 45.

[74] Ibid.

[75] National Gender Policy (2022), p. 46.

[76] Ibid.

develops networks with other bodies in Mauritius. They also evaluate women entrepreneurs' contributions to various sectors and study areas for strengthening their development.[77]

The government is expected to implement a gender-responsive budgeting strategy across various sectors. This includes establishing a Gender Cell, a Gender Focal Point, and developing sector-specific gender policy statements. The Ministry of Finance, Economic Planning, and Development is mandated to spearhead this, while Statistics Mauritius would be developing indicators and promoting gender mainstreaming.[78] The private sector has the role of partnering with the MGEFW to implement the National Gender Policy, ensuring compliance with policy at institutional and decision-making levels.[79] The Gender Technical Working Group on Gender Mainstreaming is also being established to ensure gender mainstreaming.

The National Gender Policy 2022–2030 outlines the roles and responsibilities of various organisations, including civil society organisations, media, academia, and the Parliamentary Gender Caucus. CSOs are responsible for capacity-building, sensitisation, and mobilising resources for gender mainstreaming. They also partner with the MGEFW to implement the NGP, provide emergency accommodation for victims of domestic violence, lobby for the Gender Equality Bill, support ministries in sensitisation programmes, monitor NGP implementation, and ensure government accountability.[80] Media collaborates with the MGEFW to promote gender equality messages, create awareness, and ensure gender-sensitive reporting.[81] The Parliamentary Gender Caucus recommends periodic gender assessments of government policies and research on salient gender issues and facilitates networking with organisations and institutions to promote gender equality and participation.[82]

Coordination and Resource Mobilisation

Partners in the National Gender Policy (NGP) must fulfil both implementation and oversight responsibilities as it is a multi-sectoral process. The Planning and Research Unit and the Gender Unit of the Ministry of Gender Equality and Family Welfare (MGEFW) will serve as the oversight and assessment bodies. In order to measure gender equality and women's empowerment, social indicators will be developed and reporting formats will be guided by the M&E plan.[83] For the policy to be implemented, there must be sufficient financial and human resources. The MOFEPD is researching the viability of gender-responsive budgeting, while

---

[77] National Gender Policy (2022), p. 47.

[78] National Gender Policy (2022), p. 48.

[79] Ibid.

[80] National Gender Policy (2022), p. 49.

[81] Ibid.

[82] National Gender Policy (2022), p. 50.

[83] National Gender Policy (2022), p. 52.

the MGEFW is responsible for resource assessment. Through cooperation with financial institutions, international development partners, regional development agencies, private institutions, and annual ministerial budgetary allocations, resources will be mobilised.[84]

7.2.2.2 National Strategy and Action Plan of the High-Level Committee on the Elimination of Gender Based Violence in the Republic of Mauritius 2020–2024

A National Strategy and Action Plan has been adopted by the Mauritius government in an effort to abolish gender-based violence (GBV) in the nation. The plan is survivor-focused and grounded in global best practices.[85] Understanding the nature of GBV, incorporating a variety of stakeholders, fortifying legal and policy frameworks, developing capacity, and having a reliable monitoring system are all essential components. To combat GBV, four sub-strategies have been created: detecting and correcting discriminatory practices, prioritising support services for survivors, altering cultural attitudes that oppose gender equality, and coordinating monitoring and assessment.[86] For efficient execution, a three-tiered responsibility model is developed. A systems-thinking approach, dedication to data collecting, analysis, monitoring, and capacity building for the Lead Agency are among the recommendations.[87]

7.2.3 Institutions

7.2.3.1 Gender Unit

The Gender Unit, as the National Gender Machinery, is responsible for overseeing, coordinating, monitoring, and evaluating gender mainstreaming policies, strategies, and programmes at the national level. Its main objectives are to work towards gender equality and women's empowerment through a dual approach: implementing gender mainstreaming strategies in all Ministries' policies and programmes and empowering women socially, economically, and politically. The Gender Unit is called upon to harmonise policies with international and regional human rights instruments related to women's empowerment and gender equality. These

---

[84] Ibid.

[85] NATIONAL STRATEGY AND ACTION PLAN of the High Level Committee on the Elimination of Gender Based Violence in the Republic of Mauritius 2020-2024 available at https://police.govmu.org/police/?mdocs-posts=national-strategy-and-action-plan-gender-based-violence-2020-2024 (accessed 10 July 2025) p. 7.

[86] National Strategy and Action Plan (2020-2024), pp. 15–17.

[87] National Strategy and Action Plan (2020-2024), pp. 17–27.

instruments include the Convention on Elimination of all Forms of Discrimination Against Women (CEDAW), the Beijing Platform for Action of 1995 (BFPA), and the Post-2015 Sustainable Development Goals Agenda.[88]

The Ministry of Gender Equality and Family Welfare (the Ministry) is pursuing efforts towards mainstreaming gender and empowering women and girls to ensure no-one is left behind. They have initiated actions such as the adoption of the National Gender Policy (2022–2030) in March 2022, the launch of a first National Steering Committee on Gender Mainstreaming, an Inter-Ministerial Gender Technical Working Committee, and the reinforcement of Gender Cells in all Ministries. The Ministry is also refreshing its commitment with other sectors, such as the Private Sector, Academia, Media, and Civil Society Organisations, through the Gender Technical Working Group Committee. Each sector will be assisted through a well-defined guideline that will enable the smooth integration of gender for gradual elimination of outstanding gender gaps. In addition to reaching out to the public sector, the Ministry is refreshing its commitment with other sectors, such as the private sector, academia, media, and civil society organisations, through the Gender Technical Working Group Committee.

The Ministry has implemented the Gender Responsive Budgeting Initiative (GRBI) for gender-sensitive initiatives, collaborating with Finance and Economic Development to include gender mainstreaming in government programmes. The National Women's Council and National Women Entrepreneur Council support women entrepreneurs in Mauritius.

The Gender Unit in Mauritius has revamped its decentralised network of Women Centres into Women Empowerment Centres (WCWs) in 2016, aiming to empower women to be "at par" with men. The Ministry has converted WECs into Wellness Centres for Women (WCWs) to provide targeted interventions, health services, and sports amenities for women. The Floreal WCW launched in October 2022 offers chair exercises, Tai chi, Yoga, and walking clubs for 85 women. The Gender Unit has also expanded its services to other target groups, including women and girls in deprived regions, secondary school students, and the elderly. Activities at the WCWs include implementing projects and courses, awareness campaigns, and promoting awareness campaigns on gender and other thematic areas.[89]

The Ministry celebrated International Women's Day 2023 with 10,500 guests, launching the National Strategy and Costed Action Plan for Women Entrepreneurship Development in Mauritius. The National Strategy Action Plan on the Elimination of GBV is being spearheaded by the Family Welfare and Protection Unit and implemented by all key collaborators. The Gender Unit is also implementing a project to promote women's presence and leadership within public institutions at national and

[88] Ministry of Gender Equality and Family Welfare (2025) 'Gender Unit' available at https://gender.govmu.org/Pages/Gender-Unit.aspx (accessed 10 July 2025).

[89] Ibid.

local levels, with financial assistance of $80,000 provided and a letter of agreement signed between the Ministry and UNDP.[90]

7.2.3.2 Family Welfare and Protection Unit

The Family Welfare and Protection Unit (FWPU) was established in 2003 to implement policies and programmes for families and address gender-based violence. The Protection from Domestic Violence Act (PDVA) was passed by the Government of Mauritius in 1997, providing protection orders, occupation orders, and tenancy orders. Subsequent amendments were made to the PDVA in 2004, 2007, 2011, and 2016 to provide protection to all family members living under the same roof, harsher penalties for non-compliance of court orders, and rehabilitation of perpetrators through counselling.[91]

Gender-based violence is a significant human rights violation worldwide, resulting in physical, sexual, or psychological harm or suffering to women. The United Nations General Assembly adopted the Declaration on the Elimination of Violence against Women in 1993, which defines violence as any act of gender-based violence that results in harm or suffering to women. The FWPU adopts strategies to address gender-based violence, including intervention, prevention, rehabilitation, harmonisation, and data collection. Services offered to victims include legal and psychological advice, assistance with application for protection orders, psycho-social support, counselling services to adult perpetrators, and referral to other institutions as appropriate. The FWPU also offers services through six Family Support Bureaux (FSBx) around the island, providing legal and psychological advice, assistance with application for protection orders, psycho-social support, counselling services, and referral to other institutions as appropriate.[92]

The Family Welfare and Protection Unit (FWPU) provides emergency shelters, housing, psychological support, advice, and counselling to victims of domestic violence and their children. Information, Education, and Communication (IEC) campaigns are conducted to raise public awareness on gender-based violence and family welfare. The Ministry has implemented programmes such as Men as Caring Partners (MACP), Pre-Marital Counselling Programme, Marriage Enrichment Programme, Inter-Generation Relationship Programme (IGR), and Strengthening Values for Family Life Programme (SVFL).[93]

---

[90] National Strategy and Coasted Action Plan for Women Entrepreneurship Development in Mauritius (2023) available at https://gender.govmu.org/Lists/DocumentsLinks/Attachments/20/NSCAP%20Final%20Publication.pdf (accessed 10 July 2025).

[91] Ministry of Gender Equality and Family Welfare 'Family Welfare and Protection Unit' available at https://gender.govmu.org/Pages/Family-Welfare-and-Protection-Unit.aspx (accessed 10 July 2025).

[92] Ibid.

[93] Ibid.

The Domestic Violence Perpetrators' Rehabilitation Programme aims to help perpetrators abstain from violence, manage anger, resolve conflicts peacefully, and educate them to become responsible partners. The Economic Empowerment Programme of Survivors of Domestic Violence empowers victims to join institutions for gainful employment, greater financial stability, and independence. The Victim Empowerment and Abuser Rehabilitation Policy (VEARP) is a workplace initiative to address gender-based violence, enhancing knowledge of legislations and services. The Domestic Violence Information System (DOVIS) is used to monitor and collect data on domestic violence cases. The Ministry is also developing an Observatory on Gender Based Violence to gather harmonised data for informed policy making and monitoring. Special events celebrated by the FWPU include International Day of Families, International Day Against Violence Against Women, and the Interfaith Forum. These events highlight the importance of families as fundamental units of society and the role of religious leaders in addressing and eliminating domestic violence.[94]

7.3 UN Observations on Women's Rights in Mauritius

This section focuses on the concluding observations issued against Mauritius regarding the rights of women in Mauritius. The main areas of concerns as highlighted by the various treaty-based bodies at the UN level are discussed with the aim of providing an overview of gaps and challenges that exist in Mauritius despite the existence of the legal and normative framework on women's rights as discussed in the previous section. Mauritius is a state party to the UN Convention on Elimination of All Forms of Discrimination against Women (the Convention) which it acceded to on 09 July 1984. It should be noted that Mauritius has placed a reservation on article 29(2) of the Convention as a result of which it does not accept the procedure of inter-states dispute settlement by arbitration or by International Court of Justice. In 1998, the country withdrew reservations that it had placed on article 11(1)(b) and (d) on equal employment opportunities and equal remuneration, respectively, and on article 16(1)(g) on same personal rights as husband and wife, including the right to choose a family name, a profession, and an occupation at the time of its accession to the Convention. It also ratified the Optional Protocol to the Convention on 31 October 2008 on complaints and inquiry mechanisms.

It is apposite to make mention of the non-applicability of the Convention in Mauritius which is a serious drawback in the promotion and protection of women's rights in Mauritius. In the case of *Ramar v The Mauritius Commercial Bank*, the Supreme Court stated that "the Court of Civil Appeal also declined to apply the relevant provisions of the International Covenant on Civil and Political Rights (ICCPR) and of the Convention on the Elimination of all forms of Discrimination

[94] Ibid.

Against Women in the absence of any evidence that these important UN human rights instruments—to which Mauritius has been a party since 1973 and 1984, respectively—have been incorporated in our domestic law".[95] The Supreme Court observed further that "while not questioning the decisions of the Court of Civil Appeal, I can only observe that the Human Rights Committee and the CEDAW Committee have repeatedly expressed concern that these treaties have still not been given full effect in the domestic legal order and have further recommended their full incorporation in national law to ensure their due implementation".[96]

In 2018 through its Concluding Observations on the eighth periodic report of Mauritius, the Committee on the Elimination of All Forms of Discrimination Against Women (the Committee), applauded Mauritius in undertaking legislative reforms on women's rights.[97] Specifically, it welcomes the adoption of the Protection from Domestic Violence (Amendment) Act 2016 which broadens the definition of domestic violence; the Protection of Human Rights (Amendment) Act 2012 and Independent Police Complaints Commission Act 2016, the latter of which strengthened the role of the National Human Rights Commission, among other bodies, by establishing an Independent Police Complaints Division on 9 April 2018; the Criminal Code (Amendment) Act 2012 (Act No. 11 of 2012) which decriminalises abortion in certain cases and the Equal Opportunities Act 2008 which prohibits direct and indirect discrimination on the grounds of sex and sexual orientation in certain areas such as employment and education; the Local Government Act 2011 as amended by the Local Government (Amendment) Act 2015, sections 11 (6) and 12 (6) of guarantee gender equality in local elections. A series of areas of concerns was also highlighted by the Committee which is discussed below.[98]

7.3.1 Constitutional and Legislative Framework

The Committee disapproved of Mauritius for not fully incorporating the Convention's provisions into its national law, not including a comprehensive definition of discrimination against women, and not repealing discriminatory provisions in the state party's constitutional and legislative framework. It recommended that the state party should include the Convention's provisions in its national law, adopt a comprehensive definition of discrimination against women, and ensure inclusive consultations on the review of article 16, paragraph 4 (c) of the Constitution to ensure compliance

[95] *Ramar M J S v The Mauritius Commercial Bank Ltd* 2021 SCJ 184 p.16.

[96] Ibid.

[97] UN CEDAW Concluding observations on the eighth periodic report of Mauritius (14 November 2018) UN Doc CEDAW/C/MUS/CO/8 hereafter referred to as the UN CEDAW Concluding Observations (2018).

[98] UN CEDAW Concluding Observations (2018) para 4–7.

with the Convention's provisions. Till date, there have been no amendments to the Constitution in this direction.[99]

7.3.2 *Visibility of the Convention and Legal Complaints Mechanisms*

The Committee has expressed concerns about the visibility of the Convention and the Optional Protocol in court proceedings, the low number of complaints lodged before the Equal Opportunities Commission, the lack of an explicit prohibition of discrimination in the private sector, the complexity of legal complaint mechanisms, and the limited knowledge of women's rights among legal practitioners and judicial and law enforcement officials. The Committee recommended raising public awareness of legislation prohibiting discrimination against women, amending article 16 of the Constitution to explicitly prohibit discrimination in the private sector, reviewing judicial complaint mechanisms, and strengthening capacity-building for legal practitioners and law enforcement officials to invoke or apply the Convention in court proceedings.[100]

7.3.3 *National Machinery for the Advancement of Women and Gender Mainstreaming and Gender Equality*

The Committee commended the establishment of the National Steering Committee on Gender Mainstreaming in 2010 and the appointment of gender focal points in 2017 but expressed concerns about the lack of a national action plan, complexity of national machinery, inadequate human, technical, and financial resources, absence of information on monitoring and evaluation mechanisms, and insufficient visibility of the Equal Opportunities Commission's activities. The Committee recommended Mauritius to expedite the review of the 2008 national gender policy framework, adopt a national action plan, ensure coordinated work, increase resources, involve all stakeholders, introduce effective monitoring, evaluation, and accountability mechanisms, and increase the visibility of the Equal Opportunities Commission.

Similar concerns were raised by the UN Human Rights Committee (HRC) in 2017 while considering the fifth periodic report of Mauritius submitted to the International Covenant on Civil and Political Rights. The HRC expressed concern over workplace discrimination against women, particularly in low-skilled jobs and decision-making positions. It notes that complaints are often lodged infrequently to the Equal Opportunities Commission and the Equal Opportunities Tribunal,

[99] UN CEDAW Concluding Observations (2018) para 9–10.

[100] UN CEDAW Concluding Observations (2018) para 11–12.

raising questions about access to these bodies. The HRC recommended facilitating complaints, enforcing equal pay regulations, increasing workplace inspections, investigating non-compliance, and empowering women in higher skilled roles.[101]

7.3.4 *Temporary Special Measures and Stereotypes and Gender-based Violence Against Women*

The Committee has expressed concerns about Mauritius' systematic lack of use of temporary special measures to achieve substantive gender equality. The Committee recommended that Mauritius implement these measures in areas where women are underrepresented or disadvantaged, such as political and public life and employment. It also suggested raising awareness among government officials and policymakers about the importance of temporary special measures.[102] The Committee acknowledged the Protection from Domestic Violence (Amendment) Act 2016, which expanded the scope of protection for victims of domestic violence and provided protection orders. However, it remained concerned about the prevalence of gender-based violence, discriminatory gender stereotypes, gaps in national legislation, and the lack of safeguards to prevent pardons for gender-based violence. The Committee also noted the limited availability and quality of assistance and protection services, the lack of a monitoring mechanism to evaluate the impact of existing legislation, and the lack of accurate statistical data on cases of gender-based violence against women. The Committee reiterated its recommendation to the State party to enforce existing legislation, amend, or adopt legislation to explicitly prohibit marital rape and corporal punishment, expand the scope of protection for victims of domestic violence, put safeguards in place to prevent pardons, encourage reporting of gender-based violence, ensure effective protection under protection orders, and analyse the impact of the State party's programmes and measures to prevent and address gender-based violence against women.[103]

The HRC was concerned about the persistence of violence against women in the State party, particularly gender-based violence, and the lack of criminalisation of marital rape. It urged Mauritius to strengthen efforts to combat violence against women by implementing existing legislation, intensifying awareness-raising campaigns, training police officers, judges, and prosecutors, and providing adequate assistance to victims. It also expressed concern about increased acts of violence and abuse against elderly persons, primarily within families and care institutions. The HRC recommended facilitating reporting, strengthening the Welfare and Elderly

---

[101] UN CEDAW Concluding Observations (2018) para 13–14.

[102] UN CEDAW Concluding Observations (2018) para 15–16.

[103] UN CEDAW Concluding Observations (2018) para 17.

Persons Protection Unit, conducting awareness campaigns, and training staff in care institutions.[104]

7.3.5 *Trafficking and Exploitation of Prostitution*

The Committee highlighted that Mauritius remains a major destination for trafficking in persons, with women and girls, especially those from rural areas, at the highest risk. The lack of a comprehensive anti-trafficking strategy and a national action plan limited measures to protect women, low reporting rates, inadequate shelters, and lack of regional cooperation agreements contribute to the issue. It recommended strengthening existing mechanisms and policies, accelerating the adoption of a national plan, collecting and analysing data on trafficking, providing effective redress mechanisms, supporting victims, enhancing regional cooperation with countries of origin and destination, and taking measures to protect women in prostitution from exploitation and abuse. The absence of regional cooperation agreements and a national policy framework also contributed to the problem as per the Committee.[105]

7.3.6 *Participation in Political and Public Life and Education*

The Committee has highlighted the positive impact of the Local Government Act 2011, which provides quotas for electoral lists, on increasing women's representation in local governance. It also acknowledged that women hold high-level decision-making positions in the State party and are equally represented in the public sector. However, the Committee remained concerned about the low levels of participation of women in political and public life, particularly in decision-making positions at the national level. The Committee recommended that the State party adopt temporary special measures, such as extending the application of quotas for local elections to national elections, to accelerate the achievement of substantive equality between women and men in all areas of political and public life. It also recommended addressing structural, social, and cultural barriers to women entering political life or holding public office, including providing incentives to include an equal number of women and men at equal ranks on their electoral lists and providing training to women on political campaigning, leadership, and negotiation skills.[106] In terms of education, the Committee noted the substantive measures taken by the State party to ensure universal access to education, but was concerned about insufficient data col-

[104] UN CEDAW Concluding Observations (2018) para 18.

[105] UN CEDAW Concluding Observations (2018) para 19–20.

[106] UN CEDAW Concluding Observations (2018) para 21.

lected, high absenteeism rates, low literacy rates, lack of comprehensive education on sexual and reproductive health and rights, lack of regulations and measures to address social exclusion, concentration of women and girls in traditionally female-dominated fields, and difficulties faced by women and girls with disabilities and asylum-seeking and migrant women and girls in gaining access to high-quality education.[107]

The HRC acknowledged the Local Government Act of 2012's improvement in women's representation in municipal and village councils, but expressed concern about the low percentage of women elected to the National Assembly and Cabinet. They suggest increasing women's participation in politics by 30% and promoting awareness campaigns.[108]

7.3.7 *Employment and Health*

The Committee expressed concerns about the implementation of the Equal Opportunities Act 2008 and the implementation of the Criminal Code (Amendment) Act 2012 in the country. The Committee identified several issues, including the persistent gender pay gap, underrepresentation of women in decision-making positions, limited paid maternity leave, sexual harassment, and exploitative working conditions for women migrant workers. The Committee recommended enforcing the principle of equal pay for work of equal value, improving access for women in the private sector, amending or repealing sections 30 and 54 of the Employment Rights Act 2008, strengthening labour-related complaint and dispute resolution mechanisms, and ensuring the enforcement of sections 38 and 46 of the Act 2008.[109]

The Committee also highlighted the need to address the high incidences of adolescent pregnancy and unsafe abortion, the lack of clear regulations and protocols, high maternal mortality rates, HIV/AIDS prevalence, and inadequate information on the provision of high-quality care and medical services for women and girls who are victims of gender-based violence. The Committee recommended Mauritius to increase efforts to prevent adolescent pregnancies, fully apply section 235A of the Criminal Code, collect data on access to legal abortion, reduce maternal mortality, ensure access to adequate health services, and train medical personnel to provide specialised attention and care for women and girls who are victims of sexual violence.[110]

The HRC was concerned about the 2012 Criminal Code amendments, which allow voluntary abortions in certain circumstances. It was of the view that many women resort to clandestine abortions, endangering their lives and health. The HRC

[107] UN CEDAW Concluding Observations (2018) para 22–23.

[108] UN CEDAW Concluding Observations (2018) para 24.

[109] UN CEDAW Concluding Observations (2018) para 25.

[110] UN CEDAW Concluding Observations (2018) para 27.

recommended amending legislation to ensure safe, legal, and effective access to abortions in situations where the life or health of the pregnant woman or girl is at risk and prohibits criminal sanctions against women undergoing abortion or medical service providers. It also urged Mauritius to ensure access to affordable contraceptives and quality information on sexual and reproductive rights.[111]

7.3.8 *Economic Empowerment of Women and Economic and Social Benefits*

The Committee welcomed economic and social benefit schemes such as the subsistence allowance scheme and national housing programme, as well as the adoption of a corporate social responsibility policy. It also praised Mauritius' efforts to reduce poverty, such as the Marshall Plan against Poverty and the Poverty Observatory. However, it expressed concerns about the lack of an official poverty line, lack of information on women's participation in poverty reduction strategies, insufficient statistical data, and potential adverse impact of financial policies on women's rights.[112] The Committee recommended Mauritius establish an official poverty line, assess the impact of economic and social benefits on gender equality, establish monitoring mechanisms, and undertake independent assessments of the extraterritorial effects of its financial and corporate tax policies on women's rights and equality.[113]

7.3.9 *Rural Women, Creole Women, Migrant Women, and Women with disabilities and Lesbian, Bisexual and Transgender Women and Intersex Persons*

The Committee raised concern about reports of discrimination against disadvantaged or marginalised groups of women, such as rural women, Creole women, migrant women, and women with disabilities. It noted a lack of data on their situation and their meaningful participation in political decision-making. The Committee recommended collecting data on these women and ensuring their full participation in political decision-making. It also addresses the intersecting forms of discrimination faced by lesbian, bisexual, and transgender women and intersex persons, including discriminatory practices, lack of policy measures, and underreporting of violence.[114] It recommended Mauritius adopt legislative and policy measures to combat discrimination, promote the protection of these rights, ensure law enforce-

[111] UN CEDAW Concluding Observations (2018) para 26 and 28.

[112] UN CEDAW Concluding Observations (2018) para 29.

[113] UN CEDAW Concluding Observations (2018) para 30.

[114] UN CEDAW Concluding Observations (2018) para 31.

ment mechanisms protect them, provide shelter and assistance, and provide training to medical personnel, police, and law enforcement officials.[115]

7.3.10 *Women and Climate Change, Marriage, and Family Relations*

The Committee was concerned about the lack of information on women's involvement in drafting legislation, policies, and strategies, as well as the impact of programmes aimed at engaging women as agents of change.[116] It recommended that Mauritius ensure women are meaningfully involved in the development of legislation, national policies, and programmes on climate change, disaster response, and disaster risk reduction.[117] The Committee also addressed issues related to marriage and family relations, such as the non-protection of women in unregistered Muslim marriages, the lack of legislative measures to protect women's economic and other rights, and the exclusion of women considered "at fault" for divorce from the right to alimony.[118] The Committee recommended reviewing national legislation to make mandatory registration of all marriages, criminalising noncompliance, and considering reinstatement of chapter 9 of the Civil Code. The Committee also recommended reviewing the Civil Code to protect women's property rights, establish a system of equitable division of marital property upon dissolution of de facto relationships, repeal or amend section 145 of the Civil Code to allow consent by parents or guardians, ensure women have a right to alimony, collect, analyse, and disseminate comprehensive data on child marriages, religious marriages, and polygamous marriages and conduct comprehensive awareness-raising campaigns to challenge cultural attitudes that legitimise child marriage and polygamy.[119]

7.3.11 *Data Collection, Analysis, and Dissemination of Concluding Observations*

The Committee acknowledged the development of data collection systems, such as the Domestic Violence Information System and the Child Protection Register, but noted that these systems are insufficient for accurately assessing women's situations, discrimination, and policy development.[120] It urged Mauritius to disaggregate

[115] UN CEDAW Concluding Observations (2018) para 32.

[116] UN CEDAW Concluding Observations (2018) para 35.

[117] UN CEDAW Concluding Observations (2018) para 36.

[118] UN CEDAW Concluding Observations (2018) para 37.

[119] UN CEDAW Concluding Observations (2018) para 38.

[120] UN CEDAW Concluding Observations (2018) para 39.

data by sex, age, disability, ethnicity, location, and socioeconomic status and to enhance data collection, analysis, and dissemination through a centralised system.[121] The Committee also requested the government to ensure timely dissemination of its findings to relevant state institutions, including the Government, ministries, National Assembly, and judiciary.[122]

7.3.12 Equality Between Men and Women and the Right to Work

The Committee on Economic, Social, and Cultural Rights (CESCR) was concerned about the low representation of women in public sector decision-making positions, low participation in the labour market, and the gender pay gap.[123] It recommended that Mauritius review and amend existing laws, adopt measures to end occupational gender segregation, implement the principle of equal pay for work of equal value, and eliminate strong gender role stereotypes through media campaigns, opinion leaders, and public awareness.[124] The CESCR also called for the elimination of strong gender role stereotypes in the agricultural sector and sugar and tea industries.[125] The CESCR expressed concern over the lack of suitable education and training for the labour market, leading to high unemployment rates among young people and women. It recommended intensifying efforts to improve vocational education and training, including the Youth Employment Programme and Back to Work Programme, and addressing the root causes of low female participation and high unemployment.[126]

7.4 The African Human Rights System and Women: The Maputo Protocol

Public life in Africa is still dominated by men as was the case when the OAU Charter and the African Charter were adopted, which saw the absence of any meaningful and effective contribution by women.[127] While the scenario may be changing as

[121] UN CEDAW Concluding Observations (2018) para 40.

[122] UN CEDAW Concluding Observations (2018) para 41.

[123] UN CESCR Concluding observations on the fifth periodic report of Mauritius (5 April 2019) UN Doc E/C.12/MUS/CO/5 hereafter referred to as UN CESCR Concluding Observations (2019) para 23.

[124] UN CESCR Concluding Observations (2019) para 24.

[125] Ibid.

[126] UN CESCR Concluding Observations (2019) para 26–27.

[127] Viljoen (2012), p. 249.

evidenced by a number of heads of African states as well heads of judicial and administrative bodies being women, the pace with which it is changing is alarming. Under the AU, a Solemn Declaration on Gender Equality in Africa was adopted in 2004, calling for the expansion of the principle of gender parity to all the organs of the AU, the regional economic communities (RECs) and national parliaments.[128] In 1995, the OAU Assembly endorsed a recommendation of the African Commission about the idea of having a protocol additional to the African Charter on women's rights.[129] Subsequently, the AU Assembly adopted the Protocol to the African Charter on the Rights of Women in Africa in July 2003 in Maputo (thus the Maputo Protocol) and it entered into force in November 2005.

Viljoen has argued that "the mischief that the Protocol seeks to correct is not the normative deficiency of international human rights law dealing with women's rights, but its lack of implementation".[130] It should be noted that at that time, the African Charter and the UN Convention on the Elimination of All Forms of Discrimination Against Women (the Convention) had almost universal ratification and having another legal instrument on the same subject matter could have been questionable. However, in view of undoing the defects of the existing instruments on women's rights, the Maputo Protocol adopted three strategies: the extension of the substantive scope of existing legal instruments, the improvement of legal and quasi-legal means to ensure compliance, and the extension of non-legal forms and methods of implementation.[131]

7.4.1 Expanding the Scope of Women's Rights in Africa

Prior to the adoption of the Maputo Protocol, African states were no doubt bound by the provisions of the Convention and the African Charter. For instance, discrimination on the basis of sex was prohibited by article 2 of the African Charter while article 3 provided for equality before the law. For the purpose of illustration, when article 5 of the African Charter provides for the right of "every individual" to dignity, this also includes women. However, one may not be faulted for forming an impression that the African Charter, for instance through article 18 on special treatment and specific measures, only viewed women "within the context of the family, and are deserving of special protective measures, in the same sense as are children, aged and the disabled". In addition, these special measures to protect women are not delineated in the African Charter but instead are to be found in "international declarations and conventions". Given that the Convention was passed only two years before the African Charter, there was less chances that the latter would have drawn

---

[128] AU Doc Assembly/AU/Dec.12(III)Rev.1 (July 2004).

[129] OAU Doc AHG/Res.240(XXXVI).

[130] Viljoen (2012), p. 251.

[131] Ibid.

inspiration from the former. Indeed, Oloka-Onyango and Tamale have argued that those who drafted the African Charter were "only minimally influenced by the CEDAW's provisions" given that only article 18 the African Charter deals with women's rights directly. They also contended that the wording of that article showed that the Convention was incorporated "by inference and not by name" which demonstrated a lack of enthusiasm by African leaders towards the Convention also.[132]

Focusing specifically on the additional normative value of the Maputo Protocol and in comparison with the Convention, Viljoen has argued that:

> the Protocol primarily brings into the open the Charter's shrouded premise that women are included in its protective mandate. Compared to the CEDAW, the Protocol speaks in a clearer voice about issues of particular concern to African women, locates the CEDAW in African reality, and returns some casualties of quests for global consensus into the fold. The perception that the Protocol is superfluous because the CEDAW already accords women the protection provided for under the Protocol is therefore incorrect.[133]

Indeed, the Maputo Protocol has been the first instrument to address the issue of medical abortion, HIV/AIDS, domestic violence, and polygamy in a legal binding manner. Article 11 conferred detailed and explicit protection of women in armed conflict while article 4(2)(k) emphasised the necessity to provide women refugees adequate protection under international law. The definition that the Maputo Protocol gives to issues such as discrimination against women, violence against them, and harmful practices to which they are subject is significantly expansive in comparison with the Convention. Viljoen has argued that the Maputo Protocol has provided for specificity in areas where vagueness used to prevail such as the notion of "positive African values" by clarifying that these values are "based on the principles of equality, peace, freedom, dignity, justice, solidarity and democracy".[134] It also legally oblige states to criminalise marital rape in a more specific manner compared to the Convention and stipulates that the minimum age for marriage should be 18 without any derogation. Vulnerability of women resulting from poverty, loss of spouse, disability, or old age is also addressed from articles 21 to 24 of the Maputo Protocol.

The Maputo Protocol goes beyond the scope of the rights provided by the African Charter by outlining the content of rights and by incorporating the right to adequate housing and food security. It also lays down the scope of socio-economic rights in greater detail than the Convention, which restricted some socio-economic rights to "rural women". States also have a responsibility to combat the detrimental impacts of globalisation and take into account how trade with other countries may affect women in accordance with article 19(f). The Maputo Protocol emphasises corrective and targeted positive or affirmative action, taking a fundamentally transformative attitude. While it reiterates the need for "positive" measures by placing them in diverse settings, the Convention only provides a generic clause allowing for "temporary special measures aimed at accelerating the de facto equality between

[132] Oloka-Onyango and Tamale (1995), p. 691.

[133] Viljoen (2012), p. 257.

[134] Viljoen (2012), p. 254.

men and women". Pre-empting arguments based on formal equality, the Protocol mandates that in order to maintain substantive equality, nations must implement policies that may favour women over men, including women electoral quotas. In addition, affirmative action is expressly needed to address "discrimination in law", illiteracy and education.

Given that the Committee and the African Commission have generally expanded the scope of the relevant treaties through comments, resolutions, concluding observations, and findings, one may argue that the differences between the Maputo Protocol, the African Charter, and the Convention are more "apparent than real".[135] These explanations may have a lot of persuasive weight, but they do not impose any legal requirements and obligations. The Maputo Protocol unquestionably advances norms by making such explanations legally enforceable and by adding to them.

The Protocol is a huge step forward for standard-setting, but there are some areas where it could have been improved, and its drafting is regrettable and inelegant. The text fails to reflect how HIV/AIDS disproportionately affects women in Africa. Regardless, the entitlement to receive information about one's own and one's partner's HIV status "in accordance with internationally recognised standards and best practices" is vague and therefore not to serve as the basis for the diminution of rights.[136] Furthermore, there is insufficient reflection of the feminisation of poverty, particularly in rural Africa. The "rights-holders" in the Protocol are inconsistently drafted; males are occasionally expressly included in the range of rights, but at other times excluded. The Protocol restates certain but not all existing relevant state duties and does not systematically expand upon the provisions of the African Charter due to its dearth of a "clear vision" of its status as a supplement to both the Convention and the African Charter.[137]

7.4.2 Enhancing Compliance

The African Commission and the Committee had the authority and mandate to advance women's rights in African governments even prior to the Protocol's implementation. The reporting criteria established by the African Commission mandated that states report on matters related to women's rights, going much beyond the provisions of the African Charter. Nearly all reporting states supplied some information about domestic protection of women's rights, regardless of whether they did not adhere to the Guidelines. Examining these reports included a lot of discussion and questions about gender and sex, particularly after a Special Rapporteur on the Rights of Women in Africa was appointed. Women's rights NGOs have not made use of the opportunity to submit reports alongside state reports, despite having the

---

[135] Viljoen (2012), p. 254.

[136] Article 14(1)(e) of the Maputo Protocol.

[137] Viljoen (2012), pp. 255–256.

option of doing so. Women and advocates for women's rights have always had access to the communications procedure, but they have brought very few cases, and concerns that are important to women are primarily brought up as "secondary or indirect" issues. Many African states have filed reports under the CEDAW, but no complaints have been filed under the Optional Protocol to the Convention against any of them.[138]

The implementation of the Maputo Protocol is likely to be impacted by the primary causes of the shortcomings in the supervisory procedures under the Charter and the CEDAW, which include a lack of reporting obligations compliance, a failure to domesticate treaty provisions and implement concluding observations, and a limited use of the complaint's mechanism. The Maputo Protocol does not develop new procedures or mechanisms to enhance execution. It is an addition to the African Charter and is overseen by the African Commission, which also oversees the African Charter, using the same procedures and mechanisms. The Guidelines for State Reporting under the Protocol to the African Charter on the Rights of Women in Africa were adopted by the African Commission in November 2010.[139]

These Guidelines make some progress towards integrating the reporting requirements under the African Charter with the Maputo Protocol, even if the latter did not seek to solve the problems with state reporting. States that have ratified the Protocol as well as the Charter must submit a single report, with one section covering the Maputo Protocol and the other the African Charter. Additionally, a differentiation between initial and periodic reports is made. States should use the data in their CEDAW reports to lessen these worries, even if adding another reporting requirement on women's rights could result in even more duplication and fragmentation. However, the Maputo Protocol may become more accessible to women if domestic enforcement by courts is strengthened. The Maputo Protocol goes beyond both the Convention and the African Charter, mandating that states guarantee women's efficient access to the legal system through, among other things, the provision of legal aid schemes for women. It also closes a gap in the African Charter by stating that "appropriate remedies" should be given. The legal basis of implementation is additionally reinforced by the Maputo Protocol, which not only makes certain measures mandatory but also expressly calls for their enforcement.[140]

Viljoen has argued that in the absence of increased activism and public awareness of state reporting, these steps are unlikely to enhance treaty monitoring, Interaction, as well as additional processes.[141] The Maputo Protocol will increase compliance because it serves as a clear symbol around which more awareness can be raised and social movements can be organised. Nevertheless, the most reliable means of guaranteeing implementation are still effective domestication and domestic legal action.

---

138 Viljoen (2012), pp. 257–258.

139 Viljoen (2012), pp. 258–259.

140 Viljoen (2012), p. 259.

141 Viljoen (2012), p. 257.

7.4.3 Non-legal Implementation

The Maputo Protocol seeks to address the paradox of non-compliance with the law by creating more laws by giving preference to non-legal ways of execution or "realization". To guarantee that the Maputo Protocol's commitments will undo deeply ingrained patterns and practices, states must take action beyond mere legislation. Viljoen has argued that:

To this end, a golden thread of political empowerment, education, sensitisation outreach, public awareness, and resource allocation is interwoven with the legal guarantees of the Maputo Protocol. The principle of "mainstreaming" gender into processes of decision making, policy formulation, and implementation must feature prominently.[142]

The Maputo Protocol recognises that "social and economic measures" might be employed in addition to legislation to abolish violence against women. States must also identify and address the "causes" of violence against women in order to go beyond the legislative process. The Maputo Protocol cautions governments that they need to back "initiatives" at all levels in order for them to prosper.[143] Legal prohibitions against damaging practices are supplemented by psychological support services and vocational training. Adequate budgetary allocation enhances and is directly linked to the justiciability of socio-economic rights.[144] The Maputo protocol places a great deal of emphasis on prioritising the use of existing resources, as evidenced by the requirement placed on governments to "reduce military expenditure significantly in favour of spending on social development".[145]

The Maputo Protocol addresses the frustration of unfulfilled treaty promises most effectively through the purposeful fusion of legal and non-legal means of implementation. The advancement of women's rights through the African regional system depends on the continued pursuit of this strategy. The African Commission is the only body in the AU that deals with gender-related problems and women's rights. The Directorate for Women, Gender, and Development, which is positioned under the AU Commission Chairperson, is tasked with making sure that gender mainstreaming is implemented in all AU initiatives. The African Peer Review Mechanism (APRM) under NEPAD includes gender equality mainstreaming and the advancement and upholding of women's rights as integral components. By urging states to create national policies for empowering women economically and deciding that these policies ought to be incorporated into the APRM assessment criteria, the AU Executive Council made a significant contribution to the gender-sensitive evolution of the APRM.[146]

---

[142] Viljoen (2012), p. 258.

[143] Article 2(1)(e) of the Maputo Protocol.

[144] Article 4(2)(i) of the Maputo Protocol.

[145] Article 10(3) of the Maputo Protocol.

[146] Viljoen (2012), p. 259.

7.5 Mauritius and the Maputo Protocol

Mauritius seems to be focused more on a policy-based approach to women's rights than a human-rights-based approach pertaining to the welfare and advancement of women. While one approach complements the other, the absence of one undoubtedly affects the whole system of women's rights. In relative terms, Mauritian women's rights have witnessed significant progress and evolution compared to other countries in Africa, and arguably around the world. A number of key factors, social, political, economic and cultural, have contributed to this. However, given the potential that the country has in advancing women's rights, it can be argued that not enough is being done and much more could and should be achieved.

The African human rights system, spearheaded by the Maputo Protocol, is a force to reckon with. Its boundless potential to bring positive and sustainable change and improvement to women's rights in Mauritius cannot be ignored anymore. While the policy and institutional framework on women's rights in Mauritius can be considered as being decent, the legal framework is hugely unsatisfactory and below the required standard. However, the state and other stakeholders have not focused on this issue since the apparent situation on women's rights seems decent and acceptable. This chapter has shown that there are a number of critical issues to be addressed in this field, as highlighted time and again by international treaty bodies. In this sense, Mauritius has likely been a victim of its relative success by letting a degree of complacency creep in. This explains why no state report has been submitted on the Maputo Protocol, no complaint has been submitted on issues of women's rights to the African Commission, and the African women's rights system is not known and employed enough by those working in this field.

This needs to change, and now. The State needs to interact more with the African women's rights system by submitting, diligently and meaningfully, all its state reports to the African Commission for the latter to monitor the implementation of women's rights domestically. That mentality of "mission accomplished" by submitting state reports to the CEDAW Committee and ignoring the "lesser important" Maputo Protocol's state report must be done away with. It is the legal obligation of the state to find the resources and the expertise to draft those reports in full and meaningful collaboration with civil society organisations, with their contents reflecting ground realities and with the appropriate political will for the government to act and implement measures on areas of concern that the African Commission would underline after considering those reports.

With a few exceptions such as age of marriage and property rights, a majority to the provisions of the Maputo Protocol has not been domesticated in Mauritius, and for that matter, neither have been those of the Convention. These provisions therefore cannot be invoked before judicial bodies in Mauritius, and this is a significant hurdle in the protection and promotion of women's rights. Bodies such as the Human Rights Division under the Ministry of Foreign Affairs, the National Human Rights Commission, the Equal Opportunities Commission and the Office of the Ombudsperson for Child (for the girl child) must adopt a proactive role in lobbying the government to proceed with the domestication of the provisions of the Maputo Protocol. It has to be underlined that they have been quite passive concerning this issue. Legal practitioners working on cases of women's rights should refer to these provisions more frequently and systematically in their pleadings and arguments. On the other hand, judges must use legal techniques to bypass the hurdle of dualism and interpret these provisions wherever possible and in line with their duty of judicial activism for the benefits of women's rights. Through their *obiter dicta*, they should consistently, and persistently, remind the legislature and the executive of the need to domesticate the Maputo Protocol.

Civil society organisations have a critical role to play in enhancing the interaction of the state and citizens with the Maputo Protocol and the African human rights system in general. They should be aware that, with or without the observer status, they must adopt a proactive role in advancing women's rights in Mauritius using the Protocol and available mechanisms at the African level. For instance, they should be on the forefront in submitting shadow/parallel reports to the African Commissions whenever the state submits its periodic reports. The substantive contents of these reports must guide the African Commission to accurately query the state on specific issues relating to women's rights in view of formulating concluding observations that would call on the state to act, through legislative and other means. They should also make use of the complaint mechanism of the African Commission to submit cases of women's rights violation for quasi-judicial or judicial remedies. This is crucial as it allows the African Commission to develop a set of jurisprudence on Mauritian women's rights based on the Maputo Protocol, especially given that domestic courts cannot do so because of lack of domestication. In turn, this jurisprudence can be put into use to pressurise the government to bring changes, through legislation or various other ways that the Protocol advocates for as previously discussed in this chapter.

References

Beebeejaun-Muslum ZN (2024) Gender relation, patriarchal control, and domestic violence: a qualitative study in Mauritius. Eur J Human Soc Sci *4*(3):9–19

Dey D (2014) January. Indentured laborers and the native women in Mauritius: the colonial perspectives. In: Proceedings of the Indian History Congress (Vol. 75). Indian History Congress, pp 989–995

EJS Center for Women and Development (2025) Mauritius: progress and challenges for women in politics. Available at https://ejscenter.org/mauritius-progress-and-challenges-for-women-in-politics/. Accessed 10 July 2025

Emambokus WBS, Oogarah-Pratap B (2019) Exploring parents' and teachers' perspectives about school-based sexuality education in a multicultural context: a case study in Mauritius. Educ Proc Int J 8(3):185–195

End GBV 'Mauritius' (2025). Available at https://endgbv.africa/mapping/mauritius/#:~:text=Subsequent%20amendments%20to%20the%20PDVA,and%20enhanced%20enforcement%20officer%20powers. Accessed 10 July 2025

Epstein CF (2007) Great divides: the cultural, cognitive, and social bases of the global subordination of women. Am Sociol Rev 72(1):1–22

Explanatory Memorandum of the National Women's Council Act (2016). Available at https://gender.govmu.org/Documents/legislations%202020/National%20Women's%20Council%20Act%202016.pdf. Accessed 10 July 2025

Global Gender Gap Mauritius. Available at https://npccmauritius.org/images/download/293.pdf. Accessed 15 July 2025

Hein C (1984) Jobs for the girls: export manufacturing in Mauritius. Int Lab Rev 123:251

Jansen KA (2005) Abuse and suffering. A feminist perspective on domestic violence, bodies and battered women's coping strategies in Mauritius (Master's thesis, The University of Bergen)

Mauritius Chamber of Agriculture. The Use of Pesticides Act 2018. Available at https://mauritius-chamber-of-agriculture.org/wp-content/uploads/2022/12/Use-of-Pesticides-Act-2018.pdf. Accessed 10 July 2025

McKinsey and Company (2017) Women Matter: Time to accelerate - Ten years of insights into gender diversity. Available at https://www.mckinsey.com/~/media/mckinsey/featured%20insights/women%20matter/women%20matter%20ten%20years%20of%20insights%20on%20the%20importance%20of%20gender%20diversity/women-matter-time-to-accelerate-ten-years-of-insights-into-gender-diversity.pdf. Accessed 10 July 2025

Ministry of Environment (2025a) Solid waste management and climate change 'Climate Change Information Centre'. Available at https://environment.govmu.org/Pages/CCIC.aspx. Accessed 10 July 2025

Ministry of Environment (2025b) Solid Waste Management and Climate Change 'Information and Education Unit. Available at https://environment.govmu.org/Pages/Information-and-Education-Division.aspx. Accessed 10 July 2025

Ministry of Gender Equality and Family Welfare (2022a) National Gender Policy 2022-2030. (March 2022) <https://gender.govmu.org/Lists/DocumentsLinks/Attachments/3/National%20Gender%20Policy%202022-2030.pdf> Accessed 01 July 2025

Ministry of Gender Equality and Family Welfare 'A gender approach' (2022b). Available at https://gender.govmu.org/Documents/Statistics/Statistics%20in%20Mauritius%20A%20Gender%20Approach%20Year%202022%20%20Final230224.pdf. Accessed 15 Jay 2025

Ministry of Gender Equality and Family Welfare (2025a.) 'Gender Unit' Available at https://gender.govmu.org/Pages/Gender-Unit.aspx. Accessed 10 July 2025

Ministry of Gender Equality and Family Welfare 'Family Welfare and Protection Unit' Available at https://gender.govmu.org/Pages/Family-Welfare-and-Protection-Unit.aspx. Accessed 10 July 2025b

Moghadam VM, Senftova L (2005) Measuring women's empowerment: participation and rights in civil, political, social, economic, and cultural domains. Int Soc Sci J 57(184):389–412

Mujuzi JD (2017) Marriage by foreign nationals to Mauritian citizens: a comment on Section 19A of the Civil Status Act of 1981. Int Surv Fam Law:225

National Service Framework for NCDs (2023–2028). Available at https://health.govmu.org/health/wp-content/uploads/2024/06/National-Service-Framework-for-NCDS-2023-2028.pdf. Accessed 10 July 2025

National Gender Policy 2022-2030 (2022) Available at https://gender.govmu.org/Documents/2022/NationalGenderPolicy2022-2030.pdf (Accessed 30 June 2025).

National Strategy and Action Plan of the High Level Committee on the Elimination of Gender Based Violence in the Republic of Mauritius 2020-2024. Available at https://police.govmu.org/police/?mdocs-posts=national-strategy-and-action-plan-gender-based-violence-2020-2024. Accessed 10 July 2025

National Strategy and Coasted Action Plan for Women Entrepreneurship Development in Mauritius (2023). Available at https://gender.govmu.org/Lists/DocumentsLinks/Attachments/20/NSCAP%20Final%20Publication.pdf (Accessed 10 July 2025)

Oloka-Onyango J, Tamale S (1995) The personal is political or why women's rights are indeed human rights: An African perspective on International feminism. Human Rights Quart 17:691

Packer C (2002) Using Human Rights to change tradition: traditional practices harmful to women's reproductive health in Sub-Saharan Africa. Intersentia, Antwerp

Pat MKS, Manraj M, Fauzee J, Sewsurn S, Parkin DM, Manraj S (2019) Trends in cancer incidence in the Republic of Mauritius, 1991–2015. Cancer Epidemiol 63:101616

Ramtohul R (2008) Globalisation and gendered citizenship: the Mauritian Scenario. In: CODESRIA Gender Symposium on 'Gender and Citizenship in the Age of Globalisation' (pp 8–10)

Statistics Mauritius (2022) Economic and social indicators. Available at https://statsmauritius.govmu.org/Documents/Statistics/ESI/2023/EI1730/CJS_ESI_Yr22_300623.pdf. Accessed 15 July 2025

Tandrayen-Ragoobur V (2014) Gendering governance: the case of Mauritius. Equal Diver Inclusion Int J 33(6):535–563

UN Women Africa 'Mauritius Country Profile' (2022). Available at https://africa.unwomen.org/sites/default/files/2023-11/maurituis_gender_equality_profile.pdf. Accessed 10 July 2025

UNDP (2020) The Next Frontier: Human Development and the Anthropocene. Available at https://www.undp.org/sites/g/files/zskgke326/files/migration/mu/HDR-2020%2D%2D-Mauritius-Country-Note.pdf. Accessed 15 July 2025

Viljoen F (2012) International human rights law in Africa, 2nd edn. Oxford University Press, Oxford

World Bank Group (2012) World Development Report 2012: Gender Equality and Development. Available at https://openknowledge.worldbank.org/entities/publication/51c285f6-0200-590c-97d3-95b937be3271. Accessed 10 July 2025

Chapter 8
Children's Rights in Mauritius

Abstract The rights of children in Mauritius have emerged as a crucial topic. Both the domestic legal system and international human rights documents, such as the African Charter on the Rights and Welfare of the Child (African Children's Charter) and the UN Convention on the Rights of the Child (CRC), contain these rights. The welfare of children in Mauritius, as well as the advancement and defence of their rights, are directly under the purview of domestic organisations such the Children's Court, the Child Development Unit, and the Office of the Ombudsperson for Children (OOC). In order to assess the level of protection afforded to children's rights in Mauritius, the ensuing section focusses on them as well as specific laws.

8.1 Introduction

As at July 2023, around 290,000 Mauritians were under the age of 18 which makes it around 23% of the Mauritian population to be children.[1] Children therefore represent a key population in Mauritius and the promotion, protection, respect, and fulfilment of their rights become the utmost duty and responsibility of the state and others. Through the welfare state system, Mauritius has been relatively successful to guarantee the welfare and well-being of children in terms of education[2] and health[3] with access to both free and of an acceptable quality. According to UNICEF, 95%

[1] Statistics Mauritius (2023a), p. 3.

[2] Statistics Mauritius (2023b)—The government's education expenditure for 2022/2023 was estimated at Rs 20,762 million, compared to Rs 18,434 million in 2021/2022. Pre-primary education had 769 schools, with 23,776 children enrolled. Primary education had 325 schools, with 89,001 pupils, 49.3% girls. Secondary education had 179 schools, 98,900 students, 51.7% girls, and 8992 teachers. The percentage of school candidates meeting the Primary School Achievement Certificate (PSAC) requirements increased from 80.6 in 2021/2022 to 83.1 in 2022, with a decrease in School Certificate (SC) pass rates and an increase in Higher School Certificate (HSC) pass rates. Tertiary education enrollment increased from 49,497 in 2021 to 50,566 in 2022.

[3] Statistics Mauritius (2023b), p. 6—In the Republic of Mauritius, there were 168 infant deaths (deaths to children under one year old) in 2023 compared to 172 in 2022, a 2.3% decrease. The

R. Mahadew, *Mauritius and African Human Rights Law*,
https://doi.org/10.1007/978-3-032-08832-1_8

of the child population has access to basic sanitation services and 100% to safe drinking water in Mauritius.[4]

Nevertheless, in spite of initiatives by the Mauritian government, civil society, and other stakeholders, many children continue to suffer threats such as poverty, discrimination based on race or disability, sexual exploitation, and abuse.[5] Mauritius has a significant number of street children, mostly aged 11–16, who are driven to the streets due to poor family relationships and poverty. These children are vulnerable to abuses such as violence, prostitution, drug addiction, and exploitative labour.[6] Drug addiction is a key issue, often influenced by poverty, and its use also promotes HIV/AIDS transmission among children. Mauritius faces a significant issue of sexual exploitation, particularly among girls, despite state measures. The country is a major destination for child sex offenders, with high-street children, drug abuse, lack of education, and stigma contributing to the problem. Most cases are unsolved, highlighting the urgent need for better solutions.[7] Child abuse in Mauritius is prevalent, with 5448 cases registered in 2022.[8] Common causes include poor socio-economic status, custody conflicts, drug abuse, and unstable households. Despite government efforts to eliminate violence, rehabilitation of victims remains a challenge. The main causes are usually sexual trauma, negligence, unstable family situations, school abandonment, and precarity.[9]

Against the above backdrop, the rights of the Mauritian child become an essential subject matter. These rights are to be found in the domestic legal framework and in international human rights instruments such as the UN Convention on the Rights of the Child (CRC) and the African Charter on the Rights and Welfare of the Child (African Children's Charter) specifically. Domestic institutions such as the Office of the Ombudsperson for Children (OOC), the Child Development Unit (CDU), and the Children's Court are directly responsible for the welfare of children in Mauritius and the promotion and protection of their rights. The following section focuses on them and on selected legislation in view of gauging the protection conferred to children's rights in Mauritius.

---

number of newborn deaths per 1000 live births, called the infant mortality rate, fell from 14.2 in 2022 to 13.1 in 2023.

[4] UNICEF 'Mauritius' (2024).

[5] Humanium (2025).

[6] Report on Street Children in Mauritius (2012).

[7] U.S. Department of State (2025).

[8] Ministry of Gender Equality and Family Welfare (2023).

[9] Ombudsperson for Children (2022), p. 62.

8.2 Institutional Framework on Children's Rights in Mauritius

8.2.1 The Ministry of Gender Equality and Family Welfare and its Departments

This Ministry is dedicated towards the protection of women, children, and the family as a unit with a mission statement as follows 'We undertake to design and implement policies and programmes geared towards promoting gender equality and equity, protecting the rights of children and enhancing their overall development and promoting the welfare of families'.[10] Its vision is to 'have a society free from violence and discrimination based on sex, where the fundamental rights of our citizens including children are respected and where human values within the family and the civil society are cherished'.[11] In relation to children, the main objectives of the Ministry are (1) to promote and defend children's rights as human rights, work for the elimination of all forms of violence and discrimination against children defined as being in the age bracket of 0–18 years and ensure that legal measures are taken and mechanisms are put in place to promote safety and security of children and (2) to promote the development and welfare of children from the very tender age in accordance with the Convention on the Rights of the Child (CRC), to promote family welfare and to combat gender-based violence.[12] It is noted that the African Children's Charter is not mentioned herein the objectives of the Ministry.

8.2.1.1 Planning and Research Unit

The Planning and Research Unit (PRU) is a technical support unit within the Ministry of Mauritius, responsible for designing policies, programmes, and projects promoting gender equality, child development, family welfare, and community well-being. It prepares short, medium, and long-term plans of action and reports on these issues and acts as a liaison with government institutions and non-state actors. The PRU also establishes base line data on women, family, and children in health, education, and employment fields and produces an annual report on statistics in Mauritius-A Gender Approach. As of August 17, 2020, the scope of the PRU has expanded to include licensing of places of safety, residential care institutions, and registration of child day-care centres. The PRU also initiates studies and research on

[10] Ministry of Gender Equality and Family Welfare 'Mission and Vision' available at https://gender.govmu.org/Pages/Mission-and-Vision.aspx (accessed 10 July 2024).

[11] Ibid.

[12] Ministry of Gender Equality and Family Welfare 'About the Ministry' available at https://gender.govmu.org/Pages/About-the-Ministry.aspx (accessed 10 July 2025).

social/cultural development and situation analysis for children, families, and women.[13]

8.2.1.2 Child Development Unit

The Child Development Unit (CDU) was set up in 1995. It is meant to guarantee the rights of Mauritius children to survival, protection, development, and participation are respected and promoted in the best interests of the child in accordance with the UN Convention on the Rights of the Child. In instances where parents fail to fulfil their parental responsibilities, the State, through the CDU, is required to step in and take over. The CDU is required to act promptly to protect the child. In essence, the CDU offers 24/7 protection services for victims of violence, abuse, and neglect through the provision of emergency services, follow-up sessions, legal support, and life skills training. They also provide alternative care for abused children and services for commercially and sexually exploited children. The CDU acts as a Central Authority in international child abduction cases, provides trained mentors, and promotes community safety and actions in child protection and welfare.[14]

Their strategy is based on upholding the Children's Act 2020, developing alliances with pertinent parties, strengthening and improving the efficiency of current reporting mechanisms, and promoting knowledge and instruction about children's rights in Mauritius. Additionally, it seeks to positively influence and impact regional and national child development and protection programmes. The CDU's services are intended to provide psychological assistance, counselling, and protection. To offer children who have been abused timely support and protection, the Child Protection Unit (CDU) runs nine Child Protection Services (CPS) across different regions. The CPS provides multidisciplinary help, which includes family therapy, legal advice referrals, social and psychological counselling, removal from danger, placement in shelters, reintegration/rehabilitation, and referrals to other institutions. In cases of suspected child abuse, the Ministry of Gender Equality and Family Welfare's Supervising Officer looks into the matter, takes action, and, in accordance with section 36 of the Children's Act 2020, may request an Emergency Protection Order. Children, victims, and family members can talk about abuse issues in a safe setting by attending in-person counselling sessions offered by the CDU in outstations. In order to improve parent–child relationships, they also offer parenting classes and run an integrated support centre with a 24-hour hot line service. In order to help victims deal with life's challenges, psychological support is offered.[15]

The CDU has a mandate on commercial sexual exploitation of Children in Mauritius. The Mauritius Family Planning and Welfare Association (MFPWA)

---

[13] Ministry of Gender Equality and Family Welfare 'Planning and Research Unit' available at https://gender.govmu.org/Pages/-Planning-and-Research-Unit.aspx (accessed 10 July 2025).

[14] Ministry of Gender Equality and Family Welfare 'Child Development Unit'.

[15] Ibid.

manages a Drop-in-Centre, which handles cases of sodomy, child prostitution, sexual harassment, abuse, abortion, teenage pregnancy, and rape under the monitoring of the CDU. Services include long-term counselling, medical sessions, parental counselling, home visits, prevention and sensitisation, referrals to NGOs, echography, clinical services, laboratory tests, group activity therapy, vocational courses, and radio programmes. The Residential Drop-in-Centre (GRNW) provides safe shelter, education, family mediation, medical care, and networking. All suspected child trafficking incidents are reported to the Ministry and are kept on file for social inquiry at the CDU level. The Police are notified of the cases concurrently for Criminal Inquiry.

The Child Development Unit in Mauritius handles international child abduction cases, adhering to the Hague Convention on the Civil Aspects of International Child Abduction. It provides information on a child's whereabouts and social background, applies for their return, and ensures their rights are exercised. Regular amendments to the Act's schedules and a high-level Steering Committee monitor the process are necessary. Section 14 of the Civil Status Act 1982 allows parents to declare a child within 45 days of birth. In the absence of parents or court order, the Permanent Secretary of the Ministry declares the child. The Tardy Declaration of Birth Section under the Child Development Unit facilitates tardy declarations under court order. The CDU collaborates with stakeholders to register children with shorter delays. Children with extended declaration delays are directed to the District Court for self-registration.

8.2.1.3 National Children's Council

Section 3 of the National Children's Council Act 2003 establishes the National Children's Council. The Council's objectives include implementing the Ministry's activities related to children, upholding their rights, promoting their welfare, and promoting their interests in matters of interest. Established under section 8, the National Children's Board identifies areas for improvement, develops good practices, commissions research, establishes a knowledge centre, establishes links with organisations, and performs other functions conducive to its objectives.[16] The National Children's Committee, set up under section 13, is a group of 15 young people aged 15–18, elected every 2 years from registered children's organisations. It has a President and Vice-President and meets at least once every 3 months. The Committee can discuss child welfare and provide its views to the Board. A Secretary is appointed by the Board. Children's organisations include Kids' and Teens' Clubs, Educational Institution Students' Councils, and non-governmental associations.[17]

[16] Section 9 of the National Children's Council Act.

[17] Section 13(3) - 13(6) of the National Children's Council Act.

8.2.1.4 Others

In response to court rulings, the Ministry places children considered to be at risk in Residential Care Institutions (RCI). With the aim of promoting family relations and bonding, care plans are designed and regular supervised visits are given to 14 RCIs, of which 5 are government-owned and the other 14 are administered by NGOs. Financial, emotional, social, and spiritual assistance are offered by foster parents through the Ministry's Foster Care Program for residential care facilities. The Children's Act 2020 and the Child (Foster Care) Regulations 2022 came into force in January 2022. The Adoption Unit is responsible for managing legitimation cases and assisting with the adoption of children from other nations. It governs both domestic and international adoptions and supervises international adoptions in compliance with the 1993 Hague Convention on Inter-country Adoption. The unit's objectives include ensuring best practices and eliminating abuses, advising the Minister on adoption demands, and collaborating with other countries to prevent child abduction, sale, and trafficking.[18]

8.2.2 Office of the Ombudsperson for Children

The Ombudsperson for Children Act 2003 establishes the Office of the Ombudsperson for Children (OOC) in section 3. According to section 5, the Ombudsperson is responsible for ensuring that children's rights, needs, and interests are fully considered by various authorities, promoting their rights and promoting compliance with the CRC and African Children's Charter, one of the few legislations on children that refers to the Charter. The OOC is responsible for proposing legislation, policies, and practices related to children's rights and services. It advises the Minister on residential placement facilities, protects children's rights, and ensures fair treatment. It also initiates investigations into child rights violations, investigates cases of child labour, and addresses complaints. It advises the Minister on mechanisms for children to express themselves freely and create partnerships with parents, teachers, and other stakeholders. It equally investigates cases of abandoned or street children, child labour, and complaints related to children's rights. Its role is to promote children's rights and ensure their safety.[19]

The OOC is responsible for investigating child rights complaints, including requesting information, entering premises, examining the child's environment, assessing employment, and ensuring their safety. It may also request the Commissioner of Police to investigate allegations of child rights breaches, record statements, request assistance from public bodies, summon witnesses, and obtain necessary records. After an investigation, the OOC acts as a mediator, reports to

[18] Ministry of Gender Equality and Family Welfare 'Adoption Unit'.

[19] Section 6 of the Ombudsperson for Children Act 2003.

appropriate authorities, and proposes general proposals to the Minister. They cannot investigate cases pending before a court but may refer children involved in such cases to the Ministry for advice, assistance, or counselling.[20] From July 2022 to August 2023, the Office of the Commissioner (OCO) resolved and closed 91.3% of its 446 new complaints. The complaints ranged from basic school issues to complex societal issues like family conflicts, domestic violence, abuse, neglect, and poverty. The main complaint category was school problems related to transport, transfers, admissions, and infrastructure. Other cases involved compounded difficulties, such as family conflict, child behavioural problems, and sexual abuse.[21] The annual reports of the OOC also shows that it engages in extensive thematic reporting on various issues such as teenage pregnancy, climate change and children's rights, parental alienation and education, and children with disabilities. Its proactive role during the Covid-19 pandemic and its effects on children and services available to them should also be noted.[22]

The engagement of the OCO with the African Children's Charter has been through training workshops to better understand the Charter.[23] The Charter is also often cited in its reports to specifically refer to its provisions.[24] While these are commendable efforts, the OOC should envisage making a more substantive use of the Charter especially in its advisory role to the Ministry and the state. It should take a leading role in advocating for the domestication of the Charter and for submission of state reports to the African Committee of Experts on the Rights and Welfare of the Child (ACERWC). This will enable it to fulfil its legal obligation of promoting compliance with the Charter as set out in sect. 5(c) of the Ombudsperson for Children Act 2003 in a more effective manner.

8.2.3 Children's Court

The Children Court (CC) was a much-awaited judicial creation and the CtRC welcomed 'the strengthening of the specific protections for children in contact with the justice system, including through the adoption of the Children's Court Act 2020'.[25] Section 3 of the Children's Court Act 2020 (CCA) provides that the CC consists of a Protection Division and a Criminal Division. The Protection Division has jurisdiction to hear and determine applications under Part IV of the Children's Act 2020 and other matters directed by the Chief Justice. All proceedings are conducted similar to

[20] Section 7 of the Ombudsperson for Children Act 2003.

[21] Annual Report of the OOC (2022–2023), p. 416.

[22] Annual Report of the OOC (2019–2020), pp. 19–50.

[23] Annual Report of the OOC (2022–2023), p. 18.

[24] Annual Report of the OOC (2021–2022), p. 78.

[25] Concluding Observations (2023) para 43.

civil matters before a Magistrate of the Intermediate Court.[26] The Criminal Division has jurisdiction to hear and determine criminal offences committed on a child, a child witness, a juvenile offender, and other matters in the best interests of the child, child witness, or juvenile offender. The Director of Public Prosecutions may lodge other matters, and a Magistrate of the Criminal Division can hold a preliminary inquiry involving a child. All proceedings before the Children's Court are conducted similarly to criminal matters before a Magistrate of the Intermediate Court.[27]

The CCA emphasises on a child-friendly environment for proceedings before the CC and any other court involving children. Vouching for a caring and sensitive approach towards children, court proceedings involving a child must be conducted in a simple, comprehensible language, with appropriate arrangements made for the child's evidence and their parent's presence unless otherwise determined. Courts must ensure no disrespectful treatment of the child's dignity, taking into account their personal situation, needs, age, gender, disability, and maturity. They must also not require the child to give evidence against their will or without their parents' knowledge.[28]

The CC has made mention of the African Children's Charter when referring to international obligations of the state pertaining to children's rights. However, it is noted that when it comes to the substantive interpretation of these rights, the CRC is mostly used.[29] It is contended that magistrates of the CC have a primordial duty to ensure that the African Children's Charter is referred to in their decisions. This effort from the judiciary will positively impact on compliance with the Charter as well as incite legal practitioners to use the provisions of the Charter in their legal practice. As would be discussed later in this chapter, the unique features of the Charter, in comparison with the CRC, should be utilised for a more progressive and contextual interpretation of children's rights by the CC. There is also a need for education and training for the benefits of the magistrates of the CC to enhance their use and reference to the Charter.

8.3 Legal Framework on Children's Rights in Mauritius

There are several legislations in place in Mauritius to protect children. For instance, the Criminal Code plays a critical role in protecting children from offences against them. Legislation such as the Data Protection Act, the Cybersecurity and Cybercrime Act, the Protection from Domestic Violence Act, the Education Act, the Child Sex Offenders Register Act, the Public Health Act and the Combating of Trafficking in

[26] Section 5 of the CCA.

[27] Section 8 of the CCA.

[28] Section 12 of the CCA.

[29] Police v Minor JNEP 2023 CCT 47 3; Tawun Kuttur V Police 2023 CCT 44 3; Police v Minor SNM 2023 CCT 39; Police v Asha Sufurally 2023 CCT 34; Police v Perles & anor S 2023 CCT 1.

Persons Act inter alia have all contributed towards the protection of children's rights. In the same vein, the Constitution also, through its Bill of Rights, conferred constitutional guarantees to children as individuals, regarding civil and political rights despite not mentioning them or giving them a special status which is a serious lacuna. Indeed, section 28 of the Constitution of South Africa explicitly provides that every child has the right to a name and nationality from birth, family care, basic nutrition, shelter, healthcare services, and social services. They are protected from maltreatment, neglect, abuse, and exploitative labour practices. They are not required to perform work that is inappropriate for their age or puts their well-being at risk. Detention is only as a last resort and should be kept separately from detained persons over 18. A child's best interests are paramount in all matters concerning them.[30]

In the above context, this section focuses mainly on the Children's Act 2020 (CA) as the major legislation on children's rights in Mauritius. It should be noted that the CA has regulations such as the Child (Foster Care) Regulations 2022, Children's (Conduct of Child Mentors) Regulations 2024, Residential Care Institutions for Children Regulations 2022, and the Child Day Care Centres Regulations 2022 which regulate specific matters pertaining to children.

The CA enshrines the principles provided for in the CRC and the African Children's Charter such as the best interests of the child[31] non-discrimination,[32] survival and development, and child participation.[33] Section 8 provides for a Child Services Coordinating Panel which was recommended by the CtRC in 2015.[34] The Panel is responsible for coordinating child-related public services, monitoring administrative arrangements, collaborating with stakeholders, considering cases referred by the Ministry, making recommendations, setting up committees, advising the Minister on matters governed by the CA, and fulfilling other prescribed functions.[35]

Section 11(1) of the CA provides that no person shall discriminate against a child on the ground of the child's, or the child's parent's, race, caste, place of origin, political opinion, colour, creed, sex, language, religion, property, or disability. Compared to article 3 of the African Children's Charter, this protection is not extended to a child's legal guardians but only to the parent. Additionally, grounds such as birth, fortune, and other status based on which discrimination is prohibited as per the Charter are not included in section 11(1). This limits the scope of application of section 11(1). Section 12 prohibits marriage of both civil and religious, and cohabitation with a child (which is defined as a person under 18 as per section 2 of the CA) in alignment with article 21(2) of the Charter.

[30] Section 28(2) of the Constitution of South Africa.

[31] Section 4 of the CA.

[32] Section 11 of the CA.

[33] Section 5 of the CA.

[34] Concluding Observations (2015) para 14.

[35] Section 8 of the CA.

The CA provides for ill-treatment of child, corporal and humiliating punishment on child, abandonment of child, abduction of child by parent, abduction of child by other person, removal of child from place of safety, causing, inciting or allowing child under 16 to be sexually abused, child prostitution and access to brothel, child pornography, child grooming, sale of alcohol to child, allowing child to have access to gaming house, mendicity, bullying and causing or inciting child to do unlawful act as criminal offences to which significant punishments are attached.[36] This is in line with the UN optional protocols to the CRC which Mauritius has ratified. There is no doubt that these provisions, especially as an upgrade from the previous Child Protection Act, will enhance the protection of children against these acts. The previous law catered for ill-treatment, sexual offences, child trafficking, licensed premises, and mendicity only.[37] Prohibition of some of the offences above is aligned with article 27 on sexual exploitation and article 29 on sale, trafficking, and abduction of children of the African Children's Charter.

Part IV of the CA is focused on children in need of assistance, care, and protection. Section 31 provides for a list of instances where a child can be considered to be in need of care and protection, while section 32 guarantees police assistance to a child in need. Section 33 lays down the procedure and framework within which an assessment of a child in need of care and protection is to be conducted. Section 34 imposes a duty of mandatory reporting on any person having reasonable grounds to believe that a child is being or likely to be exposed to harm. This is followed by a number of care and protection orders, namely the emergency protection order, placement order, ancillary order, long-term care order, and contact order.[38] This is an extensive upgrade from the Child Protection Act which mainly focused on emergency protection order.

Children with serious behavioural concerns are also catered for by section 41 and 42 of the CA. The Mauritius Probation and Aftercare Services can apply for parenting support intervention if a child exhibits serious hostile, aggressive, or disruptive behaviour that interferes with their care and development. The child's parent or the Police must lodge an application with the probation officer, which will include an initial psycho-social assessment, a parenting support intervention plan, at least two home visits by a parenting aide, and a follow-up assessment. The probation officer must issue a letter certifying the intervention's success.[39] The Child Mentoring Scheme, established in section 43, aims to assist children aged 8–16 who are victims of neglect, have behavioural problems, are distressed, or have social adaptation issues. The scheme is administered by a supervising officer, who receives and considers volunteer applications, registers child mentors, provides guidance and assistance, identifies children needing protection, supervises placements, forwards progress reports, and discharges other functions. No child can be placed under the

[36] Section 11–26 and 28 of the CA.

[37] Section 13–17 of the Child Protection Act 1994.

[38] Section 36–40 of the CA.

[39] Section 41 of the CA.

scheme without a mentoring order, and a child mentor cannot be assigned more than three children.

The Child Mentoring Scheme is a legal mechanism for children who need assistance from a mentor. If the supervising officer believes that the child may require assistance, the parents are unwilling to provide it, it is in the best interest of the child, and there is no alternative means, they can apply for a mentoring order to have the child placed under the scheme. The application must include a report from the supervising officer, a psychological report, and other relevant information. Upon receipt of the application, the Magistrate may summon and examine the parent, child mentor, or other appropriate person to determine the child's suitability as a mentor. The Magistrate must consider factors such as the nature and gravity of the child's problem, infrastructural facilities near the child's residence, the availability and preference of the parents, and other relevant matters.

A mentoring order, provided by section 46 of the CA, may remain in force for up to 12 months, and the supervising officer or parent may apply for a variation or discharge of the order. A mentoring order grants the supervising officer the power to gather evidence, enter the premises, cause medical examinations or treatment, request police or medical assistance, prevent a child mentor from continuing to mentor a child, and conduct investigations into complaints against a child mentor. The Commissioner of Police will provide necessary assistance to the supervising officer for the effective exercise of his powers under a mentoring order. The owner, occupier, or person in charge of the premises must provide reasonable facilities and assistance for the effective exercise of their powers under the mentoring order. Parents or persons with influence over a child subject to a mentoring order must provide assistance to the child mentor to enable them to effectively perform their duties.

The CA has also provided for a much-,needed legal framework on the child offenders, child victims and child witnesses. Regarding criminal responsibility of children, a child under 14 cannot be prosecuted for any criminal offence. If a police officer suspects a child who has committed an offence, they must conduct an enquiry and inform the Ministry responsible for probation and aftercare services. The Ministry will place the child in a safe place and arrange for an assessment by a probation officer and a psychologist. If a child is referred to a probation officer, they must conduct an assessment to establish the circumstances leading to the offence. The officer may refer the child for counselling, support services, or a meeting to help establish the circumstances and develop a plan of intervention.[40] The probation officer assesses children accused of offences before appearing before the Criminal Division of the Children's Court. They determine if the child needs care, age, and potential diversion. The officer maintains confidentiality and can conduct the assessment at any location, with the parent attending unless disrupted. They may co-opt a

[40] Section 49 and 50 of the CA.

suitable person or request a police officer if the child is at risk of escaping or endangering them.[41]

The Director of Public Prosecutions can request a probation officer to assess if a juvenile would be better off in a diversion programme or if criminal proceedings should be discontinued. If the officer finds it in the juvenile's best interests, the Director may offer the juvenile to enrol in the programme. If the officer finds it unsuitable, the Director may institute criminal proceedings against the juvenile. A diversion programme is an individualised non-residential supervision and rehabilitation scheme implemented by the Ministry to rehabilitate the juvenile without resorting to formal criminal proceedings. The programme must be for a defined period, not exceeding 3 years, and the progress of the juvenile is monitored. If the programme is not in the juvenile's best interests, the Director of Public Prosecutions will decide whether criminal proceedings should be initiated or re-instituted.[42]

The detention of a juvenile offender is a last resort measure, and the Commissioner of Police must ensure that the juvenile is separated from adults while detained, being conveyed to or from a court, or waiting for court attendance. A female juvenile must be under the care of a woman police officer. If a juvenile is charged with an offence or brought before a court, their parents must attend the court during all stages of the proceedings. The court may issue a summons to the parent, directing them to appear at a specified time and place. If the parent fails to appear, the court may issue a warrant for their arrest.[43]

The court must require a probation officer to prepare a pre-sentence report for a juvenile convicted of an offence other than a contravention. The report should include information about the juvenile's character, whether training in a Correctional Youth Centre or Rehabilitation Youth Centre is necessary, and other relevant matters. The court may remand the juvenile to the appropriate institution while seeking information or conducting a special medical examination. The court can discharge the juvenile unconditionally or conditionally, order fines and costs, commit the juvenile to the care of a parent or close relative, commit the juvenile to custody in a reform institution for juveniles, sentence them to imprisonment, or deal with the case in any other legal manner. The Commissioner of Police must provide places of remand and detention for juvenile offenders, and the authority or persons responsible for the management of any institution may agree with the Commissioner of Police for the use of the institution or any part of it as a place of detention on terms agreed upon. Juveniles detained in a place of detention are considered to be in legal custody. Those who assist or induce a juvenile to escape or harbour or conceal them are liable for penal servitude for a term not exceeding 8 years.[44] It has to be noted that the above provisions of the CA are more or less aligned with article 17 of the African Children's Charter on administration of juvenile justice.

[41] Section 51–54 of the CA.

[42] Section 55–56 of the CA.

[43] Section 57–59 of the CA.

[44] Section 61–64 of the CA.

While there is a strong institutional and legal framework on children in Mauritius, the lack of a human rights-based approach should be nevertheless highlighted. For instance, the only explicit right provided to children by the CA is the right to privacy.[45] Rights such as the rights to freedom of movement, freedom of association, freedom of thought, conscience and religion, the right to education, and the right to health and health services, which are all provided by the African Children's Charter, are not at all mentioned and therefore explicitly protected by the CA. This is a major drawback in terms of the completeness of the legal framework on children's rights in Mauritius, which is not remedied by the non-domestication of the Charter in Mauritian law. In this vein, several lacunas in the normative and legal frameworks on children's rights in Mauritius have been highlighted by the CtRC which exposes the Mauritian reality on the subject matter and negates the much-utilised welfare state system to justify some of these lacunas. The following section focuses on these gaps and challenges in Mauritius.

8.4 UN Observations on Children's Rights in Mauritius

Mauritius acceded to the UN Convention on the Rights of the Child (CRC) in 1990, and it became a state party to the Optional Protocol to the CRC on the Involvement of Children in Armed Conflict in 2009. After having signed the Optional Protocol to the CRC on the Sale of Children, Child Prostitution, and Child Pornography in 2001, it was ratified in 2011. It has to be highlighted that Mauritius has only signed the Optional Protocol to the CRC on a Communication Procedure in 2012 and has not yet ratified it till date. This implies that no complaints against abuses or violations of the rights of children can be submitted to the UN Committee on the Rights of the Child (CtRC). The CtRC has urged Mauritius to ratify the said Protocol in its Concluding Observations when the latter is submitted in state report in 2023.[46]

The CRC remains the main international standard often used as a barometer for measuring the effectiveness of the legal framework on children's rights in Mauritius. The Concluding Observations that are issued by the CtRC following the submission of state reports by the country provide for an accurate indication of the progress (or regress) made by Mauritius regarding children's rights. This section focuses on them to provide an account of the enormous work that is left to be done in this field despite advancements such as the enactment of the Children's Act 2020. Additionally, the substantive contents of these Concluding Observations often do not reach concerned stakeholders notably civil society organisations and therefore what the state has to do in terms of children's rights often remain unknown to people in general.

[45] Section 27 of the CA.

[46] Concluding Observations (2023) para 45.

8.4.1 General Measures of Implementation

The legal status of the CRC was questioned by the CtRC stating as follows:

The Committee notes that under the State party's Constitution, the Convention is not directly applicable and cannot be invoked as an enforceable source of rights unless it is enacted through Mauritian legislation and that the Convention is rarely invoked before and referred to by the domestic courts. The Committee also notes with concern that State officials and regional and municipal authorities are not sufficiently aware of their obligation to promote the implementation of the Convention.[47]

Focusing on the implementation of the provisions of the CRC, the CtRC stated that it was concerned that the National Child Protection Strategy did not incorporate all of the Convention's requirements and that the Action Plan had not been fully implemented, even though it welcomed the Strategy and its Action Plan and noted the National Human Rights Action Plan 2012–2020.[48] In order to ensure coordination with the planned update of the National Human Rights Action Plan 2012–2020 and the anticipated Ten-Year Strategic Plan for Children, the Committee recommended in 2023 that Mauritius renew the National Child Protection Strategy and Action Plan (2014–2022), making sure that it covered all areas covered by the Convention and supporting its implementation with adequate human, technical, and financial resources, as well as a clear assignment of responsibilities.[49]

The issue of coordination among the various authorities dealing with children's rights has also been underlined by the CtRC. In order to minimise duplication with the work of the National Children's Council, the Ministry of Gender Equality and Family Welfare, and the National Human Rights Monitoring Committee, the CtRC urged Mauritius to strengthen the Child Services Coordination Panel, which was established by the Children's Act 2020. This will be done by ensuring that the panel has enough authority, resources, and a clear mandate.[50] Regarding allocation of resources, it was recommended that Mauritius establish a budgeting process that incorporates a child-rights perspective, clearly allocates funds for children to the appropriate sectors and agencies, and includes specific indicators and a tracking system to monitor and evaluate the adequacy, efficacy, and equity of the distribution of resources allocated for the implementation of the Convention. The CtRC recalled its general comment No. 19 (2016) on public budgeting for the realisation of children's rights and its previous recommendation.[51]

The CtRC acknowledged Mauritius' efforts to gather data in various areas and, recalling its earlier recommendation and referring to its general comment No. 5 (2003) on general measures of implementation, has advised Mauritius to expedite the creation of the common data platform in order to gather disaggregated data on

---

[47] Concluding Observations (2015) para 7.

[48] Concluding Observations (2015) para 11.

[49] Concluding Observations (2023) para 7.

[50] Concluding Observations (2023) para 8.

[51] Concluding Observations (2023) para 9.

the circumstances surrounding children with special protection needs, such as those with HIV, disabilities, alternative care, living on the streets, victims of abuse or violence against them, including sexual exploitation and trafficking, and children in conflict with the law.[52] In relation to independent monitoring of children's rights, the CtRC specifically entrusted this responsibility to the Ombudsperson for Children Office (OCO) and recommended that it evaluates how well its communication plan (2016–2023) is working to raise children's understanding of their right to register complaints and make the necessary revisions to make sure the complaint procedures are clear, private, and kid-friendly.[53]

While tourism is one of the primary foundations of Mauritius' economy, the CtRC raised concerns that Mauritius has not yet established adequate measures to protect children from rights abuses resulting from tourist-related activities. In line with its general comment No. 16 (2013) on State obligations regarding the impact of the business sector on children's rights, the CtRC has advised the state to review and modify its civil, criminal, and administrative legal framework in order to ensure the legal accountability of businesses and their subsidiaries operating in or managed from the State party's territory, particularly in the tourism industry, and to set up monitoring mechanisms for the investigation and redress of violations of children's rights in order to improve accountability and transparency. Additionally, it was suggested that Mauritius bolster its international cooperation against the sexual exploitation of children in relation to tourism by implementing multilateral, regional, and bilateral initiatives for preventing and eradicating such practice. This would involve launching campaigns to raise awareness among the travel industry and the general public on the prevention of child exploitation in the context of travel and tourism as well as widely disseminating the World Tourism Organisation's Global Code of Ethics for Tourism among travel agents and organisations operating in the industry.[54]

8.4.2 General Principles and Civil Rights and Freedoms

Observing the principle of non-discrimination stipulated in the Children's Act 2020 and in Sustainable Development Goal targets 5. 1 and 10.3, the CtRC recommended that Mauritius tackle disparities in accessibility to all social services for children who have been excluded and disadvantaged, particularly children living on the streets, children experiencing abuse and violence, such as sexual abuse, children utilising drugs, children without a family environment, children with disabilities, and children involved in the juvenile justice system. Additionally, the CtRC recommended that Mauritius regularly assess the extent to which these children are enjoying their rights. Additionally, it urged Mauritius to undertake particular action to

[52] Concluding Observations (2023) para 10.

[53] Concluding Observations (2023) para 11.

[54] Concluding Observations (2023) para 14.

enhance the living conditions of Chagossian children by guaranteeing their efficient access to social services, housing, water, sanitation, health care, and education. It also called on Mauritius to promote the work of the Equal Opportunities Commission and encourage children, especially those who are marginalised and disadvantaged, to report instances of discrimination.[55]

The CtRC recommends strengthening efforts to integrate the right of a child to have their best interests considered in all legislative, administrative, and judicial proceedings, policies, programmes, and projects affecting children despite the fact that it has been enshrined in the Children's Act 2020. It also recommends building capacity for social workers, educators, and judges to enhance their capacity of determining the child's best interests. It equally recommended implementing legislation that recognises the right of a child to be heard. The provision of child-friendly information on child-related laws and appropriate training for professionals involved in children's care in line with its General Comment No 12 (2009) was also part of the recommendations of the CtRC.[56] It urged Mauritius to strengthen processes of birth registration, to ensure the prevention of child trafficking, to guarantee the provision of birth certificates to all children born in its territory without undue delay and to establish a national mechanism focusing on the determination of statelessness. Mauritius was also invited to ratify the Convention relating to the Status of Stateless Persons of 1954 and the Convention on the Reduction of Statelessness of 1961. It also recommended strengthening legislative provisions to protect children's privacy in the digital environment, training media and professionals, and applying deterrent sanctions for violations of children's right to privacy.[57]

8.4.3 Violence against Children

The CtRC has emphasised the importance of protecting children from corporal punishment and other cruel or degrading forms of punishment. It recommended strengthening legislative implementation, establishing protocols for action when corporal punishment occurs, and promoting attitudinal change within families and communities. The CtRC also addressed child abuse, violence, and neglect, highlighting the ineffective response to domestic violence cases, lack of awareness among children, re-traumatisation of victims, and inadequate research on the prevalence of violence and neglect.[58]

The CtRC urged the State party to strengthen the response to reports of violence, abuse, and neglect, including increasing trained first responders, finalising the renewed National Child Protection Strategy and Action Plan, ensuring children

[55] Concluding Observations (2023) para 16.

[56] Concluding Observations (2023) para 17 and 18.

[57] Concluding Observations (2023) para 19.

[58] Concluding Observations (2023) para 21 and 22.

access to child-friendly complaint mechanisms, developing child-based protocols, issuing emergency protection orders, addressing child marriage, implementing the Residential Care Institutions for Children Regulations 2022, building inspectors' capacity to identify abuse cases, raising awareness on bullying, and strengthening the Domestic Violence Information System. These measures aim to ensure the protection of children and promote a safer environment for all in line with the General Comments No 13 (2011).[59]

The CtRC acknowledges the adoption of the Child Sex Offenders Register Act 2020 and the Children's Court for sexual offences against children. However, it was concerned about the high level of sexual exploitation and abuse of children, particularly in travel and tourism, prostitution, and online sexual abuse. The CtRC also noted the lack of provisions in law to explicitly sanction such crimes and the lack of coordination among governmental institutions and civil society. It urged the State party to formulate policies to raise awareness, prosecute perpetrators, establish a comprehensive collection of data, improve software tools for detecting and investigating sexual abuse, promote accessible channels for reporting, mandate the Child Services Coordination Panel to foster cooperation, and facilitate access to restitution measures, including compensation.[60]

8.4.4 Family Environment and Alternative Care

The CtRC recommended several measures to improve the lives of children in various situations. It highlighted the need for strengthening the National Parental Empowerment Programme, promoting positive child-rearing and discipline, and ensuring capacity-building in decision-makers. It also addressed the issue of children deprived of a family environment, highlighting the insufficient resources for child rescue and protection services, inadequate monitoring of care, and lack of information about children living in alternative care arrangements. The CtRC also recommended increasing resources for professionals working with families and children, establishing quality standards for alternative care settings, providing accessible channels for reporting neglect, violence, and abuse, and providing adequate support for children leaving care. The CtRC called for the finalisation of the draft Adoption Bill, establishing a register of eligible children and identified adoptive parents, and strengthening the capacity of the judiciary to assess the best interests of children when sentencing caregivers. It equally emphasised the importance of protecting visitation rights for children of incarcerated parents and conducting a study on their situation. These measures aim to provide psychological and social support and benefits to these children.[61]

---

[59] Concluding Observations (2023) para 23.

[60] Concluding Observations (2023) para 24 and 25.

[61] Concluding Observations (2023) para 26–29.

8.4.5 Children with Disabilities

The Children's Act 2020 and the Children's Court Act 2020 both offer special attention to children with disabilities, which the CtRC applauded. However, it expressed concerns about the lack of a legal framework based on the human rights model of disability, negative attitudes and discrimination against children with disabilities, lack of social and community-based services, insufficient inclusive schools, and lack of access to early screening and intervention for developmental disabilities. It urged the State party to adopt a human rights-based model of disability and set up a comprehensive strategy for the inclusion of children with disabilities. This includes finalising the Protection and Welfare of Persons with Disabilities bill, strengthening training for professionals, implementing the Special Education Needs Authority Act 2018, supporting parents, and assessing the impact of community-based rehabilitation programmes.[62]

8.4.6 Basic Health and Welfare

The CtRC recommended Mauritius to ensure better health outcomes for children by disseminating basic health information, reducing neonatal, infant, under-5, and maternal mortality rates, and strengthening mental health services and programmes. It also highlighted the need for insufficient sexuality education in schools, restricted access to contraception, high rates of adolescent pregnancy, unsafe abortion, and maternal mortality. The CtRC also highlighted the hindering effect of stigmatisation and discrimination on early prevention efforts against HIV infections and drug and alcohol abuse on adolescents' health. Furthermore, it recommended decriminalising abortion, facilitating access to safe abortion and post-abortion care services for adolescent girls, empowering adolescents to make responsible decisions on sexual relationships, harmonising the National HIV Action Plan with policies promoting sexual and reproductive health, and reviewing the National Drug Control Master Plan to address drug use by children.[63]

The CtRC also emphasised the impact of climate change on the rights of the child, recommending that the State party involve children in its implementation of the Climate Change Act 2020 and renew climate change adaptation and mitigation strategies. It also recommended strengthening the capacities of professionals in the social assistance sector to effectively implement measures to support children living in poverty and prioritising the delivery of child-related social protection programmes.[64]

[62] Concluding Observations (2023) para 31 and 32.

[63] Concluding Observations (2023) para 34–35.

[64] Concluding Observations (2023) para 36–37.

8.4.7 *Education, Leisure, Cultural Activities, and Special Protection Measures*

The CtRC recommended that Mauritius ensures compulsory education without discrimination, particularly for children in marginalised and disadvantaged situations. This includes collecting and analysing data on children not in school, increasing the number of educational social workers conducting home visits, and supporting adolescent girls who are pregnant or have given birth. The goal is to ensure equal parenting support and support services during pregnancy, childbirth, and postnatal care.[65]

The CtRC recommended that Mauritius develops legislation and regulations to address the needs of refugee and asylum-seeking children, apply the principle of non-refoulement to children in need of international protection, guarantee cost-free access to basic social services, and consider ratifying the 1951 Convention relating to the Status of Refugees and the 1967 Protocol relating to the Status of Refugees. It also recommended conducting awareness-raising activities among businesses and within the travel and tourism industry on the prevention of economic exploitation, including child labour, and implementing the Workers' Rights Act 2019 stipulating age 16 as the minimum age of employment. Building the capacity of employers, workers, and law enforcement authorities to identify and refer to children victims of exploitation or trafficking was also recommended.[66]

The CtRC additionally recommended ensuring that the National Action Plan to Combat Trafficking in Persons 2022–2026 considers the specific needs of child victims and prioritises the allocation of resources to the provision of holistic and multidisciplinary services for their care, rehabilitation, and reintegration. Strengthening the capacity of relevant authorities, including labour inspectors, law enforcement, border management authorities, and staff of judicial and front-line services, was also recommended. The CtRC also urged Mauritius to bring its child justice system fully into line with the Convention and other relevant standards. This includes limiting the duration of pretrial detention by law, amending the Children's Act 2020, facilitating applications for legal assistance to children within the criminal justice system, promoting probation, bail, mediation, counselling, or community service, using detention as a measure of last resort, and building the capacity of all law enforcement actors to respect child criminal justice procedures.[67]

[65] Concluding Observations (2023) para 38.

[66] Concluding Observations (2023) para 39–40.

[67] Concluding Observations (2023) para 41–45.

8.5 The African Charter on the Rights and Welfare of the Child

The year 1979 was declared as the Year of the Child by the UN as a result of which the OAU adopted the Declaration on the Rights and Welfare of the African Child.[68] The Declaration served as a source of inspiration for states to undertake legal and educational measures in view of eradicating cultural practices such as female circumcision and child marriage despite its non-binding nature.[69] Pursuant to the adoption of the CRC by the UN in 1990, the OAU adopted the African Charter on the Rights and Welfare of the Child (the African Children's Charter) on the 11th of July 1990. Viljoen has argued that there were political reasons for the adoption of the African Children's Charter. On the political front, there was a perception that African states were excluded and marginalised in the drafting process of the CRC with only nine African states having actively participated in the drafting process.[70] Africans desired a legal instrument on children's rights in Africa which would demarcate itself from the CRC and would take into account the African realities that children were and still are facing today.

In comparison to the CRC, the African Children's Charter therefore presents some unique features despite the fact that the two instruments are complementary rather than oppositional. The CRC has been the product of a number of compromises given that it is a global instrument to the detriment of regional specificities. Legally speaking, there was a need to adopt an African instrument on children's rights which would take into genuine and meaningful consideration African realities. Muthoga identified key omissions from the CRC such as children living under apartheid, factors disadvantaging the female child, prevalent African practices such as female genital mutilation and circumcision not explicitly outlawed, socio-economic conditions including illiteracy and sanitary conditions, meaningful participation of children in basic programmes designed for them, a compulsory minimum age for military service in the context of African child soldiers, and the role of the family in the upbringing of children.[71]

The African Children's Charter addressed these omissions to a significant extent. It completely prohibited and outlawed the use of child soldiers in article 22(2) contrary to the CRC. It explicitly prohibited child marriage in article 21(2) while the CRC allowed it in cases where majority is acquired at an earlier age before 18 as per article 1 of the CRC. Furthermore, it extended its protection to internally displaced children in article 23(4) which the CRC does not. Article 11(6) of the African Children's Charter imposes an obligation of state parties to provide for the possibility of children 'who become pregnant before completing their education' to continue with their schooling contrary to the CRC. Article 30 favoured non-custodial

[68] OAU Doc AHG/st.4(XVI)Rev.1(1979).

[69] Ibid para 3.

[70] Viljoen (2015) 392.

[71] Muthago (1992), p. 4.

punishment for mothers who are expecting or who have found children given that they are the primary care taker of children generally in Africa, something which had not been catered for by the CRC. Article 29(b) required state parties to take all necessary measures to address the issue of children being used for begging, while article 26 accorded the 'highest priority' to the 'special needs' of children living in apartheid which remains applicable even today in cases where regimes practice racial, religious, ethnic, or other forms of discrimination. Regarding the best interests of the child, the African Children's Charter referred to it as 'the primary consideration' in article 4(1) while the CRC stipulated that it is 'a' rather than 'the' primary consideration. Thus, as argued by Viljoen, the African Children's Charter has 'fulfilled the objective of supplementing the CRC with regional specificities without eroding the notion of universality'.[72]

One of the standout African features of the African Children's Charter is the imposition of duties and responsibilities on the African child similar to the African Charter. Viljoen argued that this feature gives effect to the 'subordinate role of the children within the strict age-based hierarchy of traditional African societies'.[73] However, he underlined that these duties should be interpreted in the context of the African Children's Charter and international human rights. For instance, he argues that the duty to obey a parent at all times should be given a contextual interpretation since it is subject to the age and ability of the child and to 'such limitations as may be contained in the present Charter' as stipulated in article 31. Such a duty must be counterbalanced with the child's freedom of expression and right to privacy in addition to the parent's responsibility to 'ensure that the best interests of the child are their basic concern at all times' as per article 29(1)(a).[74] Umozurike has argued that including duties of children in the African Children's Charter obliges the state parties to 'instil these duties in their subjects'.[75]

It is apposite to underline a few weaknesses of the African Children's Charter despite the fact that its positive and unique features outweigh the weaknesses. The right to social security and to an adequate standard of living is not catered similar to the African Charter. As such, one has to rely on the African Commission's interpretation of the African Charter which provides that the right to shelter and to nutrition are 'implied' in the African Charter[76] and on the fact that the Maputo Protocol on the Rights of Women in Africa does include these rights. Therefore, this can justify an updated interpretation of the African Children's Charter as a living instrument in the light of the aforementioned instruments. Another weakness is the omission of a child's right to access information contrary to the CRC which emphasises on this particular right. Additionally, the existence of 'claw-back' clauses in article 7 and 8(3) of the African Children's Charter has also been criticised since they have the

[72] Viljoen (2015), p. 393.

[73] Viljoen (2015), p. 394.

[74] Viljoen (2015), p. 394.

[75] Umozurike (1997), p. 65.

[76] SERAC v Nigeria.

potential of eroding certain rights contained therein. Viljoen argued that this can be remedied by the interpretation of these clauses in a way that is more conducive to the realisation of children's rights as per article 1(2) of the Charter.

Kaime has argued that despite its resonance with African realities, the philosophy of the African Children's Charter, understood in the light of the CRC, is not one of 'difference or otherness' but rather 'the need for complementarity and contextualisation'.[77] He further stated that the Charter is an instrument 'both in keeping with African traditions and values and well-suited to its unique social, economic, political and cultural environment, whilst at the same time maintaining its universalist outlook'.[78]

It is thus argued that the legal obligations of Mauritius towards children's rights should be a combination of the provisions of the CRC and the African Children's Charter. However, similar to the discussion on the domestication of the CRC above, the African Children's Charter has not been domesticated in Mauritius. The Children's Act 2020 does not effectively and internally domesticate the provisions of the Charter which implies that invoking these provisions before Mauritian courts is highly challenging given the dualist nature of the country. There has been a timid attempt to cite provisions of the Charter by the Children's Court on the basis of their persuasive value but not in a legal binding manner since these provisions are not domesticated. Yet, these provisions are completely relevant to Mauritian children and their rights.

Culturally, the Mauritian realities may be different from mainland African realities of the African Children's Charter and the universal 'realities' of the CRC. It can also be agreed that Mauritian children are not affected by practices such as female genital mutilation or child soldiers. However, the unique features of the Charter can no doubt enhance the interpretation of children's rights in Mauritius in addition to those of the CRC. The domestication of the provisions of the Charter into Mauritian laws will greatly enhance the interpretation of children's rights and particularly the provisions of the Children's Act 2020 both in terms of its scope and its substantive content. Additionally, this will complete the picture in terms of children's rights in Mauritius given that the Children's Act 2020 does not necessarily provide for the full list of rights of children, especially socio-economic ones. A valid and legitimate impression is that since becoming a state party to the African Children's Charter in 1992, there has been a state lethargy, if not lack of commitment, to domesticate it. It also has to be admitted that there has been no genuine effort from the academic community, legal practitioners, and civil society organisations working on children's rights to push for its domestication. A lack of understanding of the Charter and an over-prioritisation of the CRC may arguably be reasons behind the critical non-domestication of the Charter in Mauritius. It is therefore critical for concerned stakeholders to focus on convincing the state to seriously contemplate the

[77] Kaime (2009), p. 57.

[78] Ibid.

domestication of the Charter, which by all means is a legal duty of Mauritius following the ratification of it.

8.6 Mauritius and the African Committee on the Rights and Welfare of the Child

It is important to outrightly point out the lack of interaction between Mauritius and the African Committee on the Rights and Welfare of the Child (ACERWC). The CtRC has even highlighted this issue by recommending that Mauritius should 'cooperate with the African Committee of Experts on the Rights and Welfare of the Child of the African Union on the implementation of the Convention and other human rights instruments'.[79] Yet, the ACERWC is essential and its relevance to children's rights in Mauritius cannot be undermined.

The ACERWC was founded in July 2001 in compliance with Article 32 of the African Children's Charter, which came into effect on November 29, 1999. The ACERWC is an African Union body tasked with overseeing the Charter's implementation and advancing and defending children's rights throughout the continent. Due to its unique role as a regional quasi-judicial treaty organisation that exclusively handles child-related matters, the Committee is highly specific. Articles 32 to 45 of the African Children's Charter serve as the foundation for the Committee's mandate. The primary responsibilities of the ACERWC are outlined in Article 42 of the Charter and include: monitoring the implementation of the Charter, interpreting its provisions, protecting and advancing the rights of children, and carrying out any other duties assigned to it by the Assembly of the Heads of State, Government, and Organs of the African Union.

In accordance with article 42 to 45 of the African Children's Charter and the ACERWC's Rules of Procedure, some of the primary responsibilities and activities of it are examining State Party Reports regarding the Charter's implementation status, examining communications regarding purported breaches of the Charter, conducting inquiries, and visiting countries to evaluate the Charter's execution, developing Guidelines and General Comments as Norms and Standards for subjects covered by the Charter, conduct studies and research on the continent's children's rights challenges, taking the lead in celebrating the Day of the African Child and issue declarations, letters of urgent appeal, and resolutions and monitoring the progress and implementation of the Agenda 2040. In carrying out its mandate, the ACERWC may also set up unique procedures and give particular assignments to a member or group of members for the planning of its meetings or the carrying out of unique projects, studies, and programmes.

The eleven members of the ACERWC are supposed to possess strong moral character, honesty, objectivity, and expertise in issues concerning children's rights

[79] Concluding Observations (2023) para 48.

and well-being. They are chosen by secret ballot by the Assembly of Heads of State and Government from a list of nominees provided by the State Parties to the Charter. Up to two candidates may be nominated by each State Party; these candidates must be nationals of an AU Member-State that is also a State Party to the Charter. When choosing ACERWC members, gender and regional representation are taken into account. Each member acts in their individual capacity rather than on behalf of a State. There cannot be more than one national from the same nation on the ACERWC and the members are elected once every 5 years and have a one-time term of office. Louis Pierre Robert Ahnee has served as member from 2001 to 2005.

8.6.1 State Reporting

According to article 43(1) of the African Children's Charter, a state party must submit a state report to the ACERWC initially 2 years after ratification and thereafter every 3 years. There is an obligation for a more regular submission compared to the CRC which is every 4 years. State reports allow the ACERWC to monitor the implementation of the Charter domestically by the state parties. It also allows for the ACERWC to assess measures taken by state parties to implement the concluding observations and recommendations of the ACERWC issued following any previous report submitted by the state parties. Civil society organisations and other stakeholders can be indirectly involved in the consideration of state reports through the submission of shadow reports or directly through an active participation in the drafting of the state reports. This allows the ACERWC to have an accurate overview of children's rights and the implantation of the African Children's Charter domestically.

It should be noted that Mauritius has not submitted its initial state report. Such a delay can only show the critical lack of commitment of the state towards the ACERWC and the African human rights system in general. As per the Guidelines for Reports, Mauritius is only required to 're-submit' reports already submitted under the CRC together with a 'supplementary report' dedicated to the unique provisions of the African Children's Charter without any duplication.[80] Despite this flexibility provided by the ACERWC in view of lessening the burden on States, Mauritius has failed to honour its obligations in terms of state reporting. This is contrasted with the relative seriousness with which it submits its state report under the CRC to the CtRC. One cannot be faulted to believe that there is a sense of non-committal towards the African human rights system on children's rights on this basis.

[80] Guidelines on Reports para 24–25.

8.6.2 Communications

The competence for the ACERWC to receive individuals and inter-state communications (complaints) is automatically accepted by state parties to the African Children's Charter upon its ratification.[81] The ACERWC has issued Guidelines for Communications in order to facilitate the understanding and employment of this important mechanism. It should be noted that state parties can place reservations on the powers of the ACERWC regarding communications. For instance, Egypt has placed a reservation on article 44, excluding the right of individuals to petition the ACERWC in cases of alleged violations of children's rights.[82] Viljoen has argued that such reservations 'undermines the object and purpose of the Charter, which is not only to set out substantive rights, but also a compulsory procedure through which these rights can be vindicated'.[83]

Any interested party, including victims, any group of people, CSOs, intergovernmental organisations and agencies, and State Parties, may submit a communication to the Committee in accordance with Article 44 of the Charter and Section I of the Guidelines on Communications. If a communication is prepared with the best interests of the child in mind, it may be submitted without the victims' agreement. The ACERCW therefore allows for *actio popularis* and has adopted a broad legal standing approach to submit communications before it. After receiving a communication, the ACERWC evaluates it to determine if it satisfies the requirements outlined in Section II of the Guidelines on Communications regarding form and content. It then assesses the communication's admissibility in light of the standards outlined in Section IX of the Guidelines for Communications. Following a declaration of a communication's admissibility, the ACERWC evaluates the case's merits in relation to the claimed violations. The Committee has the power to determine whether the State Party in question has breached any right of the African Children's Charter and to order that state to make amends in the merit's determination.

In cases where a right has been infringed, the state in question must provide an update on how the ACERWC's decisions are being implemented. The ACERWC monitors the application of its decisions on communications through a variety of follow-up initiatives. According to section XXII of the Guidelines on Communications, they include, among other things, follow-up country visits, implementation hearings as permitted by the Guidelines, reports to the Executive Council of the African Union, and so on. Additionally, the Committee established a Working Group on Implementation of Decisions, whose primary responsibility is to oversee the ACERWC's decisions as they are carried out.[84] A complaint to the Committee

---

[81] Article 44 of the African Children's Charter.

[82] ACERWC 'Egypt' <https://www.acerwc.africa/en/member-state/ratifications/62/egypt> accessed 01 July 2025

[83] Viljoen (2015), p. 397.

[84] ACERWC 'Communications' <https://www.acerwc.africa/en/page/about-communications> accessed 01 July 2025.

should include details about the complainant, parties involved, victims, and any public official or authority involved. The complainant may choose to withhold their identity or the victim's identity. The complainant must also provide an account of the alleged violation, the state responsible, and any attempts to remedy the issue (exhaustion of local remedies). The communication should also include submissions on the case's admissibility and merit, and if the communication has been submitted to another international settlement procedure.[85]

The above admissibility criteria have been extensively discussed in various communications before the ACERWC such as the *Legal and Human Rights Centre and Centre for Reproductive Rights (on behalf of Tanzanian girls) v United Republic of Tanzania,,*[86]*The Institute for Human Rights and Development in Africa and Finders Group Initiative on behalf of TFA (a Minor) v The Republic of Cameroon,*[87] *The African Centre of Justice and Peace Studies and People's Legal Aid Centre v The Republic of Sudan,,*[88]*The Centre for Human Rights (University of Pretoria) and La Rencontre Africaine pour la Defense Des Droits de l'homme (Senegal) V. The Government of Senegal*[89] *and Institute for Human Rights and Development in Africa (IHRDA) and Open Society Justice Initiative on behalf of children of Nubian descent in Kenya v. The Government of Kenya*[90] to name a few. Additionally, the ACERCW has extensively interpreted almost every article of the African Children's Charter on the substantive rights of children in African through the above-mentioned communications providing for a rich jurisprudence on the subject matter.

The communication mechanism of the ACERWC is an essential quasi-judicial body that has unfortunately not been employed by individuals and civil society organisations in Mauritius. There has been no communication submitted to the ACERWC by Mauritians against the state. No doubt, the reason cannot be because there are no violations of children's rights in Mauritius. Unawareness of the ACERWC, the communication mechanism is arguably a key reason for this. Yet, rights that are non-existent under Mauritian laws for children such as socio-economic rights can be invoked and enforced at the level of the ACERCW through the communication mechanism. It becomes more relevant to consider such a possibility given that Mauritius is not a state party to the Optional Protocol to the CRC on Communications. Even if Mauritius becomes one in future, the African Children's Charter still provides for some rights that do not exist in the CRC as discussed above. Despite the 'recommendatory' and non-binding nature of the decisions of the ACERWC, it has great political force and can be used as an excellent tool to put pressure on the state to better protect, promote, respect, and fulfil the rights of

[85] Para 3 Guidelines on Communications.

[86] Communication No: 0012/Com/001/2019 Decision No 002/2022.

[87] Communication No: 006/Com/002/2015 Decision No:001/2018.

[88] Communication No: 005/Com/001/2015 Decision No: 002/2018.

[89] Communication No: 003/Com/001/2012 Decision No: 003/2012.

[90] Communication: No. Com/002/2009 Decision: No 002/Com/002/2009.

children in Mauritius. There is a critical need for stakeholders to popularise this mechanism and use these decisions as tools of advocacy and lobbying.

8.7 Conclusion

The African Children's Charter has enormous potential in terms of strengthening the normative and legal framework on children's rights in Mauritius which is arguably decent but not complete. Domesticating the provisions of the Charter will add substantive content to children's rights in Mauritius conferring a better and more effective protection to children. A complete legal framework will not only benefit children but also various stakeholders such as legal practitioners, magistrates and judges, civil society organisations, policy-makers and academics, and researchers working in the field of children's rights. As discussed in this chapter, the complementary nature of the relationship between the African Children's Charter and the CRC will result in harmonising children's rights in Mauritius with international standards prescribed by the CtRC and the ACERWC. Additionally, there is a need for stakeholders to popularise and utilise the mechanisms available at the level of the ACERWC such as the communications and state reporting mechanisms to advance the agenda on children's rights in Mauritius. The state has a legal and moral duty to ensure that the provisions of the Charter are domesticated and implemented in Mauritius.

References

African Committee of Experts on the Rights and Welfare of the Child. 'Communications' <https://www.acerwc.africa/en/page/about-communications> Accessed 01 July 2025

African Committee of Experts on the Rights and Welfare of the Child. 'Egypt' <https://www.acerwc.africa/en/member-state/ratifications/62/egypt> Accessed 01 July 2025

African Committee of Experts on the Rights and Welfare of the Child. Revised Guidelines for Consideration of Communications and Monitoring Implementation of Decisions by the African Committee of Experts on the Rights and Welfare of the Child. <https://www.acerwc.africa/sites/default/files/2022-06/Guidelines-for-Consideration-of-Communications-and-Monitoring-Implementation-of-Decisions-by-the-African-Committee-of-Experts-on-the-Rights-and-Welfare-of-the-Child-English.pdf> Accessed 01 July 2025

Consortium for Street Children. Report on Street Children in Mauritius. <https://www.streetchildren.org/resources/report-on-street-children-in-mauritius/> Accessed 01 July 2025

Humanium. Children of Mauritius. <https://www.humanium.org/en/mauritius/> Accessed 01 July 2025

Kaime T (2009) The African charter on the rights and welfare of the child: a socio-legal perspective. PULP, Pretoria

Ministry of Gender Equality and Family Welfare. Adoption Unit. <https://gender.govmu.org/Pages/National-Adoption-Unit.aspx> Accessed 01 July 2025

Ministry of Gender Equality and Family Welfare. Child abuse. <https://budgetmof.govmu.org/documents/V_20_002023_24all.pdf> Accessed 01 July 2025

Ministry of Gender Equality and Family Welfare. Child Development Unit. <https://gender.govmu.org/Pages/Child-Development-Unit.aspx> Accessed 01 July 2025

Ministry of Gender Equality and Family Welfare. Mission and Vision. <https://budgetmof.govmu.org/documents/V_20_002023_24all.pdf> Accessed 01 July 2025

Ministry of Gender Equality and Family Welfare. About the Ministry. <https://gender.govmu.org/Pages/About-the-Ministry.aspx> Accessed 01 July 2025

Ministry of Gender Equality and Family Welfare. Planning and Research Unit. <https://gender.govmu.org/Pages/-Planning-and-Research-Unit.aspx> Accessed 01 July 2025

Muthago LG (1992) Introducing the African Charter on the Rights and Welfare of the Child and the Convention on the Rights of the Child. Paper presented at the international conference on the rights of the child, Community Law Centre, University of Western Cape

Statistics Mauritius (2023a) Economic and Social Indicators: Population and Vital Statistics. <https://statsmauritius.govmu.org/Documents/Statistics/ESI/2024/EI1773/Pop_Vital_Yr23_110324.pdf> Accessed 01 July 2025

Statistics Mauritius (2023b) Education Statistics. <https://statsmauritius.govmu.org/Pages/Statistics/ESI/Education/Edu_Yr23.aspx> Accessed 01 July 2025

Umozurike U (1997) The African Charter on Human and Peoples' Rights. The Hague Kluwer International

UNICEF (2024) Mauritius. <https://data.unicef.org/country/mus/> Accessed 01 July 2025

U.S. Department of State '2023 Trafficking in Persons Report: Mauritius' <https://www.state.gov/reports/2023-trafficking-in-persons-report/mauritius/> Accessed 01 July 2025

Viljoen F (2015) International human rights law in Africa. Oxford University Press UK

Chapter 9
Rights of Older Persons, Persons with Disabilities, and Sexual Minorities

Abstract This chapter offers a summary of the current institutional and legislative structure pertaining to the rights of the three aforementioned groups of Mauritius citizens. The African human rights framework is then examined, along with pertinent advancements and improvements at that level. In order to do this, it is necessary to evaluate the degree to which this system and its tools can significantly advance the rights of Mauritius' elderly, disabled, and sexual minorities. This chapter argues that the ratification and domestication of the Protocol on Older Persons would enable the enforcement of rights by domestic courts and African bodies such as the African Commission. This would apply also for the legal framework on disability rights in Mauritius. The African human rights system on sexual minorities rights presents an opportunity for NGOs working on these rights. The state is called upon to contemplate its ratification and domestication, requiring precise reports on elderly persons' rights and allowing communications on potential violations.

9.1 Introduction

An age-old phenomenon is population ageing. Almost every nation on Earth is experiencing it, having begun in the developed world. Better diet, hygiene, health care, education, and economic prosperity are all contributing factors to people living longer. Mauritius is seeing an ageing population as well. When the population's age structure shifts towards the upper end of the age distribution, it is known as population ageing. This is defined as the increase in the population's median age, which is the age at which the population is divided into two equal-sized groups, one older than the median and the other younger. By 2023, the median age had risen from 19.0 years in 1972 to 38.4 years. For statistical purposes, people 60 years of age and older are considered elderly. In 1972, 5.9% of the population was 60 years of age or older; by 2023, that percentage had dropped to 20.1%.[1] Increased

[1] Statistics Mauritius (2023), p. 11.

R. Mahadew, *Mauritius and African Human Rights Law*,
https://doi.org/10.1007/978-3-032-08832-1_9

longevity and decreased fertility are two reasons for the ageing process. Over the last 60 years, Mauritius' birth rate per 1000 people fell by 75%. Young people's proportion in the population is declining as a result of low fertility. A man was predicted to live up to 61 years and a woman up to 66 years on average in the 1970s; by 2022, those estimates were expected to rise to 70 and 77 years, respectively.[2]

There are several consequences of ageing in Mauritius. Pension plans will be impacted by ageing; There will be more beneficiaries, and they will take longer to claim payments than they do now. Along with physical and mental incapacity, an increase in the prevalence of some long-term chronic illnesses is equally associated with population ageing. The other issue is that, given that women will make up the majority of the elderly, there will likely be a greater demand for healthcare services. To reduce their reliance on others, living arrangements, including housing and transportation, must be tailored to their needs.[3] The promotion and protection of the human rights of elderly persons forming part of the ageing population also becomes a major preoccupation of the State.

From 2011 to 2022, the proportion of people with disabilities rose from 4.8% to 6.8%.[4] In 2022, some 84,500 persons reported some forms of disability, up from 59,900 in 2011.[5] Walking (36.8% of all disabled people), seeing even with glasses (17.9% of all disabled people), self-care (10.2% of all disabled people), and behaviour (8.1% of all disabled people) were the most common types of disabilities reported at the 2022 Census.[6] With the increase in the number of persons living with disabilities, it is undeniable that there would be more pressure and challenges regarding the promotion and protection of their rights in Mauritius. Members of the LGBTIQA+ group (referred to in this chapter as sexual minorities) arguably have greater issues regarding their rights and freedoms. While progress has been made through a decision of the Supreme Court that will be discussed later in this chapter, there are several gaps in the legal framework that need to be addressed.

This chapter therefore provides for an overview of the existing legal and institutional framework on the rights of the three mentioned segments of the Mauritian population. It then examines the African human rights system and relevant developments and progress made at that level. The purpose of doing so is to assess the extent to which this system and its instruments can be decisive in advancing the rights of elderly persons, persons living with disabilities and sexual minorities in Mauritius.

---

[2] Ibid 12.

[3] Bengtsson and Scott (2010), pp. 7–22.

[4] Statistics Mauritius (2022), p. 1.

[5] Ibid 16.

[6] Ibid.

9.2 The Legal and Institutional Framework on Rights of Elderly Persons, Persons with Disabilities, and Sexual Minorities

9.2.1 *Rights of Elderly Persons*

There exists a number of legislations in Mauritius that confer protection to elderly persons. The Protection from Domestic Violence Act, by extending the definition of domestic violence to 'another person living under the same roof', protects elderly persons (grandparents for example).[7] The Equal Opportunities Act prohibits discrimination on the grounds of 'age'.[8] The Mental Health Care Act also provides for special care to elderly persons admitted at a Mental health Care Centre.[9] The Senior Citizens Council Act establishes the Council which has as objectives (a) to determine the areas in which the welfare of senior citizens needs to be improved; (b) to promote generally activities and projects for the welfare of senior citizens; (c) to maintain effective communication with senior citizens; (d) to diffuse knowledge and information on gerontology; (e) to establish contacts with organisations engaged in similar activities in Mauritius and abroad; (f) to advise the Government on matters relating to the welfare of senior citizens; (g) to set up and manage homes, day care centres, recreation centres and other institutions for senior citizens; and (h) to implement such policies and programmes in favour of senior citizens, as may be specified or approved by the Minister.[10] The main legislation is the Protection of Elderly Persons Act 2005 (PEPA 2005) is the main legislation which 'set up a legal and administrative framework for greater protection and assistance to elderly persons'.[11]

Elderly person is defined as a person who has attained the age of 60.[12] Section 3 establishes the Protection of the Elderly Network which is mandated to ensure, promote, and sustain elderly people's physical, psychological, emotional, social, and economic protection and ensure, promote, and sustain elderly people's well-being so that they can contribute significantly to society.[13] The Network's responsibilities consist of advising the Minister on policies supporting the advancement of senior citizens' welfare within families and on any such action that is likely required to fulfil the objectives of the legislation and coordinating the efforts of all statutory

[7] Section 2 of the Protection from Domestic Violence Act.

[8] Section 2 of the Equal Opportunities Act 2008.

[9] Section 23(c) of the Mental Health Care Act 1998.

[10] Section 4 of the Senior Citizens Council Act 1995.

[11] PEPA 2005 Preamble.

[12] Section 2 PEPA 2005.

[13] Section 3(3) a & b PEPA 2005.

bodies, other organisations, and individual groups that support the accomplishment of the set objectives.[14]

The PEPA 2005 also establishes a Monitoring Committee to supervise the operations of the Elderly Persons' Protection Unit (the Unit) and of every Elderly Watch and give to its officers such directions of a general character as it may deem necessary and to provide adequate resources and facilities for the proper operation of the Unit and of every Elderly Watch.[15] Section 6 of the PEPA 2005 establishes the Unit which functions on the organisation's public awareness campaigns on elderly rights, receiving complaints, applying for protection orders, assisting in arranging residential care home admissions, and ensuring Elderly Watch and other authorities receive proper feedback on the situation of elderly persons in need of protection or assistance.[16] The Monitoring Committee establishes an Elderly Watch in each region, responsible for promoting the welfare of elderly persons, supporting families, preventing abuse, and reporting instances of repeated abuse to unit officers.[17]

If an officer-in-charge of the Unit finds, under oath, that there are reasonable grounds to suspect an old person has been abused or is likely to be abused, the Court may issue an elderly persons' protection order. The order will demand good behaviour towards the elderly person and prohibit the respondent from using abusive language. If there is a significant risk of injury to the old person before the case is heard, the court may grant an interim order and the application must be sent to the defendant. The order is enforceable until the court issues a final ruling regarding the application. Any party can request that the order with the other party be modified or revoked if it is still in effect.[18] Abuse occurs in cases where someone who is elderly is ill-treated physically or verbally is subject to ongoing mental or emotional stress or results in financial loss or discrimination. It is also illegal to neglect to give someone enough food, clothing, shelter, medical care, or to follow a protective order. It is also illegal to ignore a summons and fail to show up without a good explanation, presenting an application copy.[19]

In the case of *Police v Ellapen*, the District Court stated that the elements of the offence of ill-treatment of elderly are material acts of ill-treatment whether physical or verbal, inflicted by the accused, to a person who is over 60 years old and with the intent to inflict the ill-treatment.[20] Several cases have stated that the offence of ill-treatment, being a criminal one under the PEPA 2005, has to be proven beyond reasonable doubt by the prosecution.[21] The Law Reform Commission (LRC) came up with an Issue Paper on the Protection of the Rights and Interests of Elderly

[14] Section 3(4) PEPA 2005.

[15] Section 4(2) PEPA 2005.

[16] Section 6(2) PEPA 2005.

[17] Section 8(2) PEPA 2005.

[18] Section 9 PEPA 2005.

[19] Section 11 PEPA 2005.

[20] *Police v Ellapen* 2024 RDR 38.

[21] *Police v Mungul* 2024 RCR 1; *Police v Applasamy* 2024 SAV 25.

Persons in Mauritius whereby it highlighted the lack of a human rights-based approach to elderly persons in the following terms:

South Africa's Act emphasises the human rights of the elderly, aligning with the country's Constitution and the UDHR. This rights-based approach can empower the elderly and ensure their dignity and autonomy. South Africa's legislation pulses with the rhythm of human rights, harmonising with the universal human rights principles and its own Constitution. This rights-based approach could inspire Mauritius to ensure that the dignity and autonomy of its elderly population are held in high esteem.[22]

The LRC further recommended that the definition of abuse be extended in section 11 (1) to include (1) deprivation of food, shelter, clothing, medical attention, or leaving them unattended, (2) unjustly disposing of an elderly person's property without his consent, (3) deserting or neglecting an elderly persons, and (4) compelling an elderly person by force or threat to engage in any conduct or act, sexual or otherwise.[23] It also recommended the creation of shelters for elder abuse victims serving as a sanctuary for elderly persons who are victims of abuse with adequate safety, medical care, and psychological support. These shelters would provide for more adapted services compared to what the WEPPU or residential care homes, governed by the Residential care Homes Act in terms of general supervision and control of them, currently provide.[24] It also recommended penalty provisions in the PEPA 2005 by incriminating abandonment of elderly persons as well as enshrining a duty to support an elderly person in national legislation.[25]

In terms of institutional framework, under the Protection of Elderly Persons' Act 2005, the WEPPU was created to manage complaints, plan public awareness campaigns, step in when elder abuse cases arise, process applications for admission to nonprofit organisations, oversee residential care facilities, and plan activities for the well-being of the elderly. In addition, the unit runs the 172 and 199 hotlines as well as the free "Sekirite"[26] mobile app, which enables elderly victims to send distress signals and notify the closest police station. The software also gives elderly people the assistance they need.[27] The country's Medical Unit aims at offering paramedical and medical care to children with disabilities and elderly persons. It guarantees curative, promotive, rehabilitative, and preventative support and services with a team of 332 medical officers, 60 nursing officers, 9 physiotherapists, and 7 occupational therapists and therapists. Infirmary visits on a weekly basis, monthly domiciliary visits for persons over 90, and monthly domiciliary visits for bedridden persons up to 89 years of age are services provided. Bedridden Elderly persons or severely disabled ones can receive "Service de Proximité" services, and health clubs

[22] Law Reform Commission Issue Paper (2023), p. 37.

[23] Ibid 40.

[24] Law Reform Commission Issue Paper (2023), pp. 40–41.

[25] Ibid 42.

[26] This word means security in English.

[27] Welfare and Elderly Persons' Protection Unit (2024).

are established in elderly daycare centres. Monthly health debates, vaccinations for the elderly, and leisure facilities are illustrations of activities related to the promotion of health and the prevention of illnesses and diseases. Also, the facility offers individuals with minor illnesses round-the-clock nurse care.[28]

9.2.2 *Persons with Disabilities*

Mauritius ratified the UN Convention on the Rights of Persons with Disabilities in 2010 but not the Optional Protocol to it which allows for a communications mechanism. The UN Committee on the Rights of Persons with Disabilities (the CRPD) issued Concluding Observations on the initial report of Mauritius in 2015.[29] The Committee expressed concern about the medical approach to disability in the Equal Opportunities Act and Training and Employment of Disabled Persons Act, derogatory language against disabled individuals, unclear achievements from the 2007 Action Plan on Disability, and lack of consultation in the development of disability bills and strategies. The concept of reasonable accommodation is also not defined.[30]

The Committee was concerned about the unclear and inexplicit relationship between Mauritius and the Forum of Women with Disabilities. It also raised concern about the absence of statutory provisions in the Protection from Domestic Violence Act for women and girls with disabilities. It also underlined that Mauritius preferred the integrative approach compared to the elimination of barriers of a social, cultural, and physical nature for persons living with disabilities. Concerns regarding the stigma that children with disabilities had to endure, the over-reliance on non-governmental organisations to provide specialised care to children with impairments, and the absence of safeguards against placement in "centres de sauvegarde" were also highlighted as areas of concern by the Committee. The Committee also noted the absence of public transportation access for impaired children in rural regions.[31]

As a general response to the above concern, the State enacted the Protection and Promotion of the Rights of Persons with Disabilities (PPRPD) in 2024. Sections 5 and 6 of the PPRPD 2024 prohibits discrimination based on disability and abusive treatment of disabled individuals. Violations result in fines of up to 200,000 rupees and imprisonment for up to 5 years. Abuse includes degrading treatment, prolonged harassment, intentional loss, violent treatment, inadequate care, and harassment. The PPRPD 2024 outlines the rights and responsibilities of individuals with disabilities in various aspects of their lives. It emphasises the importance of special education, employment, protection, and safety in situations of risks. It also states

[28] Medical Unit (2024).

[29] Concluding Observations (2015).

[30] Concluding Observations (2015) para 5 & 9.

[31] Concluding Observations (2015) para 13, 17 & 33.

that employers must not discriminate against individuals with disabilities in terms of employment, remuneration, and conditions of employment. Employers must redeploy employees who are no longer capable of performing their duties due to a disability, provided there is no disproportionate or undue burden on them. Employers must provide reasonable accommodation to employees with disabilities, unless they can prove that the required adjustments would unduly prejudice the operation of the business. The Ministry also ensures the protection and safety of persons with disabilities in disaster situations. The text also emphasises the importance of habilitation and rehabilitation for persons with disabilities, promoting their physical, cognitive, and psychological recovery, enabling them to attain and maintain maximum independence, and promoting the development of training for professionals and staff working in these areas.[32]

The Empowerment Unit within the Ministry ensures equal protection and benefits for persons with disabilities without discrimination. It ensures effective protection against discrimination and coordinates activities related to the implementation of international instruments. The Unit works with organisations, the private sector, and stakeholders to protect and promote the rights of persons with disabilities. It conceptualises and implements disability policies, projects, and programmes and monitors national administrative arrangements. The Unit's functions include providing protection, improving social and economic status, providing support, organising public awareness campaigns, arranging safety admissions, applying for protection orders, assisting victims of violence, and advising the Minister on disability-related matters.[33]

The National Empowerment Authority is a body established to assist and support persons with disabilities in reaching their full potential. It ensures a barrier-free environment, promotes effective service delivery, conducts regular audits of programmes, and advises the Ministry on national policies. The Authority's functions include preventing discrimination against persons with disabilities, facilitating social integration, setting standards for support organisations, educating employers on employment, establishing training centres, promoting equal opportunities, ensuring employers comply with employment quotas, registering individuals with disabilities and organisations, promoting public awareness, setting up centres, and performing other functions as directed by the Minister. The Authority also promotes public awareness and promotes respect for the rights of persons with disabilities.[34] It should be noted that once the PPRPD 2024 is in force, the Lois Lagesse Trust Fund Act, the National Council for the Rehabilitation of Disabled Persons Act, and the Training and Employment if Disabled Persons Act will all be repealed.

[32] Section 8-11 PPRPD 2024.

[33] Section 15-17 PPRPD 2024.

[34] Section 25-27 PPRPD 2024.

9.2.3 Sexual Minorities

In a public opinion conducted in 2023, 48% of Mauritians believed that Mauritius is a "good place" for sexual minorities and 60% were of the view that they would accept homosexuals as their neighbours.[35] In 2017, the UN Human Rights Committee stated that it was:

> concerned about reported cases of hate speech and violence, including death threats, brutality and humiliation, against lesbian, gay, bisexual and transgender persons. The Committee is also concerned that lesbian, gay, bisexual and transgender persons are not authorised to officially enter marriage or civil partnerships and are denied other rights relating to personal status. The Committee is further concerned that the provision of article 250 of the Criminal Code of Mauritius, which criminalises "sodomy" and "bestiality", has not yet been repealed.[36]

It urges Mauritius to explicitly forbid discrimination against lesbian, gay, bisexual, and transgender people in all forms and to include sexual orientation and gender identity as grounds for discrimination in all pertinent laws, including the Criminal Code. Along with repealing article 250 of the Criminal Code, Mauritius should take all necessary steps to prohibit discrimination against lesbian, gay, bisexual, and transgender people in marriage and civil partnerships. In addition, it should guarantee that any reports of violence, including brutality and death threats, caused by prejudice against LGBT and transgender individuals are filed with the police, looked into, and the perpetrators are suitably charged and, if found guilty, punished appropriately.[37]

In 2018, during the Universal Periodic Review for Mauritius by the UN Human Rights Council, NGOs working on sexual minorities rights in Mauritius made several pertinent observations as stakeholders' submissions which are apposite to be reproduced here.[38] According to Collectif Arc en Ciel (CAEC), homosexuality was often placed within a language of sin and abnormal behaviour, and homophobic sentiments continued to exist in Mauritius. Numerous LGBT (lesbian, gay, bisexual, and transgender) individuals encountered stigma within their own families. The Civil Status Office does not accept transgender people who want their identity documents (passport, national identity card) to reflect their gender identity, according to the explanation provided by CAEC. The Young Queer Alliance (YQA) brought attention to the fact that the Equal Opportunities Act of 2008 does not address gender identification. It suggested that Mauritius hold public education campaigns about the rights of LGBT people.[39]

As a social group, sexual orientation or sexual identity were not mentioned in the definition of "racial hatred" adopted under article 282 of the Criminal Code Act

[35] Equaldex (2024).

[36] HRC 'Concluding Observations' (2017) para 9.

[37] Ibid para 10.

[38] UN HRC 'Summary of Stakeholders' submissions on Mauritius' (2018).

[39] Ibid para 6.

1838 of Mauritius, according to YQA. Therefore, under this Act, hate motivation for crimes against a person based on their gender identity or sexual orientation could not be used as a justification for a harsher sentence. It was suggested that as aggravating conditions, Mauritius added a clear statement of hate speech in article 282 of the Criminal Code Act 1838 against anyone based on their actual or perceived gender identity, gender expression, or sexual orientation.[40] As long as sodomy was carried out between consenting adults, YQA believed that it was an issue of their freedom and privacy and that the State should not infringe on their ability to engage in such sexual behaviour that is related to maintaining their bodily integrity. Article 250 of the Criminal Code, which makes sodomy illegal, was suggested to be repealed by Mauritius by CAEC because it perpetuates the stigma against transgender and homosexual men as well as lesbian and bisexual women.[41]

The CAEC stated that it seemed as though there had been a pause in the adoption of legislative legislation that would decriminalise same-sex relationships. The Human Rights Committee's recommendations on eliminating the law that criminalises sodomy and educating law enforcement, courts, and prosecutors about the rights of LGBT people have not yet been incorporated into the National Human Rights Action Plan 2012–2020, which is run by the Human Rights Secretariat/National Mechanism for Reporting and Follow-up, according to CAEC. It suggested, among other things, that the National Human Rights Secretariat/National Mechanism for Reporting and Follow-up oversee the implementation of the Human Rights Committee's observations and the tracking of any advancements made in this regard.[42]

The Employment Rights Act of 2008 and the Equal Opportunities Act of 2008 expressly prohibit discrimination on the basis of sexual orientation, although non-heterosexual couples are still not accepted in society, according to CAEC. Those who were not allowed to be married or form a civil partnership, according to YQA, were at a disadvantage because they were not entitled to the same privileges and benefits. The Commission on Asian and Pacific Education (CAEC) suggested that Mauritius change discriminatory definitions in the country's laws to include same-sex couples on the same footing as spouses of opposite sexes and that the state permit the legal recognition of a person's gender identity under national law without requiring surgery or other related medical procedures.[43]

Despite the legal protections, CAEC claimed that members of the LGBT community had reported high levels of stigma and other issues at public healthcare facilities, and transgender people experienced specific types of discrimination and stigma that hampered their access to care, among other things. It emphasised how health facilities and service providers were out of touch with gender identity and

[40] UN HRC 'Summary of Stakeholders' submissions on Mauritius' (2018) para 7.

[41] UN HRC 'Summary of Stakeholders' submissions on Mauritius' (2018) para 8.

[42] UN HRC 'Summary of Stakeholders' submissions on Mauritius' (2018) para 9.

[43] UN HRC 'Summary of Stakeholders' submission on Mauritius' (2018) para 11.

expression and did not comprehend it. Inadequate sexual and reproductive health services were provided by healthcare providers.[44]

While most of the above issues still persist in Mauritius, in 2023, the Supreme Court decriminalised sodomy on the basis of discrimination in the case of *Ah Seek v The State of Mauritius*.[45] The Supreme Court of Mauritius has ruled that a legislation that forbids consenting adult men from having same-sex relationships is unconstitutional. The 1968 Mauritius constitution is violated, according to the ruling of the Mauritian Supreme Court, by section 250 of the 1838 Mauritius Criminal Code, which makes anal sex between two consenting adult men illegal. The plaintiff, Ah Seek, a gay man from Mauritius who serves on the board of the Mauritius non-governmental organisation Collectif-Arc-en-Ciel, claimed many constitutional defences. Nonetheless, the right to protection against discrimination served as the Court's most pertinent basis for its ruling.

The Court looked to other SADC courts' decisions in resolving two matters that would work against a verdict in Ah Seek's favour.[46] The ruling rendered by Botswana's Court of Appeal in 2021 was especially noteworthy. According to this ruling, "sexual orientation" was included in the Botswana constitution's list of protected categories under "sex". The claim that discrimination based on "sexual orientation" is not expressly forbidden by Mauritius' constitution was the first point of argument. Section 16, which is pertinent, prohibits discrimination based on seven specific grounds, one of which being sex. The court in Mauritius determined that "sexual orientation" is included under the definition of "sex" in section 16 of the constitution.

The second question was whether the court needed to make a decision because prosecutions were uncommon. The Mauritius court decided, citing a ruling by the South African Constitutional Court, that homosexual males are always at danger of being arrested, charged, and found guilty. The court came to the conclusion that everyone was protected by the constitution against discrimination based on their sexual orientation, regardless of that orientation.[47] The state simply referred to same-sex relationships as a "highly sensitive issue" because of the "delicate socio-cultural and religious fabric of Mauritian society" when forced to demonstrate any justification for this type of discrimination. Dismissing them as grounds for prejudice, the court emphasised that Mauritius was a secular state.[48]

---

[44] UN HRC 'Summary of Stakeholders' submission on Mauritius' (2018) para 25.

[45] Ah Seek v The State 2023 SCJ 399; Fokeerbux N. A & Ors v The State 2023 SCJ 400.

[46] Ah Seek v The State 2023 SCJ 399 p.5-13.

[47] Ah Seek v The State 2023 SCJ 399 p.9.

[48] Fokeerbux N.A. & Ors v The State of Mauritius 2023 SCJ 400.

9.3 The Rights of Elderly Persons, Persons with Disabilities, and Sexual Minorities under the African Human Rights System

9.3.1 *Rights of Elderly Persons*

The African Charter provides for civil and political rights, socio-economic rights as well as the right to environment and development which are applicable to elderly persons. Uniquely, it also provides for the concept of duties and horizontal obligations among citizens which can also be interpreted as covering duties towards elderly persons.[49] Indeed, article 27 provides that "every individual shall have duties towards his family and society, the State and other legally recognised communities and the international community". It further provides that "the rights and freedoms of each individual shall be exercised with due regard to the rights of others, collective security, morality and common interest".[50] Having duties towards the family clearly includes duties towards elderly persons of the family and exercising rights entails exerting them in a way that takes into account the morality and common interest of elderly persons.

More specifically, the African Charter refers to elderly persons by stating that "The aged and the disabled shall also have the right to special measures of protection in keeping with their physical or moral needs".[51] Additionally, article 29(1) also provides that "the individual shall also have the duty to preserve the harmonious development of the family and to work for the cohesion and respect of the family; to respect his parents at all times, to maintain them in case of need". There exist normative and academic literature which have discussed the value and interaction of these two sections with the AU framework on the rights of elderly persons.[52] Furthermore, the Maputo Protocol on women's rights also provides for the special protection of elderly women.[53]

However, it has been argued that the AU institutions, including the African Commission and the African Courts, have not been adequately and sufficiently used to advance the rights and freedoms of elderly persons. A complete absence of claims filed with the African Court on rights of elderly persons, a complete absence of communications submitted to the African Commission on rights of elderly persons, a large number of states that completely disregard elders' rights in their state reports or only deal with them indirectly and invisibility of the NGOs themselves in the field of older persons' rights within the system of communications and claims submitted to the Commission and to the Court have been some issues and challenges

---

[49] Umozurike (1983), p. 904; D'sa (1985), pp. 72–81.

[50] Article 27(2).

[51] Article 18(4) African Charter.

[52] Sik Yuen (2011), pp. 213–233; Mbondenyi (2011).

[53] Article 22 Maputo Protocol.

highlighted by scholars.[54] Arguably, the absence of a specific instrument on the rights of elderly persons in Africa might have been one of the reasons for the "inactiveness" of stakeholders regarding this area of human rights.

As a remedial step, the Assembly of the African Union adopted the Protocol to the African Charter on Human and Peoples' Rights on the Rights of Older Persons in January 2016 during its 26th Ordinary Session in Ethiopia. This is the culmination of recommendations made in the African Union Policy Framework and Plan of Action on Ageing in 2002. Indeed, it was highlighted that "member states recognise the fundamental rights of Older Persons and commit themselves to abolish all forms of discrimination based on age; that they undertake to ensure that the rights of Older Persons are protected by appropriate legislation; including the right to organise themselves in groups and to representation in order to advance their interests".[55] The 2002 Plan of Action also called for the elaboration and adoption of "an additional Protocol" to the African Charter on rights of older persons.[56]

The Protocol on Older Persons' Rights has a number of binding and substantive provisions such as elimination of discrimination against older persons, access to justice and equal protection of the law, right to make decisions, protection against discrimination in employment, social protection, protection against abuse and harmful traditional practices, protection of older women, care and support, residential care, support for older persons taking care of vulnerable children, protection of older persons with disabilities, protection of older persons in conflicts and disaster situations, access to health services, access to education, participation in programmes and recreational activities, accessibility, awareness on ageing and preparation for old age, and duties of older persons.[57]

It should be noted that the Protocol on Older Persons' Rights has not yet come into force given that it has only 12 out of the minimum 15 ratifications required for its entry into force. Mauritius has signed it in May 2021 but it has not yet ratified it. Given the lack of a human rights-based approach to the protection of older persons in Mauritius as seen from the analysis of the PEPA 2005 above, the ratification and domestication of this Protocol would enhance the legal framework on the rights of elderly persons in the country. While institutional arrangements premised on the welfare state system can be said to be decent, the lack of a legal framework based on their human rights does not allow for enforceability and justifiability of the rights of elderly persons in Mauritius. The state is therefore called upon to genuinely contemplate its ratification and domestication. Such a step will confer an obligation on the state to submit a report precisely on the rights of elderly persons in Mauritius and will allow for individuals and civil society organisations to submit communications on potential violations to the African Commission.

---

[54] Doron et al. (2016).

[55] African Union Policy Framework and Plan of Action on Ageing (2002) para 4.1.

[56] Ibid.

[57] Article 3-20 of the Protocol on Older Persons' Rights.

9.3.2 *Persons with Disabilities*

Van Reenen and Combrinck had argued that the history of disability rights in Africa, at a continental level, has been one of "benign neglect".[58] Recently, there has been a shift in this dispensation eventually culminating towards the adoption by the AU of the Protocol to the African Charter on Human and Peoples' Rights on the Rights of Persons with Disabilities in Africa (African Disability Protocol) in January 2018. Before focusing on this new protocol, it is apposite to have a look at the existing normative framework on disability rights in Africa before the advent of the protocol.

Combrinck opined that two parallel historical dimensions should be taken into account when examining the increasing recognition of disability rights under the African human rights system.[59] The OAU was slowly moving in a human rights' direction, while, on the one hand, there was an increasingly global recognition of disability as a compelling human rights concern.[60] Taking into account that the African Charter came into existence in the early 1980s, this historical viewpoint helps to understand why there are not many references to disabilities in this fundamental document. The adoption of two Declarations on the Rights of People with Disabilities during the 1970s, the Declaration on the Rights of Mentally Retarded Persons in 1971 and the Declaration on the Rights of Disabled Persons in 1975, and the World Programme of Action concerning Disabled Persons in 1982 were signs of the conceptual and philosophical shift away from a medical or welfare approach to disability at the international level. This change was by no means systemically established at the time, though.[61]

In the African Charter, there are two articles which are of interest here. Article 2 on prohibition of discrimination and article 18(4) which provides that the disabled have the right to "special measures of protection" in keeping with their physical or moral needs. Even if article 2 does not provide explicitly for disability as a ground on the basis of which discrimination is prohibited, the phrase "other status" can be used to read in disability-based discrimination by analogy.[62] This technique of interpretation has been upheld by the African Commission in a number of communications.[63] However, article 18(4) has been viewed as more problematic and has been criticised rightly for a number of reasons, including being "vague and unclear"[64] and combining the rights of the elderly with those of those with disabilities.[65]

After the African Charter was adopted, disability rights started to gradually seep into the continental framework. For example, the Agreement for the Establishment

---

[58] Van Reenen and Combrinck (2011), p. 153.

[59] Combrinck (2013), p. 362.

[60] Biegon (2011), pp. 56–57.

[61] Quinn and Degener (2002), p. 30.

[62] Kamga (2013), p. 237.

[63] *Purohit & Another v The Gambia* (2003) AHRLR 96 (ACHPR 2003).

[64] Kamga (2013), p. 238.

[65] Secretariat of the African Decade of Persons with Disabilities (2011), p. 5.

of the African Rehabilitation Institute (ARI) was adopted by the OAU in 1985. The ARI's goals included "manpower development", being established with the technical assistance of the International Labour organisation, and placing a high priority on rehabilitation. Adoption of the African Charter on the Rights and Welfare of the Child in 1990, which included a special item on the rights of children with disabilities, was a step further.[66] Biegon has argued that the UN Decade of Persons with Disabilities (1983–1992) coincided with the 1990s wave of democratisation across Africa, allowed for a more "favourable environment for the agitation of respect for and protection of human rights".[67] The OAU Ministerial Conference on Human Rights in Africa adopted the Grand Bay (Mauritius) Declaration and Plan of Action in April 1999, which took this into consideration. This Declaration calls on all African governments to endeavour towards guaranteeing the complete respect of the rights of those with disabilities and those living with HIV/AIDS, especially women and children, noting that these rights are not always upheld.[68] The OAU Heads of State and Government notably passed a resolution designating the years 1999–2009 as the African Decade of People with Disabilities in July 1999.[69]

In 2000, the shift towards a human rights mandate for the AU was formalised with the adoption of the Constitutive Act of the African Union which stated that one of its objectives was "to promote and protect human and peoples' rights" in alignment with the African Charter and other relevant human rights instruments.[70] This shift accelerated the process of endorsing disability rights in the African human rights system. A Declaration was adopted during the first AU Ministerial Conference on Human Rights in Africa in 2003 making specific reference to disability rights.[71] Delegates urged member states "to develop a Protocol on the protection of the rights of people with disabilities and the elderly", citing "the plight of the vulnerable groups including persons with disability in general".[72] Since then and from the year 2000, human rights instruments adopted at the AU level including the Maputo Protocol, the African Youth Charter, the AU Convention for the Protection and Assistance of Internally Displaced Persons, and the African Charter on Democracy, Elections, and Governance have explicitly enshrined for disability-related provisions. Despite being criticised for their limited scope or unwieldy formulation, these provisions act as "an evolving convergence as to the standards to be achieved".[73]

[66] Combrinck (2013), p. 363.

[67] Biegon (2011), p. 58.

[68] Article 7.

[69] OAU Council of Ministers and the Assembly of State and Government in July 2000 in Lome, Togo, renewed when the AU declared 2010-2019 as the second African Decade on the Rights of Disabled Persons.

[70] Article 3(h) Constitutive Act of the AU.

[71] MIN/CONF/HRA/Decl.1(I), adopted by the First AU Ministerial Conference on Human Rights in Africa on 8 May 2003.

[72] Ibid.

[73] *MC v Bulgaria Application* [2003] ECHR 651; 40 EHRR 20.

The Kigali Declaration of 2003 called for a Protocol to protect the rights of persons with disabilities and the elderly in Africa. The African Commission appointed a "Focal Point on the Rights of Older Persons in Africa" in 2007 and expanded it to a "Working Group on the Rights of Older Persons and People with Disabilities in Africa" in 2009.[74] The Working Group was mandated to draft a concept paper for consideration by the African Commission, which would serve as the basis for the adoption of a Draft Protocol on Ageing and People with Disabilities. The Accra Draft, a document related to persons with disabilities, was criticised for being developed without the participation of persons with disabilities and presented a diluted version of international standards without introducing an "Africa-specific" perspective.[75] The Working Group was reconstituted in 2012, and the draft Protocol was finalised for adoption in 2014.

In January 2018, the African Disability Protocol was adopted. The UN Special Rapporteur on the rights of persons with disabilities stated that "the Protocol, builds on the Convention, for example by explicitly recognising people's rights to exercise legal capacity and by providing protection against any interference with such capacity, a right set out in my recent report to the Human Rights Council".[76] Msipa and Juma have accurately underlined the contribution of the Protocol towards a social and human rights approach to disability in the African human rights system as follows:

> The adoption of the Protocol to the African Charter on Human and People's Rights on the Rights of Persons with Disabilities in Africa marked a pivotal juncture in the shifting approaches to disability in the African human rights system. The African Disability Protocol abandoned the medical and charity approaches to disability that are dominant in many of the preexisting African human rights instruments, in favour of a social and human rights approach to disability...the unique lived experience of persons with disabilities in Africa dictated the shift from viewing disability in light of the medical model of disability to perceiving it as a human rights issue. Prior to the adoption of the Protocol, African human rights instruments had failed to translate into real change in the lives of persons with disabilities, making it necessary to reevaluate the approach to disability in the African human rights system. The process of rethinking approaches to disability did not take place in a vacuum. Global trends encapsulated in the Convention on the Rights of Persons with Disabilities had an enormous influence on this process. Using the social and human rights models of disability, the African Disability Protocol therefore takes stock of the unique African context while maintaining the gains and victories won in the Convention on the Rights of Persons with Disabilities.[77]

The African Disability Protocol is yet to come into force with only 10 out of the 15 mandatory ratifications required. Mauritius has not yet signed the Protocol. The social and human rights-based approach to disability adopted by the Protocol can be very effective and relevant to the rights of Mauritians living with disabilities. The

---

[74] Res 118: (XXXXII 07), adopted at 42nd Ordinary Session of ACHPR held in Brazzaville, Congo, 15-28 November 2007.

[75] Kamga (2013), p. 224.

[76] OHCHR (2018).

[77] Msipa and Juma (2023), p. 1.

PPRPD Act of Mauritius critically lacks such an approach with the focus more on institutional arrangements. While such an approach may also be relevant, the fact that it is devoid of any genuine human rights-based approach can be problematic regarding the enforceability and justiciability of disability rights in Mauritius. The ratification and domestication of the Protocol would allow for the rights to be enforced and rendered justiciable by both domestic courts and African bodies such as the African Commission. State reporting by Mauritius, communications submitted to the Commission by civil society organisations, and submission of claims to the African Court (after Mauritius submitting the declaration under article 34(6)) would enhance the legal framework on disability rights in Mauritius.

9.3.3 Sexual Minorities

Under the African Charter, the rights-holders have been identified as "everyone", "every individual", or "every human being". Therefore at the very outset, this should have applied without any possible debate to persons referred to as belonging to the sexual minorities group. The reality seems to be far from this claim compelling Viljoen to argue that "although homophobia is pervasive in societies across Africa, tormented by Christianity and Islam and further fuelled by opportunistic political rhetoric, the laws in most African states reinforce these forms of social stereotyping and facilitate violations".[78] Yet, article 2 of the African Charter does not allow for discrimination on any ground whatsoever and therefore "no person loses the protective shield of the Charter on the basis of his or her sexual orientation or gender identity".[79]

Indeed, article 2 of the African Charter provides for "sex" and "other status" as two grounds on the basis of which discrimination is prohibited. It implies that sexual orientation and gender identity can be included within these two grounds in line with the express recognition of the Human Rights Committee of such an approach in *Toonen v Australia*.[80] In addition, the enshrinement of the right to equality in article 3 and 19, as well as that of the right to dignity in article 5 of the African Charter provide for the rights on the basis of which other human rights systems have articulated the rights of sexual minorities. It has to be underlined that the right to privacy is missing from the African Charter, denying human rights claims of sexual minorities to be premised on it. However, Murray and Viljoen have argued that the right to privacy can be implied from the right to dignity, the right to life and integrity of the person, and the right to liberty and security on the basis of the concept of implied rights as adopted by the African Commission in *SERAC v Nigeria*.[81]

[78] Viljoen (2015), p. 260.

[79] Viljoen (2015), p. 265.

[80] *Toonen v Australia*, Communication 488/1992, para 8.7.

[81] Murray and Viljoen (2009), pp. 89–90.

In fact, the African Commission has interpreted these rights to include members of the LGBTI community. The African Charter's various articles were mentioned in the resolution on protection against violence and other human rights violations against people based on their real or assumed sexual orientation or gender identity. These articles serve as the resolution's foundation and the premise that the violence and violations of human rights experienced by LGBTI people are intolerable.[82] Jjuuko has argued that "by bringing LGBTI persons within the ambit of the protections of the Commission, and in essence the Charter, the resolution defeats any argument to the effect that LGBTI rights are not covered by the provisions therein".[83] The African Commission has also stated that the objective of the principle of non-discrimination and equality under the African Charter is "to ensure equality of treatment for individuals irrespective of nationality, sex…age or sexual orientation".[84] In its 2010 Guidelines on Economic, Social, and Cultural Rights in the African Charter, the African Commission again reiterated the prohibition of discrimination on the ground of sexual orientation[85] and recognised sexual minorities as a vulnerable and disadvantaged group.[86]

The non-recognition of sexual minorities rights is often justified by the general limitation clauses that is provided for in article 27(2) which is to the effect that all the individual rights and freedoms recognised in the Charter shall be exercised "with due regard to the rights of others, collective security, morality and common interest". Morality and religion has often formed part of the list of limiting grounds for sexual minorities to enjoy their rights under the African Charter. However, the interpretation of the African Commission of article 27(2) provides for a different picture contrary to popular beliefs detrimental to sexual minorities. The African Commission has adjudicated that the limitation must take the form of a law of general application[87] and that popular will and belief does not necessarily allude to what is moral or in the public interest.[88] Jjuuko argued therefore that " public opinion in Africa being largely against homosexuality does not automatically imply that the rights of LGBTI persons are not protected in the African Charter".[89] Additionally, the Maputo Protocol has defined gender as including all persons of the female gender which also consists of intersex and transgender women.[90]

---

[82] African Commission on Human and Peoples' Rights 'Resolution on the Protection against Violence and other Human Rights Violations against Persons on the Basis of their Real or Imputed Sexual Orientation or Gender Identity' (2014).

[83] Jjuuko (2017), p. 269.

[84] *Zimbabwe Human Rights NGO Forum v Zimbabwe* (2006) AHRLR 128 (ACHPR 2006) para 169.

[85] African Commission 'Guidelines and principles on Economic, Social and Cultural Rights in the African Charter on Human and Peoples' (2010) para 1(d).

[86] Ibid para 1(e).

[87] *Constitutional Rights Project and others v Nigeria* (2000) AHRLR 227 (ACHPR 1999) para 44.

[88] *Legal Resources Foundation v Zambia* (2001) AHRLR 84 (ACHPR 2001) para 69.

[89] Jjuuko (2017), p. 270.

[90] Article 1(k) Maputo Protocol.

In 2010, the African Commission adopted the Resolution 275 dedicated specifically and entirely on sexual minorities rights issues for the first time.[91] The most significant development in this area was the recent resolution on violence against people based on their gender identity and sexual orientation. The African Commission gave LGBTI issues its own comprehensive resolution for the first time. The resolution demanded that governments signatories to the Charter guarantee that human rights breaches and acts of violence against LGBTI individuals and campaigners are duly addressed. The historic nature of the resolution stemmed from the fact that it was the first resolution devoted to LGBTI rights and that it explicitly placed LGBTI rights under the African Charter's protection. Previously, the Commission had only included members of the LGBTI community in more general resolutions. One such resolution was the creation of a committee to defend the rights of those living with HIV and those who are at risk, vulnerable to, and affected by the virus, which includes men who have sex with men.[92] Sexual orientation as a ground on which discrimination is prohibited is also included in the African Commission's General Comments on article 14(1)(d) and (e) of the Maputo Protocol as well as General Comment No 2 on article 14(1)(a), (b), (c), and (f).

The African human rights system on sexual minorities rights, as described above, presents an interesting and worthwhile opportunity for the various NGOs working on the sexual minorities rights. Mechanisms such as shadows reporting and communications to the African Commission can be put to good and effective use to drive forward the agenda of sexual minorities.

References

African Commission (2010) 'Guidelines and principles on Economic, Social and Cultural Rights in the African Charter on Human and Peoples' Rights' <http://www.achpr.org/files/instruments/economic-social-cultural/achpr_instr_guide_draft_esc_rights_eng.> Accessed 01 July 2025

African Commission on Human and Peoples' Rights 'Resolution on the Protection against Violence and other Human Rights Violations against Persons on the Basis of their Real or Imputed Sexual Orientation or Gender Identity': Adopted at the African Commission on Human and Peoples' Rights (the African Commission), meeting at its 55th Ordinary Session held in Luanda, Angola, from 28 April to 12 May 2014 <http://www.achpr.org/sessions/55th/resolutions/275/> Accessed 01 July 2025

Bengtsson T, Scott K (2010) The ageing population. In: Bengtsson T (ed) Population ageing - a threat to the welfare state? Demographic research monographs. Springer, Berlin, Heidelberg

Biegon J (2011) The promotion and protection of disability rights in the African human rights system. In: Grobbelaar-Du Plessis I, van Reenen T (eds) Aspects of disability law in Africa, pp 56–57

Combrinck H (2013) Disability Rights in the African Regional Human Rights System during 2011 and 2012 (Regional Developments). Afr Disabil Rights Yearb 9:361–368

[91] Resolution on Protection against Violence and other Human Rights Violations against Persons on the basis of their real or imputed Sexual Orientation or Gender Identity.

[92] Resolution 163 adopted at the 47th session of the Africa Commission (26 May 2010).

Committee on Persons living with Disabilities (Concluding Observations on the initial report of Mauritius' (30 September 2015) UN Doc CRPD/C/MUS/CO/1

Doron I, Spanier B, Lazar O (2016) The rights of older persons within the African Union. Elder Law Rev 10:1

D'sa RM (1985) Human and peoples' rights: distinctive features of the African Charter. J Afr Law 29(1):72–81

Equaldex (2024) LBGT rights in Mauritius. <https://www.equaldex.com/region/mauritius> Accessed 01 July 2025

Grand Bay (Mauritius) Declaration and Plan of Action CONF/HRA/DECL (I), adopted by the OAU Ministerial Conference on Human Rights in Africa, meeting from 12-16 April 1999 in Grand Bay, Mauritius

Jjuuko A (2017) Protection and promotion of LGBTI rights in the African human rights system. In: Namwase S, Jjuuko A (eds) Protecting the human rights of sexual minorities in contemporary Africa. Pretoria University Law Press, Pretoria

Kamga S (2013) A call for a protocol to the African charter on human and peoples' rights on the rights of persons with disabilities in Africa. Afr J Int Comp Law 21:219

Law Reform Commission (2023) Issue Paper on the Protection of the Rights and Interests of Elderly Persons in Mauritius

Mbondenyi K (2011) International human rights and their enforcement in Africa. African Books Collective

Ministry of Social integration, social security and national solidarity 'The Medical Unit' (2024a) <https://socialsecurity.govmu.org/Pages/Services/Medical-unit.aspx> Accessed 1 July 2025

Ministry of Social integration, social security and national solidarity (2024b) 'The Welfare and Elderly Persons' Protection Unit. <https://socialsecurity.govmu.org/Pages/Services/Elderly-protection-unit.aspx> Accessed 01 July 2025

Msipa D, Juma P (2023) The African disability protocol: toward a social and human rights approach to disability in the African human rights system. In: Rioux M, Viera J, Buettgen A, Zubrow E (eds) Handbook of disability. Springer, Singapore

Murray R, Viljoen F (2009) 'Towards non discrimination on the basis of sexual orientation: the normative basis and procedural possibilities before the African commission on human and peoples' rights and the African union. Hum Rights Q 29:86–111

OHCHR (2018) African states affirm the rights of persons with disabilities in a new landmark protocol. (15 February 2018) <https://wwwohchrorg/en/press-releases/2018/02/african-states-affirm-rights-persons-disabilities-new-landmark-protocol> accessed 01 July 2025

Quinn G, Degener T (2002) Human rights and disability: the current use and future potential of United Nations human rights instruments in the context of disability. United Nations Press

Secretariat of the African Decade of Persons with Disabilities (2011) The Architecture for an African Disability Rights Mechanism

Sik Yeun J (2011) The rights of older persons and persons with disabilities in Africa. In: Ssenyonjo M (ed) The African regional human rights system: 30 years after the African charter on human and peoples' rights. Martinus Nijhoff Publishers

Statistics Mauritius (2022) Reports Available at https://statsmauritius.govmu.org/Pages/Statistics/Publication_Programme/Pub_Prog_Yr22.aspx (Accessed 30 June 2025)

Statistics Mauritius (2023) Report Available at https://statsmauritius.govmu.org/Pages/Statistics/By_Subject/Other/Other_Page.aspx (Accessed 30 June 2025)

Umozurike UO (1983) The African Charter on human and peoples' rights. Am J Int Law 77(4):902–912

UN HRC (2018) Summary of stakeholders submission on Mauritius (27 August 2018) UN Doc A/HRC/WG.6/31/MUS/3, https://upr-info.org/sites/default/files/documents/2018-10/a_hrc_wg.6_31_mus_3_e.pdf> Accessed 01 July 2025

van Reenen T, Combrinck H (2011) The UN convention on the rights of persons with disabilities in Africa: progress after 5 years. SUR Int J Human Rights 14

Viljoen F (2015) International human rights law in Africa. Oxford University Press UK

Chapter 10
The Contribution of the Judicial and Quasi-judicial Institutions of the African Union to Human Rights Law in Mauritius: Prospects for Advancing Interactions Between Mauritian and African Human Rights Law

Abstract Mauritius has not developed a culture of judicial challenges in human rights matters since independence. While individuals seek remedies and justice when they are victims, litigation for general public interest and human rights advancement has not been a part of the Mauritian way. Access to supranational human rights bodies under the UN and AU is not adequately utilised by stakeholders, including individuals and civil society organisations. Civil society organisations have been educated about these mechanisms, but researchers and academics have not made genuine attempts to popularise them. Despite multiple recommendations, access to these bodies remains largely denied. The African Commission, the African Court, and the African Children's Committee are the three AU-level organisations that are the subject of this chapter. Its main goal is to inform all parties concerned about their existence, importance, and relevance to Mauritians' human rights. Their obligation of aware ess should be followed by an obligation to make use of them.

10.1 Introduction

It is relevant to embark on this last chapter with an observation. Since independence, a culture of judicial challenges on matters regarding human rights has never been developed. Individuals do knock at the door of courts for remedies and justice when they are victims. However, litigating for a general purpose, in the interest of the public and for the advancement of human rights has never been part of the Mauritian way as arguably is the case in jurisdictions such as the South African or the Indian ones. This implies that supranational human rights bodies under both the UN and the AU are not utilised sufficiently, if not at all, by stakeholders such as individuals and civil society organisations in Mauritius. Access to them has not been given adequately except for a few ones such as the UN HRC and the CEDAW Committee. As discussed thematically in the previous chapters, access to others has

R. Mahadew, *Mauritius and African Human Rights Law*,
https://doi.org/10.1007/978-3-032-08832-1_10

been politically denied with lack of ratification of the instruments that establishes them.

While this is the main reason, there are other important ones as well. For example, civil society organisations have been taught and educated so as to enable them to employ these mechanisms. Also, researchers and academics in human rights have never made any genuine attempts to popularise these instruments and mechanisms for individuals and NGOs to engage with. Where access was given voluntarily by the state or it was automatically provided by the treaties (such as the African Commission and the African Children's Committee), NGOs and individuals barely used them and for the majority of instances where access is systematically denied, concerned stakeholders never convinced and pressurised the state to grant access in line with their obligations under international human rights law. Multiple recommendations of various bodies to which state reports have been submitted to grant access to citizens and NGOs have fallen on deaf ears and met with inaction.

This chapter focuses on three such institutions at the level of the AU: the African Commission, the African Court, and the African Children's Committee. Its primary purpose is to educate all concerned parties about their existence, relevance, and significance to human rights in Mauritius. They have a duty to know about them, which should be followed by a duty to use them.

10.2 The African Commission

The African Commission on Human and Peoples' Rights was founded by the African Charter. The Commission was established in Addis Ababa, Ethiopia, on 2 November 1987. The Gambia's Banjul is home to the Secretariat of the Commission. Eleven professionals selected by the state parties to the Charter make up the Commission, which is chosen by the AU Assembly. When choosing the members of the Commission, the Assembly takes into account fair geographic and gender representation. The Commission's members are up for re-election after serving a six-year term.

After being chosen, the commissioners work in their individual capacities rather than on behalf of their home nations. The independence of the Commission was impacted by the past political positions that a few of its members held at the federal level. Senior civil servants and diplomatic representatives were not allowed to nominate candidates for the Commission in a note verbale that the African Union delivered to member-states in April 2005.

As the Bureau of the Commission, the Commission chooses its Chairperson and Vice-Chairperson. They can run for re-election once throughout their two-year tenure of office. The Bureau oversees and evaluates the work of the Commission's Secretariat in addition to coordinating the Commission's operations. In addition, the Bureau has the authority to decide on emergency problems in between Commission sessions. Nonetheless, it must report on the state of affairs to the members at the Commission's upcoming meeting. The African Commission's Secretary and other support personnel required for the efficient execution of the Commission's mandate are appointed by the AU Commission Chairperson. The Commission receives logistical, technical, and administrative support from the Secretariat.

The Commission's mandate is outlined in Article 45 of the Charter as (1) promotion and advancement of the rights of persons and humans; the Commission uses seminars, symposia, conferences, and missions to carry out public mobilisation, sensitisation, and information dissemination; (2) defence and protection of the rights of people and human rights, through its communication process, amicable conflict resolution, state reporting (which includes reviewing the shadow reports of non-governmental organisations), urgent appeals, and other initiatives of special rapporteurs, working groups, and missions, the Commission guarantees the protection of human and peoples' rights; and (3) interpretation of the African Charter on request by a state party, AU bodies, or individuals, the Commission is tasked with interpreting the Charter's contents. No AU organ has ever requested that the Commission interpret a case involving the Charter. Nonetheless, a small number of NGOs have asked the Commission to interpret other Charter sections. In addition, the Commission has passed other resolutions that elaborate on the Charter's contents. The Commission's Rules of Procedure govern the specific actions and processes that it takes. The first set of Commission Rules of Procedure were approved in 1988 and revised in 1995. New Rules of Procedure were adopted by the Commission with the establishment of the African Court on Human and Peoples' Rights, and they became effective on 18 August 2010.

Every year, the Commission convenes twice for regular sessions. Depending on the demands and finances of each client, the session lasts anywhere from 10 to 15 days. The Commission fixes the date of an ordinary session on the recommendation of its chairperson, who confers with the chairperson of the AU Commission. The Commission may convene special meetings. The African Union Commission Chairperson or the majority of Commission members may request that extraordinary sessions be called by the Commission Chairperson. The Commission's Secretary typically drafts the agenda for a regular meeting after consulting with the Commission Bureau. The Chairperson, Commission members, state parties, AU organs, NHRIs, NGOs, and any other specialised institution of the UN may offer additional items for inclusion in the agenda in addition to those that were proposed at the previous session. The Commission Bureau, however, ultimately decides which items are included to the provisional agenda.

Every Ordinary Session of the AU Assembly receives a report from the Commission detailing its actions both during and between sessions. As the Assembly's representative, the Executive Council reviews the report. The Commission Chairperson or a representative gives a presentation of the report. Information regarding the Commission's protective missions and communications may only be made public once the Executive Council and Assembly have approved the report. Immediately following the meeting, the Commission often releases a communiqué before the AU Assembly adopts the Activity Report.

10.2.1 Communications

One tool the Commission uses to make sure nations are abiding with the human rights guaranteed by the Charter is communications (complaints). In line with its authority under articles 48, 49, and 55 of the African Charter, the Commission may hear complaints on alleged human rights abuses from states against other states (inter-state complaints) or from people and non-governmental organisations (individual complaints) against one or more states. Since its founding in 1987, the Commission has received more than 400 individual communications.

The Democratic Republic of Congo (DRC) filed a communication against Burundi, Rwanda, and Uganda in 2004, alleging grave human and peoples' rights violations. The Commission, drawing on international law, the UN Charter, and UN General Assembly resolutions, ruled that the states' actions violated the Congolese people's self-determination rights and threatened national and international peace. The Commission found that the states deprived the Congolese people of their rights to freely dispose of their natural resources, violating provisions of the African Charter.[1]

An organisation or individual may present a communication to the Commission. The subject of standing is left unsaid in the Charter, and a victim requirement is not stipulated in the Commission's Rules of Procedure. The victim or victims may submit a communication, or anybody may do so on their behalf. It is not necessary to get the victim's express authorisation when an individual or non-governmental organisation submits a communication on their behalf. Additionally, the NGO is not required to hold observer status with the Commission. It is not necessary for the person or organisation to be a citizen or registered in the state where the communication is being made. A communication can only be brought against a state that has ratified the African Charter. The Commission may grant free legal aid to the author of a communication either on its own initiative or in response to the author's request. In making this decision, the Commission must be persuaded that the author lacks the resources to cover all or a portion of the communication's costs and that legal assistance is necessary to guarantee the parties' equality and enable the Commission to carry out its obligations.

Article 56 establishes the criteria for admissibility of communications. Any communication must meet each of the following conditions before the Commission deems it admissible: They must state who are the authors, be compliant with the African Constitution and the AU Constitution, not be written in derogatory or offensive language, and not be solely based on media reports. Communications must be sent within a reasonable time after local remedies have been exhausted. Issues highlighted in the communication cannot have been resolved through other UN or AU procedures. Domestic remedies must have been exhausted, unless the domestic procedure has been unnecessarily delayed.

---

[1] *DRC v Burundi, Rwanda and Uganda* (2004) AHRLR 19 (ACHPR 2003).

The most crucial prerequisite for case admissibility before the African Commission and other international human rights organisations is the exhaustion of domestic remedies. This is a result of the international adjudicatory system's subsidiarity. The purpose of the necessity to exhaust domestic remedies is to alert the government to the infraction, giving the state time to address it, and to allow domestic courts time to consider the matter. It is necessary to exhaust only judicial remedies that are accessible, efficient, and adequate to right the error. A cure is considered effective when it has some chance of success, available when it is easily accessible without any obstacles, and sufficient when it can address the wrong.

However, if the complaints fulfil any of the following categories, the complainant is not required to pursue all available local remedies: (1) if the victims (Purohit v The Gambia) are indigent, (2) if the allegations pertain to severe or widespread infractions (Free Legal Assistance Group v Zaire), (3) if national courts lose their jurisdiction due to domestic legislation (Media Rights Agenda v Nigeria) (4) if national laws do not protect the rights asserted (SERAC v Nigeria), (5) if returning to the wrong state to exhaust the local remedy would put the complaint in danger physically (Jawara v The Gambia; Abubarkar v Ghana), (6) in the event that the lawsuit contains an "impractical number" of possible plaintiffs (Guinea v. African Institute for Human Rights and Development), and (7) if the process of seeking a domestic remedy will take an excessively long time (African Charter, article 56(5)).

The process of communication registration involves registering, submitting, allocating file numbers, acknowledging, seizing, and preparing a summary. The Secretariat distributes the summary to all Commissioners, and if not approved, the communication is presented to the Commission for approval. The state party is notified, and the Commission decides on admissibility. If admissible, parties can provide observations, and if not, a rapporteur is appointed. The Commission then makes final recommendations. Following admission of a communication, the Commission may order the state in question to implement one or more temporary measures while the communication is being finalised. Temporary steps are required to shield the victim of an alleged offence from irreversible harm. As per rule 118(2) of the 2010 Rules of Procedure, the Commission may refer a communication to the African Court if a state disregards its request for the adoption of interim measures beyond the designated timeframe. The Commission is required under its Rules of Procedure to encourage parties to settle their differences amicably. The details of the settlement must be agreeable to both parties before it is finalised. The settlement must abide by the fundamental rights of human beings. The Commission may simply declare that the state is in violation if it discovers a violation. The Commission has given several extensive recommendations in its conclusions. For example, it can suggest that the state take the required actions to abide by the Charter, such as compensating the victim or victims.

The 2010 Rules of Procedure outline follow-up procedures for the Commission's decision-making process. Parties must notify the Commission within 30 days of adopting the Activity Report, and state parties must inform the Commission within 180 days of all measures taken. If no response is received within 90 days, the

Commission may send a reminder, and the rapporteur must monitor state actions and report findings.

10.2.2 State Reporting

One way to assess how well governments are adhering to their Charter-mandated tasks is through state reporting. States are required by Article 62 of the Charter to report to the Commission on a regular basis. In October 1988, the Commission established basic guidelines for the structure and contents of official reports in order to implement that particular article of the Charter. More succinct Guidelines to Periodic Reporting were also released in 1998. States parties to the Women's Protocol are also required under Article 26 of the Protocol to report on the legislative and other actions they have taken to carry out the Protocol's provisions in their periodic report to the Commission in accordance with Article 62 of the Charter. States signatories to the Women's Protocol shall include a report in two sections, one pertaining to the Protocol and the other to the Charter. The Guidelines for Reporting on the Women's Protocol were established by the African Commission in 2009, while the Guidelines for Reporting on Economic, Social, and Cultural Rights were adopted in 2010.

The state reporting procedure provides a platform for fruitful discussion. It allows the Commission to keep an eye on how the Charter is being implemented and pinpoint any obstacles standing in the way of the Charter's goals being realised. States are allowed to evaluate their successes and shortcomings in the context of the Charter. States are required by the Charter to submit two kinds of reports: initial and periodic. States have two years from the date of ratification or accession to the Charter to submit their initial reports. After the initial report, periodic reports must be provided every two years. A state party to the Charter is required to include the following in its state report: measures taken to put the provisions of the Charter into practice, advancements made thus far, obstacles to the Charter's and the pertinent supplemental documents' implementation. In accordance with the Commission's recommendations for state reporting under the Maputo Protocol, states should additionally address the implementation of the protocol's provisions if they are ratified.

The procedure for state reporting involves states reporting to the African Commission's Secretariat, uploading the report on the Commission's website, circulating copies to commissioners and NGOs, submitting contributions to the Commission's Secretary, and inviting institutions to submit information. The Commission prepares proposals based on the report, communicates questions to all commissioners, examines the report in open session, and adopts concluding observations in closed session. After reviewing state reports, the Commission began adopting conclusions in 2001. Conclusions discuss both the good and bad things that have come to light during the report's analysis. The actions that the state should take to address the deficiencies that have been found are outlined in the concluding observations.

Commissioners are responsible for following up on recommendations from Concluding Observations and transmitting them to the AU Assembly. If state representatives cannot provide satisfactory answers, the Commission sends a follow-up letter. If a state fails to send representatives, the Commission may proceed with the report and forward its observations. The Secretary informs the Commission of non-submission of reports, with reminders sent every three months and a list attached to Commission Activity Reports.

The African Commission has a strong relationship with non-governmental organisations (NGOs), as they are required to cooperate with other African and international institutions promoting and protecting human and peoples' rights. Since 1988, the Commission has granted observer status to NGOs with over 480 NGOs granted this status. NGOs play a significant role in the Commission's activities, drawing attention to violations of the Charter, bringing communications on behalf of individuals, monitoring states' compliance, and increasing awareness about the Commission's activities. They participate in public sessions, submit shadow reports, and submit a report on their activities every two years. The NGO Forum, organised by the African Centre for Democracy and Human Rights Studies, coordinates NGOs' engagement with the Commission. National human rights institutions (NHRIs) are statutory bodies established by governments in Africa to promote and protect human rights institutions in their respective countries. The relationship between the Commission and NHRIs began in 1998 with the adoption of the resolution on the Granting of Affiliate Status to NHRIs. NHRIs are required to assist the Commission in promoting human rights at the country level and raise awareness of the Commission's activities.

10.2.3 Successes and Challenges of the African Commission

The African Commission has made significant progress in interpreting the civil and political rights provisions of the Charter, including the rights to protection of language, national and international peace and security, family life, development, existence, and self-determination.[2] The Commission has also emphasised women's rights, adopting the Women's Protocol and passing resolutions on issues such as the status of women in Africa, women and girl victims of sexual violence, and maternal mortality in Africa.[3] The Commission has a strong relationship with NGOs and NHRIs, making statements and interventions during public sessions.[4] It has been actively promoting the rights of indigenous peoples in Africa, making notable pronouncements and establishing a working group on indigenous populations and

[2] Ouguergouz (2021).

[3] Durojaye and Oluduro (2016), pp. 315–336.

[4] Mute (2021).

communities.[5] The Commission has interpreted the "claw back clauses" in the Charter progressively, ensuring that international human rights standards always prevail over contradictory national law.[6]

However, challenges remain, such as the lengthy time-lag between complaints and final decisions, delays in the adoption of reports of Special Rapporteurs, and a lack of follow-up mechanisms to monitor compliance of its recommendations.[7] States also face challenges, as many lag behind in their obligations to submit state reports under the Charter, depriving the Commission of regular opportunities for reviewing the state's human rights record.[8] The African Union (AU) political organs provide insufficient support to the Commission and sometimes stall its work, causing a lack of coordination between AU organs or bodies with human rights-related mandates.[9]

10.3 The African Court

A Protocol to the African Charter established the African Court on Human and Peoples' Rights, or African Court. On 9 June 1998, in Ouagadougou, Burkina Faso, the Protocol on the Establishment of an African Court on Human and Peoples' Rights was adopted. It came into effect on 25 January 2004. The Commission's protective function was intended to be supplemented by the Court.[10] The Protocol's state parties are obligated to abide by its final judgements.[11] Eleven judges are on the Court; they are chosen by the AU Assembly from a list of applicants submitted by AU member- states. The judges are chosen individually, but no two sitting justices may be citizens of the same state. Geographic representation and gender are also duly taken into account. The judges can only be re-elected once throughout their six-year term of office. The only person who holds office full-time is the president of the Court.[12] Ten other judges have part-time jobs. On 1 July 2006, the Court's first judges took the oath of office. The Court's headquarters are in Arusha, Tanzania. States that have ratified the Court's Protocol are the only ones over which the Court has jurisdiction. The African Charter, the Court's Protocol, and any other human rights treaty that the relevant state has ratified are among the cases and disagreements that the Court may consider. The Court also has the authority to encourage a

[5] Bojosi and Wachira (2006), pp. 382–406.

[6] Chekol and Dogan (2024), p. 1598.

[7] Okoloise (2018), pp. 27–57.

[8] Bulto (2006), p. 57.

[9] Murray (2004).

[10] Bekker (2007), pp. 151–172.

[11] Naldi (2014), pp. 366–392.

[12] Muigai (2012), pp. 265–282.

peaceful resolution of issues that are pending before it. The Court has the authority to interpret its own ruling.[13]

The AU's human rights treaties and any other human rights treaties ratified by the relevant state fall under the purview of the Court. The Court's methodology in the utilisation of its substantial authority is not impenetrable. As in the Mtikila case, the Court does not think it is necessary to take other treaties into consideration after considering the alleged infringement in light of the pertinent articles of the African Charter.[14] However, as demonstrated in the Zongo case, the Court determined that article 19 of the International Covenant on Civil and Political Rights (ICCPR) had been violated in relation to the right to freedom of expression.[15] With the exception of persistent violations, the Court's temporal jurisdiction began on the date the Court's Protocol became operative with regard to a certain state. Tanzania had ratified the African Charter and was duty bound by its provisions at the time of the alleged breach, hence the court in Mtikila case ruled the respondent accountable. It further ruled that the conduct complained of—the exclusion of independent candidates—was a prevailing practice that persisted up until the implementation of the Court's Protocol. Additionally, the Court is able to offer advisory opinions on any subject falling under its purview. The African Union (AU), its member-states, its organs, and any recognised African organisation may all obtain the Court's advisory opinion.[16]

The African Commission, states party to the Court's Protocol, and African intergovernmental organisations are among the organisations that are qualified to bring matters before the Court. The African Children's Committee was ruled to lack standing to bring cases before the court in its first advisory opinion by the African Court.[17] If the state has declared in accordance with article 34(6) of the Protocol establishing the Court, individuals and NGOs holding observer status before the Commission may bring issues directly before the Court. Only eight of the thirty-four State Parties to the Protocol have deposited the declaration admitting the Court's authority to hear cases from people and non-governmental organisations directly so far. Burkina Faso, The Gambia, Ghana, Guinea-Bissau, Mali, Malawi, Niger, and Tunisia are the eight states. Mauritius does not figure on this list implying that NGOs and individuals do not have direct access to it against the state.[18]

The relationship between the African Court and the African Commission is governed by a Protocol. The Court complements the Commission's protective mandate, transfers matters to the Commission, and can submit communications regarding

[13] Ssenyonjo (2018), pp. 1–42.

[14] Christopher Mtikila vs United Republic of Tanzania (Application No. 009/2011; Application No. 011/2011) para 123.

[15] Zongo Abdoulaye Nikiema alias Ablasse, Ernest Zongo and Blaise Ilboudo vs Burkina Faso Application 013/2011.

[16] Odinkalu (2023), pp. 365–405.

[17] Viljoen (2012), pp. 446–448.

[18] Viljoen (2004), p. 1.

human rights violations.[19] The Commission can seize the Court during consideration of a communication, submit communications due to failure or unwillingness to comply, request the Court's opinion on admissibility, and give advisory opinions upon request.[20] The Court is required to consult with the Commission when drawing up its own rules.[21] In 2011, the African Commission ordered provisional measures against Libya, citing a situation of extreme gravity and urgency.[22]

10.4 The African Committee of Experts on the Rights and Welfare of the Child

The African Children's Committee was established on 11 July 2001, during the 37th session of the Assembly of Heads of State and Government in Lusaka, Zambia, following the adoption of the Charter on 29 November 1999. The Committee is made up of people who are highly moral, honest, unbiased, and knowledgeable about issues pertaining to children's rights and welfare.[23] The AU Assembly of Heads of States and Governments elects the Committee members from nominations made by state parties. Previously, the members were chosen for a five-year term under article 37(1) of the Charter and were not eligible for reappointment. However, article 37(1) has been changed as a result of an AU General Assembly resolution, allowing Committee members to be re-elected only once.[24] The members serve in their individual capacities after being elected. The Committee chooses a Chairperson, three Vice-Chairpersons, a Rapporteur, and a Deputy Rapporteur from among its members. They are up for re-election after serving a two-year term in office. The Secretary of the Committee is chosen by the African Union Chairperson. Supporting the Committee is the responsibility of the secretariat. Its members act as a point of contact for any correspondence pertaining to the Committee and are responsible for maintaining its archives.[25]

The mandate of the Committee is outlined in Article 42 of the African Children's Charter. The protection and promotion of the Charter's guaranteed rights is a key aspect of this mandate. The Committee gathers and records data, evaluates the state of affairs regarding Africa's issues with children's rights, calls meetings, supports regional and national organisations, and, when required, offers advice and suggestions to the government. The Committee collaborates with other African, international, and regional institutions and organisations and develops corresponding

[19] Viljoen (2012), pp. 424–426.

[20] Viljoen (2018), pp. 63–98.

[21] Elsheikh (2002), p. 252.

[22] Omorogbe (2012), pp. 141–163.

[23] Lloyd (2002b), p. 320.

[24] AU General Assembly resolution (Assembly/AU/Dec.548(XXIV).

[25] Viljoen (2012), pp. 397–398.

principles and guidelines. It also ensures the protection of the rights established in the Charter and oversees its implementation. It is also entrusted with the interpretation of the African Children's Charter's provisions upon request by a state party, an AU institution, or any other individual or organisation that the AU recognises.[26]

The Committee receives complaints from individuals, groups, NGOs, and member-states regarding children's rights. It can provide free legal aid to the complainant, if necessary for the proper discharge of its duties and ensuring equality. The Committee's jurisdiction is determined by the child's age at the time of the alleged violation. Admissibility criteria include compatibility with the AU's Constitutive Act and the African Children's Charter, non-groundless information, non-pending settlement, exhaustion of local remedies, and no disparaging language. It receives communications and processes them through the Secretariat, which ensures they meet the requirements of form and content. If the communication does not meet these requirements, it may request the state party to adopt provisional measures to prevent irreparable harm to the victim. The Committee has received four communications against state parties and has given its decision on three of them.[27]

The Committee can settle disputes amicably, based on respect for child rights and welfare. Any settlement outside the Committee's jurisdiction must be reported. If a state party violates the African Children's Charter, they must report the measures taken to implement the Committee's decision within 180 days. A rapporteur is appointed to monitor the implementation of the Committee's decisions by the state party.

In *Senegalese Talibés v The Republic of Senegal,*[28] a Communication was submitted to the Committee regarding 100,000 talibés children in Senegal who were sent to Quranic schools called daaras for religious education. The Committee found that Senegal violated article 11 of the African Children's Charter by failing to provide free and compulsory education to all children. The Committee recommended that the government enforce its own laws to protect talibés from abuse and ensure that education received in daaras equips them with a rounded education.

In the Nubian case,[29] the Committee alleged that the Kenyan Government violated the right to a nationality and registration of children with Nubian descent. They found multiple violations of the African Children's Charter and recommended that the Government of Kenya take necessary legislative, administrative, and other measures to ensure that children of Nubian descent in Kenya can acquire a Kenyan nationality and proof of such a nationality at birth. In *Hansungule and Others (on*

---

[26] Viljoen (2012), p. 406.

[27] Viljoen (2012), pp. 402–404.

[28] *The Centre for Human Rights (University of Pretoria) and la Rencontre Africaine Pour la Defense des Droits de L'homme (Senegal) v Government of Senegal* Decision No. 003/Com/001/2012.

[29] *Institute for Human Rights and Development in Africa and the Open Society Justice Initiative (on behalf of children of Nubian Descent in Kenya) v The Government of Kenya* Decision No 002/Com/002/2009.

behalf of children in Northern Uganda) v Uganda,[30] the Committee found that the government failed to comply with its obligations under article 1(1) of the African Children's Charter by not specifically legislating for the banning of the recruitment of children into the armed forces.

The Committee has the authority to issue authoritative interpretations of the African Children's Charter, clarifying its meaning and scope, and explaining the corresponding obligations of state parties. The Committee has issued several general comments: General Comment No. 1 (article 30 of the African Charter on the Rights and Welfare of the Child) on "Children of Incarcerated and imprisoned Parents and Primary Caregivers" 2013 (GC 1), which deals with children of imprisoned parents; General Comment on article 6 of the African Charter on the Rights and Welfare of the Child: "Right to birth registration, name and nationality" (GC 2), which deals with the issue of birth registration, name and nationality, and the prevention of statelessness in children; General Comment No. 3: Joint General Comment of ACHPR and ACERWC on Ending Child Marriage; General Comment No. 4: on Article 31 of ACRWC on Responsibilities of the Child; General Comment No. 5: on Article 1 of ACRWC on State Party Obligations and Systems Strengthening for Child Protection; General Comment No. 6: on Article 22 of ACRWC on Children in situations of Conflict; General Comment No. 7: on Article 27 of ACRWC on Sexual Exploitation and General Comment No. 8: Joint General Comment on Female Genital Mutilation.[31]

The reporting process is an avenue for monitoring compliance of states with their children's rights obligations. Upon ratification of the African Children's Charter, each state party undertakes to submit reports on the measures it has adopted to give effect to the provisions of the Charter and on the progress made in the enjoyment of the rights guaranteed under the Charter (article 43). The Committee is empowered to receive and examine reports submitted by state parties on the measures they have adopted to give effect to the provisions of the Charter and on the progress made in the enjoyment of these rights.[32]

The report should be presented in a concise and structured manner, not exceeding 80 pages or 35,000 words, and should include copies of relevant provisions of the principal legislative, judicial, administrative, and other texts referred to in the report. The Committee has a simplified process of state reporting, which can be summarised as follows: State party submits report to the Committee, a Rapporteur is appointed to examine the situation of children's rights in relation to the state party report, civil society organisations are invited to submit complementary reports, a Committee pre-session Working Group is constituted to examine and identify issues

---

[30] *Hansungule and Others (on behalf of children in Northern Uganda) v Uganda* No. 001/Com/001/2005.

[31] ACERWC 'General Comments' available at https://reporting.acerwc.africa/en/key-documents/general-comments (accessed 15 June 2025).

[32] Viljoen (2012), pp. 400–401.

for discussion, and the Committee produces its Concluding Observations and recommendations for implementation by the State Party.[33]

The Committee on the Conduct of Investigations (CCI) conducts investigation missions to states party to the Children's Charter to gather information on the rights and welfare of children. The Committee has the power to investigate any matter falling within the ambit of the Children's Charter and may exercise its discretion to investigate a state party where allegations of violations of children's rights are reported. The Committee compiles a report, which is submitted to the Executive Council and adopted by the AU Assembly. The aim of these missions is to seek accurate and reliable information to assess the general situation of children's rights, clarify the facts and establish the responsibility of individuals and the state towards victims and their families, and promote the implementation of children's rights and welfare by the country's administrative, legal, and legislative institutions in conformity with the Charter.[34]

The Committee supports civil society organisations by granting observer status. CSOs organise CSO Forums before sessions, and the Committee assesses state reports with the help of CSOs. The Committee has developed guidelines for CSOs to complement state reports.[35] Unlike the African Commission, there is no formal engagement between the Committee and National Human Rights Institutions (NHRIs). The Day of the African Child (DAC) is celebrated annually, promoting inclusivity and improving children's rights. The DAC was established in memory of over 100 school children massacred in Soweto.[36]

References

ACERWC. Civil Society Organisations. Available at https://reporting.acerwc.africa/en/networks/csos. Accessed 15 June 2025)

ACERWC. Day of the African Child. Available at https://reporting.acerwc.africa/en/page/about-day-african-child. Accessed 15 June 2025

ACERWC. General Comments. Available at https://reporting.acerwc.africa/en/key-documents/general-comments. Accessed 15 June 2025

ACERWC. State Reporting. Available at https://reporting.acerwc.africa/en/page/about-state-reporting. Accessed 15 June 2025

AU General Assembly resolution (Assembly/AU/Dec.548(XXIV)

Bekker G (2007) The African court on human and peoples' rights: safeguarding the interests of African states. J Afr Law 51(1):151–172

[33] ACERWC 'State Reporting' available at https://reporting.acerwc.africa/en/page/about-state-reporting (accessed 15 June 2025).

[34] Viljoen (2012), pp. 404–405.

[35] ACERWC 'Civil Society Organisations' available at https://reporting.acerwc.africa/en/networks/csos (accessed 15 June 2025).

[36] ACERWC 'Day of the African Child' available at https://reporting.acerwc.africa/en/page/about-day-african-child (accessed 15 June 2025).

Bojosi KN, Wachira GM (2006) Protecting indigenous peoples in Africa: an analysis of the approach of the African Commission on Human and Peoples' Rights. Afr Human Rights Law J 6(2):382–406
Bulto TS (2006) Beyond the promises: resuscitating the sate reporting procedure under the African Charter on human and peoples' rights. Buff Hum Rights Law Rev 12:57
Chekol AT, Dogan I (2024) Championing human rights: normative insights into the African Charter on Human and Peoples' Rights. Beijing Law Rev 15:1598
Durojaye E, Oluduro O (2016) The African Commission on Human and People's Rights and the woman question. Fem Leg Stud 24(3):315–336
Elsheikh IAB (2002) The future relationship between the African Court and the African Commission. Afr Human Rights Law J 2:25
Lloyd A (2002a) Evolution of the African Charter on the Rights and Welfare of the Child and the African Committee of Experts: raising the Gauntlet. Int J Child Rights 10:179
Lloyd A (2002b) The first meeting of the African Committee of Experts on the Rights and Welfare of the Child. Afr Human Rights Law J 2:320
Muigai G (2012) From the African Court on human and peoples' rights to the African Court of justice and human rights. In: The African regional human rights system. Brill Nijhoff, pp 265–282
Murray R (2004) Human rights in Africa: from the OAU to the African Union. Cambridge University Press
Mute LM (2021) Protecting the mandate and autonomy of the African Commission on Human and Peoples' Rights: leveraging the roles of national human rights institutions June 2021. Human Rights
Naldi GJ (2014) Observations on the Rules of the African Court on Human and Peoples' Rights. Afr Human Rights Law J 14(2):366–392
Okoloise C (2018) Circumventing obstacles to the implementation of recommendations by the African Commission on Human and Peoples' Rights. Afr Human Rights Law J 18(1):27–57
Omorogbe EY (2012) The African Union, responsibility to protect and the Libyan crisis. Netherlands Int Law Rev 59(2):141–116
Ouguergouz F (2021) The African Charter of Human and Peoples' Rights: A comprehensive agenda for human dignity and sustainable democracy in Africa. BRILL
Ssenyonjo M (2018) Responding to human rights violations in Africa: Assessing the role of the African Commission and Court on Human and Peoples' Rights (1987–2018). Int Human Rights Law Rev 7(1):1–42
Viljoen F (2004) A human rights court for Africa, and Africans. Brook J Int Law 30:1
Viljoen F (2012) International human rights law in Africa, 2nd edn. Oxford University Press, Oxford
Viljoen F (2018) Understanding and overcoming challenges in accessing the African Court on Human and Peoples' Rights. Int Comp Law Quart 67(1):63–98

Bibliography

Abebe AM (2010) The African Union Convention on Internally Displaced Persons: Its Codification Background, Scope and Enforcement Challenges. Refugee Survey Quarterly 29(3): 28–57

Adetula V (2016) Principle and Practice of Regionalism in ECOWAS and the implications for regional integration in West Africa. Political Science Review 7(1): 17–34

African Commission on Human and Peoples' Rights 'Resolution on the Protection against Violence and other Human Rights Violations against Persons on the Basis of their Real or Imputed Sexual Orientation or Gender Identity': Adopted at the African Commission on Human and Peoples' Rights (the African Commission), meeting at its 55th Ordinary Session held in Luanda, Angola, from 28 April to 12 May 2014 <http://www.achpr.org/sessions/55th/resolutions/275/> accessed 01 July 2025.

African Commission on Humana and Peoples' Rights 'Concluding Observations and Recommendations on 6th to 8th Combined Report of the Republic of Mauritius on the Implementation of the African Charter on Human and Peoples' Rights' (2009).

African Commission 'Guidelines and principles on Economic, Social and Cultural Rights in the African Charter on Human and Peoples' Rights' (2010) <http://www.achpr.org/files/instruments/economic-social-cultural/achpr_instr_guide_draft_esc_rights_eng.> accessed 02 July 2025.

African Committee of Experts on the Rights and Welfare of the Child 'Communications' <https://www.acerwc.africa/en/page/about-communications> accessed 05 July 2025.

African Committee of Experts on the Rights and Welfare of the Child 'Egypt' <https://www.acerwc.africa/en/member-state/ratifications/62/egypt> accessed 105 July 2025.

African Committee of Experts on the Rights and Welfare of the Child 'Revised Guidelines for Consideration of Communications and Monitoring Implementation

R. Mahadew, *Mauritius and African Human Rights Law*,
https://doi.org/10.1007/978-3-032-08832-1

of Decisions by the African Committee of Experts on the Rights and Welfare of the Child' <https://www.acerwc.africa/sites/default/files/2022-06/Guidelines-for-Consideration-of-Communications-and-Monitoring-Implementation-of-Decisions-by-the-African-Committee-of-Experts-on-the-Rights-and-Welfare-of-the-Child-English.pdf> accessed 05 July 2025.

African Union Convention on Cyber Security and Personal Data Protection

African Union 'Solemn Declaration on Gender Equality in Africa' AU Doc Assembly/AU/Dec.12(III)Rev.1 (July 2004).

Afro Barometer 'Mauritians strongly endorse media freedom and public access to government information' (29 April 2024) <https://www.afrobarometer.org/wp-content/uploads/2024/04/AD799-Mauritians-endorse-media-freedom-and-public-access-to-government-information-Afrobarometer-28apr24.pdf> accessed 03 July 2025.

Afro Barometer 'Mauritius strong – but far from perfect – on gender equality and social tolerance' (03 August 2018) <https://www.afrobarometer.org/wp-content/uploads/2022/02/ab_r7_dispatchno225_tolerance_and_equality_in_mauritius.pdf> accessed 03 July 2025.

Ajala A Pan-Africanism: Evolution, Progress and Prospects (London: Andre Deutsch, 1974).

Akinnusi A 'The Bamako and Basel Conventions on the Transboundary Movement and Disposal of Hazardous Wastes: A comparative and critical analysis' (2001) 12 Stellenbosch Law Review 306.

Alesina, A, Murard, E & Rapoport, H (2019) Immigration and Preferences for Redistribution in Europe IZA Discussion Paper No. 12130, IZA—Institute of Labor Economics: Bonn.

Amao O (2018) African Union Law: The Emergence of a Sui Generis Legal Order, 1st edn. Routledge, London

Amao O et al. (eds) (2021) The Emergent African Union Law: Conceptualization, Delimitation, and Application. Oxford University Press, New York

Aniche ET (2020) From Pan-Africanism to African Regionalism: A Chronicle. African Studies 70(1): 70–87

Ankumah E The African Commission on Human and Peoples' Rights: The practice and procedures (1996) Brill Netherlands.

Apodaca, C., 2003. The rule of law and human rights. Judicature, 87, 292.

Appiagyei-Atua K (2006) Bumps on the Road: A Critique of how Africa got to NEPAD. African Human Rights Law Journal 6(2): 524–548

Arambulo K Strengthening the supervision of the International Covenant on Economic, Social and Cultural Rights: Theoretical and procedural aspects (1999)

Ayeni V (2011). Domestic Impact of the African Charter on Human and Peoples' Rights and the Protocol on the Rights of Women in Africa: A Case Study of Nigeria (p. 14). Unpublished LLM Dissertation, Pretoria: University of Pretoria.

Babarinde O (2007) The EU as a Model for the African Union: The Limits of Imitation. Jean Monnet/Robert Schuman Paper Series Vol. 7 No.2. https://aei.pitt.edu/8185/1/BabarindeEUasModellong07edi.pdf Accessed 25 June 2025.

Badri-Maharaj S 2016. The Mauritius-India naval relationship: naval diplomacy 2.0. Africa Trends, April-June.

Baimu E (2002) Human Rights in NEPAD and its Implications for the African Human Rights System. African Human Rights Law Journal 2: 301–319

Baimu E 'Human Rights in NEPAD and its implications for the African human rights system' (2002) 2 African Human Rights Law Journal 301, p. 302.

Baldacchino G and Wivel A (2020) Handbook on the Politics of Small States. Edward Elgar, Cheltenham

Ballgobin, V.D., 2017. Cyclones (1960–1980) and Housing Policy: Toward an Internally Controlled Migration? Revue Historique de l'Océan Indien, 14, pp.260–277.

Ballhatchet, K., 1995. The structure of British official attitudes: colonial Mauritius, 1883–1968. The Historical Journal, 38(4), pp.989–1011.

Banda, F. (2006). Blazing a Trail: The African Protocol on Women's Rights Comes into Force. Journal of African Law, 50, 72–84. https://doi.org/10.1017/S0021855306000076

Beeharry, Y., Bekaroo, G., Bussoopun, D., Bokhoree, C. and Phillips, M.R., 2021. Perspectives of leisure operators and tourists on the environmental impacts of coastal tourism activities: a case study of Mauritius. Environment, Development and Sustainability, 23, pp.10702–10726.

Bengtsson T and Scott K (2010) The Ageing Population in Bengtsson, T. (eds) Population Ageing - A Threat to the Welfare State? Demographic Research Monographs. Springer, Berlin, Heidelberg.

Bertelsmann Stiftung's Transformation Index (BTI) 2024 Germany available at https://bti-project.org/fileadmin/api/content/en/downloads/reports/country_report_2024_MUS.pdf (accessed 05 July 2025).

Bhankaraully S, Goyer M and Aroles J 'Workplace discrimination against LGBT employees in Mauritius: A sociological perspective' (2023) 44(4) Economic and Industrial Democracy 1105–1126.

Bhatt K (2018) Chagos: A Chance for the ICJ to do more for advancing human rights through the rule of law? Questions of International Law 55:85–92

Biegon J 'The promotion and protection of disability rights in the African human rights system' in I Grobbelaar-Du Plessis & T van Reenen (eds) Aspects of disability law in Africa (2011) 56–57.

Bischoff P (2021) The Politics of Regional Integration in Africa. In: Oxford Research Encyclopedia of International Studies, Oxford University Press. https://oxfordre.com/internationalstudies/view/10.1093/acrefore/9780190846626.001.0001/acrefore-9780190846626-e-612 Accessed 05 July 2025.

Bishop M et al (2021) Towards Sustained Development in Small Island Developing States: Why We Need to Reshape Global Governance. Overseas Development Institute Working Paper. https://cdn.odi.org/media/documents/SIDS_sustained_development_WP_jr.pdf Accessed 05 July 2025.

Blin, M 'Export-Oriented Policies, Women's work burden and human development in Mauritius' (2008) 34 Journal of Southern African Studies 239–253.

Borzel TA, Risse T (2016) The Oxford Handbook of Comparative Regionalism, 1st edn. Oxford University Press

Boven, T. (1986). The Relations between Peoples' Rights and Human Rights in the African Charter. Human Rights Law Journal, 7, 186.

Bueno De Mesquita, George W. Downs, Alastair Smith, Feryal Marie Cherif, Thinking Inside the Box: A Closer Look at Democracy and Human Rights, International Studies Quarterly, Volume 49, Issue 3, September 2005, Pages 439–457

C Packer Using Human Rights to change tradition: Traditional practices harmful to women's reproductive health in Sub-Saharan Africa (2002) Antwerp: Intersentia).

Carroll, B.W. and Carroll, T., 1999. The consolidation of democracy in Mauritius. Democratization, 6(1), pp.179–197.

Castellino J and S Allen Title to territory in international law: A temporal analysis (Aldershot: Ashgate, 2003).

Chan Low (2019) 'Constitutional development in the South Western Indian Ocean States' in Colom J, Rohfling-Dijoux & Schulze G (eds) The 50th Anniversary of Mauritius: Constitutional Development (Nomos, Germany).

Cheke A., 2001. Is the bird a Dodo? The wildlife of a mid-seventeenth century drawing of Dutch Mauritius. Archives of Natural History, 28(3), pp.347–351.

Claveyrolas, M., 2017. 'Indo-Mauritians' and the Indian Ocean: literacy accounts and anthropological readings. Journal of the Indian Ocean Region, 13(2), pp.174–189.

Cohen, R. (1993). Endless Teardrops: Proleg-Omena to the Study of Human Rights in Africa. In R. Cohen, G. Hyden, & W. Nagan (Eds.), Human Rights and Governance in Africa. Gainesville: University Press of Florida.

Colom J (2019) 'Equal and non-discriminatory right to health in Mauritius' in Colom J, Rohfling-Dijoux & Schulze G (eds) The 50th Anniversary of Mauritius: Constitutional Development (Nomos, Germany).

Combrinck H 'Disability Rights in the African Regional Human Rights System during 2011 and 2012 (Regional Developments)' (2013) 9 African Disability Rights Yearbook 361–368.

Committee on Persons living with Disabilities (Concluding Observations on the initial report of Mauritius' (30 September 2015) UN Doc CRPD/C/MUS/CO/1.

Consortium for Street Children 'Report on Street Children in Mauritius' <https://www.streetchildren.org/resources/report-on-street-children-in-mauritius/> accessed 05 July 2025.

Council of Europe 'Declaration from the Permanent Representative of the UK' (23 October 1953).

Cranston M What are human rights? (1973) Basic Books New York.

D'sa, R.M., 1985. Human and Peoples' Rights: Distinctive Features of the African Charter. Journal of African Law, 29(1), pp.72–81.

Dabee A 'Unfinished Business: The Journey to Women's Equality in Mauritius' (15 March 2021) <https://www.undp.org/mauritius-seychelles/blog/unfinished-business-journey-womens-equality-mauritius> accessed 05 July 2025.

Danso K (1995) The African Economic Community: Problems and Prospects. Africa Today 42(4): 31–55

Darga, L.A. and Joomun, G.D., 2005. Mauritius. South African Journal of International Affairs, 12(1), pp.95–110.

De Schutter O (2018) 'The rights-based welfare state: Public budgets and economic and social rights' Friedrich Ebert Stiftung Geneva available at https://library.fes.de/pdf-files/bueros/genf/14943.pdf (accessed 05 July 2025).

De Smith S A The New Commonwealth and its Constitutions (1964) Stevens University of California.

Doron, I., Spanier, B. and Lazar, O. 'The rights of older persons within the African Union' (2016) 10 Elder Law Review 1.

E Mengesha 'Reconciling the need for advancing women's rights in African and the dictates of international trade norms: The position of the Protocol on the Rights of Women in Africa' (2009) 9 African Human Rights Law Journal.

Environment and Land Use Appeal Tribunal <https://eluat.govmu.org/Pages/Legislations.aspx> accessed 05 July 2025.

Equaldex 'LBGT rights in Mauritius' <https://www.equaldex.com/region/mauritius> accessed 05 July 2025.

Esty DC (2006) Good Governance at the Supranational Scale: Globalizing Administrative Law. The Yale Law Journal 115(7): 1490–1562

Etzioni A (2001) Political Unification Revisited: On Building Supranational Communities. Lexington Books, Maryland

Fagbayibo B (2008) A Supranational African Union? Gazing into the Crystal Ball. De Jure 41: 493–503

Fagbayibo B (2013) Common Problems Affecting Supranational Attempts In Africa: An Analytical Overview. Potchefstroom Electronic Law Journal 16(1): 32–69

Fagbayibo B (2022) Transcending Member States: Political and Legal Dynamics of Building Continental Regionalism in Africa, 1st edn. Springer, Heidelberg

Fawcett L (2004) Exploring Regional Domains: A Comparative History of Regionalism. International Affairs 80(3): 429–446

Fawcett L, Gandois H (2010) Regionalism in Africa and the Middle East: Implications for EU Studies. Journal of European Integration 32(6): 617–636

Ferreira-Snyman A (2009) Regional Organisations and their Members: the Question of Authority. The Comparative and International Law Journal of Southern Africa 42(2): 183–209

Ferreira-Snyman A (2011) Regionalism and the Restructuring of the United Nations with Specific Reference to the African Union. The Comparative and International Law Journal of Southern Africa 44(3): 360–391

Gamble, A (2016) Can the welfare state survive? Polity Press.

Geiss, I., 1974. The pan-African movement: a history of Pan-Africanism in America, Europe, and Africa. Taylor & Francis.

Gibb R (2009) Regional Integration and Africa's Development Trajectory: Metatheories, Expectations and Reality. Third World Quarterly 30(4): 701–720

Glennerster, H (2007) The sustainability of Western welfare states - Seminar paper - Originally presented at CASE Seminar, November 2007, London School of Economics and Political Science.

Gokulsing D 'Gender, education and about market: Evidence from Mauritius' (2014) 34(9) International Journal of Sociology and Social Policy 609–633.

Gough, I & Therborn, G (2010) 'The Global Future of Welfare States', in The Oxford Handbook of the Welfare State, Edited by Francis G. Castles, Stephan Leibfried, Jane Lewis, Herbert Obinger, and Christopher Pierson, Oxford.

Gowreesunkur V (2019) African Union (AU) Agenda 2063 and Tourism Development in Africa: Contribution, Contradiction and Implications. International Journal of Tourism Cities 5(2): 288–300

Graham V, Graham S (2022) The African Small Island Developing States and Normative Coherence for Sustainable Development: The Quality of Civil Rights and Liberties. Development Policy Review 40(1): e12609

Graham, S., 2017. Drivers of the foreign policies of Southern African small states. Politikon, 44(1), pp.133–155.

Grand Bay (Mauritius) Declaration and Plan of Action CONF/HRA/DECL (I), adopted by the OAU Ministerial Conference on Human Rights in Africa, meeting from 12–16 April 1999 in Grand Bay, Mauritius.

Gray, M. and Lalljee, B., 2012. Climate change adaptation in Mauritius: considering the role of Institutions. Western Indian Ocean Journal of Marine Science, 11(1), pp.99–111.

Gray, S., 2023. Colonial continuities in Independent Mauritius: Parliamentary democracy, The British Crown, and state repression. The Journal of Indian Ocean World Studies, 7(1), pp.36–58.

Grote J (2010) The Changing Tides of Small Island States Discourse – A Historical Overview of the Appearance of Small Island States in the International Arena. Verfassung und Recht in Übersee 43(2): 164–191

Gumedze, S. (2003). Bringing Communications before the African Commission on Human and Peoples' Rights. African Human Rights Journal, 3, 119.

Gössling, S., Lindén, O., Helmersson, J., Liljenberg, J. and Quarm, S., 2007. Diving and global environmental change: a Mauritius case study. In New frontiers in marine tourism (pp. 67–92). Routledge.

Harris M, Khonje WH (2011) Regional Approaches in Sustainable Development. In: Vigilance C, Roberts JL (eds) Tools for Mainstreaming Sustainable Development in Small States. Commonwealth Secretariat, London, p 64–83

Hettne B (2005) Beyond the 'New' Regionalism. New Political Economy 10(4): 543–571

Heyns, C. (2001). The African Regional Human Rights System: In Need of Reform? African Human Rights Law Journal, 2, 157.

Heyns, C. (2004). The African Human Rights System: The African Charter. Penn State Law Review, 108, 681.

Holmberg, L., 1962. Mauritius. A study in disaster. Economy and history, 5(1), pp.3–29.

Hookoomsing, V.Y., 2003. Chota Bharat, Mauritius: the myth and the reality: The myth and the reality Preamble. In Culture and Economy in the Indian Diaspora (pp. 25–44). Routledge.

Houbert, J., 1981. Mauritius: independence and dependence. The Journal of Modern African Studies, 19(1), pp.75–105.

Humanium "Children of Mauritius' <https://www.humanium.org/en/mauritius/> accessed 05 July 2025.

ICJ Legal Consequences of the Separation of the Chagos Archipelago from Mauritius in 1965 https://www.icj-cij.org/case/169

Iroulo LC, Lenz T (2022) Global Theories of Regionalism. In Rüland J and Carrapatoso A (eds) Handbook on Global Governance and Regionalism. Edward Elgar, Cheltenham, p 36–51

Isanga, J. M. (2013). The Constitutive Act of the African Union, African Courts and the Protection of Human Rights: New Dispensation? Santa Clara Journal of International Law, 1, 271.

J Oloka-Onyango and S Tamale 'The personal is political or why women's rights are indeed human rights: An African perspective on International feminism' (1995) 17 Human Rights Quarterly 691.

Jjuuko A 'Protection and promotion of LGBTI rights in the African human rights system' in Namwase S & Jjuuko A (eds) Protecting the human rights of sexual minorities in contemporary Africa (2017) Pretoria University Law Press: Pretoria.

Johnson, D., 2006. Comparing the trajectories of educational change and policy transfer in developing countries. Oxford Review of Education, 32(5), pp.679–696.

Kadima, D.K. and Kasenally, R., 2005. The formation, collapse and revival of political party coalitions in Mauritius: Ethnic logic and calculation at play. Journal of African Elections, 4(1), pp.133–164.

Kamga S 'A call for a Protocol to the African Charter on Human and Peoples' Rights on the Rights of Persons with Disabilities in Africa' (2013) 21 African Journal of International and Comparative Law 219.

Kamga SAD and Fombad CM (2013) A Critical Review of the Jurisprudence of the African Commission on the Right to Development. Journal of African Law 57(2): 196–214

Kanbur R (2004) The African Peer Review Mechanism (APRM): An Assessment of Concept and Design. South African Journal of Political Studies 31(2): 157–166

Kannyo E "The Banjul Charter on Human and Peoples' Rights: Genesis and Political Background", in CE Welch and RI Meltzer (eds), Human Rights and Development in Africa (Albany, NY: State University of New York, 1984).

Kariseb K, Okoloise C (2019) Reflections on the African Governance Architecture: Trends, Challenges and Opportunities. In: Addaney M, Nyarko MG and Boshoff E (eds) Governance, Human Rights and Political Transformation in Africa. Springer, Cham, p 41–68

Kasenally R 'Is digitalisation endangering democracy in Mauritius' (2022) <https://www.ned.org/wp-content/uploads/2022/12/Roukaya-Kasenally_Is-

Digitalization-Endangering-Democracy-in-Mauritius.pdf> accessed 03 July 2025.

Kasenally, R., 2018. Political Leadership in Mauritius. The Mauritian paradox: Fifty years of development, diversity and democracy, p.43.

Kende M (2003) 'The South African Constitutional Court's Embrace of Socio-Economic Rights: A Comparative Perspective' Chapman Law Review 6(137) 138–160.

Khadiagala GM (2015) Pan-Africanism and Regional Integration. In: Cheeseman N, Anderson D and Scheibler A (eds) Routledge Handbook of African Politics, 1st edn. Routledge, London, p 375–389

Khalid, M., 2013. Disputed Islands of the Indian Ocean: a potential danger to Regional peace. Journal of Indian Ocean Studies, 21(2).

Kindiki K (2003) The Normative and Institutional Framework of the African Union Relating to the Protection of Human Rights and the Maintenance of International Peace and Security: A Critical Appraisal. African Human Rights Law Journal 3: 97–117

Kiwanuka, R. (1988). The Meaning of Peoples' Rights in the African Charter on Human and Peoples' Rights. American Journal of International Law, 80, 80.

Knox JH (2009) Linking Human Rights and Climate Change at the United Nations. Harvard Environmental Law Review 33: 477–498

Kotze, L.J. and du Plessis, A., 2019. The African Charter on Human and Peoples' Rights and Environmental Rights Standards. Environmental Rights: The Development of Standards, Cambridge, pp.93–115.

Kufuor KO (2005) The Collapse of the Organization of African Unity: Lessons from Economics and History. Journal of African Law 49(2): 132–144

Kumar, R. and Strazdins, N., 2021. The Digital Infrastructure Divide in the Commonwealth. Commonwealth Secretariat.

Kurecic P (2017a) Small States in the Multi-Polar World: Introduction. World Review of Political Economy 8(3): 280–294

Kurecic P (2017b) Small States and Regional Economic Integrations in the Multi-Polar World: Regional Differences in the Levels of Integration and Patterns of Small States' Vulnerability. World Review of Political Economy 8(3): 317–348

Kühnhardt L (2008) African Regional Integration and the Role of the European Union. Center for European Integration Studies ZEI Discussion Papers, University of Bonn. http://aei.pitt.edu/9046/1/dp_c184_Kuehnhardt.pdf Accessed 05 July 2025

Law Reform Commission 'Issue Paper on autonomous criminalisation of mob justice' (November 2023) <https://lrc.govmu.org/lrc/?p=4061> accessed 03 July 2024.

Law Reform Commission 'Issue Paper on the Protection of the Rights and Interests of Elderly Persons in Mauritius' (2023).

Le Matinal 'Rama Valayden's Arrest: Case Adjourned To 23 May' (17 May 2023) <https://english.lematinal.media/rama-valaydens-arrest-case-adjourned-to-23-may/> accessed 03 July 2025.

Lloyd, A., & Murray, R. (2004). Institutions with Responsibility for Human Rights Protection under the African Union. Journal of African Law, 48, 165–186. https://doi.org/10.1017/S0021855304482035

Long D, Murray R (2016) The Role and Use of Soft Law Instruments in the African Human Rights System. In Lagoutte S et al (eds) Tracing the Roles of Soft Law in Human Rights, Oxford University Press, Oxford, pp 89–108

Lubbe WD, Spijkers O (2021) Taking Stock of United Nations and African Union Constitutionalism. African Journal of International and Comparative Law 29(1): 62–81

Lyster S International wildlife law: An analysis of international treaties concerned with conservation of wildlife (Cambridge: Grotius Publications) 1985.

Magliveras KD, Naldi GJ (2003) The Pan-African Parliament of the African Union: An Overview. African Human Rights Law Journal 3: 223–234

Mahadew, R., 2015. 'The best loser system in Mauritius: An essential electoral tool for representing political minorities'. Constitutional building in Africa Nomos: Germany.

Mahadew, R., 2018. Does the Mauritian Constitution protect the right to privacy? An insight from Madhewoo v The State of Mauritius. African Human Rights Law Journal, 18(1), pp.189–204.

Mahadew, R., 2022. The Constitutionality of Legal Measures Taken by the Government of Mauritius in the Context of the Covid-19 Pandemic. In Constitutional Resilience and the COVID-19 Pandemic: Perspectives from Sub-Saharan Africa (pp. 255–281). Cham: Springer International Publishing.

Maluwa T (2003) The Constitutive Act of the African Union and Institution-building in Postcolonial Africa. Leiden Journal of International Law 16(1): 157–170

Maluwa, T. (2007). From the Organization of African Unity to the African Union: Rethinking the Framework for Inter-State Cooperation in Africa in the Era of Globalisation. University of Botswana Law Journal, 5, 10.

Mamdani M Citizen and subject: Contemporary Africa and the legacy of later colonialism (1996) Princeton University Press, New Jersey.

Mansfield ED, Solingen E (2010) Regionalism. Annual Review of Political Science 13: 145–163

Mathur, R., 1997. The Republican model of Mauritius: A short comparative study The African Review: A Journal of African Politics, Development and International Affairs, 24(1/2), pp.180–207.

Mauritius Oceanography Institute 'The Institute' <https://moi.govmu.org/about/the-institute> accessed 05 July 2025.

Mauritius Revenue Authority 'Contribution Sociale Generalisee (CSG)' available at https://www.mra.mu/business/csg (accessed 05 July 2025).

Mauthoor, S., 2017. Uncovering industrial symbiosis potentials in a small island developing state: The case study of Mauritius. Journal of Cleaner Production, 147, pp.506–513.

Mbazira C (2006) 'Enforcing the economic, social and cultural rights in the African Charter on Human and Peoples' Rights: Twenty years of redundancy, progression and significant strides' African Human Rights Law Journal 6.

Mbembe A On the post-colony (2001) University of California Press USA.

Mbondenyi, K., 2011. International human rights and their enforcement in Africa. African Books Collective.

Meetarbhan M Constitutional law of Mauritius: Constitution of Mauritius with commentaries (2015) Precigraph Mauritius.

Mehta, S.R., 1995. Power Dynamics of Indian Immigrants in Mauritius: A Study in Ethnic Relations. Indian Anthropologist, 25(1), pp.1–11.

Memorandum submitted by the Mauritius Labour Party to the Legislative Council (1961) Office of the Secretary of State Colonies.

Menon S (2020) The Rule of Law, the International Legal Order, and the Foreign Policy of Small States. The Asian Journal of International Law10(1): 50–67

Miles, W.F., 1999. The creole malaise in Mauritius. African affairs, 98(391), pp.211–228.

Ministry of Environment and Quality of Life, Government of Mauritius 'State of the Environment in Mauritius' a report prepared for presentation at the United Nations Conference on Environment and Development, Rio de Janeiro, Brazil (1992).

Ministry of Environment, Solid Waste Management and Climate Change <https://environment.govmu.org/Pages/Index.aspx> accessed 05 July 2025.

Ministry of Gender Equality and Family Welfare 'About the Ministry' <https://gender.govmu.org/Pages/About-the-Ministry.aspx> accessed 05 July 2025.

Ministry of Gender Equality and Family Welfare 'Adoption Unit' <https://gender.govmu.org/Pages/National-Adoption-Unit.aspx> accessed 05 July 2025.

Ministry of Gender Equality and Family Welfare 'Child abuse' <https://budgetmof.govmu.org/documents/V_20_002023_24all.pdf> accessed 05 July 2025.

Ministry of Gender Equality and Family Welfare 'Child Development Unit' <https://gender.govmu.org/Pages/Child-Development-Unit.aspx> accessed 05 July 2025.

Ministry of Gender Equality and Family Welfare 'Mission and Vision' <https://budgetmof.govmu.org/documents/V_20_002023_24all.pdf> accessed 05 July 2025.

Ministry of Gender Equality and Family Welfare 'National Gender Policy 2022–2030' (March 2022) <https://gender.govmu.org/Lists/DocumentsLinks/Attachments/3/National%20Gender%20Policy%202022-2030.pdf> accessed 05 July 2025.

Ministry of Gender Equality and Family Welfare 'Planning and Research Unit <https://gender.govmu.org/Pages/-Planning-and-Research-Unit.aspx> accessed 05 July 2025.

Ministry of Health and Wellness 'Strategy overview' (2022) available at https://budgetmof.govmu.org/documents/V_18_012023_24Health.pdf (accessed 05 July 2025).

Ministry of Social integration, social security and national solidarity 'The Medical Unit' (2024) <https://socialsecurity.govmu.org/Pages/Services/Medical-unit.aspx> accessed 01 July 2025.

Ministry of Social integration, social security and national solidarity 'The Welfare and Elderly Persons' Protection Unit' (2024) <https://socialsecurity.govmu.org/Pages/Services/Elderly-protection-unit.aspx> accessed 01 July 2025.

Msipa D & Juma P 'The African Disability Protocol: Toward a Social and Human Rights Approach to Disability in the African Human Rights System' In: Rioux M, Viera J, Buettgen A and Zubrow E (eds) (2023) Handbook of Disability. Springer, Singapore.

Murray R & Viljoen F 'Towards non-discrimination on the basis of sexual orientation: The normative basis and procedural possibilities before the African Commission on Human and Peoples' Rights and the African Union' (2009) 29 Human Rights Quarterly 86–111.

Murray R (2004) Historical Overview of Human Rights in the OAU/AU. In: Murray R (ed) Human Rights in Africa: From the OAU to the African Union. Cambridge University Press, New York, p 1–48

Musungu S (2003) Economic integration and Human Rights in Africa: A Comment on Conceptual Linkages. African Human Rights Law Journal 3: 88–96

Muthago LG 'Introducing the African Charter on the Rights and Welfare of the Child and the Convention on the Rights of the Child' (1992) paper presented at the International Conference on the Rights of the Child, Community Law Centre, University of Western Cape.

Mutua M (1995) The Banjul Charter and the African Cultural Fingerprint: An Evaluation of the Language of Duties. Virginia Journal of International Law 35: 339–380

Mutua M (2007) Standard Setting in Human Rights: Critique and Prognosis. Human Rights Quarterly 29: 547–630

Mutua, M. (1995). The Banjul Charter and the African Cultural Fingerprint: An Assessment of the Language of Duties. Virginia Journal of International Law, 35, 339.

Nagar D, Nganje F (2016) The African Union: Regional and Global Challenges. Centre for Conflict Resolution, Cape Town

National Human Rights Commission Website 'Home' available at https://nhrc.govmu.org/Pages/index.aspx (accessed 05 July 2025).

Neumann I, Gstöhl S (2006) Introduction: Lilliputians in Gulliver's world? In Ingebritsen C et al. (eds) Small States in International Relations. University of Washington Press, Seattle

Nkrumah K Africa Must Unite (New York: Praeger, 1963).

Nmehielle V The African human rights system: Its laws, practice and institutions (2001) Brill Netherlands.

Nmehielle VO (2003) The African Union and African Renaissance: A New Era for Human Rights Protection in Africa? Singapore Journal of International and Comparative Law 7: 412–446

North-Coombes, M.D., 2018. From Slavery to Indenture: Forced Labour in the Political Economy of Mauritius 1834–1867. In Indentured Labour in the British Empire, 1834–1920 (pp. 78–125). Routledge.

Odinkalu C ‘Implementing economic, social and cultural rights under the African Charter on Human and Peoples’ Rights’ in M Evans & R Murray The African Charter on Human and Peoples’ Rights: The system in practice, 1986–2000 (2002) Cambridge University Press UK.

OHCHR ‘African states affirm the rights of persons with disabilities in a new landmark Protocol’ (15 February 2018) <https://www.ohchr.org/en/press-releases/2018/02/african-states-affirm-rights-persons-disabilities-new-landmark-protocol> accessed 01 July 2025.

OHCHR ‘UN expert says Mauritius leads on privacy in the region, but challenges remain’ (07 December 2023) <https://www.ohchr.org/en/press-releases/2023/12/un-expert-says-mauritius-leads-privacy-region-challenges-remain> accessed 03 July 2025.

Olaniyan K (2004) The African Union Convention on Preventing and Combating Corruption: A Critical Appraisal. African Human Rights Law Journal 4(1): 74–92

Oliver R & Atmore A Africa since 1800 (1994) Cambridge University Press UK.

Olivier ME (2015) The Role of African Union Law in Integrating Africa. South African Journal of International Affairs 22(4) 513–533

Oloka-Onyango J ‘Beyond the rhetoric: Reinvigorating the struggle for economic and social rights in Africa’ University of Minnesota Human Rights Library http://www1.umn.edu/humanrts/africa/Oloka-Onyango.html (accessed 05 July 2025).

Oloruntoba SO (2020) Pan Africanism, Regional Integration and Development in Africa. Springer, Cham

Olowu D (2002) Protecting Children’s Rights in Africa: A Critique of the African Charter on the Rights and Welfare of the Child. The International Journal of Children’s Rights 10: 127–136

Ombudsperson for Children ‘Annual Report 2019-2020; <https://oco.govmu.org/Documents/Annual%20Reports/Annual%20Report%20 2019-2020%20-%20OC.pdf> accessed 05 July 2025.

Ombudsperson for Children ‘Annual Report 2021-2022’ <https://oco.govmu.org/DocumentsList/FinalAnnualReport2021-2022.pdf> accessed 05 July 2025.

Ombudsperson for Children ‘Annual Report 2022-2023; <https://oco.govmu.org/DocumentsList/FinalAnnualReport2022-2023.pdf> accessed 05 July 2025.

Ouguergouz F The African Charter on Human and Peoples’ Rights: A comprehensive agenda for human dignity and sustainable democracy in Africa (2003) Brill Netherlands.

Packer CAA, Rukare D (2002) The New African Union and its Constitutive Act. The American Journal of International Law 96(2): 365–379

Page, E (2012) ‘Bureaucracy: Disregarding public administration’ pp.101–120 in Connelly, J & Hayward, J (eds) The withering of the welfare state: Regression, Palgrave Macmillan: Basingstoke & New York.

Pakenham T Scramble for Africa: 1876–1921 (New York: Random House, 1991), Part III.

Phaala L.E. (2010) 'Development with social justice? Social democracy in Mauritius' MA Thesis Master of Arts (International Studies) Stellenbosch University.

Qobo M (2007) The Challenges of Regional Integration in Africa in the Context of Globalisation and the Prospects for a United States of Africa. Institute for Security Studies Paper 145 https://www.files.ethz.ch/isn/98933/PAPER145H.pdf Accessed 05 July 2025

Quinn G & Degener T Human rights and disability: The current use and future potential of United Nations human rights instruments in the context of disability (2002) United Nations Press.

R Murray 'Women's rights and the OAU and AU: The Protocol on the Rights of Women in Africa' in D Buss & A Manji (eds) International Law: Modern feminist approaches (2005) Oxford: Hart Publishing.

Ramtohul, R., 2016. Contested terrain: identity and women's suffrage in Mauritius. Journal of Southern African Studies, 42(6), pp.1225–1239.

Report of the Mauritius Constitutional Conference September 1965' Sessional Paper No. 6 of 1965.

Reporters without Borders 'RSF condemns harsh penalties for online content in Mauritius' <https://rsf.org/en/index> accessed 03 July 2025.

Roberts C (2023) Foundational Moments. In: (ed) Alternative Approaches to Human Rights: the Disparate Historical Paths of the European, Inter-American and African Regional Human Rights Systems, p 19–94

Rughoonundun-Chellapermal, N., 2022. Pluralism without Inclusion: The Case of Mauritius, a Linguistically Diverse Diasporic Small Island Developing State (sids). In Handbook of Language Policy and Education in Countries of the Southern African Development Community (SADC) (pp. 199–221). Brill.

Salverda, T., 2008. Maintaining an elite position: How Franco-Mauritians sustain their leading role in post-colonial Mauritius. Dilemmas of development, p.93.

Scott C and Macklem P 'Constitutional ropes of sand or justiciable guarantees? Social rights in a new South African Constitution' (1992) 141 University of Pennsylvania Law Review.

Secretariat of the African Decade of Persons with Disabilities 'The Architecture for an African Disability Rights Mechanism' (2011).

Seekings, J., 2011. British colonial policy, local politics, and the origins of the Mauritian welfare state, 1936–50. The Journal of African History, 52(2), pp.157–177.

Seetulsingh, D.B., 2004. Mauritius. Human Rights Law in Africa Online, 2(1), pp.1309–1330.

Sepulveda M The nature of the obligations under the International Covenant on Economic, Social and Cultural Rights (2003) Intersentia.

Shelton D 'Human Rights, Environmental Rights, and the Right to Environment' (1992) 28 Stanford Journal of International Law 103.

Shelton, D. L. (2007). Introduction: Law, Non-Law and the Problem of Soft Law. In D. L. Shelton (Ed.), Compliance and Commitment: The Role of Non-Binding Norms in the International Legal System (p. 1). Oxford: Oxford University Press.

Sik Yeun J 'The rights of older persons and persons with disabilities in Africa' in Ssenyonjo M (ed) The African regional human rights system: 30 years after the African Charter on Human and Peoples' Rights (2011) Martinus Nijhoff Publishers.

Singh A & Power M 'The privacy awakening: the urgent need to harmonise the right to privacy in Africa' (2019) 3 African Human Rights Yearbook 202–220.

Singh, S. (2009). The Impact of Clawback Clauses on Human and Peoples' Rights in Africa. African Security Review, 18, 95–104.

Sinjela M (2012) The African Convention on the Prevention and Combating of Corruption. In: Yusuf AA, Ouguergouz F (eds) The African Union: Legal and Institutional Framework. Brill, Leiden, p 291–301

Slade TN (2003) The Making of International Law: The Role of Small Island States. Temple International and Comparative Law Journal 17(2): 531–544

Sobhee, S.K., 2009. The economic success of Mauritius: lessons and policy options for Africa. Journal of Economic Policy Reform, 12(1), pp.29–42.

Ssenyonjo M (2012) The African Regional Human Rights System: 30 Years after the African Charter on Human and Peoples' Rights. Martinus Nijhoff Publishers, Leiden

Ssenyonjo M (2018) Responding to Human Rights Violations in Africa: Assessing the Role of the African Commission and Court on Human and Peoples' Rights (1987–2018). International Human Rights Law Review 7:1–42

Stanziani, A., 2020. Slavery and Post-Slavery in the Indian Ocean World. In Oxford Research Encyclopedia of African History.

Statistics Mauritius 'Economic and Social Indicators: Population and Vital Statistics' (2023) <https://statsmauritius.govmu.org/Documents/Statistics/ESI/2024/EI1773/Pop_Vital_Yr23_110324.pdf> accessed 05 July 2025.

Statistics Mauritius 'Education Statistics' (2023) <https://statsmauritius.govmu.org/Pages/Statistics/ESI/Education/Edu_Yr23.aspx> accessed 05 July 2025.

Statistics Mauritius 'Gender Statistics 2022' <https://statsmauritius.govmu.org/Pages/Statistics/ESI/Gender/Gender_Yr22.aspx> accessed 05 July 2025.

Statistics Mauritius 'Gender Statistics 2022' available at https://statsmauritius.govmu.org/Pages/Statistics/ESI/Gender/Gender_Yr22.aspx#:~:text=(i)%20In%202022%2C%20the,7%20years%20longer%20than%20men. (accessed 05 July 2025).

Stebbing, A & Spies-Butcher, B (2016) 'The decline of a homeowning society? Asset- based welfare, retirement and intergenerational equity in Australia', Housing Studies, 31, 2, pp. 190–207.

Subramanian, A. and Roy, D., 2001. Who Can Explain the Mauritian Miracle: Meade, Romer, Sachs or Rodrik?.

Suilleabhain AO (2014) Small States at the United Nations: Diverse Perspectives, Shared Opportunities. International Peace Institute https://www.ipinst.org/wp-content/uploads/publications/ipi_e_pub_small_states_at_un.pdf Accessed 05 July 2025.

Sunkur, R., Kantamaneni, K., Bokhoree, C. and Ravan, S., 2023. Mangroves' role in supporting ecosystem-based techniques to reduce disaster risk and adapt to climate change: A review. Journal of Sea Research, p.102449.

Sweet AS, Sandholtz W (1997) European Integration and Supranational Governance. Journal of European Public Policy 4(3): 297–317

Söderbaum F (2013) Rethinking Regions and Regionalism. Georgetown Journal of International Affairs 14(2): 9–18

Tandrayen-Ragoobur V (2019) Can Africa Serve as a Trading Hub for Mauritius?: An In-depth Analysis. In: Seetanah B, Sannassee R and Nunkoo R (eds) Mauritius: A Successful Small Island Developing State, 1st edn. Routledge, London

Tandrayen-Ragoobur V, Tengur ND, Seewooruttun B (2021) South-South Trade: The Potential for Mauritius. Journal of Economic Development 46(3): 45–65

Techane MG (2011) Where is the African Charter? Assessing the Impact of the African Charter on Human and Peoples' Rights in Mauritius. Unpublished dissertation, University of Pretoria.

Techane MG, Mahadew R (2016) The Impact of the African Charter and the Maputo Protocol in Mauritius. In Ayeni V (ed) The Impact of the African Charter and the Maputo Protocol in selected African states. Pretoria University Law Press, Pretoria

Thorhallsson B, Steinsson S (2017) Small State Foreign Policy. Oxford Research Encyclopaedia of Politics. Oxford University Press

Tinker, H., 1977. Between Africa, Asia and Europe: Mauritius: Cultural Marginalism and Political Control. African Affairs, 76(304), pp.321–338.

Toussaint A Histoire de L'île Maurice (1971) 1449.

Truth and Justice Commission (Mauritius) 'Report of the Truth and Justice Commission' Volume 1 (2011).

Tsakok I (2021) The Republic of Mauritius and the African Continental Free Trade Area: Opportunities and Challenges in a post COVID-19 environment. Policy Center for the New South, Policy Brief 39/21 https://www.policycenter.ma/publications/republic-mauritius-and-african-continental-free-trade-areaopportunities-and-challenges Accessed 05 July 2025.

Tsang Man Kin, J. (2015) Mauritius Times 'Mauritius and the African Union' available at http://www.mauritiustimes.com/mt/joseph-tsang-mang-kin-gosk-3/

Tung, O.L., 2011. Development and the balancing of interests in environmental policy and law in Mauritius. The balancing of interests in environmental law in Africa PULP: Pretoria.

Turner, B., 2014. Mauritius. The Statesman's Yearbook: The Politics, Cultures and Economies of the World 2015, pp.847–850.

U.S. Department of State '2023 Trafficking in Persons Report: Mauritius' <https://www.state.gov/reports/2023-trafficking-in-persons-report/mauritius/> accessed 05 July 2025.

Udombana NJ (2000) Toward the African Court on Human and Peoples' Rights: Better Late Than Never. Yale Human Rights and Development Law Journal 3: 45–111

Ulriksen, M.S., 2011. Social policy development and global financial crisis in the open economies of Botswana and Mauritius. Global Social Policy, 11(2–3), pp.194–213.

Umozurike U (1983) The African Charter on Human and Peoples' Rights. American Journal of International Law 77(4): 902–912

Umozurike U The African Charter on Human and Peoples' Rights (1997) The Hague Kluwer International.

Umozurike U, Five years of the African Commission on Human and Peoples' Rights (Ile-Ife: Obafemi Awolowo University, 1992).

Umozurike, U.O., 1983. The African Charter on human and peoples' rights. American Journal of International Law, 77(4), pp.902–912.

UN CESCR State Report Mauritius (2010) introductory paragraph.

UN CESCR 'Concluding observations on the combined second to fourth periodic report of Mauritius' (8 June 2010) UN Doc. E/C.12/MUS/CO/4.

UN CESCR 'Concluding observations on the fifth periodic report of Mauritius' (5 April 2019) UN Doc. E/C.12/MUS/CO/5.

UN CESCR 'Examination of the Second, Third and Fourth Periodic Reports of the Implementation by Mauritius of the ICECSR (7 May 2010)

UN CESCR 'Replies of Mauritius to the list of issues' (19 December 2018) UN Doc. E/C.12/MUS/Q/5/Add.1.

UN Committee on Economic, Social and Cultural Rights 'Concluding observations on the fifth periodic report of Mauritius' (05 April 2019) UN Doc E/C.12/MUS/CO/5.

UN Committee on the Elimination of All Forms of Discrimination Against Women 'Concluding Observations on the eighth periodic report of Mauritius' (14 November 2018) UN Doc UN Doc CEDAW/C/MUS/CO/8.

UN CtRC 'Concluding Observations on the combined sixth and seventh periodic reports of Mauritius' (23 February 2023) UN Doc CRC/C/MUS/CO/6-7.

UN CtRC 'Concluding Observations on the Combined Third to Fifth Periodic Reports of Mauritius' (27 February 2015) UN Doc CRC/C/MUS/CO/3-5.

UN HRC 'Summary of stakeholders submission on Mauritius' (27 August 2018) UN Doc A/HRC/WG.6/31/MUS/3, https://upr-info.org/sites/default/files/documents/2018-10/a_hrc_wg.6_31_mus_3_e.pdf> accessed 01 July 2025.

UN Human Rights Committee 'Concluding Observations on the fifth periodic report of Mauritius' 11 December 2017 UN Doc CCPR/C/MUS/CO/5.

UN OHCHR 'Information Note' (2022) <https://www.undp.org/sites/g/files/zskgke326/files/2023-01/UNDP-UNEP-UNHCHR-What-is-the-Right-to-a-Healthy-Environment.pdf> accessed 01 July 2025.

UN Treaty Collection 'Convention on the Elimination of All Forms of Discrimination against Women' <https://treaties.un.org/Pages/ViewDetails.aspx?src=TREATY&mtdsg_no=IV-8&chapter=4&clang=_en#41> accessed 05 July 2025.

UNEP 'Mauritius sets goals to curb the triple planetary crisis' <https://www.unep.org/news-and-stories/story/mauritius-sets-goals-curb-triple-planetary-crisis> accessed 05 July 2025.

UNICEF 'Mauritius' (2024) <https://data.unicef.org/country/mus/> accessed 05 July 2025.

UNODC 'The United Nations Standard Minimum Rules for the Treatment of Prisoners (the Nelson Mandela Rules)' available at https://www.unodc.org/documents/justice-and-prison-reform/Nelson_Mandela_Rules-E-ebook.pdf (accessed 05 July 2025).

US Department of State '2023 Country Reports on Human Rights Practices: Mauritius' <https://www.state.gov/reports/2023-country-reports-on-human-rights-practices/mauritius/> accessed 05 July 2025.

V Gite 'From Bhojpuri to dholl puri, a taste of Mauritius through the eyes of two successful women' (14 June 2022) <https://eshe.in/2022/06/14/mauritius-veidehi-gite/> accessed 05 July 2025.

Van der Linde M & Louw L 'Considering the interpretation and implementation of Article 24 of the African Charter on Human and Peoples' Rights in the light of the SERAC Communication' (2003) 3 African Human Rights Law Journal 167.

Van Kersbergen, K & Vis, B (2014) Comparative welfare state politics: development, opportunities and reform, New York: Cambridge University Press.

Van Oorschot, W, Roosma, F, Meuleman, B and Reeskens, T (eds) (2017) The Social Legitimacy of Targeted Welfare: New Perspectives on Deservingness Opinions, Cheltenham and New York: Edward Elgar Publishing.

van Reenen T & Combrinck H 'The UN Convention on the Rights of Persons with Disabilities in Africa: Progress after 5 years' (2011) 14 SUR International Journal on Human Rights.

Vaughan, M., 1998. Slavery and colonial identity in eighteenth-century Mauritius. Transactions of the Royal Historical Society, 8, pp.189–214.

Venn A (2017) Universal Human Rights? Breaking the Institutional Barriers Facing Climate-Vulnerable Small-Island Developing States. Climate Law 7(4) 322–346

Vickers B (2017) A Handbook on Regional Integration in Africa: Towards Agenda 2063. Commonwealth Secretariat, London

Viljoen (2001) Africa's Contribution to the Development of International Human Rights and Humanitarian Law. African Human Rights Law Journal 1:18–39

Viljoen F (2001) Africa's Contribution to the Development of International Human Rights Law and International Humanitarian Law. African Human Rights Law Journal 1: 18–39

Viljoen F (2009) An Introduction to the Protocol to the African Charter on Human and Peoples' Rights on the Rights of Women in Africa. Washington and Lee Journal of Civil Rights and Social Justice 16(11): 11–46

Viljoen F (2012) International Human Rights Law in Africa, 2nd edn. Oxford University Press, Oxford

Viljoen F International human rights law in Africa (2015) Oxford University Press UK.

Viljoen, F., & Baimu, E. (2004). Courts for Africa: Considering the Co-Existence of the African Court on Human and Peoples' Rights and the African Court of Justice. Netherlands Quarterly of Human Rights, 22, 241. https://doi.org/10.1177/016934410402200205

Viljoen, F., 2015. International human rights law in Africa. OUP Oxford.

Vlcek, W 'The Mauritian paradox: Fifty years of development, diversity and democracy' (2019) 108(1) The Round Table 104–106.

W Langley 'The rights of women, the African Charter, and the Economic Development of Africa' (1987) 7 Boston College Third World Law Journal 215.

Weiler J (1981) The Community System: The Dual Character of Regionalism. Yearbook of European Law 1(1) 267–306

Weisfelder R 'Human rights and majority rule in Southern Africa: The Mote in Thy Brother's Eye' in CE Welch and RI Meltzer (eds), Human Rights and Development in Africa (Albany, NY: State University of New York, 1984).

Welsh C Protecting human rights in Africa: Strategies and roles of non-governmental organisations, (Philadelphia: University of Pennsylvania, 1995).

Welz, M (2012) Integrating Africa: Decolonization's Legacies, Sovereignty and the African Union. Routledge, London

Wiebusch M et al. (2019) The African Charter on Democracy, Elections and Governance: Past, Present and Future. Journal of African Law 63(1): 9–38

World Trade Press (2010) 'Mauritius Women in Culture, Business and Travel' California.

Wurzel, R (2012) 'The environmental challenge to nation states: From limits to growth to ecological modernisation', in Connelly, J & Hayward, J (eds) The withering of the welfare state: Regression, Palgrave Macmillan: Basingstoke & New York.

Yusuf AA, Ouguergouz F (2012) The African Union: Legal and Institutional Framework: A Manual on the Pan African Organization. Brill, Leiden

MIX
Papier aus verantwortungsvollen Quellen
Paper from responsible sources
FSC® C105338

If you have any concerns about our products,
you can contact us on
ProductSafety@springernature.com

In case Publisher is established outside the EU,
the EU authorized representative is:
Springer Nature Customer Service Center GmbH
Europaplatz 3, 69115 Heidelberg, Germany

Printed by Libri Plureos GmbH
in Hamburg, Germany